MW00571074

THE WORLD SCIENTIFIC REFERENCE ON

ENTREPRENEURSHIP

Volume 4: Process Approach to Academic Entrepreneurship: Evidence from the Globe

THE WORLD SCIENTIFIC REFERENCE ON
ENTREPRENEURSHIP

Editor-in-Chief

Donald Siegel
University at Albany, SUNY, USA

Volume 4: Process Approach to Academic Entrepreneurship: Evidence from the Globe

Editors

Riccardo Fini
University of Bologna, Italy

Rosa Grimaldi
University of Bologna, Italy

W World Scientific

NEW JERSEY · LONDON · SINGAPORE · BEIJING · SHANGHAI · HONG KONG · TAIPEI · CHENNAI · TOKYO

Published by

World Scientific Publishing Co. Pte. Ltd.

5 Toh Tuck Link, Singapore 596224

USA office: 27 Warren Street, Suite 401-402, Hackensack, NJ 07601

UK office: 57 Shelton Street, Covent Garden, London WC2H 9HE

Library of Congress Cataloging-in-Publication Data
Names: Siegel, Donald S., 1959–   editor.
Title: The World Scientific Reference on entrepreneurship / edited by Donald Siegel
     (University at Albany, SUNY, USA).
Description: New Jersey : World Scientific, [2016] | "In 4 volumes."
     Contents: Vol. 1. Entrepreneurial Universities : Technology and Knowledge Transfer / edited by
     James Cunningham (Newcastle University), Maribel Guerrero (University of Deusto, Spain) and
     David Urbano (University of Barcelona, Spain) -- Vol. 2. Entrepreneurial Finance : Managerial and
     Policy Implications / edited by Na Dai (University at Albany-SUNY, USA) -- Vol. 3. Sustainability,
     Ethics, and Entrepreneurship / edited by Amy Guerber (University of Alberta, Canada), Gideon Markman
     (Colorado State University, USA) and Sherry Chih-Yi Su (National Tsing Hua University, Taiwan) --
     Vol. 4. Process Approach to Academic Entrepreneurship : Evidence from the Globe / edited by
     Riccardo Fini (University of Bologna) and Rosa Grimaldi (University of Bologna).
Identifiers: LCCN 2015033822| ISBN 9789814733304 (set : alk. paper) |
     ISBN 9789814733397 (v. 1 : alk. paper) | ISBN 9789814733403 (v. 2 : alk. paper) |
     ISBN 9789814733410 (v. 3 : alk. paper) | ISBN 9789814733427 (v. 4 : alk. paper)
Subjects: LCSH: Entrepreneurship.
Classification: LCC HB615 .W6825 2016 | DDC 658.4/21--dc23
LC record available at https://lccn.loc.gov/2015033822

British Library Cataloguing-in-Publication Data
A catalogue record for this book is available from the British Library.

Copyright © 2017 by World Scientific Publishing Co. Pte. Ltd.

All rights reserved. This book, or parts thereof, may not be reproduced in any form or by any means, electronic or mechanical, including photocopying, recording or any information storage and retrieval system now known or to be invented, without written permission from the publisher.

For photocopying of material in this volume, please pay a copying fee through the Copyright Clearance Center, Inc., 222 Rosewood Drive, Danvers, MA 01923, USA. In this case permission to photocopy is not required from the publisher.

Desk Editors: Dipasri Sardar/Philly Lim

Typeset by Stallion Press
Email: enquiries@stallionpress.com

Printed in Singapore

Contents

About the Editor-in-Chief

Dr. Donald Siegel is Dean of the School of Business and Professor of Management at the University at Albany, SUNY. He received his bachelor's degree in economics and his master's and doctoral degrees in business economics from Columbia University. Dr. Siegel is an editor of the *Journal of Management Studies* and the *Journal of Technology Transfer*, a former co-editor of *Academy of Management Perspectives*, an associate editor of the *Journal of Productivity Analysis*, and serves on the editorial boards of *Academy of Management Perspectives*, *Academy of Management Learning & Education*, *Journal of Business Venturing*, *Corporate Governance: An International Review*, *Strategic Entrepreneurship Journal*, and the *British Journal of Management*. He has also co-edited 38 special issues of leading journals in economics, management, and finance. Dr. Siegel was recently ranked #2 in the world for research on university entrepreneurship. He has published 106 articles and 10 books on issues relating to university technology transfer and entrepreneurship, the effects of corporate governance on performance, productivity analysis, the economic effects of gambling, and corporate and environmental social responsibility in leading journals in economics, management, and finance. His citation count, according to Google Scholar, is 22,807 with an h-index of 62.

About the Editors

Dr. Riccardo Fini is *Associate Professor of Entrepreneurship and Innovation Management* and *EU CIG Marie Curie Fellow* at the University of Bologna (UNIBO). He is also *Research Fellow* at Imperial College Business School in London. He is serving as the *Associate Dean for Entrepreneurship and Innovation* at the University of Bologna Business School, where he directs the Master in Entrepreneurship and the Global MBA (track in Innovation Management). Before joining UNIBO, he researched at Ecole des Mines Paris, Case Western Cleveland and University of Bozen. He was also *EU IEF Marie Curie Fellow* at Imperial College London and *Assistant Professor of Entrepreneurship and Innovation Management* at UNIBO. He holds a PhD in Management and a Master in Industrial Engineering from UNIBO. His research lies at the intersection of entrepreneurship and economics of innovation. His work is published (or forthcoming) in entrepreneurship and management journals, such as *Academy of Management Perspectives, Entrepreneurship Theory and Practice, Journal of Management Studies* and *Research Policy.* He has been invited to contribute to the *University of Chicago Handbook on Technology Transfer* and the *Palgrave Encyclopedia of Strategic Management.* He has been awarded more than €300.000 of research funds and has extensively consulted for *ANVUR,* the Italian Agency for the Evaluation of the University and Research Systems. Dr. Fini has been invited to present his research in more than 30 universities and business schools in *Asia, Australia, Europe* and *North America.* His work was also featured in *Il Sole24 Ore, Nature, Times Higher Education* and *The New York Times.*

Dr. Rosa Grimaldi is *Full Professor of Entrepreneurship and Innovation Management* at the University of Bologna, Department of Management. She is *Deputy Rector for Entrepreneurship* at Alma Mater Studiourum, University of Bologna. She is the *Director of the International PhD program in Management* and the *Director of the Executive Master in Technology and Innovation Management* (EMTIM) at BBS (University of Bologna Business School). She graduated in Industrial Engineering at the Polytechnique of Turin. She teaches 'Technology Entrepreneurship' at the School of Engineering at postgraduate and executive education levels. Most of her scientific production is about New Business Creation, Entrepreneurship, and Technology Transfer. On these topics she has publications on prestigious international journals (including *Research Policy, R&D Management, Technology and Innovation Management, Journal of Business Venturing, Small Business Economics, Scientometrics, Entrepreneurship Theory and Practice, Journal of Technology Transfer*). She is in the Editorial board of the *Journal of Technology Transfer* and she is advisory editor for *Research Policy*.

About the Contributors

Janet Bercovitz is an Associate Professor of Strategy & Entrepreneurship in the College of Business at the University of Illinois at Urbana-Champaign. Her research program consists of two main research streams. The first stream focuses on issues of organizational structure and inter-organizational contractual relationships. The second concentrates on extending understanding of academic entrepreneurship and university–industry technology transfer. Her research has been published in journal outlets such as *Organization Science, Strategic Management Journal, Management Science, Research Policy,* and the *Journal of Technology Transfer.*

Janet holds a B.S. degree in chemistry, an MBA, and a PhD from the University of California, Berkeley.

Anders Billström, PhD candidate at Chalmers University of Technology, Göteborg, Sweden is currently working at Nord University, Bodø, Norway. His main research interests are within entrepreneurship and university entrepreneurship with a specific focus on entrepreneurial teams, external/surrogate entrepreneurs, human capital and social networks. These themes are also the main themes of the coming PhD thesis. Other research areas of interest are social value of business and leadership. He has attended international conferences and published papers within relationship quality and leadership. Anders has also several years of teaching experience within business ethics, entrepreneurship, leadership and organization theory.

Daniela Bolzani holds a PhD in General Management (2013) and is currently a Postdoc at the University of Bologna. Her research interests are related to the determinants and outcomes of entrepreneurial decision-making processes, especially in the context of international, immigrant, and academic entrepreneurship. She was a visiting scholar at the Leeds School of Business, University of Colorado Boulder, and HEC Paris. Her works are presented at the BCERC, AIB, AOM, DRUID, EGOS and Alberta Institutions conferences and published in entrepreneurship and innovation journals and book chapters. In the past, Daniela worked for five years in the fields of financial audit and international development in Europe and Africa.

Bart Clarysse holds the chair of entrepreneurship at ETH Zürich and is a part-time professor in Entrepreneurship at Imperial College London Business School. Before he joined ETH Zürich in 2016, he was a tenured professor in entrepreneurship at Imperial College London Business School. He has over 20 years' experience in coaching entrepreneurs and has co-founded a portfolio of successful start-ups in businesses such as digital cinema, mobile internet and venture incubation. After his experiences in the digital economy, he entered the hospitality business in 2014 where he started to rent out holiday apartments with hotel services for city trips (www.feelathomeinghent.be) and skiing holidays and most recently he co-founded a company that commercializes a talent matching app for nascent entrepreneurs.

He has over 50 publications in the field of high tech start-ups and managing growth of these companies and has been an executive teacher for several multinationals such as KLM, Belgacom, Recticel, USG People, Johnson&Johnson, BT, EDF and Unilever in corporate venturing and innovative turnaround strategies. He is also member of the scientific advisory board of Erikshom Research Centre, a subsidiary of Oticon, a world-leading organization in hearing and a technology leader in ehealth.

His on-going research interests include the analysis of dualities in developing young ventures such as developing stability while keeping flexibility, achieving commercial objectives while keeping social objectives, making use of external forms of financing while safeguarding financial autonomy.

Pablo D'Este is currently a Tenured Scientist at INGENIO (CSIC-UPV). He has a Degree in Economics from Universitat Autònoma de Barcelona. He obtained a PhD degree in 2004 from SPRU — Science and Technology Policy Research at the University of Sussex (UK). He has been a Research Fellow at SPRU from 2002 to 2008 and at Cranfield School of Management between 2006 and 2008. His current research interests include: university–business interactions; the impact of academic research on firms' innovation perfor-mance; academic entrepreneurship; the analysis of barriers to innovation; and the relationship between research networks and innovation.

Maryann P. Feldman is the Heninger Distinguished Professor in the Department of Public Policy at the University of North Carolina. In 2013, she was awarded with the prestigious Global Entrepreneurship Research Award from the Swedish Entrepreneurship Forum and Research Institute of Industrial Economics. Her research interests focus on the areas of innovation, the commercialization of academic research and the factors that promote technological change and economic growth.

Kun Fu works as a Research Associate in the Innovation and Entrepreneurship Department at Imperial College Business School. She holds a PhD degree in Business Administration and Management from Bocconi University. Her research interests lie in the fields of technology innovation and entrepreneur-ship. She works on how entrepreneurs react to their contexts and examines the outcomes of this process such as firm creation, growth aspiration, technol-ogy innovation and diversification. Kun also undertook consultancy assign-ments for national government (e.g., The Swedish Agency for Growth Policy Analysis), international organization (e.g., The World Intellectual Property Organization), and private sector enterprise (e.g., Shell).

Lisa A. Goble is currently the Export Control and Conflict of Interest Official at The University of North Carolina at Greensboro, managing the institu-tional compliance programs for these federal policies. Her PhD is in Public Policy from the University of North Carolina at Chapel Hill, she also holds a Bachelor of Science degree from UNC Greensboro in Information Systems and Operations Management, and a minor in Economics. Her research inter-ests include evaluating US federal policies that have an impact upon institu-tions of higher education and understanding their influence upon research partnerships, entrepreneurship, and other community engagement activities in the academic environment.

Maximilian Goethner is a postdoctoral researcher at the University of Jena, Germany and a research fellow at the DFG Graduate School "Economics of Innovative Change" (DFG-GRK 1411), funded by the German Research Foundation. He received his PhD in Economics from the University of Jena, Germany in 2012, studying determinants and effects of technology entrepre-neurship. His research interests include entrepreneurial cognition, university–industry interactions and the economics of innovation. His current research focuses on the influence of innovation and entrepreneurship on economic inequality.

Jonas Van Hove is a PhD candidate at ETH Zurich, Chair of Entrepreneurship where he conducts research on entrepreneurial ecosystems, incubation models, and academic entrepreneurship at Imperial College Business School and ETH Zurich. He is managing and designing experiential programmes to equip STEM students and academics with an entrepreneurial mind set so they are able to identify and exploit entrepreneurial opportunities (equally relevant to starting-up, scaling-up or steady-state organizations).

Oscar Llopis is Assistant Professor at the Rennes School of Business, France. In 2013, he received a PhD degree in Business Management from the University of Valencia, Spain and INGENIO (CSIC-UPV). He has been a visiting scholar in the Copenhagen Business School, Denmark (2011) and in the University of Pisa, Italy (2012). Between 2014 and 2015, he has been a post-doctoral fellow at GREThA, University of Bordeaux. His current research interests include: innovation management, social networks and innovation performance, university–business interactions and academic creativity.

Marius Tuft Mathisen is a PhD candidate at the Norwegian University of Science and Technology (NTNU). He also teaches at the NTNU School of Entrepreneurship. He received his MSc degree in Industrial Economics in 2007, and later worked professionally as an entrepreneur and in various consulting and management positions. He has broad international experience working across Europe and the US. His doctoral research is centered on academic entrepreneurship, more specifically the growth processes and outcomes of research-based spin-off companies from universities and research institutions. He is particularly focused on the dynamic and complex nature of firm growth, including the role of structural growth through acquisitions. During his PhD he has been a visiting scholar at New York University and the University of California, Berkeley.

Ayoub Moustakbal, In 2013, Ayoub Moustakbal got his doctorate in business administration at the School of Management, Université du Québec à Montréal (ESG UQAM). He is a lecturer at the same university since 2010. He also holds the position of advisor to business start-up in a Canadian organization of economic development. Ayoub Moustakbal is interested in entrepreneurship and innovation management at high-tech SMEs. He published the results of his research in refereed seminars and journals such as the Conference of Portland International Center for Management of Engineering and Technology (PICMET) and *International Journal of Biotechnology* (IJBT).

Jorge Niosi is Professor in the Department of Management and Technology at the Université du Québec à Montréal since 1970. He received his doctorate at the Ecole pratique des hautes études in Paris in 1973. He is the author, co-author, editor or co-editor of 15 books, as well as some 60 articles in refereed journals including the *Cambridge Journal of Economics, Industrial and Corporate Change, Journal of Business Research, Journal of Development Studies, Journal of Evolutionary Economics, Journal of Technology Transfer, Management International Review, Research Policy, R&D Management, Small Business Economics, Technovation* and *World Development.*

Adam Novotny received his PhD degree in Economics and Management from the Budapest University of Technology and Economics in 2011 with his research on university–industry technology transfer. In spring 2012, he was a visiting scholar at Georgia College & State University, Milledgeville, Georgia, US. The same year he was appointed as Associate Professor at the Institute of Economic Science, Eszterházy Károly University of Applied Sciences, Eger, Hungary. He is presently a researcher of the Business School at Nord University, Bodø, Norway. His research interests include academic entrepreneurship, science-based firms, and knowledge transfer between higher education institutions and industry.

Einar Rasmussen is Professor of Technology Management at Nord University Business School, Norway. He has been visiting scholar at University of Nottingham, University of Strathclyde, University of Twente and University of Bologna. His main research interests are entrepreneurial processes, academic entrepreneurship and university–industry technology transfer. He has managed several research and development projects funded by research councils, ministries and government agencies. He is Consulting Editor of *International Small Business Journal* and publish regularly in international journals such as *Journal of Management Studies, Journal of Business Research, Research Policy, International Small Business Journal, Entrepreneurship and Regional Development, Technology Analysis and Strategic Management, Journal of Technology Transfer and Technovation.*

Rosana Silveira Reis has 30 years of experience in HRM, 15 of them she had been a Manager in large companies. Since 2000 she has been teaching HRM,

IHRM and Cross Cultural Management in graduation and MBA courses. Currently, she is Associate Professor at ISG — Paris, France. She is also regular visiting professor at Fundação Dom Cabral — FDC, Brazil and Invited professor in MBA programs at IMPS Business School in Brno (Czech Republic) and at University of Bologna (Italy). In 2000, she received her scientific master in Business Administration from the Federal University of Santa Catarina (Brazil) and in 2010, her PhD in Management from the University of Bologna (Italy). Her research focuses on Culture and Innovation, Creativity, Leadership, International HRM, Cross-Cultural Management and Global Teams.

Marcos Mueller Schlemm, has completed his doctoral work at USC in Public Policy and Development and has had a wide spread experience in management praxis both in private and public organizations. Is Professor at the Business School at the Pontifícia Universidade Católica do Paraná, since 1998 teaching and focusing his research on entrepreneurship and innovation. In 2000 he brought to Brazil, the **GEM — Global Entrepreneurship Monitor**, a global research on the entrepreneurial activity led by London Business School and Babson College, and a network of Universities in more than 50 countries. Has spent the years of 2013 to 2015 as Visiting Scholar at the University of California at Berkeley, studying and completing his research on the culture of innovation identified in the Silicon Valley ecosystem. His current research interests are innovation, design-thinking and innovation ecosystems.

Luiz Márcio Spinosa is Visiting Scholar at University of California Berkeley (US), full professor and researcher in the Pontifical Catholic University of Paraná (BR). He earned his PhD degree in Production and Informatics and his Diplôme d'études approfondies in CIM Systems from Université d'Aix-Marseille III (FR), his Master of Science in Mechanical Engineering degree and his Bachelor of Computer Science degree from Universidade Federal de Santa Catarina (BR), his Specialization in Innovation Management degree from the University of Texas (US) and Simon Fraiser University (CA). His present research concerns theoretical and field study of innovation ecosystems, innovation management and knowledge representation.

Aurora A.C. Teixeira is Associate Professor at the University of Porto (Portugal), where she holds the chairs of Macroeconomics and Innovation Management. She received her PhD from SPRU — Science Policy Research Unit (University of Sussex, UK). Her current research interests include technology commercialization, U-I linkages, economic growth, structural change, entrepreneurship, scientometrics, and academic ethics. She has published in journals such as *Cambridge Journal of Economics, China Economic Review, Ecological Economics, European Planning Studies, Industrial and Corporate Change, Journal of Evolutionary Economics, Portuguese Economic Journal, Regional Studies, Research Policy, Scientometrics, Social Indicators Research,* and *Structural Change and Economic Dynamics.*

Mike Wright is Professor of Entrepreneurship at Imperial College Business School, Director of the Centre for Management Buyout Research, and a visiting professor at the University of Ghent. He is currently co-editor of *Strategic Entrepreneurship Journal* and of *Academy of Management Perspectives.* His research focuses on management buyouts, entrepreneurial ownership mobility, academic entrepreneurship, returnee entrepreneurs, habitual entrepreneurs, technology transfer, family firms, venture capital, private equity, business angels, crowdfunding, and related topics. He is Chair of the Society for the Advancement of Management Studies, a Past Chair of the Academy of Management Entrepreneurship Division and a recipient of that Division's Mentor Award.

Alfredo Yegros was born in Valencia, Spain. He received his PhD in Library and Information Sciences from the Technical University of Valencia in 2012. That year he moved to work as a researcher at the Centre for Science and Technology Studies (CWTS) at Leiden University, in the Netherlands. His research focuses on public–private interactions and knowledge flows, the study of science-technology linkages and the development of metrics on science and technological developments. Before joining CWTS, he worked at the technology transfer office of the Spanish National Research Council (CSIC) in Valencia and at the Institute of Innovation and Knowledge Management (CSIC-UPV).

Chapter 1

A Multicountry, Process-Based Approach to Academic Entrepreneurship

Riccardo Fini* and Rosa Grimaldi[†]

University of Bologna, Italy
*riccardo.fini@unibo.it
[†]rosa.grimaldi@unibo.it

Academic entrepreneurship is a hot topic that is drawing increasing attention from policymakers, university administrators, and the scientists who engage in it. By adopting a process view of academic entrepreneurship, in this book, we aim to contribute to the conversation on how to effectively commercialize university research. We collect evidence from twelve countries and three continents. We use both qualitative and quantitative research methods to illuminate how and to what extent entrepreneurship unfolds from universities worldwide.

Overview of Academic Entrepreneurship

In recent years, academic entrepreneurship has received increased attention in the literature from scholars, practitioners, and policymakers. By academic entrepreneurship (Grimaldi *et al.*, 2011), we refer to diverse technology-based economic development initiatives, focused mainly on stimulating technological entrepreneurship in universities via patenting, licensing, start-up creation, and university–industry partnerships. The commonality among such efforts is the commercialization of innovations developed by academic scientists. Within this broad definition, great attention has been paid to the creation of new businesses based on university-developed knowledge, also known as academic start-ups or spin-outs (Fini *et al.*, 2013).

In line with the definition above, as well as with the general entrepreneurship literature, academic entrepreneurship can be seen as a multifaceted phenomenon that involves many actors, operating at different levels and engaging in processes that unfold over extended time periods. Accordingly, extant research has addressed the phenomenon at different levels of analysis, emphasizing individual, organizational, and environmental approaches.

Individual agency is the engine of entrepreneurship. Research on individuals has addressed scientists' personal characteristics (Roberts, 1991; Mosey & Wright, 2007), their motivation and preferences (Baron, 1998; Shane *et al.*, 2003), as well as their entrepreneurial orientation and human capital (Cooper *et al.*, 1994; Colombo & Grilli, 2005) as key drivers of the entrepreneurial process. At the organizational level, studies have examined the characteristics of the institutions where the research is conducted and, more specifically, the effectiveness of organizational mechanisms that foster and incentivize the commercial exploitation of research results (Sørensen & Fassiotto, 2011). Such characteristics include the organizational structure of opportunities (Lee *et al.*, 2011), the nature of knowledge (Clarysse *et al.*, 2011), the networks' characteristics (Greve & Salaff, 2003), as well as the vast array of support mechanisms (e.g., university incubators and TTOs) and internal regulations (spin-off and patent policies) that university administrators may introduce to facilitate university-knowledge commercialization (Phan & Siegel, 2006; Lockett *et al.*, 2005; Siegel *et al.*, 2007; Baldini *et al.*, 2014). Environmental-level perspectives have also addressed the phenomenon. Policies, institutional regulations (Mowery *et al.*, 2004; Kenney & Patton, 2009; Grimaldi *et al.*, 2011), environmental aspects, and the characteristics of the local context and the availability of supporting institutions and science parks (Florida, 2003; Degroof & Roberts, 2014) may promote enterprising behaviors at universities.

The increased research on academic entrepreneurship has been coupled with growing university engagement in science commercialization (Perkmann *et al.*, 2015a). The rationale for this increased engagement is that a university can address forms of market failure and contribute to socioeconomic and technological advancement while simultaneously producing benefits for the university through start-ups' revenues. Consequently, we have seen increased university investment to create legal frameworks (Leydesdorff & Etzkowitz, 1996; Di Gregorio & Shane, 2003; O'Shea *et al.*, 2005; Clarysse *et al.*, 2007) and organizational conditions (Siegel *et al.*, 2003; Lockett *et al.*, 2005) to foster the commercial exploitation of their research results.

A Process Approach to Academic Entrepreneurship

The idea behind this book is to address academic entrepreneurship from a process perspective and, at the same time, to empathize its global nature. Previous research highlights how entrepreneurial behaviors may unfold according to an intentional, planned, process — moving from the generation of an idea to its implementation (Krueger *et al.*, 2000) — or according to a more unstructured, emergent, approach, which is also referred to as *effectuation* (Sarasvathy, 2001). The former view emphasizes a planned engagement in entrepreneurship, rooted in individuals' intentionality (Bird, 1988). Intentions are driven by individuals' psychological characteristics as well as by the perception of the surrounding context in which entrepreneurship will take place (Fini *et al.*, 2012). Effectuation, by contrast, emphasizes the non-intentional nature of entrepreneurial behaviors, as part of which entrepreneurs create their own odds of success by taking incremental steps, thus moving closer to their goals. This incremental approach is called effectuation because it takes advantage of the compounding effects that entrepreneurs themselves create via their own actions.

Regardless of the specific cognitive framework leading to the entrepreneurial event (causal versus effectual), it is possible to identify a few major steps in the entrepreneurial journey. In this book, by emphasizing a process view of entrepreneurship, we deconstruct the journey into three major phases: namely, the evaluation of the business idea, the implementation of the entrepreneurial opportunity, and the strategies for entrepreneurial growth.

We believe this approach is methodologically sound because it permits different levels of analysis that correspond to different phases of the entrepreneurial journey (employing both qualitative and quantitative techniques). In the evaluation phase, individuals are, indeed, central because they are the engines of the process. In the implementation phase, individuals remain important (as they do throughout the process), but the organizational context comes to the forefront to set the boundary conditions for how entrepreneurship unfolds. Finally, in the growth phase, other environmental factors will come into play to influence the development of the new company, as well as its internationalization and merger-and-acquisition (M&A) strategies.

Additionally, we consider location to highlight how country specificities represent additional ingredients, with the potential to influence the enactment of entrepreneurship. We believe that a global take is timely and needed because, to the best of our knowledge, no studies have contributed evidence on more than two continents at the same time. This book also complements the notable efforts by Shane (2004) focused on the US context; by Wright *et al.* (2007) on Europe; and Wong (2011) on Asian countries. A global perspective emphasizes the specificities and idiosyncrasies of individual countries and the reality that there is no universal formula for successful academic entrepreneurship. More specifically, history, culture, socio-political conditions, and economic climate all influence successful commercialization of academic knowledge. Indeed, *individual behaviors matter, but context shapes how entrepreneurship unfolds.*

This book brings together contributions from twelve countries located on three continents; it covers the entire entrepreneurial process from evaluation of the business idea to the strategies that academic spin-off firms pursue to achieve sustainable growth. In Table 1, we characterize the contributions in terms of geographical coverage, position within the entrepreneurial process, and key features.

Academic Entrepreneurship: Evidence from Around the Globe

Business idea evaluation

The first contribution related to the business idea evaluation phase is by *D'este, Llopis and Yegros.* The authors look at individual characteristics that enhance academic entrepreneurship in its various forms, with particular emphasis on new venture creation. They rely on data from 1,295 scientific researchers as representative of the population of scientists in the Spanish Council for Scientific Research.

The study reveals the existence of a set of research-related behaviors (namely, pro-social research behaviors) that are performed by scientists in framing their research agendas and projects. These conducts are closely linked to scientists' subsequent participation in university-science commercialization. One of the main findings of this chapter is that pro-social research conducts are shaped by previous knowledge-transfer experiences, cognitive diversity, and research excellence.

A relevant implication of the study is that technology transfer would benefit from a change in the reward system in scientific fields. For instance, including knowledge transfer activity as a criterion for academic promotion could reduce the perceived obstacles to adopting pro-social research conduct for many scientists. Given the centrality of individuals to the academic entrepreneurial process, this contribution highlights the importance of cultural and cognitive dimensions that could affect the nature of research.

Table 1.   Exhibits.

Chapter Order	Contributors	Geo-coverage	Phase 1 Business idea evaluation	Phase 2 Implementation of the entrepreneurial opportunity	Phase 3 Strategies for entrepreneurial growth
2	D'este, Llopis and Yegros	Spain	The focus is on pro-social behaviors as determinants of entrepreneurial behaviors among academics. The study relies on a sample of 1,295 Spanish scientists and it employs quantitative methods.	—	—
3	Goethner	Germany	The study focuses on the determinants of entrepreneurial intentions among academics. It uses a sample of 247 German scientists and it employs quantitative methods	—	—
4	Billström	Sweden	The focus is on the role of external entrepreneurs' human capital, and social networks in the formation of Swedish university spin-offs. The study relies on 6 case studies and employs a qualitative research design.		—
5	Goble, Bercovitz and Feldman	USA	—	The chapter investigates how the organizational reporting structure of the university TLO and the educational background and experience of the TLO director affect academic entrepreneurship. The study focuses on a sample of 76 US universities and employs quantitative methods.	—

(*Continued*)

Table 1. (*Continued*)

Chapter Order	Contributors	Geo-coverage	Phase 1 Business idea evaluation	Phase 2 Implementation of the entrepreneurial opportunity	Phase 3 Strategies for entrepreneurial growth
6	Noyotny	Hungary	—	The focus is on factors influencing the inception and success of Hungarian academic spin-offs. It relies on a sample of 80 academic entrepreneurs and employs both quantitative and qualitative methods.	
7	Fu and Wright	UK	—	The chapter focuses on the creation and performance of UK university spin-out firms. It employs data on the population of 113 universities and their 1359 spin-outs during the 2000–2012 period. It employs quantitative methods.	
8	Moustakbal and Niosi	Canada	—	—	The study focuses on the performance of 213 academic spin-outs, established in Canada, between 1990 and 2010, operating in the biotech sector. It employs a quantitative approach.
9	Rasmussen and Tuft Mathisen	Norway	—	—	The focus is on exit strategies by Norwegian academic spin-offs, with particular emphasis on M&A. The study uses a sample of 471 science-based firms and employ quantitative methods.

10	Bolzani, Fini and Grimaldi	Italy	—	—	The focus is on the extent to which Italian academic spin-outs go international. The study relies on a sample of 120 firms and employs quantitative methods.
11	Texeira	Portugal	—	—	The focus is on how international academic partnerships created in the last decade have contributed to academic entrepreneurship in Portugal. The study relies on a sample of 101 firms and employs quantitative methods.
12	Spinosa, Schlemm and Reis	Brasil	—	—	The study addresses how the introduction of an ICT platform at the Pontifical Catholic University in Curitiba Brazil fostered the creation of an entrepreneurial ecosystem in the region. It employs a case study approach and relies on qualitative data.
13	Van Hove and Clarysse	Belgium	—	—	The study addresses the propensity of Belgium-based higher education institutions to create an entrepreneurial and knowledge-driven ecosystem. It focuses on 4 institutions and employs a qualitative case study approach.

Goethner also looks at individual-level determinants of entrepreneurial intentions among academic scientists. Specifically, he investigates how the process of knowledge production by individual scientists (i.e., whether their research is performed on a national or international scale) influences academic entrepreneurship. The study draws on a sample of 247 German scientists.

The starting point of the contribution is the lack of studies addressing the process of knowledge production by university scientists. The central tenet of the paper is that scientists' international research collaborations may influence the ways in which entrepreneurship occurs. The main findings show that consistent with the theory of planned behavior, attitudes, and perceived behavioral control predict intentionality. Moreover, scientific and technical human capital moderate these relationships; in particular, if the scientific and technical human capital is high (i.e., a scientist's international research network is large), the effect of perceived control on intentionality is diminished.

One key aspect that is highlighted by this research is that although there is a small yet growing body of literature dealing with this topic (D'Este *et al.*, 2012; Erikson *et al.*, 2015), more research is needed on the role of scientific productivity in the prediction of entrepreneurial behaviors. The contribution by Goethner represents a first step in this direction, shedding light on the mechanisms through which skills and networks — which are key for the practice of science and the career growth of scientists — may impact academic entrepreneurship.

By focusing on opportunity recognition and the different steps that characterize the inception and evolution of academic spin-offs, the contribution by *Billstrom* bridges the evaluation and inception phases. Specifically, it emphasizes the role of external — non-academic — entrepreneurs' human capital, and social networks in the formation of Swedish university spin-offs. The author employs a qualitative case study design and focuses on six Swedish companies, suggesting a conceptual framework for the role of social network actors (in terms of network content, network governance, and network structure) in the formation of university spin-offs managed by external and inventor entrepreneurs.

His findings suggest that some university spin-off firms grow slowly or fail to grow because academic researchers sometimes lack sufficient industry networks. External entrepreneurs — who come from outside academia and who typically have more extensive industry networks — may represent a key asset in the formation and growth of such firms. These findings have implications for policymaking related to university incubators and for the support of university–industry collaborations. This evidence may also lead to an increased number of university spin-offs established by external entrepreneurs; it also significantly contributes to the development of external non-university-linked entrepreneurial firms.

Implementation of the entrepreneurial opportunity

As for the implementation phase, *Goble, Bercovitz, and Feldman* investigate how the organizational reporting structure of the university technology licensing office (TLO), and the educational background, and experience of the TLO director affect the technology transfer process, and, in particular, the creation of spin-off firms in the US. The study relies on data from different sources, including the AUTM annual licensing survey and Feldman and Bercovitz's 2010 survey of AUTM respondents (as part of which technology transfer outcome data were collected for 76 universities over a three-year period from 2008 to 2010).

One of the main findings is that TLOs that reported directly to the university leader (or to an economic/business development office) are relatively more effective in working with university spin-offs than TLOs that report to an office of research; by contrast, TLOs that report to multiple functions are relatively more effective in licensing than TLOs that report directly to the office of research (or to an economic/business development office).

Moreover, the study provides evidence of a positive relationship between business and commercialization skills taught through an MBA educational degree and increased disclosure and start-up activity compared to TLO directors with a PhD. Findings also suggest that, although legal knowledge is an important element for the technology transfer process, in intellectual property (IP) protection and contractual language, legal wrangling in negotiation practices may limit successful licensing opportunities. Overall, the findings suggest that the technology transfer activities of US research universities continue to evolve and expand, and, as a result, the influence of university characteristics on commercialization outcomes will continue to change.

By bridging the implementation and growth phases, *Novotny* addresses the motivations, characteristics, and performance of spin-off firms established by university faculty members in Hungary. In particular, the study draws attention to the role of motivations in evaluating the success of academic entrepreneurship. The study represents one of the first efforts to provide robust evidence on university–industry technology-transfer activities in post-socialist economies in Central and Eastern Europe.

Among the main findings, we highlight extrinsic motivation (i.e., the need to maintain specific families' living standards) as an important trigger for Hungarian academic entrepreneurs. Moreover, the low growth potential of many university spin-offs can be largely attributed to the fact that their founder–managers are only part-time entrepreneurs who do not want to give up their relatively secure university positions and jeopardize their social status, and university income to focus on their firms full time.

It is also interesting to highlight that the majority of academic entrepreneurs run their firms 'outside' the institution (i.e., without shared ownership with the university). The support received from the university, when available, does not seem to affect the success of the spin-off firms. This finding is especially interesting in light of recent changes to the national Hungarian innovation policy that encourage universities to increase their involvement in commercializing inventions stemming from university research.

Similarly, *Fu* and *Wright* overview both the determinants and performance of academic spin-offs in UK. The study is based on the full population of the UK Higher Education Institutions. Several aspects are discussed in the empirical analysis. First, an interesting argument relates to the scant attention paid to start-ups involving less formal IP (Fini *et al.*, 2010). Increasing emphasis has been traditionally granted to university spin-offs by faculty who are involved with formal IP. However, notwithstanding their small size, start-ups involving less formal IP may generate significant local employment benefits, often having a larger impact on the society.

Second, the authors show a decline in spin-offs by faculty members and illuminate the interesting albeit scantly researched phenomenon of venture creation by students. Universities are, in fact, responding to and stimulating this trend through the creation of creativity labs and entrepreneurial garages, such as CreateLab at Imperial College, which provides pre-accelerator support for early stage ventures.

Overall, their contribution provides new insights into the variety of the UK landscape that opens up questions for both policy development and further research in this field.

Strategies for entrepreneurial growth

As for the actions that academic spin-off firms may undertake to achieve sustainable growth, *Moustakbal* and *Niosi* look at a sample of 213 university Spin-offs, operating in bio-related sectors, drawn from the population of more than 1,000 biotech start-ups in Canada (for which longitudinal data and information are available from 1990 to 2010).

The study presents an up-to-date portrait of these firms, analyzing the factors that influence the survival or disappearance of these companies. As for the latter, the authors look at two distinct forms of disappearances of USOs: namely, M&A and bankruptcies. The factors explaining the failure of start-ups may significantly differ from those that are at the origin of M&A. In fact, M&A transactions can be regarded as a strategic choice, thoughtful and adapted to the realities of Canadian companies whose financial resources are limited. Such a choice also seems justified by the biotechnology product-development process, which is costly and uncertain. Moreover, strategic alliances and interference of stakeholders in the lifecycle of biotechnology spin-off could play an important role in the governance model adopted by the management team and, therefore, in firms' forms of disappearance.

According to the evidence provided, the authors suggest that the Canadian government at both federal and provincial levels should rethink their intervention strategies in the biotechnology sectors and implement new programs and policies that address both the creation as well as the development of spin-offs.

By focusing on post-entry strategies, *Rasmussen* and *Tuft Mathisen* use the real option approach to analyze the performance of science-based spin-offs in Norway. The study assesses, in detail, the portfolios of all 471 firms that are supported by technology transfer offices, incubators, and science parks in Norway from 1995 to 2012.

The findings reveal that 97 of these firms have reached a successful outcome, 126 have most likely failed, and the remaining 251 may still be considered as real options with an uncertain outcome. Furthermore, acquisitions appear to be an important mode of successful outcomes for these ventures. One important implication of the study is that slow-growing science-based spin-offs can also play an important role in bringing technology to the market. These firms can create value through their indirect role as a mechanism to translate scientific findings into application in society.

In line with Rasmussen and Tuft Mathisen, *Bolzani, Fini, and Grimaldi*, move from the difficulties associated with gauging the performance of newly established high-tech companies, and focus on internationalization strategies. The chapter reviews the existing studies on academic spin-offs' internationalization strategies, connecting these to the international business and international entrepreneurship literature. It also describes the internationalization patterns followed by 120 academic spin-off firms in Italy that were established between 2000 and 2008.

The results show that more than 60% of these companies operate in international markets. The internationalized firms exhibit different capital structures (i.e., they have more financial institutions among the shareholders and benefit from a higher amount of equity invested by public institutions and individual shareholders); they employ more people and have higher revenues compared to the spin-off companies that do not internationalize. Data also show that non-internationalized companies display significantly less positive attitudes towards the exploitation of international opportunities and challenges; in other words, both observable and unobservable characteristics should be carefully considered to understand and properly predict internationalization growth strategies.

Based on a sample of 101 spin-offs associated with the University Technology Enterprise Network (UTEN) in Portugal, *Texeira* extends this line of research and links the economic performance of academic spin-off firms to the context in which entrepreneurship takes place. The economic performance of the firms was regressed not only on founders' and firms' characteristics but, also, on the availability of infrastructures to support science and technology-based entrepreneurship (e.g., TTOs, Incubators, Science Parks).

Results show that the steady investment in science and technology support infrastructures has a partial payoff. Indeed, support from incubators (or by more than two infrastructures) significantly contributes to firms' economic performance. Additionally, access to skilled labor, and the services of business mentoring, and counseling provided by science and technology support infrastructures are fundamental to these companies' sustainability. Nonetheless, the results indicate that university spillovers (proxied by the stock of scientific publications and patents, and the quality of research centers) have not yet yielded noticeable economic returns to academic spin-offs in Portugal.

Following this line of inquiry, *Reis, Schlemm,* and *Spinosa* examine the environmental characteristics that may favor the enactment of entrepreneurial behaviors. They focus on ecosystems and their constituting elements (namely a set of innovation clusters structured as cooperation networks). One of the tenets of this contribution is that to capture all components of an innovation ecosystem, we need a process-based approach that accounts for all actors creating value within the ecosystem (i.e., both producers and final users of innovation-related activities).

Conducted in the Brazilian context, the study uses a process-based approach implemented as an information and communications technology (ICT) platform called PIA — developed at the Pontifical Catholic University in Curitiba (and involving global partners such as Nokia and Siemens) — to manage a Brazilian innovation ecosystem. By providing practical tools to support the evolution of the innovation ecosystem in the region of Curitiba, this chapter sheds light on how complex multifaceted environments can support the emergence of technology-based enterprising behaviors.

Finally, *Clarysse* and *Van Hove* conclude by exploring the factors that determine the propensity of Belgium-based Higher Education Institutions (HEIs) to create an entrepreneurial and knowledge- driven ecosystem. Specifically, the authors focus on Flanders, the largest autonomous region of Belgium, and examine how the role of Flemish universities has evolved from closed powerhouses to boundary-spanning organizations. This evolution is mainly based on applying an inter- organizational network perspective.

In this chapter, the authors examine the case of IMINDS, one of the four independent research institutes of Flanders, and its contribution to the creation of an entrepreneurial ecosystem and to the support of regional academic entrepreneurship. By comparing IMINDS to Imperial College London (which is recognized as one of the world's most successful technology innovation ecosystems), the authors explore the emerging ecosystem in Belgium, envision what an entrepreneurial university would look like, and examine the barriers to achieving this. They also suggest ways to strive for a vibrant entrepreneurial community with a balanced representation of university, corporate, entrepreneurial, and government stakeholders.

Directions for Future Research

By addressing academic entrepreneurship via a process perspective, we had the opportunity to compose a book that examines the different phases of the entrepreneurial journey, using different levels of analysis, employing either qualitative or quantitative methods. We thus looked at academic entrepreneurship from diverse angles, systematizing some of the knowledge available in the field but also identifying some aspects that may be worthy of further investigation. In the following, we streamline some of these.

First, given its holistic nature and origins in transparent organizations (i.e., universities), academic entrepreneurship may represent a fertile and easy-to-research context suitable to advance knowledge in diverse disciplines, such as organizational theory, sociology, psychology, geography, and institutional and evolutionary theories. Although some notable contributions have recently been made (Rasmussen *et al.*, 2011; Fini *et al.*, 2012; Kotha *et al.*, 2013; Pitsakis *et al.*, 2015), we still see room for advancing management studies by using academic entrepreneurship as a "laboratory" to test general management theories.

Second, notwithstanding investigators' efforts to explore different levels of analysis, studies that adopt a multilevel perspective represent a significant gap in the literature. Indeed, interesting research questions may lie at the interface of the institutional, organizational, and individual domains (Hitt *et al.*, 2007). Moreover, process perspectives would also provide new insights into the evolution of academic entrepreneurship (McMullen & Dimov, 2013). Both aspects are underexplored in the literature, and this paves the way for future studies. However, notwithstanding its desirability, feasibility aspects may be detrimental. Gathering reliable, cross-level, longitudinal data may present, in reality, quite a challenge. To fill part of this void, the following chapters present some of the latest advancements in the research on this domain (see for example, Bolzani *et al.*, 2014 and Perkmann *et al.*, 2015b for a multilevel, longitudinal study on university-science commercialization).

The third aspect relates to the cross-country perspective. In compiling evidence from different nations, we appreciated once more the relevance of country-level factors in influencing the outcome of academic entrepreneurship. Along these lines, it would be desirable to see cross-country studies that address how — and to what extent — the national cultural, and normative idiosyncrasies impact the enactment of academic entrepreneurship.

Finally, we stress the importance of investigating additional 'un-structured' aspects of academic entrepreneurship. There are other mechanisms, less familiar to statistics and more difficult to be traced, through which university-related knowledge flows to the market. One of these includes student or alumni entrepreneurship: specifically, entrepreneurial firms started by undergraduate students in the three years immediately after graduation or during enrollment (Astebro *et al.*, 2012). The conditions favoring student entrepreneurship and, most importantly, its impact deserve further attention.

All this notwithstanding, by systematizing the latest global trends in the field, we aimed to provide a sound contribution to state-of-the-art research on academic entrepreneurship.

References

Astebro, T., Bazzazian, N. & Braguinsky, S. 2012. Startups by recent university graduates and their faculty: Implications for university entrepreneurship policy. *Research Policy*, 41(4), 663–677.

Baldini, N., Fini, R., Grimaldi, R. & Sobrero, M. 2014. Organisational change and the institutionalisation of university patenting activity in Italy. *Minerva*, 52, 27–52.

Baron, R. A. 1998. Cognitive mechanisms in entrepreneurship: why and when entrepreneurs think differently than other people. *Journal of Business Venturing*, 13(4), 275–294.

Bird, B. 1988. Implementing entrepreneurial ideas: the case for intention. *Academy of Management Review*, 13(3), 442–453.

Bolzani, D., Fini, R., Grimaldi, R., Santoni, S. & Sobrero, M. 2014. *Fifteen Years of Academic Entrepreneurship in Italy: Evidence from the Taste Project*. Technical Report, University of Bologna.

Clarysse, B., Tartari, V. & Salter, A. 2011. The impact of entrepreneurial capacity, experience and organizational support on academic entrepreneurship. *Research Policy*, 40(8), 1084–1093.

Clarysse, B., Wright, M., Lockett, A., Mustar, P. & Knockaert, M. 2007. Academic spinoffs, formal technology transfer and capital raising. *Industrial and Corporate Change*, 16(4), 609–640.

Colombo, M. & Grilli, L. 2005. Founders' human capital and the growth of new technology-based firms: a competence based view. *Research Policy*, 34(6), 795–816.

Cooper, A. C., Gimeno-Gascon, G. J. & Woo, C. Y. 1994. Initial human and financial capital as predictors of new venture performance. *Journal of Business Venturing*, 9(5), 371–395.

Degroof, J. & Roberts, E. 2004. Overcoming weak entrepreneurial infrastructures for academic spin- off ventures. *The Journal of Technology Transfer*, 29(3), 327–352.

Di Gregorio, D. & Shane, S. 2003. Why do some universities generate more start-ups than others? *Research Policy*, 32, 209–227.

Fini, R., Grimaldi, R., Marzocchi, G. L. & Sobrero, M. 2012. The determinants of corporate entrepreneurial intention within small and newly established firms. *Entrepreneurship Theory and Practice*, 36(2), 387–414.

Fini, R., Lacetera, N. & Shane, S. 2010. Inside or outside the IP-system. Business creation in Academia. *Research Policy*, 39, 1060–1069.

Fini, R., Lacetera, N. & Shane, S. 2013. Academic entrepreneurship. In *The Palgrave Encyclopedia of Strategic Management*, D. Tcccc & M. Augier (eds.). Palgrave Macmillan, Basingstoke. DOI: 10.1057/978113729467.

Florida, R. 1999. The role of the university: leveraging talent, not technology. Issues formal technology transfer and capital raising. *Industrial and Corporate Change*, 16, 609–640.

Greve, A. & Salaff, J. W. 2003. Social networks and entrepreneurship. *Entrepreneurship Theory and Practice*, 28(1), 1–22.

Grimaldi, R., Kenney, M., Siegel, D. & Wright, M. 2011. 30 years after Bayh–Dole: reassessing academic entrepreneurship. *Research Policy*, 40(8), 1045–1057.

Hitt, M. A., Beamish, P. W., Jackson, S. E. & Mathieu, J. E. 2007. Building theoretical and empirical bridges across levels: multilevel research in management. *Academy of Management Journal*, 50(6), 1385–1399.

Kenney, M. & Patton, D. 2009. Reconsidering the Bayh–Dole Act and the current university invention ownership model. *Research Policy*, 38, 1407–1422.

Kotha, R., George, G. & Srikanth, K. 2013. Bridging the mutual knowledge gap: coordination and the commercialization of university science. *Academy of Management Journal*, 56(2), 498–524.

Krueger, N. F., Reilly, M. D. & Carsrud, A. L. 2000. Competing models of entrepreneurial intentions. *Journal of Business Venturing*, 15(5–6), 411–432.

Lee, L., Wong, P. K. & Der Foo, M. 2011. Entrepreneurial intentions: the influence of organizational and individual factors. *Journal of Business Venturing*, 26(1), 124–136.

Leydesdorff, L. & Etzkowitz, H. 1996. Emergence of a triple helix of university-industry- government relations. *Science and Public Policy*, 23(5), 279–286.

Lockett, A., Siegel, D., Wright, M. & Ensley, M. 2005. The creation of spin-off firms at public research institutions: managerial and policy implications. *Research Policy*, 34(7), 981–993.

McMullen, J. S. & Dimov, D. 2013. Time and the entrepreneurial journey: the problems and promise of studying entrepreneurship as a process. *Journal of Management Studies*, 50(8), 1481–1512.

Mosey, S. & Wright, M. 2007. From human capital to social capital: a longitudinal study of technology-based academic entrepreneurs. *Entrepreneurship Theory and Practice*, 31(6), 909–935.

Mowery, D. C. & Sampat, B. N. 2005. The Bayh–Dole Act of 1980 and university industry technology transfer: a model for other OECD governments? *Journal of Technology Transfer*, 30, 115–127.

O'Shea, R. P., Allen, T. J., Chevalier, A. & Roche, F. 2005. Entrepreneurial orientation, technology transfer and spinoff performance of U.S. universities. *Research Policy* 34, 994–1009.

Perkmann, M., Fini, R., Ross, J. M., Salter, A., Silvestri, C. & Tartari, V. 2015a. Accounting for universities' impact: using augmented data to measure academic engagement and commercialization by academic scientists. *Research Evaluation*, 24(4), 380–391.

Perkmann, M., Fini, R., Ross, J. M., Salter, A., Silvestri, C. & Tartari, V. 2015b. Accounting for Impact at Imperial College London: A Report on the Activities and Outputs by Imperial Academics Relevant for Economic and Social Impact. Technical Report, Imperial College London.

Phan, P. & Siegel, D. S. 2006. The effectiveness of university technology transfer: lessons learned, managerial and policy implications, and the road forward. *Foundations and Trends in Entrepreneurship* 2(2), 77–144.

Pitsakis, K., Souitaris, V. & Nicolaou, N. 2015. The peripheral halo effect: do academic spinoffs influence universities' research income? *Journal of Management Studies*, 52(3), 321–353.

Rasmussen, E., Mosey, S. & Wright, M. 2011. The evolution of entrepreneurial competencies: a longitudinal study of university spin-off venture emergence. *Journal of Management Studies*, 48(6), 1314–1345.

Roberts, E. B. 1991. *Entrepreneurs in High Technology*. Oxford University Press, Oxford, UK.

Sarasvathy, S. D. 2001. Causation and effectuation: toward a theoretical shift from economic inevitability to entrepreneurial contingency. *Academy of Management Review*, 26(2), 243–263.

Shane, S., Locke, E. A. & Collins, C. J. 2003. Entrepreneurial motivation, human resource. *Management Review*, 13(2), 257–279.

Shane, S. A. 2004. *Academic Entrepreneurship: University Spinoffs and Wealth Creation*. Edward Elgar Publishing, Cheltenham.

Siegel, D., Veugelers, R. & Wright, M. 2007. University commercialization of intellectual property: policy implications. *Oxford Review of Economic Policy*, 23(4), 640–660.

Siegel, D. S., Waldman, D. A., Atwater, L. & Link, A. N. 2004. Toward a model of the effective transfer of scientific knowledge from academicians to practitioners: qualitative evidence from the commercialization of university technologies. *Journal of Engineering and Technology Management* 21(1–2), 115–142.

Siegel, D. S., Waldman, D. A. & Link, A. N. 2003. Assessing the impact of organizational practices on the productivity of university technology transfer offices: an exploratory study. *Research Policy*, 32(1), 27–48.

Sørensen, J. B. & Fassiotto, M. A. 2011. Organizations as fonts of entrepreneurship. *Organization Science*, 22(5), 1322–1331.

Wong, P. K. (ed.). 2011. *Academic Entrepreneurship in Asia: The Role and Impact of Universities in National Innovation Systems*. Edward Elgar Publishing, Cheltenham.

Wright, M., Clarysse, B., Mustar, P. & Lockett, A. 2007. *Academic Entrepreneurship in Europe*. Edward Elgar Publishing, Cheltenham.

Chapter 2

Conducting Pro-Social Research: Exploring the Behavioral Antecedents to Knowledge Transfer Among Scientists

Pablo D'Este

INGENIO (CSIC-UPV), Universitat Politècnica de València, Camino
de Vera s/n, 46022 Valencia, Spain
pdeste@ingenio.upv.es

Oscar Llopis

Rennes School of Business, 2 Rue Robert d'Arbrissel
35065 Rennes, France
oscar.llopis-corcoles@esc-rennes.com

Alfredo Yegros

Centre for Science and Technology Studies (CWTS),
Leiden University, Wassenaarseweg 62A 2333 AL Leiden, The Netherlands
a.yegros@cwts.leidenuniv.nl

We propose the concept of pro-social research to describe the adoption of behavior by scientists who consider societal relevance to be a critical objective of research. We argue that pro-social research is a behavioral antecedent to scientists' engagement in knowledge transfer activities, including firm creation. Our study investigates the impact of various cognitive aspects on the development of pro-social research behavior. In particular, we investigate whether cognitive diversity and research excellence positively shape pro-social research behavior, and more critically, whether they act as substitutes for prior experience in knowledge transfer activity. Our data are from a large scale survey of scientists in the Spanish Council for Scientific Research (CSIC) and administrative and bibliometric sources.

Introduction

Numerous academic studies recognize that the transfer of knowledge and technology between academia and industry is crucial for boosting economic growth and improving social welfare (Bercovitz & Feldman, 2006; Feller, 1990; Spencer, 2001). The growing emphasis in government policy agendas on encouraging knowledge exchange between the scientific and societal domains is being accompanied by increasing academic interest in the micro-foundations of scientists' engagement in this activity (Ankrah *et al.*, 2013, Bercovitz & Feldman 2008; Jain *et al.*, 2009, Rothaermel *et al.*, 2007). This interest stems in part from the complex challenges faced by academic scientists working at the interface between the academic and business environments, which requires reconciliation among different (often conflicting) norms, priorities, and incentives (Philpott *et al.*, 2011; Sauermann & Stephan, 2013; Tartari & Breschi, 2012). Researchers who adopt an individual approach to academic entrepreneurship point to the importance of individual differences for explaining academic involvement in firm creation (Clarysse *et al.*, 2011; Fini *et al.*, 2012; Goethner *et al.*, 2012).

However, academic entrepreneurship as a channel for the flow of scientific research to society, is very specific and rather exceptional channel. The complexity and multifaceted nature of the interactions between the academic and the societal spheres has been receiving greater attention (Gilsing *et al.*, 2011; Murray, 2004; Salter & Martin, 2001) and these studies reveal a range of formal and informal channels which are allowing academic science to be exploited by non-academic audiences. These channels range from patenting and licensing of research results to participating in consulting activities with non-academic agents such as firms or public organizations. Although a number of studies have proposed factors associated with scientists' participation in specific knowledge transfer channels (e.g., Ankrah *et al.*, 2013; Perkmann *et al.*, 2011), much less is known about the extent to which cognitive and motivational factors shape the adoption of a research mode that accounts explicitly for an underlying preference for a societal impact via research activities (Audretsch & Erdem, 2004).

The current paper addresses this issue and focuses on individual level characteristics to understand why and how scientists' construct and nurture explicit awareness of the societal impact of their research activities. This micro-perspective is aimed at understanding why scientists exhibit very different levels of engagement in knowledge transfer activities (Agrawal

& Henderson, 2002; Haeussler & Colyvas, 2011), and which types of skills induce this engagement despite little previous experience. To be precise, we propose adoption of the concept of pro-social research behavior. Drawing on the organizational behavior and social psychology fields (Brief & Motowidlo, 1986; Grant & Sumanth, 2009; Grant, 2007; Penner *et al.*, 2005), we define pro-social research as a set of observable and deliberate behaviors reflecting the critical goal of societal relevance in the scientists' research agendas. We argue that explicit consideration of this concept is important both theoretically and practically, in showing that researchers who exhibit an awareness of the societal impact of their research, demonstrate this concern by more frequent engagement in an extensive set of activities to transfer knowledge to non-academic agents, ranging from consulting activities to the creation of companies. We also investigate whether different cognitive aspects at the individual level (i.e., cognitive diversity, research excellence) have a significant influence on shaping pro-social research behaviors, and more important, whether they act as substitutes for prior experience in knowledge transfer activities.

This article offers two main contributions to the existing knowledge. The first contribution is a theoretical (and empirical) integration of research on pro-social behavior and knowledge transfer studies. Specifically, the concept of pro-social research is proposed as a novel mechanism to explain scientists' heterogeneous participation in various forms of knowledge transfer activities with actors located beyond the boundaries of academia. It offers a new perspective to investigate the antecedents to academic entrepreneurship, and scientists' involvement in firm creation. Second, we show that three individual-level differences among scientists are salient to explain scientists' heterogeneous levels of pro-social research behavior, and thus, to partly explain why certain scientists are particularly active with regard to engagement in a wide range of knowledge transfer activities. Both these contributions should add to the knowledge on the micro-foundations of science in relation to knowledge transfer to society (Ankrah *et al.*, 2013; Tartari & Breschi, 2012).

By investigating the mechanisms underlying the observed heterogeneity in scientists' participation in knowledge transfer activities, we try to disentangle whether there is a uniform set of behaviors underpinning these observed differences. Our findings show the existence of a set of related behaviors (namely, pro-social research) performed by scientists when framing their research agendas and projects. The importance of an explicit focus on pro-social research rests on the fact that it is closely linked to the subsequent participation of scientists in a range of different knowledge transfer activities. Crucially, we find that pro-social research is shaped by previous knowledge transfer experience, cognitive diversity, and research excellence.

We test our hypotheses on a sample of 1,295 scientific researchers, representative of the population of scientists in the CSIC, the largest public research organization in Spain. We begin by reviewing the knowledge transfer and organizational psychology literatures, to provide a context for our proposed explicit focus on pro-social research as an antecedent to participation in knowledge transfer activities. We postulate the potential influence of previous knowledge transfer experience, cognitive diversity, and research excellence as determinants of pro-social research behavior. We describe our methodology, test the hypotheses, and present the results. The paper concludes with a discussion of the results and directions for future research.

Theoretical Background

Science and the societal impact of research

Research in the sociology of science suggests that scientist' behaviors respond to an "academic logic" based on the classical model of science (Merton, 1973; Sauermann & Stephan, 2013) whose norms and incentive structures prioritize the quest for fundamental understanding and the open dissemination of scientific knowledge. In this model, scientists' rewards come mainly in the form of peer recognition and academic reputation within the scientific community. However, in recent years the system of science has undergone several changes. Proposed new models of knowledge production such as "Mode 2" research (Gibbons *et al.*, 1994), "academic capitalism" (Slaughter & Leslie, 1997), "entrepreneurial science" (Etzkowitz, 1998), and "post-academic science" (Ziman, 2002), have provoked discussion on the different ways that science is organized and performed. Common to these potential new configurations of knowledge production is a greater effort to interact with other societal spheres such as government and industry. According to Hessels and Van Lente (2008, p. 742), *"Mode 2 knowledge is rather a dialogic process, and has the capacity to incorporate multiple views. This relates to researchers becoming more aware of the societal consequences of their work (social accountability). Sensitivity to the impact of the research is built from the start"*. Researchers are being pushed by public funding agencies towards producing knowledge with clear societal and economic utility (Bornmann, 2013; Olmos-Peñuela *et al.*, 2014). This implies that academics need to be more conscious of the particular needs and interests of other actors in society, and ensure that their work has a clearer social orientation. The quest for societal impact from scientific research is reflected in what Stokes (1997) calls "Pasteur's Quadrant". Research in this mode suggests that scientists' efforts may be directed towards the generation of fundamental knowledge and simultaneously inspired by the potential use of their research results. In other words, considering the potential impact of scientific research on non-academic agents is an individual-level preference irrespective of the basic or applied nature of the research performed (Stokes, 1997).

However, switching from a scientific system governed by the traditional norms of science to one governed by new socio-economic rules related to a more distributed knowledge production process, poses significant challenges for the scientist. In this regard, prior research indicates that an explicit focus on the scientists' attitudes and behaviors towards knowledge transfer reveals considerable heterogeneity. Scientists differ widely in how they manage and respond to the tensions between scientific advance, commercial gains, and career progression (Gittelman & Kogut, 2003; Owen-Smith & Powell, 2001). There are also individual differences in scientists' "taste for science" (Sauermann & Roach, 2011; Stern, 2004), and their predisposition, attitude, and skills to recognize and exploit opportunities to bring scientific knowledge into the societal sphere (Azoulay *et al.*, 2007). There are also differences in scientists' capacity to reorient their research priorities or consider what their research could mean for society (Jain *et al.*, 2009). Thus, the existing evidence in part explains why participation in knowledge transfer activities is systematically concentrated in a few researchers (Haeussler & Colyvas, 2011). It also points to the existence of individual-level factors accounting for those differential preferences. We draw on the pro-social behavior literature to suggest pro-social research as accounting for differences in scientists' engagement in various forms of knowledge transfer.

Pro-social organizational behaviors

A useful approach to an analysis of the differential capacity and disposition of scientists to address societal and economic needs explicitly in their research agendas, is provided by the existing literature on pro-social behavior. Research on pro-social behavior has attracted the attention of organizational behavior scholars (De Dreu & Nauta, 2009; Grant & Sumanth, 2009; Grant, 2007, McNeely & Meglino, 1994), and has been conceptualized in organizational settings as:

> *behavior which is (a) performed by a member of an organization, (b) directed toward an individual, group, or organization with whom he or she interacts while carrying out his or her organizational role, and (c) performed with the intention of promoting the welfare of the individual, group, or organization toward which it is directed.*
>
> (Brief and Motowidlo, 1986, p. 711).

Acts such as helping, sharing, and cooperating are forms of pro-social behavior and are actions that encompass the central notion of the intent to benefit others not formally specified as a role requirement. The organizational behavior literature shows clearly that individuals differ in their tendency to engage in pro-social behaviors, and engage with their pro-social values (Audrey *et al.*, 1997; Meglino & Korsgaard, 2004). Pro-social behavior is consistently related to increased levels of commitment and dedication to the job (Grant & Sumanth, 2009; Thompson & Bunderson, 2003), better coordination and cohesion among the organization's members (Organ *et al.*, 2005), and higher levels of work-group performance (Puffer, 1987). Also, engagement in pro-social behaviors helps individuals to experience their work as more meaningful, and enhances their feeling of social worth in the workplace (Perry & Hondeghem, 2008).

The importance of pro-social behavior for organizational functioning was the motivation for a substantial body of research explaining its determinants. It has been suggested that pro-social behavior is influenced by a myriad factors ranging from biological and psychological (Buck, 2002) to social and contextual (Kerr & MacCoun, 1985). Moreover, the particularities of the workplace exert a considerable effect on the emergence of pro-social identities and pro-social behaviors among individuals (Penner *et al.*, 2005).

The emergence and maintenance of pro-social behaviors is particularly interesting in the context of mission-driven organizations (Brickson, 2007). Such organizations include hospitals, government agencies, universities, and public research centers whose objectives transcend economic profit (Hammer, 1995) and are aimed at making a positive contribution to society. However, there is evidence that not all individuals working in mission-driven organizations are clear about the positive effects that their work might have on potential beneficiaries (Grant & Sumanth, 2009). For instance, it may take many years before biomedical researchers can see the positive impact of their work on patients. Similarly, research has yet to fully integrate the insights and explicit consequences of exhibiting pro-social research behavior in an academic environment. The next section proposes a theoretical conceptualization of pro-social research behavior and justifies its potential relevance as a behavioral antecedent to engagement in a range of knowledge-transfer activities among academic scientists.

Conceptualizing pro-social research behavior

As previously stated, engagement of research scientists in knowledge transfer activity would seem desirable from a policy perspective. However, there is evidence suggesting that implementing policy initiatives does not result automatically in a higher level of scientist participation in such activities. Scientists differ in their adaptation to new rules of the game because their behavior is shaped by a range of different personal and institutional incentives (Bercovitz & Feldman, 2008). Because of the set of norms and incentives particular to the academic environment, the transition between academic research and engagement in knowledge transfer activity is non-trivial (Jain *et al.*, 2009; Owen-Smith & Powell, 2001; Philpott *et al.*, 2011; Tartari & Breschi, 2012) and entails significant modifications to the scientists' role identity (Jain *et al.*, 2009). This suggests that psychological processes related to the perceived usefulness of the research may foster or deter scientists' participation in knowledge transfer. Thus, the perception of task significance and social worth associated with adopting pro-social behavior (Grant *et al.*, 2007) may help to explain why some scientists are more prone than others to adopt a mode of scientific knowledge production that involves strong interaction with the context of application and the potential beneficiaries of the research.

We take the research scientist as our unit of analysis, and examine scientists' adoption of a research mode whose central focus is societal relevance. Employing the concept of pro-social research behavior allows us to adopt a socio-psychological perspective to study the individual-level determinants and consequences of explicit pro-social research conducts in setting up the research agenda. Specifically, we define pro-social research behaviors as conducts that positions societal relevance as the primary research goal, and thus, reflect scientists' revealed preferences for a societal impact from their research activities. We argue that this societal awareness is reflected in three different but related scientist research behaviors. First, an explicit identification of research results that could have a *potential societal impact* on other people or groups (Shane & Venkataraman, 2000). Second, an explicit identification of the *potential users* of the research (Gibbons *et al.*, 1994; Stokes, 1997). Third, an explicit identification of the *intermediate agents* which might help to channel the social benefits of the research to potential users (Jain *et al.*, 2009).

A common feature in all three behaviors is an explicit interest in an impact beyond the academic context. An interest in the research findings benefiting others, and explicit recognition of the channels through which this social impact might be materialized, are clear indications of the adoption of a research mode that diverges from the Mertonian model of science. Work in organizational psychology shows that if the individual perceives that his/her work will have a positive impact on society, there is a greater willingness to go beyond the formal job requirements (Grant, 2008; McNeely & Meglino, 1994) and to aim at professional goals based on the wider community's needs. Additionally, it has been shown that professionals with other-focused outcome goals tend to be more committed to these goals

(Thompson & Bunderson, 2003). Adopting research conduct that prioritizes societal impact is more likely to lead to engagement in knowledge transfer, even if it is not a requirement of the particular job role.

Pro-social behaviors and pro-social motives have recently been incorporated in the academic entrepreneurship and knowledge transfer literatures. Lam (2011) studied the determinants of scientists' engagement in the commercialization of research, and finds that the positive impact on others is an underlying reason for their engagement in commercialization activity. Weijden *et al.* (2012) interviewed 188 leaders of biomedical research groups and found that scientists' participation in activities and outputs to benefit non-academic audiences is explained largely by a positive attitude towards the societal impact of their work. Similarly, Hobin *et al.* (2012), who interviewed biomedical scientists, showed that nearly three-quarters of their respondents had engaged in knowledge transfer activities from a motivation to have an impact on patients and human health.

Hypotheses

Antecedents to pro-social research behavior

We add to the knowledge transfer literature by examining the factors that contribute to the configuration of pro-social research behavior among scientists. We are interested specifically in identifying individual-level features that are conducive to pro-social research by scientists, particularly those with no (or very little) prior experience in knowledge transfer. Drawing on the academic entrepreneurship and organizational behavior literatures, we examine the role of prior experience and investigate two potentially relevant determinants of pro-social research behavior: research excellence and cognitive diversity.

Knowledge transfer experience

It is reasonable to expect that experience of knowledge transfer matters for shaping pro-social research behavior. Those scientists with previous entrepreneurial or other knowledge transfer experience are likely to have developed mindsets and skills that promote further engagement in knowledge transfer (Goethner *et al.,* 2012; Hoye & Pries, 2009; Krueger *et al.,* 2000; Landry *et al.,* 2006). Previous experience of knowledge transfer activity also implies that the scientists will have interacted with the potential beneficiaries of their academic research. The literature emphasizes that contact with beneficiaries is an important driver of development of pro-social attitudes (Goldman & Fordyce, 1983; Grant *et al.,* 2007; Grant, 2007). Thus, we hypothesize that previous knowledge transfer experience will increase pro-social research behavior. From a scientists' perspective, previous contact with potential beneficiaries allows scientists to understand their needs and to focus on their demands (Brief & Motowidlo, 1986). Organizational research shows that developing interpersonal interactions with the potential beneficiaries of research is a source of task significance (Grant *et al.*, 2007) which allows work to be experienced as more meaningful (Morgeson & Humphrey, 2006).

Building on this logic, we would expect that previous contact with the beneficiaries of research should be relevant for inspiring and promoting pro-social research behavior among scientists. In an institutional work environment where there is pressure to perform according to academic metrics (Bercovitz & Feldman, 2008), previous experience in knowledge transfer may motivate the scientist to go beyond the Mertonian norms of science (Merton, 1973). Compared with scientists with little or no previous knowledge transfer experience, it should promote the development of a greater concern for the societal impact of subsequent research. Experience should make the scientist more willing to expend efforts to meet the needs of potential non-academic beneficiaries, and to embrace a broader range of behaviors that reflect stronger awareness of the social impact of the research activities. Research in academic entrepreneurship highlights that previous experience provides the opportunity to acquire task-relevant knowledge and skills (Dokko *et al.*, 2009; Owen-Smith & Powell, 2003). Some scholars invoke the concept of self-efficacy to argue that scientists previously involved in knowledge transfer to non-academic actors are likely to have more confidence in their ability to interact successfully with such actors (Clarysse *et al.*, 2011), and to respond to their particular needs. Accordingly, we hypothesize that:

Hypothesis 1: *Prior experience in knowledge transfer is positively associated with pro-social research behavior.*

Research excellence

Several studies suggest that research excellence[1] can have a substantial effect on scientists' disposition to consider non-academic agents in their research activities (Calderini *et al.*, 2007; Link *et al.*, 2007; Perkmann *et al.*, 2011). Research shows that scientists whose research performance is outstanding

---

[1] We use the term research excellence in a rather narrow and limited sense, to refer to the impact within the scientific community. It is often measured by citation counts to capture the actual influence of research work on surrounding research activities at a given period of time (Irvine & Martin, 1983).

measured by the scientific impact of their research (e.g., citations), may enjoy greater visibility and greater prestige, which has a signaling effect for potential users of their findings (Landry *et al.*, 2006; Perkmann *et al.*, 2011). Scientists considered to be excellent researchers are seen as embodying more valuable human and social capital (Fuller & Rothaermel, 2012) which increases the likelihood that these star scientists will send credible signals to external actors (Spence, 1973). Scientists with high scientific visibility may attract the attention of non-academic actors, facilitating research oriented to their specific needs. Since self-perception of effectiveness and competence is thought to increase a positive disposition towards a positive impact on others (Penner *et al.*, 2005), we contend that greater competence, and greater confidence in their research abilities may contribute to a positive attitude among scientists towards helping others and interacting with the potential beneficiaries of their research (see Brief & Motowidlo, 1986; Mowday *et al.*, 1982).

While research excellence may predict pro-social research behaviors, the relationship may not be homogeneous across all levels of research ability. The relation may exhibit a J-shape if less prestigious scientists show reluctance to engage in pro-social research conducts. This might be because scientists fear that pro-social conduct may threaten his or her commitment to research, and reduce their recognition among peers by shifting the focus of knowledge transfer/ dissemination of research findings away from the scientific community towards non-academic stakeholders (Stephan, 2010; Weijden *et al.*, 2012). While these negative effects might be irrelevant once a scientist has achieved high status and recognition from peers, they can be important for shaping the behavior of scientists in the early stages of their scientific careers. Building on this discussion, we propose the following alternative hypotheses:

Hypothesis 2a: *Research excellence is positively associated with pro-social research behavior.*

Hypothesis 2b: *There is a curvilinear J-shaped relationship between research excellence and pro-social research behavior such that scientists exhibit lower levels of pro-social research behavior at low and intermediate levels of research excellence.*

Cognitive diversity

Cognitive diversity refers to the knowledge breadth of the research scientist, measured as the diversity and balance of the scientists' research area (Rafols & Meyer, 2010). Based on previous research, we contend that cognitive diversity is positively linked to pro-social research behavior. Entrepreneurship research (Fitzsimmons & Douglas, 2011; Philpott *et al.*, 2011) suggests that scientists with expertise in more scientific fields are likely to engage in more distant external search and develop gatekeeper roles (within and outside academia) which provide opportunities to identify new lines of enquiry and increase awareness of the social relevance and commercial possibilities of their research (D'Este *et al.*, 2012; Fleming *et al.*, 2007). Following a similar logic, recognizing and assimilating societal needs as an explicit research goal will be facilitated by a wider scope of knowledge. Researchers with higher cognitive diversity will be more likely to integrate potential users' needs into their research agendas, and therefore, to show higher levels of pro-social research behavior. The capability to integrate distant knowledge allows researchers to conduct research that will be more useful to practitioners (Grant & Berry, 2011; Mohrman *et al.*, 2001). Also, addressing and solving societal problems will be optimized by scientists with greater cognitive breadth (Stirling, 1998). Research shows that scientists with more experience outside academia report higher levels of scientific knowledge breadth (van Rijnsoever & Hessels, 2011). Management research on diversity emphasizes the many benefits of a broad pool of knowledge. For instance, Milliken and Martins (1996) suggest that higher levels of diversity in a group facilitate the creation of linkages with people outside the group, allowing better identification and integration of their particular needs. At the level of the scientist, we expect that those with higher cognitive diversity will be more able to consider the potential needs of non-academic actors in the conduct of their research.

However, broad knowledge bases have some drawbacks. Scientists with high levels of cognitive diversity face increasing problems of knowledge integration and coordination in the case of more distant bodies of knowledge (Cummings & Kiesler, 2005; Rafols, 2007). These coordination costs stem from the difficulties involved in integrating disparate bodies of knowledge, including lack of a common scientific language, and problems associated with coordinating the heterogeneous meanings and norms governing different scientific fields.

Taken together, the above arguments imply that cognitive diversity can have both negative and positive effects on pro-social research behaviors. High cognitive diversity is associated with high coordination costs derived from the integration of distant bodies of knowledge. However, low cognitive diversity means that the scientist may lack the ability to identify and adopt the potential user's needs. Thus, scientists with moderate levels of cognitive diversity may be the most likely to conduct pro-social research. Hence, we propose two alternative hypotheses:

Hypothesis 3a: *Cognitive diversity is positively associated with pro-social research behaviors.*

Hypothesis 3b: *There is curvilinear (inverted U-shaped) relationship between cognitive diversity and engagement in pro-social research behavior. Scientists with low and high cognitive diversity will exhibit lower tendencies to engage in pro-social research than scientists with moderate cognitive diversity.*

Substitution effects

Finally, we hypothesize that both research excellence and cognitive diversity are likely to act as substitutes for knowledge transfer experience. We expect these two factors to play a stronger role in eliciting pro-social research behavior among scientists with no (or little) knowledge transfer experience compared to scientists with a strong experience in these interactions who are, therefore, likely to have developed the skills required for pro-social research behavior. We expect that high scientific visibility and confidence in one's research abilities will compensate for the absence of knowledge transfer experience and contribute to promoting pro-social attitudes particularly among scientists with little or no prior knowledge transfer experience. In other words, the positive effect of experience in knowledge transfer on the conduct of pro-social research will be greater for scientists who do not have the scientific reputation to attract non-academic actors. This means that the ability, skills, and self-efficacy acquired in previous knowledge transfer activities with external agents will be particularly relevant for promoting engagement in pro-social research behavior among less renowned academic researchers.

Similarly, we expect that cognitive diversity will play a particularly strong role in the formation of pro-social research behavior among researchers with no prior knowledge transfer experience, compared to scientists who have established interactions with non-academic actors. As already mentioned, cognitive diversity is related to a greater capacity to integrate distant bodies of knowledge. We expect that the set of skills related to high cognitive diversity may compensate for lack of ability and specific skills in scientists with less knowledge transfer experience. Therefore, we propose the following hypotheses:

Hypothesis 4: *Research excellence will have a higher impact on engagement in pro-social research behavior for researchers with less experience in knowledge transfer activities.*

Hypothesis 5: *Cognitive diversity will have a higher impact on engagement in pro-social research behavior for researchers with less experience in knowledge transfer activities.*

Figure 1 depicts the conceptual model and the hypotheses proposed in this section.

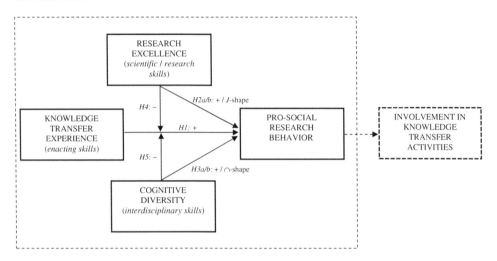

Figure 1.   Theoretical model.

Method

Data and sample

The main source of data for this study is a large scale survey of all (tenured) scientists in CSIC — the main public research organization in Spain. The sample consists of 3,199 CSIC scientists who were invited to participate in the online survey. CSIC scientists cover all scientific fields including Biomedicine, Physics, Chemistry, Engineering, and Social Sciences and Humanities (see Table 1 for details). The survey was conducted between April and May 2011. We achieved a 40% response rate, and 1,295 valid responses. These responses are representative of the population of CSIC scientists in terms of age, gender, and academic rank.[2] However, Table 1 shows that although response rates generally are similar across scientific fields, some disciplines are overrepresented (e.g., Agriculture, Chemistry, Food Science) while Social Sciences and the Humanities is significantly underrepresented.

We also collected data from secondary sources: (i) administrative data on the socio-demographic characteristics of our population of scientists (i.e., gender, age, academic rank, institute of affiliation), and (ii) bibliometric data

---

[2] In both the target population and our sample of respondents, the average age is 50, and 35% of the sample are women. In the target population, professors account for 25% of the sample, and 23% of the respondent sample.

Table 1.   Response rates by field of science ($N = 1295$).

Scientific field	Surveyed population	Valid responses	Response rate
Agriculture Sc. & Tech.	365	191	52%*
Biology & Biomedicine	547	199	36%
Chemistry Sc. & Tech.	381	179	47%*
Food Sc. & Tech.	246	119	48%*
Natural Resources	482	190	39%
Physics Sc. & Tech.	424	163	38%
Social Sc. & Humanities	321	90	28%*
Tech. for New Materials	433	164	38%
Total	**3199**	**1295**	**40%**

*The response rates of these four scientific fields significantly differ (chi-square, $p < 0.05$) when compared to the overall response rate for the other fields in our sample.

from Thomson Reuters' Web of Science (WoS), to obtain publication and citation profiles, and scientific field of specialization. Since we combine three different data sources, potential problems of common method bias (CMV) are largely controlled for (Podsakoff *et al.*, 2012). However, a potential concern related to our data is that respondents might tend to provide "socially desirable" answers to our pro-social research conduct question. To minimize the possibility of social desirability bias (SDB) (Moorman & Podsakoff, 1992), respondents were guaranteed anonymity. In addition, our respondents hold permanent positions and promotions are mainly based on demonstration of production with a high scientific impact. Therefore, we think it unlikely that respondents would inflate their responses to the questionnaire.

Measures

Our dependent variable, *Pro-social research behavior*, is built based on the responses to a question asking scientists to report the frequency (on a 4-point Likert scale from 1 'never' to 4 'regularly') of their engagement, in the course of their research, in the following three activities: (i) identifying potential results from research, (ii) identifying potential users of the research, and (iii) identifying intermediate actors to help transfer the results of research. We compute the averages for the responses to these items since they are strongly correlated, suggesting that all items are measuring the same construct and the scale is consistent (Cronbach's alpha of 0.80). Table A.1 presents the survey questions. Our measure of pro-social research behavior follows a bell-shaped, close-to-normal distribution, with mean, median, and mode around 2.5, and a degree of skewness well within the expected values for a normal distribution.[3] This indicates that overall, scientists engage at intermediate or moderate levels in the three activities used to measure pro-social research, with almost no differences across scientific fields.[4] Finally, since our dependent variable corresponds to a scale comprising three items with values ranging from 1 to 4, the estimation procedure chosen is a Tobit regression model.

We next describe the explanatory variables. *Knowledge transfer experience* is the total value (in €s) of a scientists' R&D contracts, consulting activities, and income from intellectual property rights (i.e., patents) during 1999–2010, based on administrative data provided by CSIC. Because of its highly asymmetric distribution we transformed this variable into logarithms. The mean value of income from knowledge transfer activities for the scientists in our sample is €89.6 thousand; however, note that 57% of the scientists who responded to the survey were not involved in any of these activities (i.e., reported no income from these activities).[5]

We measure *research excellence* as the mean citation score (mcs), which is the mean number of citations of each scientist's publications, excluding self-citations. For each scientific article, we considered a fixed-length four years citation window, thus averaging citations received during the publication year and the following three years. The resulting measure displays an asymmetric distribution indicating that a few individuals achieve very high scores (10% of our scientists scored 11.03 or above), while the rest scored an average of 4.46. A very few of our sample (4.86% of our scientists) received zero citations to their work.

Our measure of *cognitive diversity* is derived from the number of WOS subject categories (SC) of each researcher's journal articles. To build this measure, we used the Shannon entropy index which has the advantage that scores depend on both number of subject categories, and balance in the distribution across subject categories. For instance, scientists whose publications are distributed evenly across subject categories are assigned a higher score than scientists whose publications cover a similar range of subject categories but are unevenly distributed, that is, they are concentrated in a

---

[3] The distribution departs from normal due to significant Kurtosis levels.

[4] There are mostly no significant differences in pro-social research across fields, except in Food Sc. & Tech., and Biology and Biomedicine, which show significantly higher and lower levels respectively compared to other fields.

[5] Because of the high proportion of zeros, this variable was logarithmically transformed after adding 1 to the original values, in order to retain the cases with zero levels for R&D contracts and consulting.

few subject categories. Thus, a higher Shannon score reflects expertise in a wide range of scientific fields. This index can be written as:

$$\text{Cognitive Diversity} = \sum_{i=1}^{i=N} p_i \ln(1/p_i),$$

where p_i is the proportion of articles corresponding to the ith subject category, and N is the number of subject categories covered by the scientists' journal articles.[6] The scores for this measure range from zero to 3.5, following a close to normal distribution with a spike at zero, reflecting large number of scientists whose research is concentrated in a single subject category.

To illustrate the type of information provided by this measure in more detail, we provide the following two contrasting cases from our sample. (i) A scientist who had a score for cognitive diversity of 2.05, which is close to the mean, based on 25 publications assigned to 10 different subject categories, including Applied Physics (11 articles), Materials Science (5 articles), Physical Chemistry (4), Spectroscopy (1) among other subject categories. (ii) A scientist who had the same number of publications (25) but scored zero for cognitive diversity because all his/her publications were in a single category (Astronomy & Astrophysics).

To account for other individual attributes that might shape pro-social research, we considered some alternative individual-level control variables. First, we included the socio-demographic characteristics of the scientists in our sample, such as researcher age (*Age*), gender (whether the researcher is *Male*), and academic status (i.e., whether the researcher is a *Professor*). This information was obtained from the administrative data provided by CSIC. Second, motivational aspects are likely to play an important role in shaping the disposition of scientists to adopt pro-social research behavior (Grant, 2008; Grant *et al.*, 2007). We take account of that by including a number of motivational features connected to the different types of benefits expected by scientists from their interaction with non-academic agents. These expected benefits included: (a) fostering the research agenda of the focal scientist (*Advancing Research*), (b) expanding the scientists' professional network (*Expanding Network*), and (c) increasing the scientists' personal income (*Personal Income*). The first two are computed as three-item

---

[6] Since an article may belong to more than one subject category, we considered the total number of subject categories attached to all a scientist's articles and used this number (which might be higher than the total number of papers) to compute the proportion of papers attached to each subject category.

scales, the third is measured as a single-item scale. Additionally, we consider two more general types of motivations regarding the main drivers of the scientists' engagement in research activities: *Autonomous* and *Controlled* motivations. Third, we include information on number of articles per scientist (i.e., log transformation of the total number of papers, *Number Publications*), and average number of co-authors of this work (i.e., log transformation of average number of co-authors, *Average No Co-authors*).

Finally, we include a number of controls for the institutional environment in which the scientist operates. Drawing on information from the responses to the survey, we built a measure of institutional climate to capture the extent to which scientists consider that their research institute offers a climate supportive of knowledge transfer activities, *Climate*. We also consider a set of dummy variables to control for the scientific disciplines in our sample of scientists: Agriculture Science & Technology, Biology & Biomedicine, Chemistry Science & Technology, Food Science & Technology, Natural Resources, Physics Science & Technology, Social Sciences & Humanities; New Materials Technologies. Description and details of all these variables can be found in Appendix Table A.1. Table 2 presents descriptive statistics for all the variables in our analysis (the correlation matrix is provided in Appendix Table A.2).

Table 2.   Descriptive statistics.

Variables	Mean	S.D.	Median	Min.	Max.	Obs.
1. Pro-social research behavior	2.516	0.731	2.333	1.000	4.000	1219
2. Knowledge transfer experience (ln)	4.736	5.588	0.000	0.000	15.852	1249
3. Research excellence	5.845	5.648	4.500	0.000	114.000	1249
4. Cognitive diversity	1.676	0.644	1.764	0.000	3.482	1249
5. Motive 1: Advancing research	1.108	0.522	1.000	0.000	2.000	1237
6. Motive 2: Expanding network	0.859	0.509	1.000	0.000	2.000	1235
7. Motive 3: Personal income	0.261	0.552	0.000	0.000	2.000	1239
8. Controlled motivation	2.843	0.712	3.000	1.000	4.000	1239
9. Autonomous motivation	3.642	0.475	4.000	1.667	4.000	1248
10. Age	49.826	8.245	49.000	31.000	70.000	1249
11. Gender (Male = 1)	0.649	0.477	1.000	0.000	1.000	1249
12. Professor	0.230	0.421	0.000	0.000	1.000	1249
13. Number Publications*	32.609	32.032	25.000	1.000	286.000	1249
14. Average No. Co-authors*	7.563	44.225	3.950	0.000	1183.500	1249
15. Climate	2.131	1.782	2.000	0.000	4.000	1249

*The figures for these three variables correspond to the original values, not to the log transformed ones.

Results

Engagement in pro-social research behavior and knowledge transfer

Drawing on our conceptual framework, the adoption of pro-social behavior in the context of academic research can be understood as a precursor to engagement in knowledge transfer activity. This is a critical point since it provides theoretical justification for our study of pro-social research behavior. This section offers some preliminary empirical evidence of the validity of the premise that pro-social behavior is strongly associated with engagement in knowledge transfer. While the analysis in this paper is not aimed at demonstrating causality, we believe it is important to investigate whether a systematic connection is observed between the extent to which scientists adopt pro-social research behavior and their degree of involvement in knowledge transfer activities. To do so we examine the relationship between conducting pro-social research and engaging in knowledge transfer activities, using information gathered by the survey. We distinguish scientists with high scores for pro-social research behavior, defined as those with pro-social levels in the highest quartile (i.e., the 25% of scientists who score highest for pro-social research behavior), and compared them with scientists whose pro-social scores are in the first (lowest) quartile. We examined the pattern of their responses to a survey question asking whether the researcher had been involved in any of the following interactions or technology transfer activities with businesses: (i) R&D contracts, (ii) joint research activities, (iii) consulting activities, (iv) licenses from patents, and (v) creation of new firms.

Figure 2 shows that regardless of which type of knowledge transfer channel we consider, scientists with the highest scores for pro-social behavior are at least twice as likely to engage in knowledge transfer activities compared to those with low scores. Figure 2 shows that more than half of the researchers with high scores for pro-social research behavior had been involved in R&D contracts with businesses (53%), compared to only 17.8% of researchers scoring low for pro-social research behavior. Similarly, about 5% of the scientists with pro-social scores engage in firm creation, compared with a proportion that is below 1% for those scientists with low pro-social scores. This pattern is consistent across all types of knowledge transfer activities examined. These results provide confirmatory evidence about the existence of a strong link between pro-social research behavior and engagement in knowledge transfer activities and firm creation.

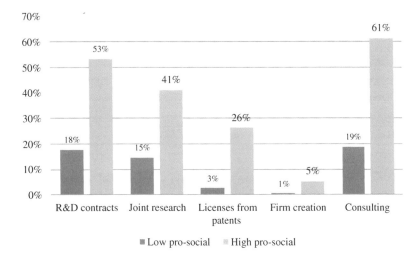

Figure 2.   Pro-social research behavior and engagement in knowledge transfer.

Antecedents to pro-social research behavior

We run a Tobit regression analysis since our dependent variable, *Pro-social research behavior*, is a continuous variable that takes values between 1 and 4. We investigate the direct impact of prior experience in knowledge transfer, of research excellence, and of cognitive diversity on pro-social research behavior, and the extent to which cognitive-related skills moderate the relationship between knowledge transfer experience and pro-social research behavior conducts.[7] Table 3 presents the results. First, we see that, as expected, previous knowledge transfer experience is a strong predictor of pro-social research behavior. This result is consistent across all our specifications (see columns 2–6) and supports hypothesis 1. Second, Table 3 shows that research excellence is important for explaining pro-social research but contrary to our expectations, we find no significant linear relationship (see column 2). Thus, we find no support for hypothesis 2a of a positive relationship between research excellence and conducting pro-social research (see also Table A.3).

However, we find that the relationship between research excellence and pro-social research behavior is U-shaped; that is, scientists are comparatively reluctant to conduct pro-social research at intermediate levels of research excellence but exhibit high levels of pro-social research at low or high research excellence. In column 3, we observe a positive and significant

---

[7] We centered the variables used for the squared and the interaction terms before entering them into the regression analysis, in order to minimize potential mulitcollinearity problems (Aiken & West, 1991)

Table 3.   Tobit estimates. Dependent variable: pro-social research behavior.

	1	2	3	4	5	6
Knowledge transfer experience (KTE)		0.030*** (0.00)	0.030*** (0.00)	0.030*** (0.00)	0.027*** (0.00)	0.031*** (0.00)
Research excellence (RE)		−0.007 (0.00)	−0.020*** (0.01)	−0.006 (0.00)	−0.026*** (0.01)	−0.006 (0.00)
Cognitive diversity (CD)		0.093** (0.04)	0.090** (0.04)	0.100** (0.04)	0.092** (0.04)	0.087** (0.04)
RE^2			0.000*** (0.00)		0.001*** (0.00)	
CD^2				0.022 (0.04)		
KTE*RE					−0.001 (0.00)	
$KTE*RE^2$					0.000* (0.00)	
KTE*CD						−0.012** (0.01)
Motive 1: Advancing Research	0.214*** (0.05)	0.204*** (0.05)	0.194*** (0.05)	0.202*** (0.05)	0.199*** (0.05)	0.208*** (0.05)
Motive 2: Expanding Network	0.311*** (0.05)	0.300*** (0.05)	0.300*** (0.05)	0.301*** (0.05)	0.296*** (0.05)	0.294*** (0.05)
Motive 3: Personal Income	−0.033 (0.04)	−0.019 (0.04)	−0.013 (0.04)	−0.018 (0.04)	−0.013 (0.04)	−0.019 (0.04)
Controlled motivation	0.058* (0.03)	0.051 (0.03)	0.051 (0.03)	0.050 (0.03)	0.051 (0.03)	0.051 (0.03)
Autonomous motivation	−0.078 (0.05)	−0.066 (0.05)	−0.057 (0.05)	−0.064 (0.05)	−0.055 (0.05)	−0.063 (0.05)
Age	0.009*** (0.00)	0.004 (0.00)	0.002 (0.00)	0.004 (0.00)	0.002 (0.00)	0.004 (0.00)
Gender (Male = 1)	0.087* (0.05)	0.066 (0.05)	0.065 (0.05)	0.067 (0.05)	0.068 (0.05)	0.066 (0.05)
Professor	0.019 (0.06)	−0.004 (0.06)	0.006 (0.06)	−0.007 (0.06)	0.009 (0.06)	−0.002 (0.06)
Number of publications	−0.006 (0.02)	−0.057** (0.03)	−0.048* (0.03)	−0.055** (0.03)	−0.047* (0.03)	−0.055** (0.03)
Av. number of co-authors	0.020 (0.04)	0.039 (0.04)	0.059 (0.04)	0.038 (0.04)	0.065 (0.04)	0.040 (0.04)

(*Continued*)

Table 3.   (*Continued*)

	1	2	3	4	5	6
Climate	0.020	0.008	0.006	0.008	0.006	0.007
	(0.01)	(0.01)	(0.01)	(0.01)	(0.01)	(0.01)
Scientific field dummies	Included	Included	Included	Included	Included	Included
Constant	1.323***	1.785***	1.817***	1.769***	1.797***	1.771***
	(0.28)	(0.28)	(0.27)	(0.28)	(0.27)	(0.28)
Observations	1195	1195	1195	1195	1195	1195
Log Likelihood	−1339.500	−1305.866	−1300.714	−1305.688	−1298.537	−1303.939
LR Chi^2 (d.f.)	201.69***	268.96***	279.27***	269.32***	283.62***	272.82***
Pseudo R^2— McKelvey & Zavoina	0.157	0.203	0.210	0.204	0.213	0.206

$*p < 0.10$; $** \, p < 0.05$; $*** \, p < 0.01$. Standard errors in parentheses.

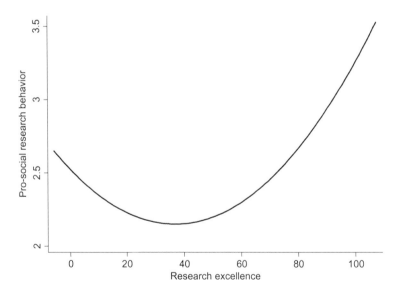

Figure 3.   Relationship between research excellence and pro-social research behavior.

effect of research excellence and a negative and significant effect of research excellence squared. This result is in line with hypothesis 2b *of a* curvilinear relationship for the positive effect of research excellence but only above a certain excellence threshold. Figure 3 depicts this curvilinear relationship between research excellence and pro-social research behavior.

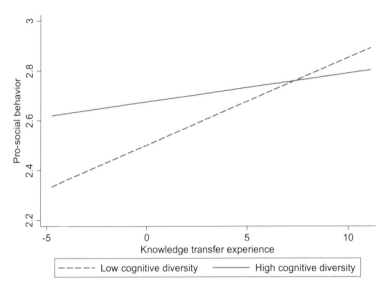

Figure 4.   Regression slopes for the interaction of KT experience and cognitive diversity.

Third, our results show that cognitive diversity has a positive and significant impact on pro-social research behavior, and this result is consistent in all the specifications in Table 3, supporting hypothesis 3a. It suggests that interdisciplinary research skills (the capacity to integrate multiple bodies of knowledge in research activities) contribute positively to fostering pro-social research behavior among scientists. However, we find no evidence of a curvilinear relationship. The quadratic term for *Cognitive Diversity* is not statistically significant (see column 4); thus, we find no support for hypothesis 3b.

Finally, while our results show that past experience in knowledge transfer activities is a strong predictor of pro-social research behavior, we find that cognitive diversity acts as a substitute for experience in knowledge transfer: see the negative sign of the interaction terms in Table 3, column (6). Following Aiken and West (1991), we interpret the form of the interaction by plotting simple slopes at one standard deviation above and below the means (see Figure 4). The slopes suggest that previous knowledge transfer experience is more strongly associated with pro-social research behavior as scientists' cognitive diversity decreases. That is, the impact of cognitive diversity on pro-social research behavior is stronger for scientists who exhibit little or no previous knowledge transfer experience. This result supports hypothesis 5.

We did not find that research excellence moderated the relationship between knowledge transfer experience and pro-social research behavior in any significant way (with the qualification that the interaction term between previous knowledge transfer experience and the square of research excellence, is positive and weakly statistically significant, see Table 3, column 5). Thus, we find no support for hypothesis 4: there is no substitution effect between previous experience in knowledge transfer and research excellence.

Discussion

Contribution and practical implications

This study aimed to provide a deeper understanding of the drivers of knowledge and technology transfer engagement among scientists. In this sense, it responds to call for research on the micro-foundations of scientists' engagement in knowledge transfer activities and academic entrepreneurship (Jain *et al.*, 2009; Shane, 2004), by highlighting the concept of pro-social research behavior. We propose that pro-social research behavior includes: (i) identification of research results that could have *potential social impact* on other people or groups, (ii) identification of the *potential users* of the research findings, and (iii) identification of *intermediate agents* which could channel the social impact of research. A fundamental argument in this research is that a scientists' adoption of such behavior in his/her research helps to bridge between academic and business logics, and to some extent, predicts subsequent engagement in a range of knowledge transfer activities, including the creation of new companies.

We found preliminary evidence of a close relationship between scientists' pro-social research behaviors and subsequent participation in knowledge transfer activities. Specifically, we found that scientists who exhibit a stronger awareness of the societal impact of their research through activities associated with the identification of the potential results from research, or identification of potential beneficiaries, are more likely to be involved in contract R&D, joint research activities with business, firm creation (among others). Our findings also indicate that while extremely high levels of pro-social research conducts are rare, a large proportion of scientists exhibit intermediate levels of this type of research.

By drawing on research on pro-social behaviors from the social psychology literature (De Dreu & Nauta, 2009; Grant & Berry, 2011; Grant, 2008), our study offers some insights into the sources of individual heterogeneity regarding engagement in knowledge transfer. We examined the role of three types of experience for individual scientists: previous knowledge transfer activity, research excellence, and cognitive diversity. Our findings suggest first that experience in knowledge and technology transfer activities is a strong predictor of pro-social research. This type of experience is likely to enhance self-efficacy and contribute to a better capacity to understand the needs and demands of potential beneficiaries of research. Second, the empirical analysis indicates that cognitive diversity is an important driver of pro-social research. It highlights that an interdisciplinary research track enhances the formation of favorable attitudes towards engagement in knowledge transfer activities. The importance of interdisciplinary research is amplified by its moderating effect on knowledge transfer experience: cognitive diversity has a particular influence on shaping pro-social research behavior among scientists with no previous experience of knowledge transfer activity. Third, we show that there is a curvilinear relationship between scientific impact and pro-social research. This suggests that for scientists exhibiting intermediate levels of research excellence, engagement in pro-social research might conflict with the search for peer recognition through scientific impact. However, these findings suggest also that the search for academic impact does not conflict with the development of pro-social research among researchers who exhibit high levels of scientific excellence.

Facilitating scientists' engagement in knowledge transfer activities has become a priority for policy. Our study has implications for scientists, research managers, and policymakers. Although there are good reasons for policies that facilitate an institutional environment that promotes knowledge transfer, this study suggests that the individual level is also important. When academic and commercial incentives are misaligned, some scientists will prioritize furthering their academic careers over the societal impact of the knowledge they produce. Our results suggest that policies to encourage knowledge transfer would be more effective if accompanied by changes to the reward system in science. For instance, including knowledge transfer activity as a criterion for academic promotion could reduce the perceived obstacles to engagement in pro-social research for a large proportion of scientists. Our findings point to the importance of cognitive diversity to substitute for previous experience in knowledge transfer. The results of our study should encourage scientists with less experience of knowledge transfer to increase the breadth of their knowledge by collaborating with scientists from a diverse range of research communities. In the adoption of pro-social research conducts, the types of skills brought by high cognitive diversity can compensate for lack of knowledge transfer experience. Also, research managers might consider encouraging researchers to engage in interdisciplinary research, or to promote interdisciplinary research training tracks at early stages in the academic career, as they seem to instill favorable attitudes to engagement in knowledge transfer, and to promote pro-social research behavior.

Limitations and future directions

Our study has some limitations that suggest useful directions for further research. First, the empirical study focuses on scientists from a single research organization — the Spanish Council of Scientific Research. While this allows us to control for potential organizational level factors that might influence scientists' pro-social research behavior, restricting the investigation to just one organization questions the generalizability of the results presented here. CSIC scientists mainly perform scientific research, and the adoption of pro-social research behavior among university researchers might be driven by a different set of determinants. Future research should include samples from a wider range of organizations. Although our analysis controls for scientists' scientific field, we cannot rule out that the adoption of pro-social research behavior might be field-specific. Future work could expand the target population and examine the determinants of pro-social research behavior separately for each scientific field to determine whether there are differences across scientific disciplines.

We are aware that adoption of pro-social research behavior at the individual-level is difficult to predict given that the large number of potential individual factors might promote a favorable attitude towards knowledge transfer. Although our research controls for a range of motivational variables, further work is needed to unpack the role of other individual level differences that might influence the individual propensity for knowledge exchange. Analyzing how different personality traits promote pro-social research modes is a critical avenue for future research.

References

Agrawal, A. & Henderson, R. 2002. Putting patents in context: exploring knowledge transfer from MIT. *Management Science*, 48(1), 44–60.

Aiken, L. S. & West, S. G. 1991. *Multiple Regression: Testing and Interpreting Interactions*. Sage, Newbury Park, CA.

Ankrah, S. N., Burgess, T. F., Grimshaw, P. & Shaw, N. E. 2013. Asking both university and industry actors about their engagement in knowledge transfer: what single-group studies of motives omit. *Technovation*, 33(2), 50–65.

Audretsch, D. & Erdem, D. 2004. Determinants of scientist entrepreneurship: an integrative research agenda. *Discussion Papers on Entrepreneurship, Growth and Public Policy*, 42.

Audrey, M., Meglino, B. M. & Lester, S. W. 1997. Beyond helping: do other-oriented values have broader implications in organizations? *Journal of Applied Psychology*, 82(1), 160–177.

Azoulay, P., Ding, W. & Stuart, T. 2007. The determinants of faculty patenting behavior: demographics or opportunities. *Journal of Economic Behavior and Organization*, 63(4), 599–623.

Bercovitz, J. & Feldman, M. 2006. Entrepreneurial universities and technology transfer: a conceptual framework for understanding knowledge-based economic development. *The Journal of Technology Transfer*, 31(1), 175–188.

Bercovitz, J. & Feldman, M. 2008. Academic entrepreneurs: organizational change at the individual level. *Organization Science*, 19(1), 69–89.

Bornmann, L. 2013. What is societal impact of research and how can it be assessed? A literature survey. *Journal of the American Society for Information Science and Technology*, 64(2), 217–233.

Brickson, S. L. 2007. Organizational identity orientation: the genesis of the role of the firm and distinct forms of social value. *Academy of Management Review*, 32(3), 864–888.

Brief, A. P. & Motowidlo, S. J. 1986. Prosocial organizational behaviors. *The Academy of Management Review*, 11(4), 710–725.

Buck, R. 2002. The genetics and biology of true love: prosocial biological affects and the left hemisphere. *Psychological Review*, 109(4), 739–744.

Calderini, M., Franzoni, C. & Vezzulli, A. 2007. If star scientists do not patent: the effect of productivity, basicness and impact on the decision to patent in the academic world. *Research Policy*, 36(3), 303–319.

Clarysse, B., Tartari, V. & Salter, A. 2011. The impact of entrepreneurial capacity, experience and organizational support on academic entrepreneurship. *Research Policy*, 40(8), 1084–1093.

Cummings, J. N. & Kiesler, S. 2005. Collaborative research across disciplinary and organizational boundaries. *Social Studies of Science*, 35(5), 703–722.

D'Este, P., Mahdi, S., Neely, A. & Rentocchini, F. 2012. Inventors and entrepreneurs in academia: what types of skills and experience matter? *Technovation*, 32(5), 293–303.

Dokko, G., Wilk, S. L. & Rothbard, N. P. 2009. Unpacking prior experience: how career history affects job performance. *Organization Science*, 20(1), 51–68.

De Dreu, C. K. W. & Nauta, A. 2009. Self-interest and other-orientation in organizational behavior: implications for job performance, prosocial behavior, and personal initiative. *Journal of Applied Psychology*, 94(4), 913–926.

Etzkowitz, H. 1998. The norms of entrepreneurial science: cognitive effects of the new university–industry linkages. *Research Policy*, 27(8), 823–833.

Feller, I. 1990. Universities as engines of R&D based economic growth: they think they can. *Research Policy*, 19(4), 335–348.

Fini, R., Grimaldi, R., Marzocchi, G. L. & Sobrero, M. 2012. The determinants of corporate entrepreneurial intention within small and newly established firms. *Entrepreneurship Theory and Practice*, 36(2), 387–414.

Fitzsimmons, J. R. & Douglas, E. J. 2011. Interaction between feasibility and desirability in the formation of entrepreneurial intentions. *Journal of Business Venturing*, 26(4), 431–440.

Fleming, L., Mingo, S. & Chen, D. 2007. Collaborative brokerage, generative creativity, and creative success. *Administrative Science Quarterly*, 52(3), 443–475.

Fuller, A. W. & Rothaermel, F. T. 2012. When stars shine: the effects of faculty founders on new technology ventures. *Strategic Entrepreneurship Journal*, 6(3), 220–235.

Gibbons, M., Limoges, C., Nowotny, H., Schwartzman, S., Scott, P. & Trow, M. 1994. *The New Production of Knowledge: The Dynamics of Science and Research in Contemporary Societies*. Sage Publications Inc., Thousand Oaks, CA, US.

Gilsing, V., Bekkers, R., Bodas Freitas, I. M. & van der Steen, M. 2011. Differences in technology transfer between science-based and development-based industries: transfer mechanisms and barriers. *Technovation*, 31(12), 638–647.

Gittelman, M. & Kogut, B. 2003. Does good science lead to valuable knowledge? Biotechnology firms and the evolutionary logic of citation patterns. *Management Science*, 49(4), 366–382.

Goethner, M., Obschonka, M., Silbereisen, R. K. & Cantner, U. 2012. Scientists' transition to academic entrepreneurship: economic and psychological determinants. *Journal of Economic Psychology*, 33(3), 628–641.

Goldman, M. & Fordyce, J. 1983. Prosocial behavior as affected by eye contact, touch, and voice expression. *The Journal of Social Psychology*, 121(1), 125–129.

Grant, A. 2007. Relational job design and the motivation to make a prosocial difference. *Academy of Management Review*, 32(2), 393–417.

Grant, A. M. 2008. Does intrinsic motivation fuel the prosocial fire? Motivational synergy in predicting persistence, performance, and productivity. *Journal of Applied Psychology*, 93(1), 48–58.

Grant, A. M. & Berry, J. W. 2011. The Necessity of others is the mother of invention: intrinsic and prosocial motivations, perspective taking, and creativity. *Academy of Management Journal*, 54(1), 73–96.

Grant, A. M., Campbell, E. M., Chen, G., Cottone, K., Lapedis, D. & Lee, K. 2007. Impact and the art of motivation maintenance: The effects of contact with beneficiaries on persistence behavior. *Organizational Behavior and Human Decision Processes*, 103(1), 53–67.

Grant, A. M. & Sonnentag, S. 2010. Doing good buffers against feeling bad: prosocial impact compensates for negative task and self-evaluations. *Organizational Behavior and Human Decision Processes*, 111(1), 13–22.

Grant, A. M. & Sumanth, J. J. 2009. Mission possible? The performance of prosocially motivated employees depends on manager trustworthiness. *Journal of Applied Psychology*, 94(4), 927–944.

Haeussler, C. & Colyvas, J. A. 2011. Breaking the ivory tower: academic entrepreneurship in the life sciences in UK and Germany. *Research Policy*, 40(1), 41–54.

Hammer, M. 1995. *The Reengineering Revolution: A Handbook.* 1ˢᵗ edition. Harper Business.

Hessels, L. K. & Van Lente, H. 2008. Re-thinking new knowledge production: a literature review and a research agenda. *Research policy*, 37(4), 740–760.

Hobin, J. A., Deschamps, A. M., Bockman, R., Cohen, S., Dechow, P., Eng, C. & Galbraith, R. 2012. Engaging basic scientists in translational research: identifying opportunities, overcoming obstacles. *Journal of Translational Medicine*, 10(72).

Hoye, K. & Pries, F. 2009. Repeat commercializers, the habitual entrepreneurs of university–industry technology transfer. *Technovation*, 29(10), 682–689.

Jain, S., George, G. & Maltarich, M. 2009. Academics or entrepreneurs? Investigating role identity modification of university scientists involved in commercialization activity. *Research Policy*, 38(6), 922–935.

Kerr, N. L. & MacCoun, R. J. 1985. Role expectations in social dilemmas: sex roles and task motivation in groups. *Journal of Personality and Social Psychology*, 49(6), 1547–1556.

Krueger Jr, N. F., Reilly, M. D. & Carsrud, A. L. 2000. Competing models of entrepreneurial intentions. *Journal of Business Venturing*, 15(5–6), 411–432.

Lam, A. 2011. What motivates academic scientists to engage in research commercialization: Gold, ribbon or puzzle? *Research Policy*, 40(10), 1354–1368.

Landry, R., Amara, N. & Rherrad, I. 2006. Why are some university researchers more likely to create spinoffs than others? Evidence from Canadian universities. *Research Policy*, 35(10), 1599–1615.

Link, A. N., Siegel, D. S. & Bozeman, B. 2007. An empirical analysis of the propensity of academics to engage in informal university technology transfer. *ICC*, 16(4), 641–655.

McNeely, B. L. & Meglino, B. M. 1994. The role of dispositional and situational antecedents in prosocial organizational behavior: an examination of the intended beneficiaries of prosocial behavior. *Journal of Applied Psychology*, 79(6), 836–844.

Meglino, B. M. & Korsgaard, M. A. 2004. Considering rational self-interest as a disposition: organizational implications of other orientation. *Journal of Applied Psychology*, 89(6), 946–959.

Merton, R. K. 1973. *The Sociology of Science: Theoretical and Empirical Investigations.* University of Chicago Press.

Milliken, F. J. & Martins, L. L. 1996. Searching for common threads: understanding the multiple effects of diversity in organizational groups. *Academy of Management Review*, 21(2), 402–433.

Mohrman, S. A., Gibson, C. B. & Mohrman Jr, A. M. 2001. Doing research that is useful to practice: a model and empirical exploration. *The Academy of Management Journal*, 44(2), 357–375.

Moorman, R. H. & Podsakoff, P. M. 1992. A meta-analytic review and empirical test of the potential confounding effects of social desirability response sets in organizational behaviour research. *Journal of Occupational and Organizational Psychology*, 65(2), 131–149.

Morgeson, F. P. & Humphrey, S. E. 2006. The work design questionnaire (WDQ): developing and validating a comprehensive measure for assessing job design and the nature of work. *Journal of Applied Psychology*, 91(6), 1321–1339.

Mowday, R. T., Porter, L. W. & Steers, R. M. 1982. *Employee-Organization Linkages: The Psychology of Commitment, Absenteeism, and Turnover*. Academic press, New York.

Murray, F. 2004. The role of academic inventors in entrepreneurial firms: sharing the laboratory life. *Research Policy*, 33(4), 643–659.

Olmos-Peñuela, J., Benneworth, P., Castro-Martinez, E. 2014. Are 'STEM form Mars and SSH from Venus?: challenging disciplinary stereotypes of research's social value. *Science and Public Policy*, 41(3), 384–400.

Organ, D. W., Podsakoff, P. M. & MacKenzie, S. B. 2005. *Organizational Citizenship Behavior: Its Nature, Antecedents, and Consequences*. Sage.

Owen-Smith, J. & Powell, W. W. 2001. To patent or not: faculty decisions and institutional success at technology transfer. *The Journal of Technology Transfer*, 26(1–2), 99–114.

Owen-Smith, J. & Powell, W. W. 2003. The expanding role of university patenting in the life sciences: assessing the importance of experience and connectivity. *Research Policy*, 32(9), 1695–1711.

Penner, L. A., Dovidio, J. F., Piliavin, J. A. & Schroeder, D. A. 2005. Prosocial behavior: multilevel perspectives. *Annual Review of Psychology*, 56, 365–392.

Perkmann, M., King, Z. & Pavelin, S. 2011. Engaging excellence? Effects of faculty quality on university engagement with industry. *Research Policy*, 40(4), 539–552.

Perry, J. L. & Hondeghem, A. 2008. *Motivation in Public Management: The Call of Public Service*. Oxford University Press.

Philpott, K., Dooley, L., O'Reilly, C. & Lupton, G. 2011. The entrepreneurial university: examining the underlying academic tensions. *Technovation*, 31(4), 161–170.

Podsakoff, P. M., MacKenzie, S. B., & Podsakoff, N. P. 2012. Sources of method bias in social science research and recommendations on how to control it. *Annual Review of Psychology*, 63, 539–569.

Puffer, S. M. 1987. Prosocial behavior, noncompliant behavior, and work performance among commission salespeople. *Journal of Applied Psychology*, 72(4), 615–621.

Rafols, I. 2007. Strategies for knowledge acquisition in bionanotechnology: Why are interdisciplinary practices less widespread than expected? *Innovation*, 20(4), 395–412.

Rafols, I. & Meyer, M. 2010. Diversity and network coherence as indicators of interdisciplinarity: case studies in bionanoscience. *Scientometrics*, 82(2), 263–287.

Rothaermel, F. T., Agung, S. D. & Jiang, L. 2007. University entrepreneurship: a taxonomy of the literature. *ICC*, 16(4), 691–791.

Salter, A. J. & Martin, B. R. 2001. The economic benefits of publicly funded basic research: a critical review. *Research Policy*, 30(3), 509–532.

Sauermann, H. & Roach, M. 2011. Not all scientists pay to be scientists: heterogeneous preferences for publishing in industrial research. *SSRN Working paper* 1696783.

Sauermann, H. & Stephan, P. 2013. Conflicting logics? A multidimensional view of industrial and academic science. *Organization Science*, 24(3), 889–909.

Shane, S. & Venkataraman, S. 2000. The promise of entrepreneurship as a field of research. *Academy of Management Review*, 25(1), 217–226.

Shane, S. A. 2004. Academic Entrepreneurship: University Spinoffs and Wealth Creation. Edward Elgar Publishing. Cheltenham.

Slaughter, S. & Leslie, L. L. 1997. *Academic Capitalism: Politics, Policies, and the Entrepreneurial University*. Eric.

Spence, M. 1973. Job market signaling. *The Quarterly Journal of Economics*, 87(3), 355–374.

Spencer, J. W. 2001. How relevant is university-based scientific research to private high-technology firms? A United States–Japan comparison. *Academy of Management Journal*, 44(2), 432–440.

Stephan, P. E. 2010. The economics of science. *Handbook of the Economics of Innovation*, 1, 217–274.

Stern, S. 2004. Do scientists pay to be scientists? *Management Science*, 50(6), 835–853.

Stirling, A. 1998. On the economics and analysis of diversity. Science policy research unit (*SPRU*), *Electronic Working Paper Series*, Paper 28.

Stokes, D. E. 1997. *Pasteur's Quadrant: Basic Science and Technological Innovation*. Brookings Institution Press.

Tartari, V. & Breschi, S. 2012. Set them free: scientists' evaluations of the benefits and costs of university–industry research collaboration. *Industrial and Corporate Change*, 21(5), 1117–1147.

Thompson, J. A. & Bunderson, J. S. 2003. Violations of principle: ideological currency in the psychological contract. *Academy of Management Review*, 28(4), 571–586.

Van Rijnsoever, F. J. & Hessels, L. K. 2011. Factors associated with disciplinary and interdisciplinary research collaboration. *Research Policy*, 40(3), 463–472.

Weijden, I., van der, M., Verbree, P. & van den Besselaar. 2012. From bench to bedside: the societal orientation of research leaders: the case of biomedical and health research in the Netherlands. *Science and Public Policy*, 39(3), 285–303.

Ziman, J. 2002. *Real Science: What it is, and What it Means*. Cambridge University Press, Cambridge, NY.

Appendix

Table A.1. Details of measures.

Variable	Source	Description
Pro-social Research behavior	Questionnaire	Please, indicate the frequency you engage in each of the following activities when you conduct a research project (1 = never; 4 = regularly): 1. Identify the potential results of your research that can benefit users 2. Identify the potential users who can apply the results of your research 3. Identify intermediaries in order to transfer the results of your results
Knowledge Transfer Experience	Administrative data	Total value (in €s) of R&D contracts, consulting activities and income from licences of intellectual property rights (i.e., patents) in which the scientists were engaged over the period 1999–2010, as reported in the administrative data provided by CSIC. This variable was transformed logarithmically for the empirical analysis (x_new = ln (x_original +1)).
Research Excellence	ISI-SCI database	Average number of citations per paper and year. For each single paper p published in the year n we computed a score for the average received citations per year in the following four years ($n + 1$ to $n + 4$). Then, we proceed to sum the scores for all the papers corresponding to each scientist.
Cognitive Diversity	ISI-SCI database	To build this measure, we use the Shannon entropy index. The actual expression of this index is as follows: $\sum_{i=1}^{N} p_i \ln(1/p_i)$, where p_i is the proportion of articles corresponding to the ith subject category, and N is the total number of subject categories of the journal articles published by a scientist.
Age	Administrative data	The scientist age, as we know the year in which each scientist was born.
Gender	Administrative data	A dichotomous variable that takes the value 1 if the scientist gender is Male, and zero if female.
Professor	Administrative data	A dichotomous variable that takes the value 1 if the scientist academic status corresponds to the category of Professor.

(Continued)

Table A.1.   (Continued)

Variable	Source	Description
Advancing Research	Questionnaire	Please, indicate the degree of importance you attach to each of the following items, as personal motivations to establish interactions with non-academic organizations (firms, public administration agencies, non-profit organizations) (1 = not at all; 4 = extremely important): 1. To explore new lines of research 2. To obtain information or materials necessary for the development of your current lines of research 3. To have access to equipments and infrastructure necessary for your lines of research (Cronbach $\alpha = 0.72$) We computed the average response to these three items.
Expanding Network	Questionnaire	Please, indicate the degree of importance you attach to each of the following items, as personal motivations to establish interactions with non-academic organizations (firms, public administration agencies, non-profit organizations) (1 = not at all; 4 = extremely important): 1. To keep abreast of about the areas of interest of these non-academic organisations 2. To be part of a professional network or expand your professional network 3. To test the feasibility and practical application of your research 4. To have access to the experience of non-academic professionals (Cronbach $\alpha = 0.68$) We computed the average response to these four items.
Personal Income	Questionnaire	Please, indicate the degree of importance you attach to 'Increase your personal income' as a personal motivation to establish interactions with non-academic organizations (firms, public administration agencies, non-profit organizations) (1 = not at all; 4 = extremely important).
Autonomous Motivation	Questionnaire	When you think of your job as a researcher, what is the importance attached to the following items? (1 = no importance; 4 = extremely important): 1. To face intellectual challenges 2. To have greater independence in your research activities 3. To contribute to the advance of knowledge in your scientific field (Cronbach $\alpha = 0.65$). We computed the average response to these three items.

Controlled Motivation	Questionnaire	When you think of your job as a researcher, what is the importance attached to the following items? (1 = no importance; 4 = extremely important): 1. Salary 2. Job security. 3. Career advancement. (Cronbach α = 0.71). We computed the average response to these three items.
Number of Publications	ISI-SCI database	Total number of publications over the scientist career until 2010 (included). This variable was transformed logarithmically for the empirical analysis (x_new = ln (x_original +1)).
Average Number of Co-authors	ISI-SCI database	Average number of co-authors per article, for each scientist. This variable was transformed logarithmically for the empirical analysis (x_new = ln (x_original +1)).
Climate	Questionnaire	Number of items assessed by the respondent as 'very positively', from the following question: Assess the experience you have had in your relationships with the personnel at your institute, regarding the following issues (1 = very negatively; 4 = very positively): 1. Attitudes of the personnel at your institute to address your queries and requests 2. Accessibility to the human resources and services available at your institute 3. Capacity to solve the problems in due time and form 4. Technical capacity of the institute's personnel We have computed the count of items assessed as 'very important'.
Discipline dummies	Administrative data	Dichotomous variables for each of the 8 scientific disciplines. We have considered Biology and Biomedicine as the reference category.

Table A.2.   Correlation matrix*.

	1	2	3	4	5	6	7	8	9	10	11	12	13	14	15
1. Pro-social research behavior	1														
2. Knowledge transfer experience (ln)	0.258*	1													
3. Research excellence	−0.129*	−0.092*	1												
4. Cognitive diversity	0.043	0.161*	0.050	1											
5. Motive 1: Advancing Research	0.252*	0.031	−0.003	0.022	1										
6. Motive 2: Expanding Network	0.298*	0.041	−0.053	−0.024	0.583*	1									
7. Motive 3: Personal Income	0.073	−0.023	−0.006	−0.073*	0.261*	0.226*	1								
8. Controlled motivation	0.084*	0.030	0.020	−0.051	0.103*	0.124*	0.377*	1							
9. Autonomous motivation	−0.012	0.001	0.093*	−0.079*	0.162*	0.139*	0.073*	0.249*	1						
10. Age	0.083*	0.236*	−0.180*	0.064*	−0.021	−0.056	0.005	−0.029	−0.096*	1					
11. Gender (Male = 1)	−0.018	0.071*	0.049	0.053	−0.181*	−0.194*	0.016	0.037	0.039	0.099*	1				
12. Professor	0.038	0.235*	0.030	0.077*	−0.029	−0.028	0.003	0.060*	0.090*	0.436*	0.162*	1			
13. Number of publications (ln)	−0.019	0.166*	0.051	0.597*	−0.012	−0.064*	−0.078*	−0.035	−0.031	0.105*	0.065*	0.287*	1		
14. Av. number of co-authors (ln)	−0.012	−0.052	0.293*	0.186*	0.080*	−0.017	−0.061*	−0.011	−0.078*	−0.080*	0.015	−0.031	0.221*	1	
15. Climate	0.125*	0.136*	−0.038	0.041	0.127*	0.156*	−0.023	0.028	−0.008	0.006	0.024	−0.006	−0.004	0.037	1

*$p < 0.05$.

Table A.3.   OLS results. DV: Pro-social research behavior.

	1	2	3	4	5	6
Knowledge transfer experience (KTE)		0.028***	0.028***	0.028***	0.025***	0.029***
		(0.00)	(0.00)	(0.00)	(0.00)	(0.00)
Research excellence (RE)		−0.006	−0.018***	−0.006	−0.024***	−0.005
		(0.01)	(0.01)	(0.01)	(0.01)	(0.01)
Cognitive diversity (CD)		0.089**	0.086**	0.096**	0.088**	0.084**
		(0.04)	(0.04)	(0.04)	(0.04)	(0.04)
RE^2			0.000***		0.001***	
			(0.00)		(0.00)	
CD^2				0.024		
				(0.04)		
KTE*RE					−0.001	
					(0.00)	
KTE*RE^2					0.000**	
					(0.00)	
KTE*CD						−0.010*
						(0.01)
Motive 1: Advancing Research	0.201***	0.191***	0.182***	0.189***	0.186***	0.195***
	(0.05)	(0.05)	(0.05)	(0.05)	(0.05)	(0.05)
Motive 2: Expanding Network	0.278***	0.268***	0.268***	0.270***	0.265***	0.263***
	(0.05)	(0.05)	(0.05)	(0.05)	(0.05)	(0.05)
Motive 3: Personal Income	−0.035	−0.022	−0.016	−0.021	−0.016	−0.022
	(0.04)	(0.04)	(0.04)	(0.04)	(0.04)	(0.04)
Controlled motivation	0.058*	0.052*	0.051*	0.050	0.052*	0.052*
	(0.03)	(0.03)	(0.03)	(0.03)	(0.03)	(0.03)
Autonomous motivation	−0.078*	−0.067	−0.059	−0.065	−0.057	−0.065
	(0.04)	(0.04)	(0.04)	(0.04)	(0.04)	(0.04)
Age	0.008***	0.003	0.002	0.003	0.002	0.003
	(0.00)	(0.00)	(0.00)	(0.00)	(0.00)	(0.00)
Gender (Male = 1)	0.086**	0.067	0.067	0.068	0.068	0.067
	(0.04)	(0.04)	(0.04)	(0.04)	(0.04)	(0.04)
Professor	0.024	0.002	0.011	−0.001	0.014	0.004
	(0.05)	(0.05)	(0.05)	(0.05)	(0.05)	(0.05)
Number of publications	−0.006	−0.054**	−0.046*	−0.053*	−0.045	−0.053*
	(0.02)	(0.03)	(0.03)	(0.03)	(0.03)	(0.03)
Av. number of co-authors	0.013	0.030	0.049	0.029	0.054	0.031
	(0.04)	(0.04)	(0.04)	(0.04)	(0.04)	(0.04)

(*Continued*)

Table A.3. (*Continued*)

	1	2	3	4	5	6
Climate	0.019*	0.008	0.007	0.008	0.006	0.007
	(0.01)	(0.01)	(0.01)	(0.01)	(0.01)	(0.01)
Intercept	1.428***	1.855***	1.883***	1.836***	1.866***	1.843***
	(0.25)	(0.25)	(0.25)	(0.25)	(0.25)	(0.25)
Observations	1195	1195	1195	1195	1195	1195
FR^2	13.75	15.84	16.44	15.32	16.34	15.34
	0.158	0.205	0.212	0.206	0.215	0.208

$*p < 0.10$; $** p < 0.05$; $*** p < 0.01$. Standard errors in parentheses.

Chapter 3

International Research Collaboration and Academic Entrepreneurship: Evidence from Germany

Maximilian Goethner

Department of Economics and Business Administration and
Graduate College "The Economics of Innovative Change" (DFG-GRK-1411)
Friedrich Schiller University, Carl-Zeiss-Str. 3
07743 Jena, Germany
maximilian.goethner@uni-jena.de

How does the internationalization of science influence entrepreneurial career aspirations of scientists? Applying the theory of planned behavior (TPB), this chapter investigates the role of S&T human capital, approximated by the international scope of scientists' research network, as determinant of academic entrepreneurial intentions. The analysis is based on comprehensive survey data from a sample of 247 German scientists. Information on international research activity is collected from the ISI Web of Science (WoS) database. The results show that entrepreneurial intentions are predicted by attitude and perceived behavioral control, but not by social norms. Furthermore, S&T human capital moderates the control-intentions link. The importance of control beliefs as driver of intentions diminishes with an increasing scope of international research activity. This chapter, in sum, provides a first step to better understand the mechanisms through which professional skills and networks — which are key for the practice of science and the growth of scientific careers — may also impact academic entrepreneurship.

Introduction

While traditional science is seen as an individual endeavor, increasingly scientific knowledge is produced by collaborative groups of scientists (de Solla Price, 1986; Katz & Martin, 1997), and the groups are growing larger (Adams *et al.*, 2005; Wuchty *et al.*, 2007). Using a comprehensive dataset of 19.9 million research articles and 2.1 million patents, Wuchty *et al.* (2007) documented that collaborative research has become increasingly prevalent in virtually all fields of science, engineering, and the social sciences since the 1950s. These developments are owing to a variety of factors, including, among others, the need to pool resources due to escalating costs of conducting scientific research, an increasing division of labor among specialized scholars, and the emergence of interdisciplinary research fields such as biotechnology (de Solla Price, 1986; Jones, 2005; Stephan, 2012). Moreover, the growth in scientific collaboration activities is not bound within national borders but shows an international outreach. As Adams *et al.* (2005) demonstrated for the top 110 US research universities, the rate of national collaborations were more than double and the rate of international collaborations increased five-fold in the period 1981–1999. Not only is there a pervasive shift towards international research but the knowledge produced by international research teams also seems to have a higher impact. Evidence suggests that, throughout almost all scientific disciplines, international collaboration leads to multi-authored publications that tend to be of higher quality and more influential, as measured by citations, than research reported in single-authored publications (Narin *et al.*, 1991; Wuchty *et al.*, 2007).

These significant changes in the production and dissemination of scientific knowledge also raise the question whether and how the internationalization of science affects the pathways by which scientists commercialize their research. Most closely related to the present paper are studies that link career mobility of scientists to academic entrepreneurship. This literature suggests a positive relationship between work experience in many different environments and the likelihood to become an entrepreneur (Krabel *et al.*, 2012; Stuart & Ding, 2006). While these studies focus on the influence of job changes and thus changes in the professional environment of scientists, they do not explicitly investigate the process of knowledge production the individual scientist is engaged in, e.g., the international scope of scientific research as a predictor of academic entrepreneurship. This chapter aims to help in filling this gap. Following previous research, international research collaboration is regarded as a prominent way to increase the individual scientist's embeddedness in professional networks and the resources available which translates into higher scientific and technical (S&T) human capital

(Bozeman *et al.*, 2001). I propose that S&T human capital related to international science critically influences the cognitive processes that, according to the theory of planned behavior (TPB; Ajzen, 1991; Fishbein & Ajzen, 2010) underlies the formation of entrepreneurial intentions. While S&T human capital may be important for the practice of science and the growth of scientific careers, such knowledge, skills, and network ties may in fact hamper an entrepreneurial career choice.

I test this hypothesis using extensive survey data from a sample of 247 German scientists. Additional information on respondent's international research activity is retrieved from research articles published in scientific journals that are indexed by the ISI Web of Science (WoS) database.

The remainder of this chapter is organized as follows. Section 2 provides an overview of the policy measures and legislations introduced by the German government to facilitate technology transfer and research commercialization. Section 3 then turns the attention to the current study and discusses the relevance of entrepreneurial intentions for researching the emergence of academic entrepreneurship and sets out the theoretical framework and related hypothesis. This is followed in Section 4 by the presentation of the data and variables used. Section 5 contains the findings of the empirical analysis. Finally, Section 6 discusses the findings, concludes, and draws implications for future research and potential policy interventions.

Academic Entrepreneurship in Germany

In Germany, academic entrepreneurship, i.e., the creation of university spin-offs, is a relatively new phenomenon. Traditionally, engineering research in Germany has been an area of excellence with close collaboration with industry and organized in well-resourced large research groups (Grimpe & Fier, 2010). However, entrepreneurship as means to economically valorize scientific knowledge and skills is not as common and recognized yet as the university spin-off creation is still considered to be a controversial behavior in certain universities and areas of study. For example, entrepreneurship research and teaching played almost no role in the university curricula until the 1990s. While in the U.S. the number of entrepreneurship education programs (majors, minors, certificates) has more than quadrupled — from 104 in 1975 to more than 500 in 2006 (Kauffman, 2006) — similar programs emerged in Germany only in the late 1990s. After the establishment of the first entrepreneurship chair at the European Business School in Oestrich-Winkel in 1998, the number of professorships at German universities offering entrepreneurship programs to students grew rapidly to 128 in 2015 (FGF e.V., 2015).

Since the 1990s public programs to support university spin-offs have also been rising in numbers and fund volume. At the national level, the most prominent example is the program "EXIST: Promotion of university-based start-ups" (www.exist.de). Started in 1998, EXIST is a federally funded part of the German government's "Hightech Strategy for Germany" and is co-financed by the European Social Funds (ESF). The program aims to establish an entrepreneurial culture at universities and to improve sustainably the conditions for academic entrepreneurship (Kulicke, 2014). EXIST comprises three pillars:

(1) "Business start-up grant" is a one-year salary stipend of €2,500 per month for PhDs (€2,000 for Master's degree students up to five years after degree completion, €800 for current students) for up to three founders plus an additional €22,000 for other start-up costs. The grant aims to enable founders to develop a viable business model and to reduce the personal financial risks involved in starting up.
(2) "Transfer of research" promotes sophisticated technology-based start-up projects in technology fields that involve expensive and risky development activities such as in biotechnology, medical technology, optics, and material sciences. Depending on project-specific requirements, founders can get funding of up to €550,000 to finance development work to verify technological feasibility (funding phase I) and to start business operations in the newly created technology venture as well as meeting the prerequisites for external financing (funding phase II).
(3) "Culture of entrepreneurship" supports projects at universities and research institutions to strengthen their spin-off activities and technology transfer infrastructure. Universities taking part are supported in developing and implementing a university-wide strategy of developing their status as institution with a reputation for entrepreneurship and to establish an entrepreneurial profile.

Fostering the commercialization of public-funded research in Germany has also meant significant regulatory changes in the last decades. With the amendment of the Higher Education Framework ("Hochschulrahmengesetz") in 1998, the Federal Ministry of Science and Education (BMBF) emphasized the responsibility of public universities for the transfer of knowledge and technology (§2, clause 7, HRG), introducing technology transfer as a third mission to the two traditional missions of research and teaching.

Furthermore, a Bayh-Dole Act type of legislation came into force in 2002 when the BMBF altered clause 42 in the German "Gesetz über Arbeitnehmererfindungen" (§42 ArbnErfG) or Employee Invention Law

(BMBF, 2002; Grimm, 2011). Prior to this revision, faculty members were allowed to retain ownership of inventions resulting from academic research, which was known as the "professor's privilege". Once derived from Article 5 of the German constitution, which pertains to the freedom of science and research, the "professor's privilege" determined that professors were the only occupational group in Germany that had the right to use their scientific results for private commercialization even if the underlying research was financed by the university (Kilger & Bartenbach, 2002).

In contrast to the U.S., the German suspicion was not that university inventions might be shelved because IPR negotiations between university administrations and federal agencies were obstructed by red tape. Rather, German policy-makers were concerned that the efforts, costs and financial risks involved would prevent university scientists to pursue the commercial exploitation of their inventions (Kilger & Bartenbach, 2002).

Under the new law, the "professor's privilege" was abandoned and universities were given the right to claim ownership on any invention resulting from on-campus research. In case the university decides to file for patent protection, the law specifies that 30% of the revenues from exploiting his or her invention should go to the academic inventor. Additionally, the university takes over the financial risk and the patent application procedure, further decreasing academic scientists' opportunity costs of engaging in commercial activities.

Despite numerous support measures and legislations set up to foster academic entrepreneurship in Germany, evidence suggests that research scientists' right to commercialize inventions privately before 2002 — when the "professor's privilege" was abolished — is still reflected by a rather low number of German university patents and university spin-offs compared to the US (Grimm, 2011). There seems to be a deficit of entrepreneurship among academics in Germany (as well as in other European countries) that we still need to understand. The present chapter aims to contribute to this endeavor by studying determinants of academic scientists' intentions to engage in the creation of science-based new ventures.

Theoretical Background and Hypotheses

Academic entrepreneurial intentions

In recent years, the study of entrepreneurial intentions has become a key approach in entrepreneurship research dealing with the complex factors underlying an individual's transition to entrepreneurship (Krueger, 2009). Scholars are increasingly adopting an intentions-based view on entrepreneurship because entrepreneurial intentions can be seen as a conceptual hub connecting entrepreneurial behavior with a wide range of factors, both psychological and economic, that may influence this behavior through such intentions (e.g., Carsrud & Brännback, 2009; Fini *et al.*, 2012; Krueger & Carsrud, 1993).

It is widely acknowledged that entrepreneurial behavior is inherently intentional because acting entrepreneurially is something that people choose or plan to do (Bird, 1988; Krueger & Carsrud, 1993). Consistent with longitudinal findings (e.g., Lee *et al.*, 2011), the most proximal and important predictor of the engagement in entrepreneurial behavior is seen in entrepreneurial intentions (Bird, 1988). Simply put, these are cognitive representations of a person's readiness to engage in entrepreneurship. Entrepreneurial intentions signal how intensely one is prepared and how much effort one is planning to commit in order to carry out entrepreneurial behavior. Even if people may have significant potential, they will refrain from making the transition into entrepreneurship when they lack the intentions (Krueger *et al.*, 2000).

Theory of planned behavior

A widely researched framework for understanding and predicting behavioral intentions is the theory of planned behavior (TPB; Ajzen, 1991; Fishbein & Ajzen, 2010). This parsimonious and coherent model of behavioral intentions received strong empirical support in a wide range of studies predicting very different kinds of planned behavior (Ajzen, 2001; Conner & Armitage, 1998). Past research showed that the TPB is able to predict substantial amounts of entrepreneurial intentions in general (e.g., Krueger *et al.*, 2000; Kautonen *et al.*, 2013; Liñán & Chen, 2009). Given the general and basic nature of the TPB approach, this framework also applies in the specific domain of academic entrepreneurship with its special focus on scientists' active participation in the entrepreneurial exploitation of scientific research and inventions (Obschonka *et al.*, 2012; Prodan & Drnovsek, 2010; Shane, 2004). The core assumption of the TPB is that behavioral intentions are an additive function of three conceptually independent factors: attitudes, social norms, and perceived behavior control.

Attitudes reflect an individual's enduring evaluation — positive or negative — of engaging in a particular behavior. Existing literature suggests that academic scientists allocate their efforts and time towards entrepreneurship if they have a favorable appraisal of entrepreneurial activity (e.g., Gulbrandsen, 2005; Owen-Smith & Powell, 2001), and when they expect to gain reputation or other rewards (i.e., financial) as a likely consequence of commercializing their research (Goethner *et al.*, 2012; Guerrero & Urbano, 2014; Huyghe & Knockaert, 2015; Prodan & Drnovsek, 2010).

The second predictor of entrepreneurial intentions, social norms, refers to perceived normative pressure from a specific reference group towards engaging or not engaging in a particular behavior (Ajzen, 1991). In line with the literature on academic entrepreneurship (Bercovitz & Feldman, 2008; Stuart & Ding, 2006), this study considers individual scientists' workplace peers as salient referents determining their entrepreneurial behavior. Previous research suggested that scientists feel pressure to become involved with the commercial exploitation of technology or knowledge, and are thus more likely to do so, if they sense that their academic peers look favorably on such activity (Rahm, 1994). Whereas some decades ago scientists' active involvement in the commercialization of their academic research knowledge was met with consternation among academic peers, the scientific community has recently experienced a significant change of view (Owen-Smith & Powell, 2001). University faculties have come to accept and, in many institutions, to endorse the participation in entrepreneurial endeavors. As Etzkowitz (1998, p. 824) stated, "the norms of science which traditionally condemn profit-making motives are beginning to change to allow for . . . entrepreneurship."

Perceived behavioral control is closely related to Bandura's (1997) concept of self-efficacy and reflects the perceived ease or difficulty of performing a particular behavior successfully. Following the TPB, scientists who do not perceive themselves to have control over entrepreneurial behavior and its outcome are unlikely to form strong entrepreneurial intentions, even if social norms and personal attitudes towards entrepreneurship are favorable. This is supported by entrepreneurship research which stressed the importance of self-efficacy as a mechanism for overcoming perceptions of higher financial, technological, and legal uncertainties that are often associated with the commercialization of university inventions (Markman *et al.*, 2002; Obschonka *et al.*, 2010). In line with the TPB, the following hypothesis applies:

Hypothesis 1: Scientists' entrepreneurial intentions are positively predicted by respective attitudes, social norms, and perceived behavioral control.

International research collaboration and S&T human capital

In this chapter, research collaboration is defined following the well-established co-authorship concept of research collaboration (for a critical review see Katz & Martin, 1997). Hence, the presence of two or more authors on the byline of a journal article is used as an indicator of collaborative research. Furthermore, this study is focusing on international research collaboration, which implies that a co-publication involves authors who belong to foreign organizations.

According to Bozeman *et al.* (2001), one can think of the dynamics of scientific collaboration in terms of researchers accumulating S&T human capital. S&T human capital has been defined as the unique set of scientific, technical and social knowledge, skills, and resources embodied in the individual scientist (Bozeman *et al.*, 2001; Ponomariov & Boardman, 2010). It encompasses not only human capital endowments, such as formal education, but also tacit knowledge, craft knowledge, and technical skills that are acquired through professional learning and training. Learning may partially occur through connections to scientific collaborators. These professional ties may help scientists to acquire formal and tacit knowledge, technical and cognitive skills to engage in further problem solving (Ponomariov & Boardman, 2010). International research collaboration might thus serve as a prominent way to increase the individual scientist's embeddedness in professional networks and the resources available which translates into higher S&T human capital (Edler *et al.*, 2011).

S&T human capital and entrepreneurial intentions

Besides its importance for the practice of science and the career growth of scientists, several pathways exist by which scientists may reap economic returns from their S&T human capital, including the creation of university spin-offs (Corolleur *et al.*, 2004; Zucker *et al.*, 1998). In fact, the S&T human capital approach to scientific productivity may help to get a better understanding of scientists' transitioning to entrepreneurship.

In the present study, I assume that S&T human capital operates as a moderator in the TPB framework. This assumption follows identity theory (Stets & Burke, 2000; Stryker, 1987), self-consistency theories (e.g., Festinger, 1957), and Super's (1963) occupational self-concept theory, which together indicate that people have a strong motivation to avoid a misfit between self-identity and behavior, particularly when the behavior in question is as "far-reaching" for the individual (in terms of enduring self-verification versus the inhibition of enduring self-verification) as an entrepreneurial occupational choice.

Researchers with higher levels of S&T human capital may also show a stronger commitment to their scientific work and anchor their self-identity in their profession (Henkel, 2005). For them, science is a 'vocation' (Weber, 1958) imbued with personal and social meaning. When deciding whether to engage in enterprising behavior or not, these research scientists will not follow their attitudes, norms, and control beliefs when this new occupational role does not fit the individual occupational self-concept — when such a "far-reaching" decision like engaging in entrepreneurship would stand against the person's fundamental psychological nature and would come at the cost of a (persisting) self-behavior misfit, which may produce cognitive dissonances (Festinger, 1957) and hamper enduring self-verification (Lecky, 1945; McCall & Simmons, 1966) in the occupational life-context (Super, 1963).

To illustrate, research scientists with higher levels of S&T human capital may have a positive attitude towards entrepreneurship, may perceive a social norm that is positive about entrepreneurship (for example because peers at the department generally value and expect such a behavior), and they may also feel capable of performing this behavior. At the same time, however, these researchers may not identify themselves with an entrepreneurial role — this does not fit to their scientific self — and thus do not choose to become an entrepreneur. Therefore, I propose:

Hypothesis 2: *S&T human capital has a moderating effect on the relationship between attitudes, norms, and perceived control (the predictors) and entrepreneurial intentions (the criterion), such that when S&T human capital is low the relationship is stronger and when S&T human capital is high the relationship is weaker.*

Research Methodology

The data presented in this chapter stemmed from the Thuringian Founder Study ("Thüringer Gründer Studie"), which is an interdisciplinary research project that examines the entrepreneurial process and its antecedents from the perspective of economics and psychology. The research was carried out on a regional basis with a focus on the German state of Thuringia. Located in the center of Germany, Thuringia is the smallest of the new German "Laender" with 2.16 mio. (2014) inhabitants. GDP hast constantly increased since 1991 amounting to €48 billion (2011). However, productivity is on average 30% lower than in West Germany. The Thuringian per capita income amounted to €14.898 in 2011 (German average is €18.411). Thuringia has a broad spectrum of research organizations, comprising nine public universities and eleven non-university research institutes, among them the Leibnitz Association, the Max-Planck Institutes and the Fraunhofer Society, providing a fertile ground for the emergence of academic entrepreneurship.

Thuringia has a long tradition of producing manufacturing but also high-quality goods and products, for example, in the optical and automotive industry. Furthermore, recent state policy places emphasis on environmental technologies with special focus on solar energy.

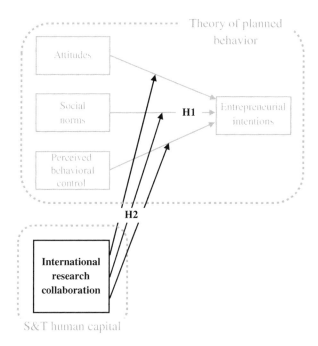

Figure 1.   Conceptual model for the prediction of research scientists' entrepreneurial intentions.

Data were collected using an online survey of university faculty and academic research staff. Internet-based surveys allow for highly standardized data collection at low cost and have been shown to collect data in a valid way (Gosling *et al.*, 2004). Furthermore, such surveys are expected to increase the response rate because the questionnaire can be completed without having to mail any forms (Mann & Stewart, 2000). Before this study was conducted we pilot-tested and optimized the questionnaire and the procedure in an independent sample of 133 scientists in the Federal State of Saxony, Germany.

To test the hypothesized relationships (see Figure 1), hierarchical OLS regression is employed. Hierarchical regression allows for examining the influence of predictor variables in a sequential way. The relative importance of a predictor variable entered later in the analysis can be judged on the basis of how much it adds to the prediction of the dependent variable, over and above that which can be accounted for by predictors entered earlier in the analysis. As a precaution, I used the robust regression to account for possible violations regarding the usual assumptions of normal distribution and homoscedasticity in the underlying data.

As a first step of sample selection, websites of public research organizations were accessed and prospective participants of the survey were identified. A total of 4,638 contact names and e-mail addresses were collected, comprising scientists from all scientific disciplines. From this initial list of names, a random sub-sample consisting of 2,319 individuals was drawn. These scientists were then sent an e-mail containing a cover letter and a link to the online questionnaire. Two weeks later a reminder was sent to the non-respondents, which was set up the same way as the initial e-mail. After another two weeks data collection was completed. In June 2008, we received completed questionnaires from 565 participants, representing a response rate of 24.4%. Compared to other web-based studies, this is an acceptable rate (Cook *et al.*, 2000). Before conducting our analysis, we excluded 15 participants due to incomplete data. We also excluded 54 participants who reported that they do not conduct any research, as this study targeted scientists' intentions to commercialize their own research. The final sample consists of 496 scientists.

Compared with official statistics on research personnel in Germany (Statistisches Bundesamt, 2008), this survey sample appeared to be representative in terms of age, gender, and academic rank.

Dependent variable

Three items assess scientists' intentions to engage in entrepreneurial activity (Ajzen, 2002; Krueger *et al.*, 2000) (Item 1: "In the foreseeable future, do you intend to participate in the founding of a firm to commercialize your research?"; five-point Likert scale; 1 = no, 5 = yes; Item 2: "In your opinion, how high is the probability that, in the foreseeable future, you will participate in the founding of a firm to commercialize your research?"; 1 = 0%; 6 = 100%; Item 3: "I have recently sought information about the ways and means of founding a firm with the object of commercializing my research."; five-point Likert scale; 1 = "no" to 5 = "yes"). The three items are z-standardized and averaged to create the final variable entrepreneurial intentions (α = 0.86). In a follow-up survey 18 months after the baseline survey it was tested whether this entrepreneurial intentions measure indeed forecasts entrepreneurial behavior. In December 2009 (T2), respondents were asked whether they had pursued entrepreneurship since T1, using the item "Since the last survey in June 2008, did you participate in the development of a business idea to commercialize your research?". For this study, this information was available for 119 of the participants. It turned out that entrepreneurial intentions (mean of the three z-standardized intention variables) indeed predicted entrepreneurial activity (r_s = 0.46, $p < 0.001$).

Independent variables

Intention predictors in the TPB (attitudes, social norms, perceived behavioral control)
Research scientists' *attitudes* towards academic entrepreneurship were measured

with the mean of four five-point bipolar adjective scales ("My personal attitude towards participation in the founding of a firm to commercialize my own research is that this is…; Item 1: 1 = "uninteresting" versus 5 = "interesting"; Item 2: 1 = "unattractive" versus 5 = "attractive"; Item 3: 1 = "boring" versus 5 = "exciting"; Item 4: 1 = "waste of time" versus 5 = "worth investing as much time as possible"; $\alpha = 0.89$) (Ajzen, 2001; 2002).

Social norms were assessed with the mean across two items, each referring to academic workplace peers (Ajzen, 2002) ("Most of my colleagues whose opinions matter to me…"; Item 1: "…think I should participate in the founding of a firm to commercialize my research."; Item 2: "…would encourage my participation in the founding of a firm to commercialize my research."; five-point Likert scale; 1 = "not at all correct" to 5 = "totally correct"; $\alpha = 0.68$).

Following Ajzen and Madden (1986), *perceived behavioral control* was measured with the mean of three items (Item 1: "I believe I can meet the demands posed by a participation in the founding of a firm to commercialize my research."; Item 2: "I am convinced that I would find it generally easy to participate in the founding of a firm to commercialize my research."; Item 3: "If I wanted to participate in the founding of a firm to commercialize my research, I am confident that I would succeed."; five-point Likert scale; 1 = "not at all correct" to 5 = "totally correct"; $\alpha = 0.84$).

International research collaboration
Information on respondents' international research activity has been extracted from research articles published in scientific journals that are indexed by the ISI Web of Science (WoS) database. WoS is a bibliographical database produced by Thomson Reuters, indexing approximately 9,000 journals worldwide and considered to be one of the most comprehensive and reliable sources of information on research activity across all countries and fields of science. Its indexed research articles all occur in peer-reviewed journals. These sources are selected on the basis of a minimum quality assessment carried out by Thomson Reuters. As such, the database can be considered representative of all scientific research that exceeds some minimum quality threshold.

For the analysis, I considered all research articles contained in the WoS that were published in the period 1998–2008. A publication was indicating research collaboration when two or more authors were listed on the byline. Although collaboration may take a number of different forms, a key outcome is a co-authored paper. International research collaboration thus implies that at least one author belongs to a foreign organization. These data were used to approximate the scope of the respondents' international research network. Following Scellato *et al.* (2015), the variable *network size* takes the value of 1 for those with no international collaborations, 2 for those with collaborations in just one other country, 3 for those with collaborations in two to four countries and 4 for those with collaborations in five or more countries. These levels correspond to the thresholds identified in previous summary statistics for the number of countries where the respondents' co-authors came from (not shown here). The resulting discrete ordered variable network size allows to identify no international network, small network, medium network and large network, respectively.

Control variables

The empirical analysis employs several control variables suggested by previous research on academic entrepreneurship and entrepreneurial intentions. As the likelihood to shift towards entrepreneurship may vary with an individual's background and life experience (Bercovitz & Feldman, 2008; Lee *et al.*, 2011; Murray & Graham, 2007), I control for *age* (measured in years) and *gender* (0 = female, 1 = male). I account also for academic seniority effects. Several authors have found a positive relationship between academic rank and scientists' engagement in entrepreneurial efforts (see Perkman *et al.*, 2013). I hence consider three levels of seniority in the analysis: *doctoral student* (0 = no, 1 = yes), *postdoctoral researcher* (0 = no, 1 = yes), and *professor* (0 = no, 1 = yes). The latter measure served as reference category. Patenting has been found to relate positively to academic entrepreneurial intentions (Prodan & Drnovsek, 2010). The dummy variable *academic inventor* thus captured whether participants had applied for at least one patent (0 = no, 1 = yes). This information was retrieved from matching the names of the individual researchers with the names of inventors on patents applied for at the German Patent and Trademark Office (DPMA) in the period 2004–2008. Prior entrepreneurial experience (whether positive or not) adds to the academic scientists' specific human capital by providing direct learning and episodic knowledge about the entrepreneurial process, which in turn predicts recurrent entrepreneurial activity (Hoye & Pries, 2009). As a proxy for entrepreneurial experience, the dummy variable *academic entrepreneur* represents the answer to the following question: "Have you already participated in the founding of a firm in the past to commercialize your research?" (0 = no, 1 = yes). It has been widely acknowledged that the scientific discipline constitutes an important work context that influences the disposition of research scientists to engage in entrepreneurship (D'Este *et al.*, 2012; Perkman *et al.*, 2013). To control for variation in entrepreneurial intentions across disciplines five dummy variables (0 = no, 1 = yes) were included representing the following categories: clinical medicine and pharmacy (*Medicine*), engineering, technology and computer science (*Engineering*), life and agricultural sciences (*Life*), social and behavioral sciences (*Social*), and natural sciences and mathematics (*Natural*). The latter category served as reference category in the analysis.

Common method variance

Several procedural and statistical remedies were employed to mitigate and examine the potential for common method variance (CMV) in the dataset (Podsakoff *et al.*, 2012). CMV occurs when respondents systematically distort their replies to survey questions, e.g., according to social desirability or their lay theory of the purpose of the questionnaire. Procedural remedies implemented in the survey design stage include protecting respondent anonymity, reducing item ambiguity, and separating scale items for the different measures of the explanatory and dependent variables in the questionnaire. These remedies together with the complex and comprehensive nature of the questionnaire made it almost impossible for respondents to outguess the survey goals and give socially desirable answers. Statistical remedies include Harman's one-factor test to check whether variance in the data can be largely attributed to a single factor (Podsakoff *et al.*, 2012). Entering all study variables into an exploratory factor analysis, the unrotated factor solution revealed the presence of five factors with eigenvalues larger than 1 rather than a single factor. The five factors together accounted for 61% of the total variance; the first (largest) factor did not account for a majority of the variance (19%). Thus, no general factor is apparent. As another statistical test, all study variables were loaded on one factor to examine the fit of the confirmatory factor analysis (CFA) model. If the one-factor CFA model fits the data well, it is considered that common method variance is largely responsible for the relationship among the variables (Mossholder *et al.*, 1998). The one-factor CFA model did not represent the data well (χ^2 (105) = 987.854, p = 0.000, CFI = 0.365, RMSEA = 0.153), providing evidence that the study variables were not merely different aspects of one underlying construct. Taken together, the procedural and statistical remedies applied leave us confident that common method variance is of limited concern in this dataset and thus is unlikely to confound the interpretations of our results.

Results

Table 1 provides descriptive statistics and correlation coefficients for all study variables. Mean age of the respondents is 39.72 years (*SD* = 11.31 years) and

Table 1. Descriptive statistics and correlations.

Variables	[1]	[2]	[3]	[4]	[5]	[6]	[7]	[8]	[9]	[10]	[11]	[12]	[13]	[14]	[15]
[1] Entrepreneurial intentions	1														
[2] Age	0.052	1													
[3] Gender (1 = male)	0.176**	0.273***	1												
[4] Doctoral student	−0.009	−0.690***	−0.244***	1											
[5] Postdoctoral researcher	0.049	0.309***	0.082	−0.694***	1										
[6] Academic inventor	0.247***	0.260***	0.152*	−0.216**	0.115	1									
[7] Academic entrepreneur	0.293***	0.306***	0.211**	−0.169**	0.058	0.223***	1								
[8] Medicine	−0.025	−0.008	−0.222***	−0.006	−0.029	0.046	0.009	1							
[9] Engineering	0.233***	0.054	0.148*	0.029	−0.037	0.154*	0.134*	−0.192**	1						
[10] Life	−0.070	0.007	−0.161*	−0.056	0.102	0.040	0.002	−0.175**	−0.225***	1					
[11] Social	−0.020	−0.081	0.047	−0.015	−0.051	−0.137*	−0.099	−0.105	−0.135*	−0.123	1				
[12] Attitudes	0.584***	−0.084	0.074	0.084	0.015	0.206**	0.218**	0.033	0.118	0.027	−0.052	1			
[13] Social norms	0.276***	−0.017	0.012	0.017	−0.022	0.133*	0.148*	0.021	0.129*	−0.038	−0.070	0.413***	1		
[14] Perceived behavioral control	0.523***	0.116	0.206**	−0.079	0.003	0.146*	0.285***	−0.054	0.130*	−0.043	0.066	0.524***	0.376***	1	
[15] Network size	−0.134*	0.417***	0.194**	−0.427***	0.134*	0.105	0.093	0.127*	−0.163*	−0.027	−0.192**	−0.047	−0.048	0.040	1
Mean	0.030	39.725	0.749	0.320	0.506	0.202	0.117	0.130	0.198	0.170	0.069	−0.037	0.065	−0.042	2.117
SD	0.887	11.309	0.434	0.467	0.501	0.403	0.323	0.336	0.4	0.376	0.254	1.014	0.975	0.951	1.168
Min	−0.713	24	0	0	0	0	0	0	0	0	0	−2.516	−2.558	−1.928	1
Max	3.477	65	1	1	1	1	1	1	1	1	1	1.654	2.406	2.03	4

Note: ***$p < 0.001$, **$p < 0.01$, *$p < 0.05$; $n = 247$.

74.9% are male. About one-third are doctoral students (32%), 50.6% are postdoctoral researchers, and 17.4% are professors or university lecturers. 54 (20.2%) of the researchers had prior patenting experience and 30 (11.7%) reported to have been involved in the creation of new businesses in the past. Furthermore, the international scope of the respondents' research networks on average is small (M = 2.12), indicating collaborations in just one other country. Researchers in the sample are conducting research activities in different scientific disciplines: 32 (13%) are involved in clinical medicine and pharmaceutical research, 59 (19.8%) in engineering, technology and computer science, 45 (17%) in life and agricultural sciences, 18 (6.9%) in social and behavioral sciences, and 111 (43.3%) in natural sciences and mathematics.

Hierarchical OLS regressions were conducted to test all hypotheses. Table 2 presents the results. Model 1 is the baseline model and analyzes the effect of the control variables; Model 2 considers the extra effect of the TPB variables, whereas Model 3 examines the additional effect of the size of respondents' international research network. The hypothesized interaction effects between the TPB variables and network size are tested in Model 4. All models are statistically significant, and the addition of extra variables considerably improves the variance explained as indicated by the change in R^2. To control for the existence of multicollinearity, variance inflation factors (VIF) were calculated for the variables used in each step of the regression analysis (not shown here). VIF scores ranged from 1.20 (academic inventor) to 3.73 (postdoctoral researcher). These values are below the critical value of 5 (Hair *et al.*, 2010), and thus multicollinearity is unlikely to be a concern in the present study.

Among the control variables (Model 1), males reported significantly higher levels of entrepreneurial intentions than females (β = 0.230, $p <$ 0.05). Postdoctoral researchers more strongly intended to engage in entrepreneurship than doctoral students and professors (β = 0.261, $p <$ 0.10). Furthermore, the effects of being an academic inventor (β = 0.410, $p <$ 0.05) and being an academic entrepreneur (β = 0.663, $p <$ 0.01) were positive and significant. Those respondents who previously engaged in commercialization activities (i.e., patenting, business creation, consulting to industry) also showed higher current intentions to become an entrepreneur. Finally, significant discipline effects exist with respondents active in engineering, technology and computer science showing greater entrepreneurial intentions (β = 0.372, $p <$ 0.05).

Model 2 adds the intention predictors described in the theory of planned behavior (TPB). This model additionally explains 27.6% variance in

Table 2. Hierarchical OLS regression for the prediction of research scientists' entrepreneurial intentions.

	Model 1		Model 2		Model 3		Model 4	
	β	SE	β	SE	β	SE	β	SE
Constant	−0.544	(0.377)	−0.367	(0.334)	−0.047	(0.373)	0.006	(0.357)
Control variables								
Age	−0.002	(0.007)	0.002	(0.006)	0.004	(0.006)	0.006	(0.006)
Gender (1 = male)	0.230*	(0.116)	0.091	(0.100)	0.128	(0.099)	0.094	(0.101)
Doctoral student	0.336	(0.212)	0.205	(0.187)	0.030	(0.202)	0.003	(0.187)
Postdoctoral researcher	0.261†	(0.141)	0.172	(0.126)	0.084	(0.124)	0.021	(0.115)
Academic inventor	0.410*	(0.171)	0.207	(0.139)	0.199	(0.133)	0.182	(0.121)
Academic entrepreneur	0.663**	(0.214)	0.266	(0.172)	0.248	(0.170)	0.332*	(0.159)
Medicine	0.079	(0.169)	0.006	(0.133)	0.033	(0.129)	0.008	(0.118)
Engineering	0.372*	(0.156)	0.255*	(0.125)	0.173	(0.129)	0.080	(0.126)
Life	−0.035	(0.142)	−0.099	(0.122)	−0.132	(0.120)	−0.168	(0.118)
Social	0.195	(0.218)	0.074	(0.203)	−0.078	(0.212)	−0.072	(0.214)
TPB variables								
Attitudes			0.346***	(0.051)	0.352***	(0.052)	0.498***	(0.105)
Social norms			−0.025	(0.052)	−0.034	(0.052)	0.047	(0.114)
Perceived behavioral control			0.245***	(0.060)	0.249***	(0.060)	0.471***	(0.124)
International research collaboration								
Network size					−0.130**	(0.044)	−0.157***	(0.044)
Interaction effects								
Network size × Attitudes							−0.060	(0.040)
Network size × Social norms							−0.042	(0.045)
Network size × Perceived behavioral control							−0.106*	(0.047)
F-statistic	3.790***		11.964***		11.635***		11.384***	
R^2	0.179		0.455		0.474		0.518	
Adjusted R^2	0.144		0.424		0.442		0.483	
R^2 change			0.276***		0.019**		0.045***	

Note. Robust standard errors in parentheses; ***$p < 0.001$, **$p < 0.01$, *$p < 0.05$, †$p < 0.10$; $n = 247$.

entrepreneurial intentions, indicating a large effect (Cohen, 1988). In terms of relative contributions, attitudes ($\beta = 0.346$, $p < 0.001$) and perceived behavioral control ($\beta = 0.245$, $p < 0.001$) predicted intentions, but not social norms ($\beta = -0.025$, $p = 0.624$). In sum, Hypothesis 1 received partial support.

In Model 3, network size was introduced to the regression equation. This variable showed a negative and significant direct effect on scientists' entrepreneurial intentions ($\beta = -0.130$, $p < 0.01$) and explained additional 1.9% of variance in the dependent variable.

In the last step of the regression analysis (Model 4), interaction effects between the TPB predictors and network size were tested. Following Aiken and West (1991), z-standardized variables were used to calculate the interaction terms. One interaction effect showed up significant: the interaction between network size and perceived behavioral control ($\beta = -0.106$, $p < 0.05$). Figure 2 shows that the influence of perceived behavioral control on entrepreneurial intentions diminishes with an increasing international scope of respondents' research activity. On the other hand, the control-intentions link seems to be strongest for scientists who do not publish with international co-authors at all (i.e., scientists without an international research network). Overall, Hypothesis 2 is partially supported by the data (as I do not find support for such an interaction effect for the other two TPB predictors, attitudes and social norms).

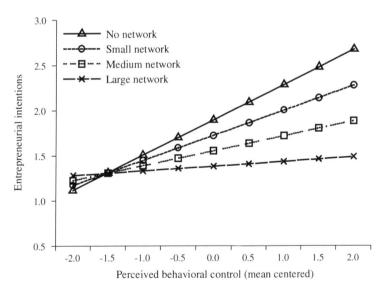

Figure 2.   Interaction between perceived behavioral control and the international scope of scientists' research network.

Discussion and Conclusion

Acknowledging and demonstrating the intentionality of academic entrepreneurship, in this chapter a model is tested that combines previous research on the internationalization of science (Katz & Martin, 1997) and the theory of planned behavior approach (TPB), which is a universal model of behavioral intentions (Ajzen, 1991; Fishbein & Ajzen, 2010). It was expected that the scientific and technical (S&T) human capital (Bozeman *et al.*, 2001) related to scientists' international research collaborations critically influences the cognitive processes that, according to the TPB underlie the formation of entrepreneurial intentions. In the following, I first briefly discuss the findings on the TPB-intention link, and then turn to the main results, namely the effect of S&T human capital via the TPB.

The TPB would predict that planned behavior such as entrepreneurship is mainly a function of the respective behavioral intentions, which in turn can be best explained by attitude, norms, and perceived behavioral control. The results presented in this study are very much in line with this proposition. First, by means of prospective data it could be shown that entrepreneurial intentions are indeed a powerful predictor of future entrepreneurial behavior. Second, the TPB proves to be a useful framework to study the emergence of entrepreneurial intentions, explaining a large amount of variance in this variable (around 52%). This compares favorably to both the 35–42% of explained variance in previous entrepreneurship studies applying intentions-based models (e.g., Krueger *et al.*, 2000; Souitaris *et al.*, 2007) and the 39% of the variance typically explained across a wide range of other planned behaviors (e.g., dieting, quitting smoking, seatbelt usage) (for a review see Armitage & Conner, 2001).

Referring to the intention predictors described in the TPB (attitudes, social norms, perceived behavioral control), only social norms turned out not to be relevant in the prediction of intentions. While this result contrasts with previous research proposing that scientist's decision to found an own firm is socially conditioned (Bercovitz & Feldman, 2008; Stuart & Ding, 2006), it is in line with more general TPB studies on entrepreneurial intentions, which also found non-significant effects of social norms (Liñán *et al.*, 2011). It thus seems that entrepreneurial intentions are mainly driven by the personal TPB factors (attitudes and perceived control), whereas norms associated with the social context (in our case perceived expectations and behaviors of scientists' workplace peers) are less important. Hence, when deciding whether to start a new business or not, research scientists may be more "inner-directed" (Krueger *et al.*, 2000). On the other hand, and in line with social identity theory, it may well be that the effect of social norms on entrepreneurial intentions is moderated by group identification (Terry *et al.*, 1999). Accordingly, perceived expectations and behaviors of scientists' workplace peers may only matter for entrepreneurial intentions when the scientists strongly identify with these peers (Obschonka *et al.*, 2012).

Regarding moderating effects, S&T human capital, approximated by the international scope of respondents' research network, moderated the TPB-entrepreneurial intentions link. From the three tested interactions, one showed up significant and the plot is consistent with the expected interaction pattern. If S&T human capital was high (i.e., scientist's international research network was large), the effect of perceived control was diminished. Control is a key construct in theories on vocational choice in general (Lent, Brown, & Hackett, 1994), and also figures prominently in entrepreneurship research (e.g., self-efficacy and locus of control, Rauch & Frese, 2007) and research on entrepreneurial intentions (Krueger *et al.*, 2000; Lee *et al.*, 2011; Obschonka *et al.*, 2010; Zhao *et al.*, 2005). One basic result in past entrepreneurship studies is that interindividual differences in control beliefs (e.g., higher levels of self-efficacy or internal locus of control) are among the most influential personal determinants on entrepreneurial career decisions (Rauch & Frese, 2007). This study adds to this research by suggesting that the control-intentions relationship may be conditional on the carrier growth and renown of the individual scientist. It seems that, for accomplished scientists with research contacts all over the world, higher levels of entrepreneurial self-efficacy do not necessarily translate into higher levels of entrepreneurial career aspirations. Although one should be careful not to overinterpret these results until they are replicated in other studies, these findings might provide some explanation for the so-called "commitment paradox" (Corolleur *et al.*, 2004), that is the observation that star scientists usually do not leave academia to engage in commercial activities but rather work part-time as scientific advisors whereas less famous scientists leave academia at some point and start new firms to create their own jobs.

This study has implications for future research. Although the results discussed above are correlational in nature and further longitudinal evidence is needed to infer more causal interpretations, they add an important perspective to the study of the entrepreneurial scientist by tackling the question how the internationalization of science may be relevant for understanding scientists' transition to the entrepreneurial arena. One aspect that deserves further scrutiny refers to the role of scientific productivity in the prediction of entrepreneurial intentions and behavior. While there is a small and emerging literature dealing with this topic (D'Este *et al.*, 2012; Erikson *et al.*, 2015), clearly more research is needed to better understand the mechanisms through which the skills and networks that are important for the practice of science and the career growth of scientists may also impact on their entrepreneurial career aspirations. Moreover, to enhance the robustness of the present findings, it would be interesting to replicate this study in the US and UK, which are often referred to as powerhouses of academic entrepreneurship, and China, the world's largest developing economy. A cross-cultural validation of this study may further provide promising opportunities for future research, as cultural aspects have recently been shown to be relevant in explaining entrepreneurial intentions (Liñán & Chen, 2009; Prodan & Drnovsek, 2010). Finally, future research could further examine how entrepreneurial intentions of scientists with different levels of S&T human capital precipitate into entrepreneurial behavior.

For higher education leaders and policymakers who wish to stimulate academic entrepreneurship implications from this study are as follows. The present results suggest that respective policy interventions could follow the logic of the TPB and target a person's attitudes and control beliefs. Interventions informed by intentions-based models, such as the TPB, have already proven to be efficacious in changing intentions and behavior of very different kinds (Fishbein & Ajzen, 2005) and also in the context of entrepreneurship (Fayolle, 2005; Krueger, 2007; Souitaris *et al.*, 2007). Public support schemes may further benefit from understanding that the scientific collaboration pattern of researchers may critically influence the intention formation process. In particular, policy interventions may be limited in their effectiveness when targeting competences and perceptions of control in order to stimulate entrepreneurship among internationally renowned scientists who publish with international peers.

This study has several limitations. Although the proposed conceptual model is grounded in well-established theories, the correlational design of this study does not allow for strictly causal testing. Nevertheless, the results concur with past empirical research employing the TPB to predict entrepreneurial intentions. Second, all information is collected from the same source, namely from the individual scientist, and by means of the same method (online questionnaire), except for secondary data on scientists' publication record. Future research may take into account multi-informant/multi-method procedures to consider other sources and methods as well. A third caveat is the study's focus on the population of German research scientists to investigate the relationship between international research collaborations and the cognitive processes underlying the formation of entrepreneurial intentions. At first glance, this might come at the expense of a more general application of the results in other national contexts. One should keep in mind, however, that the approach chosen for this study bases on general and well-established theories, which have proven their usefulness in a variety of studies on entrepreneurial career transitions. Thus, the results may well apply to other countries and populations.

Acknowledgments

Financial support by the Thuringian Ministry of Education (Thüringer Kultusministerium) and the Hans Böckler Foundation (Hans-Böckler-Stiftung) within the research project "Success and Failure of Innovative Start-Ups — A Process-Oriented Analysis of Economic and Psychological Determinants" is gratefully acknowledged. The author also thanks the German Science Foundation for financial support with the doctoral program DFG-GRK 1411 "The Economics of Innovative Change".

References

Aiken, L. S. & West, S. G. 1991. *Multiple Regression: Testing and Interpreting Interactions.* Sage, Newbury Park.

Adams, J. D., Black, G. C., Clemmons, J. R. & Stephan, P. E. 2005. Scientific teams and institutional collaborations: evidence from US universities, 1981–1999. *Research Policy,* 34(3), 259–285.

Ajzen, I. 2002. Construction of a standard questionnaire for the theory of planned behavior. Available at: http://www-unix.oit.umass.edu/~aizen/ (Accessed on June 10, 2008).

Ajzen, I. 2001. The nature and operation of attitudes. *Annual Review of Psychology,* 52, 27–58.

Ajzen, I. 1991. The theory of planned behavior. *Organizational Behavior and Human Decision Processes,* 50, 179–211.

Ajzen, I. & Madden, T. J. 1986. Prediction of goal-directed behavior: attitudes, intentions and perceived behavioral control. *Journal of Experimental Social Psychology,* 22(5), 453–474.

Bandura, A. 1997. *Self-efficacy: The Exercise of Control.* W. H. Freeman, New York, NY.

Bercovitz, J. & Feldman, M. 2008. Academic entrepreneurs: organizational change at the individual level. *Organization Science,* 19(1), 69–89.

Bird, B. J. 1988. Implementing entrepreneurial ideas: The case for intention. *Academy of Management Review,* 13(3), 442–453.

BMBF (Bundesministerium für Bildung und Forschung). 2002. *Zur Einführung der Neuheitsschonfrist im Patentrecht — ein USA–Deutschland–Vergleich bezogen auf den Hochschulbereich.* BMBF, Bonn.

Bozeman, B., Dietz, J. & Gaughan, M. 2001. Scientific and technical human capital: an alternative model for research evaluation. *International Journal of Technology Management,* 22(7/8), 636–655.

Cohen, J. (1988). *Statistical Power Analysis for the Behavioral Sciences*. Lawrence Erlbaum, Hillsdale.

Conner, M. & Armitage, C. J. 1998. Extending the theory of planned behavior: A review and avenues for future research. *Journal of Applied Social Psychology*, 28(15), 1429–1464.

Cook, C., Heath, F. & Thompson, R. L. 2000. A meta-analysis of response rates in web- or internet-based surveys. *Educational and Psychological Measurement*, 60(6), 821–836.

Davidsson, P. & Honig, B. 2003. The role of social and human capital among nascent entrepreneurs. *Journal of Business Venturing*, 18(3), 301–331.

D'Este, P., Mahdi, S., Neely, A. & Rentocchini, F. (2012). Inventors and entrepreneurs in academia. *Technovation*, 32(5), 293–303.

de Solla Price, D. J. 1986. *Little Science, Big Science...and Beyond*. Columbia University Press, New York, NY.

Edler, J., Fier, H. & Grimpe, C. 2011. International scientist mobility and the locus of knowledge and technology transfer. *Research Policy*, 40(6), 791–805.

Erikson, T., Knockaert, M. & Foo, M. D. 2015. Enterprising scientists: The shaping role of norms, experience and scientific productivity. *Technological Forecasting & Social Change*, 99, 211–221.

FGF e.V. (Förderkreis Gründungs-Forschung e.V.). (2015). *Entrepreneurship-Professuren an öffentlichen und privaten Hochschulen in Deutschland*. http://www.fgf-ev.de/wp-content/uploads/2015/03/E-Professuren-17-03-2015.pdf.

Fini, R., Grimaldi, R., Marzocchi, G. L. & Sobrero, M. (2012) The determinants of corporate entrepreneurial intention within small and newly established firms. *Entrepreneurship: Theory & Practice*, 36(2), 387–414.

Fishbein, M. & Ajzen, I. 2010. *Predicting and Changing Behavior: The Reasoned Action Approach*. Taylor, New York, NY.

Fritsch, M. & Krabel, S. 2012. Ready to leave the ivory tower?: Academic scientists' appeal to work in the private sector. *Journal of Technology Transfer*, 37(3), 271–296.

Goethner, M., Obschonka, M., Silbereisen, R. K. & Cantner, U. 2012. Scientists' transition to academic entrepreneurship: Economic and psychological determinants. *Journal of Economic Psychology*, 33(3), 628–641.

Gosling, S. D., Vazire, S., Srivastava, S. & John, O. P. 2004. Should we trust web-based studies? A comparative analysis of six preconceptions about internet questionnaires. *American Psychologist*, 59(2), 93–104.

Göktepe-Hulten, D. & Mahagaonkar, P. 2010. Inventing and patent activities of scientists: In the expectation of money or reputation? *Journal of Technology Transfer*, 35(4), 401–423.

Gulbrandsen, M. 2005. "But Peter's in it for the money" — The liminality of entrepreneurial scientists. *VEST Journal for Science and Technology Studies*, 18(1–2), 49–75.

Grimm, H. M. 2011. The diffusion of Bayh–Dole to Germany: Did new public policy facilitate university patenting and commercialisation? *International Journal of Entrepreneurship and Small Business*, 12(4), 459–478.

Guerrero, M. & Urbano, D. 2014. Academics' start-up intentions and knowledge filters: An individual perspective of the knowledge spillover theory of entrepreneurship. *Small Business Economics*, 43(1), 57–74.

Hair, J. F., Black, W. C., Babin, B. J. & Anderson, R. E. 2010. *Multivariate data analysis: A Global Perspective*. 7th ed. Pearson, Prentice Hall, NJ.

Huyghe, A. & Knockaert, M. 2015. The influence of organizational culture and climate on entrepreneurial intentions among research scientists. *Journal of Technology Transfer*, 40(1), 138–160.

Henkel, M. 2005. Academic identity and autonomy in a changing policy. *Higher Education*, 49(1–2), 155–176.

Kauffman. 2010. *Entrepreneurship in American Higher Education, A Report from the Kauffman Panel on Entrepreneurship Curriculum in Higher Education, Kansas City, US*: Kauffman: The foundation of entrepreneurship.

Kautonen, T., Van Gelderen, M. & Tornikoski, E. T. 2013. Predicting entrepreneurial behaviour: A test of the theory of planned behaviour. *Applied Economics*, 45(6), 697–707.

Katz, J. S. & Martin, B. R. 1997. What is research collaboration? *Research Policy*, 26(1), 1–18.

Kilger, C. & Bartenbach, K. 2002. New rules for German professors. *Science*, 298(8), 1173–1175.

Krabel, S., Siegel, D. S. & Slavtchev, V. 2012. The internationalization of science and its influence on academic entrepreneurship. *Journal of Technology Transfer*, 37(2), 192–212.

Krueger, N. F. & Carsrud, A. L. 1993. Entrepreneurial intentions: Applying the theory of planned behavior. *Entrepreneurship & Regional Development*, 5(4), 315–330.

Krueger, N. F., Reilly, M. D. & Carsrud, A. L. 2000. Competing models of entrepreneurial intentions. *Journal of Business Venturing*, 15(5, 6), 411–432.

Krueger, N. F. 2009. Entrepreneurial intentions are dead: Long live entrepreneurial intentions. In *Understanding the Entrepreneurial Mind: Opening the Black Box*, Carsrud, A. L. & Brännback, M. (eds.). Springer, New York, NY, pp. 51–72.

Lee, L., Wong, P. K., Foo, M. D. & Leung, A. 2011. Entrepreneurial intentions: the influence of organizational and individual factors. *Journal of Business Venturing*, 26(1), 124–136.

Liñán, F. & Chen, Y.-W. 2009. Development and cross-cultural application of a specific instrument to measure entrepreneurial intentions. *Entrepreneurship: Theory & Practice*, 33(3), 593–617.

Mann, C. & Stewart, F. 2000. *Internet Communication and Qualitative Research. A Handbook for Researching Online*. SAGE Publications Inc., Thousand Oaks, CA.

Markman, G. D., Balkin, D. B. & Baron, R. A. 2002. Inventors and new venture formation: The effects of general self-efficacy and regretful thinking. *Entrepreneurship: Theory & Practice*, 27(2), 149–165.

Mossholder, K. W., Bennett, N., Kemery, E. R. & Wesolowski, M. A. (1998). Relationships between bases of power and work reactions: The mediational role of procedural justice. *Journal of Management*, 24(4), 533–552.

Narin, F., Stevens, K. & Whitlow, E. (1991). Scientific co-operation in Europe and the citation of multinationally authored papers. *Scientometrics*, 21(3), 313–323.

Obschonka, M., Goethner, M., Silbereisen, R. K. & Cantner, U. 2012. Social identity and the transition to entrepreneurship: The role of group identification with workplace peers. *Journal of Vocational Behavior*, 80(1), 137–147.

OECD. 2009. Strengthening entrepreneurship and economic development in East Germany: Lessons from local approaches. Final report prepared by the Organisation for Economic Co-operation and Development, OECD, Paris/Trento.

Podsakoff, P. M., MacKenzie, S. B. & Podsakoff, N. P. 2012. Source of method bias in social science research and recommendations on how to control it. *Annual Review of Psychology*, 63, 539–569.

Ponomariov, B. L. & Boardman, P. C. 2010. Influencing scientists' collaboration and productivity patterns through new institutions: University research centers and scientific and technical human capital. *Research Policy*, 39(5), 613–624.

Preacher, K. J. & Hayes, A. F. 2008. Asymptotic and resampling strategies for assessing and comparing indirect effects in multiple mediator models. *Behavior Research Methods*, 40, 879–891.

Prodan, I. & Drnovsek, M. 2010. Conceptualizing academic-entrepreneurial intentions: An empirical test. *Technovation*, 30(5), 332–347.

Rahm, D. 1994. Academic perceptions of university-firm technology transfer. *Policy Studies Journal*, 22, 267–278.

Scellato, G., Franzoni, C. & Stephan, P. 2015. Migrant scientists and international networks. *Research Policy*, 44(1), 108–120.

Schultz, T. W. 1980. Investment in entrepreneurial ability. *Scandinavian Journal of Economics*, 82, 437–448.

Schumpeter, J. A. 1934. *The Theory of Economic Development.* Harvard University Press, Cambridge, MA.

Shane, S. A. 2004. *Academic Entrepreneurship: University Spin-offs and Wealth Creation.* Edward Elgar Publishing, Cheltenham, UK.

Statistisches Bundesamt. 2008. *Bildung und Kultur. Personal an Hochschulen [Education and Culture. Personnel at Universities].* Statistisches Bundesamt, Wiesbaden, Germany.

Stephan, P. E. 2012. *How Economics Shapes Science.* Harvard University Press, Cambridge, MA.

Stuart, T. E. & Ding, W. W. 2006. When do scientists become entrepreneurs? The social structural antecedents of commercial activity in the academic life sciences. *American Journal of Sociology*, 112(1), 97–144.

Weber, M. 1958. Science as a vocation. *Daedalus*, 87(1), 111–134.

Wuchty, S., Jones, B. & Uzzi, B. 2007. The increasing dominance of teams in the production of knowledge. *Science*, 316(5827), 1036–1039.

Chapter 4

The Role of Social Network Actors in the Formation of University Spin-Offs — Case Studies of External and Inventor Entrepreneurs in Sweden

Anders Billström

Nord University, Business School
N-8049 Bodø, Norway
School of Business, Engineering and Science
Halmstad University, P.O. Box 823, SE-301 18 Halmstad, Sweden
Anders.Billstrom@hh.se

In recent decades, policy makers and researchers have taken an increased interest in university spin-offs. Entrepreneurship research provides limited knowledge of the role of the social network actors of external entrepreneurs in the formation process of university spin-offs. External entrepreneurs, who come from outside the university, are likely to use other network actors than academic researchers. This may influence the subsequent development of the firm. The purpose is to develop a conceptual framework for the role of social network actors in the formation of university spin-offs managed by external and inventor entrepreneurs. Literature of social networking, university spin-off formation and external and inventor entrepreneurs guide this study. This study employs a case study design that contains three external and three inventor entrepreneurs of Swedish university spin-offs. The results demonstrate that business actors, support actors and technology actors influence the firm formation process. The study also shows that external entrepreneurs have strong ties (direct access) to business actors while inventor entrepreneurs have weak ties (indirect access) to business actors via the university incubator. University incubators are less important for external entrepreneurs than inventor entrepreneurs because of their strong ties to business actors. The chapter provides implications for researchers and policy makers.

Introduction

In recent decades, policy makers, practitioners, and scholars have taken an increased interest in university spin-offs. In Pinay, Surlemont, and Niemvo's definition, a university spin-off is a "new firm created to exploit commercially some knowledge, technology or research results developed within the university" (2002, p. 356). Such firms are important because they may contribute to regional development, promote universities' reputations (Steffensen *et al.*, 2000), create new jobs, and produce breakthrough products (Shane, 2004).

However, most of university spin-offs do not grow, or grow slowly (Mustar *et al.*, 2008), or perform not as well as other technology-based firms (e.g., Ensley and Hmieleski, 2005; Wennberg *et al.*, 2011). One reason may be that academic researchers, when they assume the role of inventor entrepreneur, do not always have the business experience and industrial networks needed to develop these firms (Vohora *et al.*, 2004). These limitations create challenges for the firms as they work to establish opportunity recognition, entrepreneurial commitment, market credibility, and sustainable returns. As a result, policy makers and practitioners have created business support systems such as university incubators to support commercialization of university technologies. While university incubators can provide business infrastructure and business coaching, and mediate network contacts, they have nevertheless been criticized for producing rather few successful firms (Peters *et al.*, 2004). Consequently, university incubators, working with inventor entrepreneurs, do not always provide assistance needed for the creation of successful university spin-offs.

In contrast, researchers have found that external entrepreneurs (also termed surrogate entrepreneurs) are more successful at generating firm growth. An external entrepreneur refers to the individual from outside the university who has not previously been engaged in technology development (Politis *et al.*, 2012) but initiated a university spin-off. Lundqvist (2014) suggests that surrogate entrepreneurs create higher growth and produce more revenue than non-surrogate entrepreneurs. Billström *et al.* (2014) conclude that external entrepreneurs have greater direct access to centrally positioned business networks than inventor entrepreneurs whose business networks have a more peripheral position. Thus, it appears that external entrepreneurs rely on other network actors more than inventor entrepreneurs.

This chapter addresses three limitations of previous entrepreneurship research. First, most entrepreneurship research focuses on established firms. The research on the theories related to firm formation (Davidsson & Wiklund, 2001; Phan, 2006) and to university spin-off formation is limited (Druilhe & Garnsey, 2004; De Cleyn *et al.*, 2014). Firm formation is worthy of investigation because a firm's characteristics at its founding influence its later development (Boeker, 1989). For example, it is important to identify a radically innovative firm's strong and weak network ties (Elfring & Hulsink, 2003). The implication is that entrepreneurs' social networks influence firm formation.

Second, the literature on entrepreneurship proposes that all network elements (i.e., network content, governance, and structure) should be investigated if the aim is to provide a more extensive picture of the start-up process (Hoang & Antoncic, 2003; Slotte-Kock & Coviello, 2010). Most university spin-off studies focus on only one or two network elements such as network structure (e.g., Nicolaou & Birley, 2003) or network content and network structure (e.g., Pérez Pérez & Martinez Sánchez, 2003). The author of this chapter identified only two studies that address all network elements. One study investigates the relationships between human capital and social networking by inventor entrepreneurs (Mosey & Wright, 2007); the other study investigates social networking of external and inventor entrepreneurs (Billström *et al.*, 2014). However, neither of these two studies focuses explicitly on firm formation and the network actors. The conclusion is that research on social networking in university spin-offs is fragmented as far who provides the resources and when these resources are provided.

Third, university spin-off research assumes that academic researchers initiate university spin-offs. As a result, the research presents a rather one-sided picture of university spin-off formation. To date, very few, mostly fragmented, studies of external entrepreneurs in university spin-offs are available. The one exception concerns the research into social networking that reveals that external and inventor entrepreneurs have similar network contents although they coordinate and position their network structures differently (Billström *et al.*, 2014). Hence, theoretical knowledge on external entrepreneurs' social networks is scarce. Two literature reviews (Djokovic & Souitaris, 2008; Rothaermel *et al.*, 2007), in their call for more research on surrogate entrepreneurs, suggest we need to develop our theoretical knowledge of their role in university spin-off formation.

The purpose of this chapter is to develop a conceptual framework for the role of social network actors in the formation of university spin-offs that are managed by external and inventor entrepreneurs.

The chapter is structured as follows. The frame of reference follows and includes studies of university spin-off formation, social networking, and external and inventor entrepreneurs. The method section, which follows, describes the research context, case selection, data collection, and data analysis. The empirical findings section presents the cases for this study. Thereafter a case analysis follows. The last section presents the research conclusions and implications.

Frame of Reference

The formation of university spin-offs

This study uses the conceptual framework of development phases and critical junctures proposed by Vohora *et al.* (2004). The framework consists of the research phase, the opportunity-framing phase, the pre-organization phase, the re-orientation phase, and the sustainable return phase. Critical junctures emerge in the interstices between these phases if the firm lacks the resources needed to progress to the next phase. These junctures are the following: opportunity recognition, entrepreneurial commitment, threshold of credibility, and threshold of sustainability.

In the *research phase,* the research team's role is to identify a technological and business opportunity (Vohora *et al.*, 2004). However, the team may require assistance from its peers, technology transfer officers (TTO), and incubator coaches in this phase (Vanaelst *et al.*, 2006). Parents, friends, and neighbors of the team members who have business experience can influence the opportunity recognition (Davidsson & Honig, 2003). Therefore, actors with research and entrepreneurial experience are needed to move beyond opportunity recognition and to progress to the opportunity framing phase.

In the *opportunity framing phase,* the key activities are the evaluation of the technology outside the laboratory and the framing of the business opportunity based on identifying, accessing, and targeting customers (Vohora *et al.*, 2004). In this phase, it is necessary to develop proof of the concept, the market, and interactions with market actors. In addition to the inventor entrepreneurs, industrial partners, external entrepreneurs (Wright *et al.*, 2004) and privileged witnesses referring to peers from the scientific community, the TTO and incubator coaches may be essential (Vanaelst *et al.*, 2006). Hence, actors with technological and entrepreneurial experience are needed to progress to the pre-organization phase.

In the *pre-organization phase*, the key activities are identifying and segmenting the market, gaining credibility, and acquiring start-up resources (Vohora *et al.*, 2004). The inventor entrepreneur may not advance to commercialization owing to a lack of commitment or to university policy restrictions. In such cases, the inventor entrepreneur may return to previous employment in academia (Vanaelst *et al.*, 2006). Thus, business people, external entrepreneurs, business angels (Vohora *et al.*, 2004), privileged witnesses, industrial partners, and venture capitalists are essential actors (Vanaelst *et al.*, 2006). In particular, actors with business experience and industrial networks are needed to progress to the re-orientation phase.

In the **re-orientation phase**, the key activities are establishing legitimacy and gaining market acceptance by offering customer value (Vohora *et al.*, 2004). Resource re-configuration, based on knowledge acquired from interactions with customers, suppliers, competitors. and potential investors, is often necessary. The entrepreneur's knowledge acquisition and interactions with key actors in previous phases are paramount. In particular, actors with business and entrepreneurial experience and industrial networks are needed to progress to the sustainable return phase.

In the **sustainable return phase**, the key activities are realizing the business model (revised in earlier phases), acquiring a major market share and scaling production (Vohora *et al.*, 2004). This phase requires financial capital from investors such as venture capitalists. External entrepreneurs can contribute the necessary market information (Billström *et al.*, 2014). Other essential actors are the privileged witnesses and the boards of directors. In particular, actors with business experience and industrial networks are needed to maintain the position in the sustainable return phase instead of regressing to earlier phases.

Social networks in the formation of university spin-offs

University spin-offs require social networks for the acquisition of critical resources and for the management of various challenges such as those that emerge in the critical junctures in firm formation (Vohora *et al.*, 2004; Wright *et al.*, 2004). Soetanto and Van Geenhuizen (2011, p. 308) define social networks as "networks of important 'partners' that potentially provide valuable resources for firms' growth".

Social networking is especially important for entrepreneurs who must complement their own resources (Jack, 2005). While some inventor entrepreneurs face significant challenges in building network ties to industry, other inventor entrepreneurs face smaller challenges, depending on their entrepreneurial human capital (Mosey and Wright, 2007). In short, university spin-offs founded by inventor entrepreneurs may have different needs as far as social networks.

Hoang and Antoncic (2003) identify three network elements that are critical for successful entrepreneurship: (i) the nature of *network content* that is exchanged between network actors, (ii) the *network governance* of mechanisms that coordinate relationships between network actors, and (iii) the *network structure* that consists of network ties that connect network actors.

Network content is generally defined as the various resources that network actors exchange. Network content includes, for example, financial capital, emotional support, legitimacy measures (Hoang & Antoncic, 2003) as well as advice and expertise on patents, legal issues, business plans, product testing, technology development, market identification, and internationalization activities (Neergaard, 2005). Network content is useful in recruiting employees, creating an entrepreneurial team, capturing investors' interest, and connecting with other network actors. Experienced entrepreneurs usually have greater access to a larger variety of resources than less experienced entrepreneurs who rely on the limited resources from social networks (Mosey *et al.*, 2006). Although professional actors are generally most capable of providing such resources, family members and friends can also contribute to both firm formation and reputation enhancement (e.g., Jack, 2005).

Network governance is generally defined as the coordinating mechanisms that manage relationships between network actors (Hoang & Antoncic, 2003). Formal contracts are often a necessity in the resource exchanges between network actors. Trust between actors is another form of network governance (Anderson *et al.*, 2007). Trust comes from respect, familiarity, and confidence in the counterpart's ability and knowledge (Jack, 2005). Trust is important in maintaining goodwill when firms pool their resources (Anderson *et al.*, 2007). Governance mechanisms can also be useful for acquiring technical credibility and market credibility. Experienced entrepreneurs may rely more on trust than on formal contracts (Billström *et al.*, 2014).

Network structure is generally defined as the pattern of relationships between actors in social networks (Hoang & Antoncic, 2003). Network structure includes network size, centrality, density, and strong/weak bridging ties. Differences in network position can influence resource flows and firm development. Strong and weak ties refer to the frequency of contact and the quality and intensity of relationships (Granovetter, 1973). Strong ties connect entrepreneurs with first-order actors while weak ties connect them to second-order actors (Jack, 2005). Network ties contribute to firm formation by linking customers and by providing business support, knowledge, and experience with firm development.

Inventor entrepreneurs and external entrepreneurs in university spin-offs

Various descriptive titles are used for academic researchers who initiate university spin-offs: for example, academic entrepreneurs (Franklin *et al.*, 2001), technology entrepreneurs (Marvel & Lumpkin, 2007), and inventor entrepreneurs (Radosevich, 1995a). In this chapter, the term used is inventor entrepreneur.

External entrepreneurs are individuals coming from outside the university and initiate university spin-offs (e.g., Franklin *et al.*, 2001; Nicolaou and Birley, 2003; Politis *et al.*, 2012). These individuals have not participated in the technology development but play a role in the formation of the university spin-off. As noted above, these individuals are sometimes called surrogate entrepreneurs. The two descriptive titles differ only with respect to who involves them in the spin-off (see Franklin *et al.*, 2001). Technological sources involve the surrogate entrepreneur in the spin-off whereas external entrepreneurs become involved through their own initiative. Thus, 'external entrepreneur' is a broad term that encompasses the term 'surrogate entrepreneur'. In this chapter, the term used is external entrepreneur.

Radosevich (1995a), who introduced the concepts external and surrogate entrepreneurs, suggests that both entrepreneurial types have greater business and entrepreneurial experience, more industrial networks, lower dependencies on business support systems, and larger proclivities for focusing on business aspects than inventor entrepreneurs. See Table 1.

Empirical studies of external entrepreneurs indicate they rely on assistance from technological sources, have access to risk capital, focus on business and managerial issues, and experience few entrepreneurial challenges (Radosevich, 1995b). More recent studies of external entrepreneurs suggest they are more knowledgeable than inventor entrepreneurs about business planning, manufacturing and management expertise, industrial networking, and management team creation. In addition, they are more skilled at securing additional funding and resolving firm problems (Kassicieh, 2011). Kassicieh also claims that venture capitalists prefer funding external entrepreneurs than funding inventor entrepreneurs.

Other recent studies conclude that external entrepreneurs have both business and entrepreneurial human capital (van der Steen *et al.*, 2013) as well as an inclination to prioritize private financial sources and private equity

Table 1. Stereotypical characteristics of external and inventor entrepreneurs.

Characteristics	Type of entrepreneur	
	External entrepreneur	Inventor entrepreneur
Experience	Business and entrepreneurial experience	Research and technology experience
Social networks	Industrial networks	Technology networks
Support systems	Independent on support systems	Dependent on support systems
Focus in firm operation	Business operations	R&D operations

partners (e.g., business angels and venture capitalists) over public financial sources (e.g., grants and 'soft loans'; Politis *et al.*, 2012). This distinction is consistent with Billström *et al.*'s (2014) finding that external and inventor entrepreneurs receive similar resources from their social networks. These authors also argue that external entrepreneurs (who exist at the center of both business and technology networks) rely primarily on trust in managing their network relationships and secondarily on formal contracts.

In addition, external entrepreneurs appear to generate greater firm growth in university spin-offs than in corporate spin-offs (Lindholm Dahlstrand, 2008) and greater firm growth and more revenue than inventor entrepreneurs (Lundqvist, 2014). As a result, external entrepreneurs offer a different contribution to university spin-off formation than inventor entrepreneurs. Other studies show that the strategic use of external entrepreneurs contributes to the success of the TTO (Lockett *et al.*, 2003) and that a TTO with a positive attitude towards external entrepreneurs creates more start-ups than other TTO (Franklin *et al.*, 2001).

Method

The Swedish context

This study was conducted in Sweden, a country of about nine million inhabitants. Despite its small population, Sweden is well known for its innovation and knowledge production (Andersson *et al.*, 2013). These authors argue that Sweden's higher than average expenditure (compared to other OECD countries) of its gross domestic product (GDP) on research and development (R&D) explains the country's impressive innovation and knowledge production. However, Sweden ranks somewhat lower in total entrepreneurship activity than other Global Entrepreneurship Monitor economies (Singer *et al.*, 2014). Lindholm Dahlstrand (2001, 2004) shows that among new firms in Sweden, about 15% are new technology based firms. Of these firms, 8% are corporate spin-offs, 2.6% are university spin-offs, and 4.4% originate with an external or founder idea.

Sweden differs from most other European countries in that academic employees are legally allowed to own the rights to their research. This right is sometimes referred to as teachers' exemption or professors' privilege. Nevertheless, in Sweden university spin-offs have achieved lower growth than corporate spin-offs (Lindholm Dahlstrand, 2001; Wennberg *et al.*, 2011) despite greater innovativeness (Lindholm Dahlstrand, 2001). This situation is perhaps explained by the fact that university spin-offs require 10 years or more before they begin to grow and also by the fact that different entrepreneurial types perform differently (see Lindholm Dahlstrand, 2008).

Lundqvist (2014) recently suggested that Swedish external entrepreneurs generate higher growth and more revenue than inventor entrepreneurs. In a presentation of the distribution of entrepreneurs among Swedish university spin-offs, Lindholm Dahlstrand (2008) reveals that 24% of such firms were direct university spin-offs (i.e., initiated by an inventor entrepreneur), 62% were indirect university spin-offs (i.e., initiated by an inventor entrepreneur from private industry), and 14% were initiated by external entrepreneurs.

Case selection

Theoretical sampling was used in this research to reach theoretical generalizations rather than empirical generalizations. The following four criteria were used in the case selection. All cases originated at the same Swedish technological university so as to minimize potential variations in technology transfer policies related to particular types of entrepreneurs or technologies. (see Rasmussen *et al.*, 2011). All cases used university-developed technology and fit the definition of a university spin-off. The cases selected originated with external or inventor entrepreneurs. Vohora *et al.*'s (2004) phases were used to identify entrepreneurs at various stages of their development.

To identify potential cases, the author contacted the university incubator manager by e-mail and telephone to request suggestions for firms to contact. The incubator is well known for actively working with the commercialization of university-developed technologies. The author asked respondents at the firms to confirm that the selection criteria were met and to minimize selection bias (see Yin, 2003).

The six cases chosen fit these four criteria. Three cases had external entrepreneurs, and three cases had inventor entrepreneurs. All cases had passed the research phase and were in a later phase. Firms with external entrepreneurs were distributed among the opportunity recognition, pre-organization, and re-orientation phases; firms with inventor entrepreneurs were distributed among the opportunity- recognition, pre-organization, and sustainable return phases. At the time of this research, no firm with an external entrepreneur had reached the sustainable return phase.

Data collection

Various documents such as annual reports,[1] press releases, project descriptions, and incubator and firm websites were used to gather relevant

---

[1] For one firm (Optical, see upcoming sections), it was impossible to gain access to its annual reports because of its early development phase.

information about social networking and case contexts (see Yin, 2003). However, face-to-face interviews with the CEOs of the firms and the inventor entrepreneurs for the external entrepreneur cases were the primary data source. Data collection began in January 2011 and concluded in February 2015. Fifteen face-to-face interviews were conducted.

A semi-structured interview-guide was used to ensure the interviews were driven by the respondents' own experiences. Each respondent was asked to explain the firm's formation — from the idea generation until the interview date. Each respondent was asked to make a written list of the most critical incidents in the firm formation. Next they were asked about the entrepreneurs' networking activity in the firm, the network actors, and their contributions to the firm's formation, the relationship of the network actors to the firm, and the relative ranking of network actors' contributions to the firm's formation. Each interview lasted between two and three hours. All interviews were recorded and later transcribed.

Data analysis

Data analyses was conducted in a systematic process of identifying empirical findings, of categorizing these findings by pattern detection in the cases, and of reaching conclusions on the findings (see Eisenhardt, 1989). The analysis began by analyzing the cases separately (within-case analysis) and then jointly (cross-case analysis). This analysis resulted in a summarized account of the contribution, coordination, and network type linked to each network actor for the external and inventor entrepreneurs.

To increase the internal validity of the analysis, the unique findings for each case were recorded (see Yin, 2003). Potentially contradictory findings as well as original findings among the cases were analyzed. The goal was to investigate if the findings were specific to the various cases, or if the findings revealed similarities among the cases (see Miles and Huberman, 1994). Last, the findings were analyzed in relation to previous research.

Empirical Findings

The empirical findings derive from six cases (at various phases of firm development) in which different technologies were commercialized. Table 2 presents an overview of the six cases. The firm names are fictitious.

Table 2. General description of the six firms.

Firm	External entrepreneurial firms			Inventor entrepreneurial firms		
	Carbon	Computer software	Nanotech	Computer	Climate	Optical
Project initiated	2005	2006	2006	2005	2000	2011
Incubator entrance	2005	2007	2007	2006	2004	2011
Firm registration	2005	2008	2008	2006	2006	Not reg.
Technology	Carbon technology	Industrial networks	Nano technology	Computer software	Climate control	Optical modulation
Industry class (NACE code)	Technical consultancy and industrial techniques (71122)	Other software publishing (58290)	Manufacture. of other general purpose machinery (28290)	Not reg. anymore	Manufacture. of instrument and appliances for measuring, testing, and navigation (26510)	Not yet reg.
Current formation phase	Opportunity-framing phase	Pre-organization phase	Re-orientation phase	Pre-organization phase	Sustainable return phase	Opportunity-framing phase

External entrepreneur — Carbon

Carbon originated from research conducted in an electronics department at the university. The firm was founded and transferred to the incubator in 2006 by a doctoral student and a business student. The firm bases its operations on carbon nanotechnology for applications in the semiconductor industry. The business student took the CEO position, and the doctoral student was responsible for technology development. Carbon also employed two additional scientists who worked in the technology development; however, one of these scientists left Carbon to join another company.

After about four years, the business student stepped down as the CEO, and an external entrepreneur joined the firm as CEO. The doctoral student and the business student remained the firm's owners. The external entrepreneur had about 20 years of international experience coordinating project management in the semiconductor industry or related industries. A new researcher was employed to work with technology development and patenting.

At the time of this research, Carbon was in the opportunity framing phase because the firm was still developing its technology and filing patents. The firm has four employees although no paying customers. The most valuable network actors are a professor and former advisor of the original inventor, potential customers, a fund, an incubator coach, a patent attorney, and a local public financier. These actors contribute to Carbon with R&D support, ideas for industrial application, investments, and patent advice. The network relationships with the professor and the potential customers are based in trust; the other actor relationships are mainly controlled by formal contracts. The fund and the patent attorney are indirectly involved with the firm via connections with the university incubator. The other actors are directly involved through connections with the CEO or the founder.

External entrepreneur — computer software

Computer Software originated from research conducted in the university's physics department. The firm was founded in 2006 and transferred to the incubator in 2007 by two academic researchers who were colleagues and co-entrepreneurs in a previous university spin-off. The firm develops computer software technology for industrial network optimization in the automotive industry. After about two years, when one academic researcher left the company, the current external entrepreneur was employed as CEO. The external entrepreneur has 20 years of experience with software development for manufacturing corporations in the telecom and medical industries. One academic researcher is still the firm owner and has the title of Chief Technology Officer (CTO).

Computer Software has frequently worked with the students at the university on their degree projects. An individual with experience in technology development and testing was hired after the hiring of the CEO but left the firm after a cutback. Computer Software is in the pre-organization phase because it has framed its business opportunity into prototypes and has investigated potential markets. Previously, the firm stepped back from the re-orientation phase when it changed strategy. Currently, the firm focuses on the international market. The firm has no paying customers.

Computer Software's most valuable network actors are its R&D partners, potential customers, a former board member, an incubator coach, and venture capitalists. These actors contribute to Computer Software with business advice, patent support, industrial application, identification of user needs, investments, prototyping, and tests as well as industry networking. The relationship with its R&D partner, potential customers, and former board member is based on trust; the relationships with the incubator coach and the venture capitalists are mainly controlled by formal contracts. The venture capitalists were indirectly involved with the firm through the incubator. The CEO or the original inventor directly involved the other network actors.

External entrepreneur — nanotech

Nanotech originated from research conducted in the university's microtechnology and nanotechnology department. Two researchers founded the firm in 2006 and transferred to it to the incubator in 2007. The firm's main activity is the development of filters for high-performance filtration and purification in the biotechnology industry. One researcher took the CEO position and then became the CTO. The owners employed a student entrepreneur whose task was to identify a market opportunity. When the student left the firm, an external entrepreneur with previous university spin-off experience in the construction industry was hired. No other entrepreneurs have been involved with the firm.

Nanotech has reached the re-orientation phase because the external entrepreneur and the academic researcher have sold some products. However, because of its limited market, the firm has not yet reached the sustainable return phase. The firm has no employees although it does have some paying customers. Recently, the external entrepreneur left the firm and joined another start-up firm.

Nanotech's most valuable network actors are the incubator and the incubator coach, a patent attorney, users, an industrial expert, a new venture fund, a prototype producer, and the institute for product testing. These actors contribute business and patent support, market information, industrial application, funds, product verification, networks, and prototype testing. The relationships with the network actors are mainly controlled by contracts except for the relationships with users and the industrial expert that are based on trust. The external entrepreneur and the original inventor have involved all the network actors.

Inventor entrepreneur — optical

Optical originated from research conducted at the university's micro-technology and Nano-science department. Two doctoral students, with their advisor-professor, started the project in 2011. In the same year they transferred it to the incubator. Optical, which works with optical technology from mathematics, aims to increase data speed and improve communications in optical networks. One doctoral student became the CEO while continuing studies at the university.

Optical's founders had frequent contact with an incubator coach who helped them formulate a business plan and identify a potential market. Therefore, Optical is in the opportunity framing phase. Some thought has been given to leaving the commercialization process because of the very narrow and immature market. Thus far, Optical has not filed the forms required to become a registered company. Furthermore, it has no employees and no paying customers.

Optical's most valuable network actors are its incubator coach, a fund, a market consultant, potential customers, and research colleagues. These actors contribute R&D support, industrial application experience, board experience, business advice, and financial resources. The network relationships with potential customers and research colleagues are based on trust. The relationships with the incubator coach, the fund, and the market consultant are mainly controlled by formal contracts. The inventor entrepreneur directly involved the incubator coach, the fund, and the research colleagues. The market consultant and potential customers were indirectly involved via contacts with the incubator.

Inventor entrepreneur — computer

Computer originated from research in the university's computer department. An academic researcher, two doctoral students, and two engineers founded the firm in 2005 and transferred it to the incubator in 2006. The firm's activities are based on technology aimed at increasing computer memory capacity for applications used with computers, mobile phones, and other consumer electronics. The academic researcher employed three engineering students and a product manager with technology experience and an engineering education. This researcher is a professor, who has more than 20 years of research experience at Swedish and international universities, was the project leader and CEO until 2009. The professor, the incubator coach, and a venture capitalist were the original board members

When Computer was in the pre-organization phase, it ended its operations owing to the firm's technical problems and the lack of paying customers. Computer's most valuable network actors were its research colleagues, the incubator coach, funds, patent attorneys, a business advisor, and potential customers. These actors provided R&D, social support, business support, funds, networks, patent advice and assistance with industrial applications. The firm's relationships with its research colleagues, business advisor, and potential customers were based on trust while the relationships with the incubator coach, funds, and patent attorneys were mainly controlled by contracts. The business advisor was indirectly involved in the firm via the incubator. The inventor entrepreneurs directly involved the research colleagues, the incubator coach, the funds, patent attorneys, and potential customers.

Inventor entrepreneur — climate

Climate originated from research at the university's construction engineering department. An academic researcher and a doctoral student founded the firm in 2000 and transferred it to the incubator in 2004. Climate's goal was to investigate whether and how its technology could be applied in practice. Climate works with technology aimed at controlling in-house climate for industry and households. Two student entrepreneurs tried to operate the firm (sequentially), but left because of costs resulting from a legal action. The academic researcher, with more than 20 years of research experience at Swedish and international universities, is now the CEO and Board Chairman.

Climate is now a registered company. However, the firm currently has no employees although it has sold about 100 products through a re-seller. Thus, Climate has recently reached the sustainable return phase. Climate's most valuable network actors are the incubator and its coach, its R&D partner, a trade organization, a fund, the re-seller, and a producer. These actors provide business, R&D, and social support, as well as funds, sales activity, distribution channels, and production support. The relationship with the trade organization is based on trust, while the other relationships are controlled by formal contracts. The trade organization, the re-seller, and the producer were involved via the incubator. The inventor entrepreneur directly involved the incubator and its coach, the R&D partner, and the fund.

Analysis

Network actors in university spin-off formation

The external entrepreneurs ranked potential customers and users as the most important network actors in all formation phases. A professor, an R&D partner, and industrial experts were also highly ranked. This finding indicates that both business and technology actors are highly valued in all formation phases. However, the university incubator and its coach were ranked relatively low in all formation phases. The explanation probably relates to the central location of the business and technology networks (Billström *et al.*, 2014) and to the business and entrepreneurial human capital of the external entrepreneurs (van der Steen *et al.*, 2013). Therefore, the external entrepreneurs seem to have little need for the incubator assistance.

The external entrepreneurs also highly valued the financial actors, such as venture capitalists and the funds. This finding is consistent with findings by Politis *et al.* (2012) who suggest external entrepreneurs prioritize private financial sources. In addition, the external entrepreneurs ranked patent attorneys highly. All these business, technology, and support actors form a 'core group of network actors' needed to manage the critical junctures associated with the formation of university spin-offs (see e.g., Vohora *et al.*, 2004).

The rankings differ for the inventor entrepreneurs as far as the importance of the network actors. They ranked the incubator and its coach much higher than the external entrepreneurs in all formation phases. Thus, inventor entrepreneurs need more business support than external entrepreneurs. The explanation probably relates to the peripheral location of their business networks (Billström *et al.*, 2014), to their somewhat low level of business and entrepreneurial human capital, and to their peripheral position in the industrial networks (Mosey & Wright, 2007).

The external entrepreneurs, instead of relying on the university incubator as the inventor entrepreneurs do, provide their own support or rely on other network actors. The external entrepreneurs have a wider variety of network actors in the opportunity-framing and pre-organization phases than the inventor entrepreneurs. The reason may be, as experienced entrepreneurs, they can access a number of resources (Mosey *et al.*, 2006).

Two similarities were observed between the external and inventor entrepreneurs. First, the number of network actors seems to increase in the formation phases. Second, both entrepreneur types value the same three groups of actors; *business actors* (e.g., boards of directors, potential customers, suppliers, producers, and re-sellers); *technology actors* (e.g., research colleagues and R&D partners); and *support actors* (e.g., the incubator and its coaches, patent attorneys, market consultants, business advisors, trade organizations, venture capitalists, and funds). In contrast with previous research (e.g., Jack, 2005) none of the entrepreneurs find family members or friends highly important for firm formation.

Network content in university spin-off formation

Network content refers to the different resources entrepreneurs receive from their network actors (Hoang & Antoncic, 2003). The external entrepreneurs' network actors provide R&D support (e.g., materials and equipment) and other support including industrial applications, development advice and services, patent work, funds, and network links.

Market information seems to be more important when the firms approach the market and strive to establish contacts with customers. At this point, the firms are in the re-orientation and sustainable return phase (see Vohora *et al.*, 2004). As the variety of network actors increases over time, so also does the network content.

Inventor entrepreneurs receive their basic network content in the opportunity framing and the pre-organization phases. External entrepreneurs receive market information and industry specific contacts from potential customers and from board members, respectively. Direct access to both business and technology networks of external entrepreneurs and indirect access to business networks of inventor entrepreneurs (Billström *et al.*, 2014) may explain this finding. However, in general, external and inventor entrepreneurs receive similar network content in the cases that are in the re-orientation and sustainable return phases. This finding agrees with Billström *et al.* (2014) who found that external entrepreneurs receive more market information, perhaps because of their business and industrial experiences (van der Steen *et al.*, 2013).

Network governance in university spin-off formation

Network governance coordinates the management of the exchange of resources between network actors and entrepreneurs (Hoang & Antoncic, 2003). Trust and formal contracts are mechanisms the control the exchange of resources. The findings show that external entrepreneurs rely on both trust and formal contracts in all development phases. They rely on trust in their relationships with business actors (Billström *et al.*, 2014) probably because they are familiar with the industry network actors they have previously dealt with. Jack (2005) argues that familiar network contacts are more trusted by entrepreneurs. External entrepreneurs' previous industry experience (van der Steen, 2003) may explain why they seek industrial applications and market information from their industrial partners. In particular, such trust is very important in technology-based firms, as Anderson *et al.* (2007) claim, because they often pool their resources in cooperative arrangements. Hence, trust, which derives from mutual respect and familiarity, can increase both market and technical credibility (Jack, 2005). The external entrepreneurs may also trust the network technology actors because their original inventor entrepreneurs are still active in the firms.

The findings reveal that inventor entrepreneurs rely on trust with technology actors and on contracts with the university incubator. Furthermore, the university incubator mediates their network contacts (Peters *et al.*, 2004) among other network actors such as market consultants. Thus, the university incubator is essential for inventor entrepreneurs who sometimes lack industrial networks (e.g., Mosey & Wright, 2007). For this reason, inventor entrepreneurs receive support with industrial applications from industrial partners while external entrepreneurs also receive market information. Such market information may increase their market credibility. As previous studies claim, this is difficult for inventor entrepreneurs (e.g., McAdam & Marlow, 2008).

Network structure in university spin-off formation

Network structure primarily refers to the actors' position in the network of actors (Hoang & Atoncic, 2003). Network structure also refers to the relationships among network actors: namely, the strong and weak ties or direct/first order and indirect/second order ties (Jack, 2005). Using Jack's (2005) classifications, the findings reveal that external entrepreneurs have many strong ties and few weak ties in all development phases. Their central position in business and technology networks (Billström *et al.*, 2014) may explain this finding. Their few weak or indirect ties are connected to their boards of directors. As a result, external entrepreneurs are independent from most of their network actors.

The findings reveal that inventor entrepreneurs have weaker ties to business actors although stronger ties to technology and support actors. Their peripheral position in business networks and their central position in technology networks (Billström *et al.*, 2014) may explain this mixture of strong and weak ties. Compared to external entrepreneurs, internal entrepreneurs have more confidence in the university incubator coaches who seem to serve as gatekeepers to business contacts. Thus, the inventor entrepreneurs are more distance from industry. However, this finding seems only applicable in the opportunity framing and pre-organization phases. Figure 1 summarizes the relationship between the two types of entrepreneurs and their business, technology, and support actors.

The dashed lines in Figure 1 represent the weak ties via university incubator and its coaches (in the support actor group) to business actors. The three groups — business actors, support actors, and technology actors — are at the end of university spin-off formation phases (i.e., the sustainable

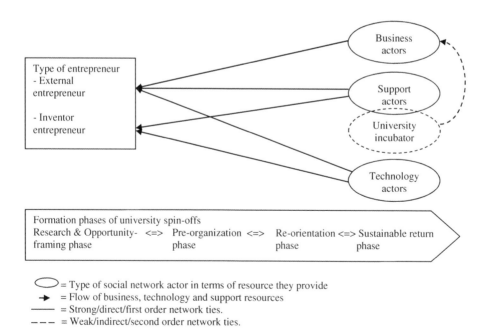

Figure 1. A conceptual framework of the role of social network actors in the formation of university spin-offs initiated by external and inventor entrepreneurs.

return phase), which illustrates the importance of these network actors in all development phases.

Conclusions and Implications

Some university spin-off firms often grow slowly or fail to grow because academic researchers supported by university incubators sometimes lack sufficient industry networks. External entrepreneurs, who come from outside academia and who typically have more extensive industry networks, can be useful in the formation of such firms.

In the research reported on in this chapter, the purpose was to develop and relate a conceptual framework of social network actors to the formation of university spin-offs initiated by external and inventor entrepreneurs. This use of the conceptual framework contributes to entrepreneurship research in three ways. First, it enhances our theoretical knowledge of firm formation because many previous studies have investigated established firms. The findings of this research indicate that the formation phases may progress differently depending on the interaction between the entrepreneurial type, the involvement of the university incubator, and the various social network actors. This research also adds different types of social network actors (i.e., business, technology and support actors) to previous research on university spin-off formation (e.g., Vohora *et al.*, 2004; Wright *et al.*, 2004).

Second, the findings contributes to entrepreneurship research on social networking (e.g., see Nicolaou & Birley, 2003; Pérez Pérez & Martinez Sánchez, 2003) in its original investigation of network actors, content, governance, and structure in firms' formation phases. The external entrepreneurs' central position in business networks and their access to industrial actors are advantages that inventor entrepreneurs generally lack. Because external entrepreneurs can acquire more market information from potential customers than inventor entrepreneurs, they rank the university incubator as relatively unimportant and rank potential customers as highly important. External entrepreneurs, at the center of business networks, are better prepared for the challenges of firm formation.

Third, this research contrasts the stereotypical picture of inventor entrepreneurs who commercialize university technology with that of external entrepreneurs. The research complements previous research on the influence of external entrepreneurs in university spin-offs (e.g., Billström *et al.*, 2014; Politis *et al.*, 2012). In short, the study provides a more nuanced picture of university spin-off formation by its inclusion of both external and inventor entrepreneurs.

The findings from this research may be used in policy decisions about university incubators and for the support of academia-industry collaborations. These findings may lead to an increase in the number of university spin-offs initiated by external entrepreneurs and contribute to the opportunity framing, pre-organization and re-orientation phases of external entrepreneurial firms.

Some limitations of this research, which may be of value in future research should be noted. First, it was not possible, despite the author's ambition, to follow one external entrepreneurial firm and one inventor entrepreneurial firm in every formation phase longitudinally. The reason was the lack of external entrepreneurs. Future researchers may be able to overcome this limitation and thereby increase our theoretical knowledge of firm formation.

Second, only the key network actors (at the time of the research) were studied. Interviews with social network actors, who have left entrepreneurial firms and had a central role in the early phases of firm formation, could be informative. Research in this area may increase research of social networking and even explain why some university spin-offs do not grow or grow very slowly. In addition, the role of university incubators in external entrepreneurial firms can also extend our theoretical knowledge of social networking and early phases of firm formation.

References

Anderson. A., Park, J. & Jack, S. 2007. Entrepreneurial social capital: Conceptualizing social capital in new high-tech firms. *International Small Business Journal*, 25(3), 245–272.

Andersson, M., Anonkhin, S., Autio, E., Ejermo, O., Lavesson, N., Lööf, H., Savin, M., Wincent, J. & Ylinenpää, H. 2013. *Det Innovative Sverige: Sverige Som Kunskapsnation I En Internationell Context*. Vinnova, Stockholm.

Billström, A., Politis, D. & Gabrielsson, J. 2014. Entrepreneurial networks in technology commercialization — An analysis of the 'external-entrepreneur' model. In *RENT XXVI, Research in Entrepreneurship and Small Business Anthology*, R. Blackburn (ed.). Edward Elgar, Cheltenham.

Boeker, W. 1989. Strategic change: The effects of founding and history. *The Academic Management Journal*, 32(3), 489–515.

Davidsson, P. & Honig, B. 2003. The role of social capital and human capital among nascent entrepreneurs. *Journal of Business Venturing*, 18(3), 301–331.

Davidsson, P. & Wiklund, J. 2001. Levels of analysis in entrepreneurship research: Current research practice and suggestions for the future. *Entrepreneurship Theory & Practice*, 25(4), 81–100.

De Cleyn, S. H., Braet, J. & Klofsten, M. 2014. How human capital interacts with early development of academic spin-offs. *International Entrepreneurship and Management Journal*, 11(3), 599–621.

Djokovic, D. & Souitaris, V. 2008. Spinouts from academic institutions: A literature review with suggestions for further research. *Journal of Technology Transfer*, 33(3), 225–247.

Druilhe, C. & Garnsey, E. 2004. Do academic spin-outs differ and does it matter? *Journal of Technology Transfer*, 29(3–4), 269–285.

Eisenhardt, K. M. 1989. Building theories from case study research. *Academy of Management Review*, 14(4), 532–550.

Elfring, T. & Hulsink, W. 2003. Networks in entrepreneurship: The case of high-technology firms. *Small Business Economics*, 21(4), 409–422.

Ensley, M. D. & Hmieleski, K. M. 2005. A comparative study of new venture top management team composition, dynamics and performance between university-based and independent start-ups. *Research Policy*, 34(7), 1091–1105.

Franklin, S. J., Wright, M. & Lockett, A. 2001. Academic and surrogate entrepreneurs in university spin-out companies. *Journal of Technology Transfer*, 26(1–2), 127–141.

Granovetter, M. 1973. The strength of weak ties. *American Journal of Sociology*, 78(6), 1360–1380.

Hoang, H. & Antoncic, B. 2003. Network-based research in entrepreneurship: A critical review. *Journal of Business Venturing*, 18(2), 165–187.

Jack, S. 2005. The role, use and activation of strong and weak network ties: A qualitative analysis. *Journal of Management Studies*, 42(6), 1233–1259.

Kassicieh, S. 2011. Benefits from using surrogate entrepreneurs in technology commercialization. *International Journal of Innovation and Technology Management*, 8(4), 522–534.

Lindholm Dahlstrand, Å. 2001. Entrepreneurial origin and spin-off performance: A comparison between corporate and university spin-offs. In *Corporate and Research-based Spin-offs: Drivers for Knowledge-based Innovation and Entrepreneurship*, P. Moncada-Paternò-Castello, A. Tübke, R. Miège and T. B. Yaquero (eds.), pp. 43–66. European Commission, IPTS Technical Report Series, EUR 19903 EN.

Lindholm Dahlstrand, A. 2004. *Teknikbaserat nyföretagande, tillväxt och Affärsutveckling*. Studentlitteratur, Lund.

Lindholm Dahlstrand, Å. 2008. University knowledge transfer and the role of academic spin-offs. In *OECD Report. Entrepreneurship and Higher Education*, J. Potter (ed.).

Lockett, A., Wright, M. & Franklin, S. 2003. Technology transfer and universities' spin-out strategies. *Small Business Economics*, 20(2), 185–200.

Lundqvist, M. A. 2014. The importance of surrogate entrepreneurship for incubated Swedish technology ventures. *Technovation*, 34(2), 93–100.

Marvel, M. R. & Lumpkin, G. T. 2007. Technology entrepreneurs' human capital and its effects on innovation radicalness. *Entrepreneurship Theory and Practice,* 31(6), 807–828.

McAdam, M. & Marlow, S. 2008. A preliminary investigation into networking activities within the university incubator. *International Journal of Entrepreneurial Behaviour and Research,* 14(4), 219–241.

Miles, M. & Huberman, A. 1994. *Qualitative Data Analysis,* 2nd edn. Sage Publications, Thousand Oaks.

Mosey, S., Locket, A. & Westhead, P. 2006. Creating network bridges for university technology transfer: The Medici fellowship scheme. *Technology Analysis and Strategic Management,* 18(1), 71–91.

Mosey. S. & Wright, M. 2007. From human capital to social capital: A longitudinal study of technology-based academic entrepreneurs. *Entrepreneurship Theory and Practice,* 31(6), 909–935

Mustar, P., Wright, M. & Clarysse, B. 2008. University spin-off firms: Lessons from ten years experience in Europe. *Science and Public Policy,* 35(2), 67–80.

Neergaard, H. 2005. Networking activities in technology-based entrepreneurial teams. *International Small Business Journal,* 23(3), 257–278.

Nicolaou, N. & Birley, S. 2003. Academic networks in a trichotomous categorisation of university spinouts. *Journal of Business Venturing,* 18(3): 333–359.

Pérez Pérez, M. & Martinez Sánchez, A. 2003. The development of university spin-offs: Early dynamics of technology transfer and networking. *Technovation,* 23(10), 823–831.

Peters, L., Rice, M. & Sundarajan, M. 2004. The role of incubators in the entrepreneurial process. *Journal of Technology Transfer,* 29(1), 83–91.

Phan, P. H. 2004. Entrepreneurship theory: Possibilities and future directions. *Journal of Business Venturing,* 19(5), 617–620.

Pirnay, F., Surlemont, B. & Nlemvo, F. 2002. Toward a typology of university spin-offs. *Small Business Economics,* 21(4), 355–369.

Politis, D., Gabrielsson, J. & Shvekina, O. (2012). Early-stage finance and the role of external entrepreneurs: The commercialization of university-generated knowledge. *Venture Capital,* 14(2–3), 175–198.

Radosevich, R. 1995a. A model for entrepreneurial spin-offs from public technology sources. *International Journal of Technology Management,* 10(7/8), 879–893.

Radosevich, R. 1995b. A test of the surrogate-entrepreneurship model of public-technology commercialization. *Proceedings of the 28th Annual Hawaii International Conference on System Sciences* (HICSS '95).

Rasmussen, E., Mosey, S. & Wright, M. 2011. The evolution of entrepreneurial competencies — A longitudinal study of university spin-off venture emergence. *Journal of Management Studies,* 48(6), 1314–1345.

Rothaermel, F. T., Agung, S. D. & Jiang, L. 2007. University entrepreneurship: A taxonomy of the literature. *Industrial and Corporate Change,* 16(4), 691–791.

Shane, S. 2004. *Academic Entrepreneurship — University Spin-offs and Wealth Creation.* Edward Elgar Publishing, Cheltenham, United Kingdom.

Singer, S., Amorós, J. E. & Moska, D. (eds.). 2014. *Global Entrepreneurship Monitor (GEM) 2014 Global Report.* Global Entrepreneurship Research Association, London Business School, London.

Slotte-Kock, S. & Coviello, N. 2010. Entrepreneurship research on network processes: A review and ways forward. *Entrepreneurship Theory and Practice,* 34(1), 31–57.

Soetano, D. P. & Van Geenhuizen, M. 2011. Social networks, university spin-off growth and promises of "living labs". *Regional Science Policy & Practice,* 3(3), 305–321.

Steffensen, M., Rogers, E. M. & Speakman, K. 2000. Spin-offs from research centers at a research university. *Journal of Business Venturing,* 15(1), 93–111.

Vanaelst, I., Clarysse, B., Wright, M., Lockett, A., Moray, N. & S'Jegers, R. 2006. Entrepreneurial team development in academic spinouts: An examination of team heterogeneity. *Entrepreneurship Theory and Practice,* 30(2), 249–271.

van der Steen, M., Englis, P. D. & Englis, B. 2013. Team effectiveness and external CEOs — A study of biotechnology university spin-offs. *Industry and Higher Education,* 27(1), 15–25.

Vohora, A., Wright, M. & Lockett, A. 2004. Critical junctures in the development of university high-tech spinout companies. *Research Policy,* 33(1), 147–175.

Wennberg, K., Wiklund, J. & Wright, M. 2011. The effectiveness of university knowledge spillovers: Performance differences between university spin-offs and corporate spin-offs. *Research Policy,* 40(8), 1128–1143.

Wright, M., Vohora, A. & Lockett, A. 2004. The formation of high-tech university spin-outs: The role of joint ventures and venture capital investors. *Journal of Technology Transfer,* 29(3–4), 287–310.

Yin, R. K. 2003. *Case Study Research: Design and Methods.* Sage, London.

Chapter 5

Organizing for Innovation: Do TLO Characteristics Correlate with Technology Transfer Outcomes?

Lisa Goble
University of North Carolina, Greensboro
lagoble@uncg.edu

Janet Bercovitz
University of Illinois, Urbana-Champaign
jbercov@illinois.edu

Maryann Feldman
University of North Carolina, Chapel Hill
maryann.feldman@unc.edu

There is great heterogeneity across American Research Universities in terms of the technology transfer process and office characteristics that influence academic technology commercialization outcomes. This study investigates how the organizational reporting structure of the university technology licensing office (TLO) and the educational background and experience of the TLO director affect the technology transfer process. We find that TLOs reporting directly to the university leader or to an economic/business development office are relatively more effective in working with university startups than TLOs reporting to an office of research, whereas TLOs reporting to multiple functions are relatively more effective in licensing than TLOs reporting directly to the office of research or to an economic/business development office. We also find TLO directors with an MBA degree to be more effective in obtaining invention disclosures and working with startups than TLO directors with a PhD, and TLO directors with an MBA or a PhD degree are more effective at licensing activities than TLO directors with a legal degree. Our analysis finds TLO directors with Juris Doctor (Doctor of Law degree) to be less effective in licensing outcomes than all other educational backgrounds, suggesting that legal wrangling may reduce university licensing counts.

Introduction

The university's technology licensing office (TLO) is the organizational unit responsible for documenting, protecting, marketing, and commercializing innovations with commercial value.[1] While considerable attention has been paid to the growth in university patenting, licensing, revenue generation and startup formation, as well as the many individual-level researcher attributes and university-level characteristics that influence the technology transfer process (Siegel *et al.*, 2007a, 2007b; Rothaermel *et al.*, 2007; Bradley *et al.*, 2013), fewer studies have adopted an organizational unit level of analysis and focused on the TLO itself.

Research finding on the influence of TLO characteristics on technology-transfer outcomes were mixed. Some studies found positive correlations between older TLOs and licensing and startup formation (Friedman & Silberman, 2003; Powers & McDougall, 2005a, 2005b; Chukumba & Jensen, 2005; O'Shea *et al.*, 2005), while others found older TLOs less effective at startup creation (Markman *et al.*, 2004). Findings for TLO size have also been varied; some studies show larger TLOs may be less effective or have little influence upon licensing and startup formation (Thursby & Kemp, 2002; Chukumba & Jensen, 2005); while others show larger TLOs to be more effective at licensing and generating revenues and startups (Siegel *et al.*, 2003, 2008; Markman *et al.*, 2009; Jensen & Jones, 2011). Capturing additional features that can help differentiate TLO organizations is clearly needed.

---

[1]A requirement set in place with the passage of the federal Bayh–Dole Act, (P.L. 96-517), Patent and Trademark Act Amendments of 1980, enables universities to retain title to inventions made under federally-funded research programs, putting responsibility for commercializing research based inventions with the university. This act requires federally sponsored inventions research be disclosed to the university's TLO. Available at: http://www.autm.net/Bayh_Dole_Act/7698.htm.

Some progress has been made on this front by looking at the corporate form and financial autonomy of TLOs (Markman *et al.*, 2005a; Feldman *et al.*, 2002). Three corporate forms have been identified: whether the TLO is organized and supported as an integral unit within the university (the traditional structure), organized as an external non-profit (501(c)3) organization, or as a for-profit structure focused upon economic development and university startups. The data indicate that different corporate forms of TLOs do influence upon technology transfer outcomes and the speed at which technologies are transferred to the public. Traditional forms of TLOs have a negative relationship with both revenues and startup formation in comparison to the external non-profit groups. The for-profit form of the TLO had no significant direct relationship; however, this latter form did have a significant influence upon reducing time to a startup formation, while a traditionally organized TLO significantly increased time to a startup formation (Markman *et al.*, 2005a). There is also some evidence that the TLO's financial organization can influence licensing and startup efforts (Bercovitz *et al.*, 2001; Markman *et al.*, 2005a). For example, in evaluating use of equity as a licensing mechanism, Feldman *et al.* (2002) find that self-funded TLOs are less likely to utilize equity as a licensing mechanism than otherwise funded offices, potentially due to the short term focus upon obtaining a revenue stream to meet obligations for operating budgets. Though these studies are a start, building greater understanding of how differences in organizational structure, staffing and other resources generate disparities in technology transfer outcomes would be valuable (Merrill & Mazza, 2010, pp. 43 & 45).

This study adds to the literature by investigating how the organizational reporting structure of the university technology licensing office (TLO) and the educational background and experience of the TLO director affect the technology transfer process. Both of these attributes are important as, in-line with behavioral theory of the firm reasoning, professional backgrounds can be expected to cause directors with different backgrounds to focus attention on different aspects of the transfer process while different reporting structures dictate different decision-making processes, which in turn influences technology-transfer outcomes (Cyert & March, 1963; March & Simon, 1958). We find that TLOs reporting directly to the university leader or to an economic/business development office are relatively more effective in working with university startups than TLOs reporting to an office of research, whereas TLOs reporting to multiple functions are relatively more effective in licensing than TLOs reporting directly to the office of research or to an economic/business development office. We also find TLO directors with an MBA degree to be more effective in obtaining invention disclosures and working with startups than TLO directors with a PhD, and directors with either an MBA or PhD degree to both be more effective at licensing activities than TLO directors with a legal degree. Our analysis finds TLO directors with JDs to be less effective in licensing outcomes than all other educational backgrounds, suggesting that legal wrangling may reduce university licensing counts.

The chapter proceeds as follows. In the following two sections we review the technology-transfer literature to delineate relationships between organizational reporting structures, director's professional orientation and technology transfer outcomes. We then provide details about our data, methodology, and empirical results. We conclude with a discussion of findings and comments regarding the implications of our findings for TLO structure decisions.

Organizational Reporting Structure

Organizational reporting structures of the TLO may have an influence upon various technology transfer outcomes. The degree of centralization of an office is expected to have an impact on the organizational effectiveness and ability of the office to manage information flows as alternative organizational structures both direct and reflect processes of decision-making, coordination and behavioral routines of individuals (Lam, 2000; Zheng *et al.*, 2010). As such, how a TLO is organized within the university and its ability to make decisions regarding licensing negotiations can be expected to have an effect upon technology transfer outcomes. Using case studies of three universities adopting different decision and coordination archetypes — centralized, decentralized, and matrix, Bercovitz *et al.* (2001) explore how different TLO reporting structures may coordinate efforts with the larger university environment. Preliminary findings from these case studies indicate that the increased integration and coordination capacity of a TLO with a matrix decision structure can have a positive effect on invention disclosures. Further, effective TLO integration with other university functions, even with lower autonomy of the TLO, can have a positive influence on licensing activity (Bercovitz *et al.*, 2001; Feldman & Bercovitz, 2010). These benefits from increased integration and coordination are likely a product of the additional opportunities to interact with faculty and industry representatives. In related work, Markman *et al.* (2009) note the choice of organizational form can pose dilemmas for university administration; the centralization of a university TLO provides standardization and reliability, but may restrict the ability of the TLO to negotiate licensing contracts in response to dynamic market conditions. Their study finds low autonomy TLOs are negatively related to licensing revenues, while high autonomy TLOs are significantly and positively related to startup formation (Markman *et al.*, 2009), suggesting the ability of TLOs to coordinate with external resources and form independent ties with the local industry, entrepreneurs, investors and other resources may have a positive influence on startup formation. These prior studies highlight the value of exploring different TLO organizational reporting relationships to better understand variation in technology transfer outcomes. We extend this line of research by analyzing the specific reporting structure of the TLO, as the office to which the TLO reports is likely to have a say in the goals and objectives of TLO, and may have an influence upon its outcomes.

When TLOs report to the institutional leader, the importance of technology transfer is emphasized, sending strong signals of legitimacy to the campus. This type of centralized reporting structure for the TLO can benefit from strong leadership driving coordination efforts (Bercovitz *et al.*, 2001), potentially influencing all stages of technology commercialization. A TLO reporting to a research office tends to emphasize increasing awareness of the TLO with academic researchers and the coordination between these academic researchers, other research support units, and funding agencies. Such structures have potential for positive influence on invention disclosure activity as a result of TLO engagement with researchers and campus education efforts. Similarly, TLOs organized under the office of research may have access to industry networks from industry support of research, increasing opportunities for licensing. A TLO organized under an economic or business development office structure may be able to coordinate efforts with other externally focused departments (such as alumni offices or public relations) as well as entities and resources outside of the university. A TLO focused on economic development activities, with high autonomy in decision-making is shown in previous studies to have a positive influence upon startup formation (Markman *et al.*, 2009); potentially through access to external business and entrepreneurial support mechanisms. A TLO reporting to multiple operations may positively influence technology commercialization outcomes through increased visibility and coordination efforts. The effectiveness of the TLO in managing the increased complexity generated from multiple reporting relationships (Bercovitz *et al.*, 2001) may moderate that influence. The different organizational structures may focus efforts of the TLO on strategic technology commercialization outcomes, and suggests there may be some variation in commercialization outcomes further described in Table 1.

Director's Professional Orientation

Concomitant with organizational structure, the attributes of key employees may also impact TLO performance. Specialized knowledge and skills are

Table 1. Predicted relationships between reporting structure and technology transfer outcomes.

| | Reporting structures | | | |
	Research	Leadership	Econ/Bus Dev.	Multiple
Input				
Invention Disclosures	+ Increased coordination with research faculty and funding sources	+ Strong signal in support of tech transfer	– Potential less direct interaction with researchers	+ Increased coordination activities may increase interface with inventors
Commercial path				
Licenses	+ Coordination with faculty researchers provides access to increased network for licensing	+ Depends upon strategic direction of leadership, expect positive relationship	– Less coordination with researchers may reduce access to networks and funding agencies	+ Increased coordination with internal & external entities may create increased opportunities for licensing
Startups	– Less coordination with external organizations may limit access to entrepreneurs and investment	+ Depends upon strategic direction of leadership, expect positive relationship	+ Increased coordination with units focused on economic development, access to external support	+ Increased coordination with multiple units may provide increased opportunities for startup activities

developed through professional training and employment experience (Rodan & Galunic, 2002). Further, professional norms instilled via education and training focus the attention of managers with different educational backgrounds on different elements of the technology transfer process. As such, managers build different types of expertise overtime generating a unique portfolio of routines that facilitate certain activities of the TLO. Past successes have a positive influence on subsequent outcomes (Owen-Smith & Powell, 2001), suggesting prior experience and successes in licensing and startup formation may have a positive influence upon subsequent activities of the university TLO. Similarly, as the tenure of a TLO director increases, prior work suggests their integration within the university expands, creating a positive influence upon invention disclosure submission (Feldman & Bercovitz, 2010).

The technology transfer process requires a variety of skills: knowledge of university research, business marketing and commercialization skills, networking and links to business development organizations (Siegel *et al.*, 2003; Markman *et al.*, 2005a; McGee, 2007). Identifying how different professional degrees and skillsets influence the technology transfer process and its outcomes can inform those who wish to strategically align skills of the TLO with other university characteristics in order to target particular outcomes. Educational training provides expert understanding on how resources can be managed and leveraged in industry (Galunic & Rodan, 1997). This suggests educational background differences among TLO directors can cause directors to promote certain activities over others. To date, there has not been an examination of the TLO director's education as an influence on technology transfer activities. Several studies identify TLO business and commercialization skills as important to academic technology transfer efforts, particularly for startup formation (O'Shea *et al.*, 2005; Siegel & Phan, 2005; Siegel *et al.*, 2007a; Swamidass, 2013), but for licensing efforts as well (Markman *et al.*, 2005a). Many business and commercialization skills may be developed through specific educational training, or through experience working with industry, entrepreneurs, or investment managers. The importance of hiring personnel in the TLO with a variety of these key business qualifications is important for successful commercialization efforts (ipHandbook, 2012). Using high salaries of TLO licensing professionals as a proxy for commercialization skillsets in the TLO, Markman *et al.* (2009) find that higher salaries for those individuals charged with licensing the university's intellectual property have a positive relationship with both licensing revenues coming into the university and startup formation. A deficit of commercialization skills, (specifically financial, technical, commercial industry linkages and entrepreneurial backgrounds) is identified as a potential barrier to successful academic technology transfer activities (Metz *et al.*, 2000; Siegel *et al.*, 2004, 2007b; Siegel, 2012; Markman *et al.*, 2005a; Litan & Cook-Deegan, 2011; Swamidass, 2013). The findings from these previous studies provide justification for evaluating the variety of skillsets of the individuals responsible for managing TLOs; their educational degree is used as a proxy for this difficult to measure characteristic.

A TLO director with an MBA degree may facilitate commercialization efforts due to training in strategic and business planning, financial management, asset valuation and other business related skills, which may support both licensing and startup activity. Dissimilar cultural and educational norms (Zheng *et al.*, 2010) may create a barrier for a TLO director with an MBA in obtaining invention disclosures from PhD research faculty, while a TLO director with a PhD who is well versed in the research logic may be able to positively influence invention disclosure submission. Additionally, subject matter expertise developed through a PhD in the scientific field of an invention may provide access to industry or practitioner networks, potentially increasing licensing outcomes. TLO directors with legal degrees (JD) may have advanced IP & legal contract skills, which may not be an advantage for licensing efforts if those skills result in a tougher negotiation stance as suggested by Siegel *et al.*'s (2003) field research. The presence of a law school is shown to have a positive relationship with university startup activity (Feldman & Bercovitz, 2010), suggesting there may be some positive correlation between TLO directors with a JD and startup formation. A JD may be able to help university startups with business legalities and contractual work that can facilitate university startup formation. As the technology transfer profession has become more established, advanced degrees are increasingly a requirement for director positions as indicators of professional success. Thus, TLO directors who have bachelor degrees are likely to be in leadership positions due to a level of experience and skills specific to technology commercialization or industry partnerships such as those identified by Siegel (2012) and Markman *et al.* (2005a). TLO directors with different educational backgrounds may have variation in commercialization outcomes further described in Table 2.

Data & Method

In evaluating the influence of TLO characteristics on technology transfer metrics, data are used from two surveys: the AUTM annual licensing survey

Table 2.   Predicted relationships between TLO Director's education and outcomes.

		TLO director's education		
	PhD	**Legal (JD)**	**MBA**	**BS**
Input				
Invention Disclosures	+	–	–	+
	Direct interaction with researchers, common educational foundation	Less coordination with research faculty, skills related to IP protection	Dissimilar cultural and educational norms from research faculty	Coordination with research faculty, previous experience
Commercial path				
Licenses	+	–	+	+
	Scientific domain can facilitate placement with industries best capable of utilizing invention	Increased legalities in agreements add difficulties in getting to license finalization.	Marketing skills, industry contacts, and financial knowledge	Depends on previous licensing experience, industry networks
Startups	+	+	+	+
	No 'broad based' commercial skills; scientific knowledge can facilitate transfer to startup	Access to contractual and legal resources may facilitate startup activity	Market, financial and commercialization knowledge, access to entrepreneurs and investment	Depends on previous entrepreneurial experience, networks

and Feldman and Bercovitz's (2010) survey of AUTM respondents, collected in 2007. Technology transfer outcome data is collected for 76 universities for a 3-year period (2008–2010) to analyze the influence of the 2007 reporting structure and TLO director's educational background on subsequent invention disclosure, licensing and startup activity. We limit outcome data to a three-year period to minimize potential variability that may be introduced by TLO reorganizations due to administrative or other changes (Feldman & Bercovitz, 2010). The AUTM annual licensing survey provides yearly measures for the dependent variables and information on total research funding, industry funding, TLO age and size. Industry research funding divided by total research dollars provides a percentage of industry funding, and a ratio of licensing staff per million of total research funding provides a normalized variable to control for the size of the university and the size of the TLO. Feldman and Bercovitz's (2010) survey of AUTM members in 2007 provides the independent variables of interest: the TLO reporting structure, last educational degree of the TLO director, and the directors' tenure in their position. This survey also provides institutional controls indicators for private universities and the presence of medical and law schools. A list of the dependent and independent variables of interest for this current study is included in Table 3, with descriptive names, the percentages for each structure and education, the variable type, and source of the data. The control variables and their sources are further described in Table 8, and a full set of descriptive statistics for all variables included in this analysis is provided in Table 9.

Dependent variables

The dependent variables of this study include the number of invention disclosures received, licenses completed, and startups formed. Patents are not included in the regression analysis as decisions regarding intellectual property protection can be driven by many factors including budget availability, patenting strategies, decisions by patent committees and licensee expectations, among others (Livne, 2007). For the representative universities in our sample from 2008 to 2010, annual invention disclosure submissions ranged between 6 and 513, US issued patents between 1 and 155, licenses between 1 and 104, and startups between 0 and 19. In comparison to the AUTM population, the 76 universities included in this study seem to reflect the general characteristics of the population of AUTM respondents (Table 4).

Table 3.   Dependent and independent variables.

Variable		Percentage	Type	Source
Dependent variables (yearly measures)				
Invention Disclosures	Invention Disclosures received			
Licenses	Executed Licenses		Continuous (logged averages)	AUTM STATT
Startups	Startups from the university			
Independent variables				
Reporting Office				
Report to Research	Research Office	47 (62%)		
Report to Leader	Chancellor/President	12 (16%)	Binary	Feldman and Bercovitz survey, independent verification
Report to Econ/Bus	Economic/Business Development.	11 (14%)		
Report to Multiple Off.	Multiple Offices	6 (8%)		
Education & Experience				
Director PhD	PhD degree	30 (40%)		
Director Lawyer	Law degree	14 (18%)	Binary	Feldman and Bercovitz survey, independent verification
Director MBA	MBA	18 (24%)		
Director BS/BA	Bachelors	14 (18%)		
Dir. Tenure	Years in current position		Continuous	

Table 4.   Study sample comparisons to AUTM population, 2008–2010.

Variable	AUTM population (148 universities)				Sample (76 Universities)			
	Obs	Mean	Min	Max	Obs	Mean	Min	Max
Invention Disclosures	148	110.19	1	744	76	111.02	6	512.67
Licenses	148	23.15	0	214	76	24.98	0.67	103.67
Startups	146	3.46	0	33	76	3.63	0	19
Issued US Patents	147	20.57	0	180	75	25.42	1	155
Staff/Total Research ($M)	145	0.03	0	0.18	76	0.025	0.0059	0.11
Licensing Staff	145	5.38	0	60	76	5.90	0.5	60
Total Research ($M)	147	$291	$3	$2,547	76	$327	$16	$1,518
Industry Research %	147	7%	0%	38.5%	76	10.8%	1.0%	34.7%
TLO Age	147	20.89	0	85	76	20.89	1	82

Independent variables

Organizational reporting structures for the university TLOs in this current study consist of four reporting types. Offices that report to: (1) the university research function, (2) an economic or business development function, (3) the leadership of the university, and (4) multiple offices. Forty-seven university TLOs report to the research function within the university, 11 report to an economic development or business development function, 12 report directly to the leader of the university, while 6 report to multiple university functions.

Average invention disclosures received, licenses completed and startups formed for each of the four organizational structures evaluated in this study are presented in Table 5.

The multiple educational backgrounds of the TLO directors analyzed in this study reflect the widespread and multidisciplinary nature of university commercialization efforts, and the range of multidisciplinary skills that can support the technology transfer process. Thirty TLO directors in the current sample have PhDs, 14 have legal degrees (JD), 18 have MBA degrees, and 14 TLO directors have BS degrees. Average invention disclosures received, licenses completed and startups formed for each of the TLO director's different educational backgrounds from 2008 to 2010 are presented in Table 6.

Between the organizational reporting structure and the TLO director's education, there are 16 possible combinations that could result. The two most common organizations in this study are TLOs reporting to an office of

Table 5. Data statistics by TLO organizational structure, 2008–2010.

Invention disclosures	Obs	Mean	Min	Max
Office of Research	47	114	13	513
Leader	12	151	11	338
Econ/Bus Dev.	11	108	6	311
Multiple	6	147	33	357

Licenses	Obs	Mean	Min	Max
Office of Research	47	23	1	104
Leader	12	27	2	81
Econ/Bus Dev.	11	22	2	69
Multiple	6	40	13	50

Startups	Obs	Mean	Min	Max
Office of Research	47	3	0	18
Leader	12	4	0	11
Econ/Bus Dev.	11	5	0	19
Multiple	6	3	0	4

Table 6. Data statistics by TLO director education, 2008–2010.

Invention Disclosures	Obs	Mean	Min	Max
MBA	18	145	12	513
Lawyer	14	119	32	357
PhD	30	118	6	359
BS	14	100	13	450

Licenses	Obs	Mean	Min	Max
MBA	18	28	2	69
Lawyer	14	23	2	81
PhD	30	22	2	49
BS	14	30	1	104

Startups	Obs	Mean	Min	Max
MBA	18	5	0	19
Lawyer	14	4	1	11
PhD	30	3	0	10
BS	14	3	0	9

Job Tenure	Obs	Mean	Min	Max
MBA	18	9.78	2	23
Lawyer	14	6.25	2.5	13
PhD	30	7.1	3	13
BS	14	10.5	3	26

Table 7.   Combinations of organizational structure and director's degree.

Reporting office/ director's educ.	Multi	EDBD	Leader	Research	N
PhD	0	6	9	15	30
Law	4	1	2	7	14
MBA	0	3	0	15	18
BS	2	1	1	10	14
N	6	11	12	47	76

research with a PhD director (15), or TLOs reporting to an office of research with an MBA director (15). The different combinations of TLO organizations are shown in Table 7. These two dominant structures are compared against all others to determine if there is any statistical difference between the two most commonly found TLO organizations and the remaining in obtaining invention disclosures from faculty, licensing to industry, or forming startups. The results of these comparisons are discussed in the results section below.

Control Variables

Other institutional characteristics such as private versus public status and the type of affiliated schools with the university are included to help control for any influence they may have upon technology commercialization efforts in addition to controlling for some of the differences between the universities. Many previous studies have included public or private indicators to control for differences and their potential influence on licensing and startup activity (Friedman & Silberman, 2003; Chukumba & Jensen, 2005; Markman *et al.*, 2005a, 2009; Bulut & Moschini, 2009). Medical schools are often included in prior analysis due to the high volume of biomedical research that has garnered the attention of industry and produced high revenue generating licenses for universities (Bulut & Moschini, 2009). The presence of an engineering school was also considered for potential inclusion, but tests for significance indicated the presence of an engineering school had little direct impact upon disclosure activity, licenses or startups for these 76 universities. Twenty-one universities in the current study (28%) are identified as private institutions. Fifty (66%) have a medical school, and 34 (45%) have a law school. Twenty-seven (36%) have both academic programs, while 23 (32%) have a medical school without a law school, and 7 (9%) have a law school with no medical school.

The annual research levels of the 76 universities range from about $16 million to about $1.5 billion.[2] A ratio of the number of full-time licensing staff per million in research funding normalizes the resource commitment for technology transfer. For the sample in this analysis, this ratio stands at 0.025 or about 1 licensing staff member for every $40 million in research funding. Industry sponsored research percentages (industry research$/total research$) for the universities in the current study average about 10.8% during 2008–2010, ranging from 1% to 34.6%, similar to the AUTM population, which averaged about 7% industry funding, ranging from 0% to 38.5%. The age of the TLO provides additional controls for general experience in academic technology transfer, and ranges from a single year to 82 years of operation in the current sample; the AUTM population ranges from 0 to 85.

Previous experience of the TLO can facilitate subsequent efforts (Friedman & Silberman, 2003; O'Shea *et al.*, 2005; Jensen & Jones, 2011); suggesting measures of previous activities can be useful for the current analysis. Invention disclosures from 2003 to 2006 are included as historical inputs for licensing activity and startup formation. In estimating startup formation, historical license activity from 2003 to 2006 is also included to evaluate how prior licensing activity might influence subsequent startup efforts. The historical variables are logged to address over dispersion, normalize the data and reduce variable variance, and minimize multicollinearity. The control variables and their sources are further described in Table 8 below with descriptive names, type of variable, and percentages.

Descriptive statistics of the variables utilized in the model (Table 9) help to understand the variety of institutions included in the current study. The dependent and historical variables for invention disclosures, licenses, and startups are averaged to account for internal unobserved university characteristics, and logged to address any nonlinearity issues.

Table 10 provides the Pearson correlation coefficients between the dependent and the independent variables of interest. The technology licensing outcomes are positively related to each other; specifically invention disclosures are highly correlated with both licensing and startup activity, highlighting the pipeline effect of the technology transfer process, and of invention disclosures as the primary input into this process; no other commercialization activity happens without this critical first step (Bercovitz &

---

[2]The full set of universities participating in the AUTM annual licensing survey during this same time frame ranges from $3.2 million to about $5.4 billion in research funding, indicating the sample in the current study is missing the highest and lowest funded universities in this analysis (see Table 4).

Table 8.   List of controls.

Control variables		Percentage	Type	Source
University controls				
Private	Indicator	21 (28%)		
Medical school	Indicator	50 (66%)	Binary	Feldman and Bercovitz survey
Law school	Indicator	34 (45%)		
Technology licensing office controls				
TLOAGE	Age of TLO		Count	
LICFTE/TOTRES($M)	# Licensing Staff per million in research $		Continuous	AUTM Statistics Access for Tech Transfer (STATT)
Industry Research %	Industry % of research		Continuous	
History and input controls				
Past Invention Disc.	Average 2003–2006			AUTM Statistics
Past Licenses	Average 2003–2006		Continuous (logged)	Access for Tech
Past Startups	Average 2003–2006			Transfer (STATT)

Table 9.   Descriptive statistics.

Variable	Obs	Mean	Std. Dev.	Range	Frequency
Log Avg. Inv. Disclosures 2008–2010	76	4.40	0.95	1.95–6.24	
Log Avg. Licenses 2008–2010	76	2.81	1.02	0.511–4.65	
Log Avg. Startups 2008–2010	76	1.27	0.69	0–2.995	
Log Avg. Disclosures 2003–2006	75	4.31	0.90	2.3–6.22	
Log Avg. Licenses 2003–2006	75	2.81	1.02	0.69–5.12	
Log Avg. Startups 2003–2006	75	1.17	0.69	0–3.045	
Research Office	76	0.15	0.36	0–1	47
Institutional Leader	76	0.61	0.48	0–1	12
Economic or Business Dev.	76	0.14	0.35	0–1	11
Multiple Reporting	76	0.07	0.27	0–1	6
PhD	76	0.39	0.49	0–1	30
Lawyer	76	0.18	0.39	0–1	14
MBA	76	0.23	0.42	0–1	18
BS	76	0.18	0.39	0–1	14
Director years at job	76	8.19	4.91	2–26	
Private	76	0.27	0.45	0–1	21, 55 public
Medical school	76	0.65	0.47	0–1	50
Law School	76	0.44	0.50	0–1	34
Average Industry Res %	76	0.10	0.08	0.01–34.66%	
TLO age	76	20.89	14.37	1–82	
Licensing Staff/Total Res. $M	76	0.02	0.01	0.006–0.11	

Table 10.   Pearson correlations, dependent and independent variables.

	(a)	(b)	(c)	(d)	(e)	(f)	(g)	(h)	(i)	(j)	(k)	(l)
LogAVGInvDisc (a)	1											
LogAVGLicenses (b)	0.79	1										
LogAVGSTRTUP (c)	0.75	0.55	1									
Office of Research (d)	-0.10	-0.11	-0.15	1								
Institutional Leader (e)	0.11	0.03	0.06	-0.55	1							
Economic/Bus. Dev. (f)	-0.07	-0.06	0.14	-0.52	-0.18	1						
Multiple Offices (g)	0.11	0.24	0.00	-0.37	-0.13	-0.12	1					
Director PhD (h)	0.01	0.00	-0.02	-0.20	0.31	0.13	-0.24	1				
Director JD (i)	0.02	-0.08	0.08	-0.12	-0.02	-0.10	0.36	-0.38	1			
Director MBA (j)	0.06	0.03	0.13	0.25	-0.24	0.03	-0.16	-0.45	-0.26	1		
Director BS (k)	-0.10	0.05	-0.20	0.09	-0.11	-0.10	0.11	-0.38	-0.23	-0.26	1	
Director tenure (l)	0.01	0.10	-0.09	0.08	-0.11	-0.12	0.18	-0.19	-0.19	0.18	0.22	1

Feldman, 2008). Tests for multicollinearity after each regression suggest an absence of strong correlation between most of the independent variables, with variance inflation factors less than 10 for each.

Method

Ordinary least squares (OLS) is used to estimate the influence of university and TLO characteristics, including the variables of interest: the organizational structure of the TLO, educational background, and tenure of the TLO director on invention disclosures, licenses and startups. Historical measures are included to model the pipeline effect and evaluate how past efforts might impact subsequent activities. Regression results for base-line comparisons are provided in Table 11.

The averaged variables are transformed (increased by 1 and logged) to normalize the data and to correct for skewness and over dispersion. Logging variables is a common transformation practice in normalizing data; adding one to the transformation on the dependent variable ($\ln(1) = 0$) allows the inclusion of any observations of zero for that metric.

Table 11.   OLS, logged averages, office of research reporting & PhD held as comparison.

	(1)		(2)		(3)	
OLS (08-10)	Invention disclosures		Licenses		Startups	
Institutional Leader	0.171	18.65%	0.186	20.44%	0.310*	**36.34%**
	(0.300)		(0.204)		(0.142)	
Economic/Bus. Dev.	−0.394	−32.56%	−0.0288	−2.84%	0.257+	**29.30%**
	(0.329)		(0.226)		(0.143)	
Multiple Offices	0.205	22.75%	0.664+	**94.25%**	−0.0640	−6.20%
	(0.305)		(0.354)		(0.211)	
Director JD	−0.0579	−5.63%	−0.455*	**−36.56%**	0.117	12.41%
	(0.294)		(0.203)		(0.178)	
Director MBA	0.451*	**56.99%**	0.0380	3.87%	0.295+	**34.31%**
	(0.216)		(0.209)		(0.168)	
Director BS	0.0833	8.69%	0.359	43.19%	0.238	26.87%
	(0.280)		(0.273)		(0.171)	

(*Continued*)

| **Table 11.** (*Continued*) | | | | | |
OLS (08-10)	(1) Invention disclosures		(2) Licenses		(3) Startups	
Director tenure	−0.0237	−2.34%	−0.0103	−1.02%	−0.0115	−1.14%
	(0.0185)		(0.0147)		(0.0127)	
Private	**0.393***	**48.14%**	−0.349*	**−29.46%**	−0.237*	**−21.10%**
	(0.186)		(0.154)		(0.106)	
Medical School	**0.556***	**74.37%**	−0.170	−15.63%	0.0831	8.67%
	(0.212)		(0.206)		(0.122)	
Law School	0.334+	**39.65%**	0.0868	9.07%	0.269*	**30.87%**
	(0.172)		(0.178)		(0.114)	
Licensing Staff/ M$ Research Funding	−12.24*	**−1.00%**	−6.574	**−1.00%**	−4.966+	**−0.99%**
	(5.300)		(4.873)		(2.605)	
Industry Research %	2.303*	**9.00%**	−0.110	−0.10%	1.463+	**3.32%**
	(0.924)		(0.884)		(0.874)	
TLO Age	0.0307***	**3.12%**	0.0000600	0.01%	0.00729	0.73%
	(0.00684)		(0.00535)		(0.00447)	
Log Avg Inv. Disc.T1			0.859***	**0.858%**	0.659***	**0.658%**
			(0.0938)		(0.126)	
Log Avg Licenses T1					−0.235+	**−0.234%**
					(0.135)	
_cons	3.291***		−0.500		−1.303***	
	(0.380)		(0.458)		(0.343)	
N	76		75		75	
R^2	0.524		0.711		0.679	
adj. R^2	0.424		0.643		0.597	
F	10.38		27.80		10.12	

Standard errors in parentheses

$^{+}p < 0.10$, $^{*}p < 0.05$, $^{**}p < 0.01$, $^{***}p < 0.001$

Interpreting the coefficient estimates for the independent variables when the dependent variables are log transformed requires a reverse transformation to understand how changes might affect the different commercialization outcomes. With a log transformed dependent variable, the effect size can be shown by $100(e^{\beta i} - 1)$, to measure the impact of a 1 unit increase in the independent variable on each of the technology transfer outcome measures (Cameron & Trivedi, 2010; Wooldridge, 2006). For the logged historical averages, the coefficients (βi) are elasticities, and measure the expected percentage change for each of the dependent variables associated with a potential 1% increase in the lagged historical variable (Greene, 2003). The transformations are included in the tables and indicate the effect sizes for a one unit change in each of the independent variables.

Results

The results suggest the different TLO reporting structures and different educational backgrounds of the TLO director may have an influence upon academic technology commercialization outcomes. Results presented in Table 11 utilize the office of research reporting structure and a TLO director with a PhD educational background as initial baseline comparisons. Results comparing each organizational structure and educational background of TLO directors to the others are presented in Tables 12 and 13. The results comparing the performance of TLOs under each organizational structure and educational background of the TLO director show how the different reporting structures and educational characteristics may influence activities along the technology transfer process relative to the others. Consideration of the implications of the findings for university administrators coordinating the technology transfer process at US research universities and those legislators involved in policy discussions regarding academic technology transfer follows the discussion of the results.

Table 12 compares the effectiveness of each structure. No significant difference is found for invention disclosures receipt, suggesting other characteristics outside of the TLO may influence disclosure rates (Bercovitz & Feldman, 2008). Different structures influence the quantity of licenses and startups. The economic/business development reporting structure may be 23–29% more effective at startup formation than the default reporting to an office of research. Reporting to an economic/business development office is found to be significantly less effective at licensing efforts, potentially 50–100% less effective at licensing the invention disclosures received than those TLOs reporting to multiple offices. Similar results are found with

Table 12. Organizational structure comparison.

Comparison structure (Base line)	Alternate structure effectiveness			
	Office of research	Econ/Bus Dev.	Leader	Multiple
Office of Research	—	Startups: **29.30%** ($p < 0.10$)	Startups: **36.34%** ($p < 0.05$)	Licenses: **94.25%** ($p < 0.10$)
Econ/Bus Dev.	Startups: **−22.66%** ($p < 0.10$)	—	NS	Licenses: **99.97%** ($p < 0.10$)
Leader	Startups: **−26.66%** ($p < 0.05$)	NS	—	Startups: **−31.20%** ($p < 0.10$)
Multiple	Licenses: **−48.52%** ($p < 0.10$)	Licenses: **−49.99%** ($p < 0.10$)	Startups: **45.35%** ($p < 0.10$)	—

Table 13. Professional background comparison.

Comparison education (Base line)	Alternate education effectiveness			
	PhD	MBA	BS	JD
PhD	—	Inv. Disc.: **56.99%** ($p < 0.05$) Startups: **34.31%** ($p < 0.10$)	NS	Licenses: **−36.56%** ($p < 0.05$)
MBA	Inv. Disc.: **−36.30%** ($p < 0.05$) Startups: **−25.55%** ($p < 0.10$)	—	NS	Licenses: **−38.92%** ($p < 0.05$)
BS	NS	NS	—	Licenses: **−55.69%** ($p < 0.01$)
JD	Licenses: **57.62%** ($p < 0.05$)	Licenses: **63.72%** ($p < 0.05$)	Licenses: **125.69%** ($p < 0.01$)	—

those TLOs reporting to multiple offices; they can be 49–94% more effective in licensing than TLOs reporting to the office of research. TLOs reporting to the institutional leader are more effective at startup formation than reporting to the office of research by 27–36%; and are 31–45% more effective than those TLOs reporting to multiple offices.

The increased effectiveness of the economic/business development TLO reporting structure for startup formation in comparison to the TLO reporting to an office of research provides some support for Markman *et al.*'s (2009) finding that ability of the TLO to coordinate with external resources has a positive influence on startup formation. This analysis also finds TLOs reporting to the institutional leader have a positive influence upon startup formation, more so than a TLOs reporting to an office of research or multiple offices, suggesting TLOs reporting directly to the institutional leader may have a strategic focus upon startup formation, or have access to similar resources that can facilitate startup activity. We find TLOs reporting to multiple offices more effective in licensing activities during 2008–2010 than either the office of research or economic/business development reporting structure, but less effective at startup formation than TLOs reporting to an institutional leader, suggesting TLOs under multiple reporting structures may be strategically focused upon licensing, or may have access to resources, such as ties to a wider range of potential licensees, that can facilitate licensing efforts.

The summary of the analysis of educational backgrounds of TLO directors in Table 13 compares the influence of different educational backgrounds to each other for each of the technology transfer outcome measures. In comparison to all other TLO directors with different educational backgrounds, directors with a legal background (JD) are less effective in licensing university inventions; potentially 37–58% less effective than those TLO directors with a PhD, potentially 39–64% less effective than those TLO directors with a MBA, and potentially 56–125% less effective than TLO directors with a bachelor's degree, all else equal. We find TLO directors with MBA backgrounds more effective at obtaining invention disclosures and at startup formation than TLO directors with PhDs, about 36–57% more effective at invention disclosure receipt, and 26–34% more effective at startup formation, all else equal. Directors with PhD backgrounds seem to be more effective (37–57%) than directors with legal backgrounds in licensing. No significant difference is indicated between TLO directors with bachelor's degrees and TLO directors with PhDs or MBAs for any of the outcome measures. The negative relationship between TLO directors with JDs and licensing efforts in comparison to all TLO directors with alternative educational backgrounds provides support for Siegel *et al.*'s (2003) finding from their analysis of external legal expenditures and qualitative interviews that suggest legal wrangling from lawyers may have a negative influence upon licensing efforts. Further analysis might consider the relationship between TLO directors with a JD and revenue streams received by the university, considering Siegel *et al.*'s (2003) finding that external expenditures are correlated with higher licensing revenues.

TLO directors with an MBA background seem to be more effective in obtaining invention disclosures and forming startups compared to TLO directors with a PhD, and more effective at licensing than TLO directors with legal backgrounds. Those directors with PhD scientific background and understanding may have more success in licensing efforts by being selective in commercializing scientific innovations they understand. These findings provide additional support for those suggesting a need for expanded commercialization skillsets in university TLOs (Metz *et al.*, 2000; Litan & Cook-Deegan, 2011; Siegel *et al.*, 2007b; Siegel, 2012; Swamidass, 2013), through hiring individuals with strong licensing, technical and commercial skills and entrepreneurial backgrounds that can facilitate licensing and startup activity (Siegel, 2012).

The estimate for the TLO director's tenure variable indicates a slight negative relationship with invention disclosures, licensing and startup activity, but it is not significant. Indicators for private institutions suggests they may be more effective than public institutions at obtaining invention disclosures (48%, $p < 0.05$), however private universities may be less effective than public at licensing (-29%, $p < 0.05$) or forming startups (-21%, $p < 0.05$) from the disclosures received by the TLO. The presence of a medical school is also shown to have a positive influence upon invention disclosure receipt (74%, $p < 0.05$), but is not significantly related to licensing or startup formation. The indicator for the presence of a law school is shown to have a positive relationship with invention disclosure receipt (40%, $p < 0.10$), and is positive and strongly significant for startup activity (31%, $p < 0.05$).

Findings from previous studies indicate universities with high research funding are able to generate more invention disclosures (Thursby & Kemp, 2002; Friedman & Silberman, 2003), and are effective at licensing and startup formation (O'Shea *et al.*, 2005; Markman *et al.*, 2004; Thursby & Thursby, 2007; Bulut & Moschini, 2009; Jensen & Jones, 2011). Findings from several studies also indicate larger TLOs facilitate licensing and startup activities (Markman *et al.*, 2005a; Thursby & Thursby, 2007; Markman *et al.*, 2009; O'Shea *et al.*, 2005; Jensen & Jones, 2011). Larger universities may also have larger TLOs to facilitate the technology transfer process, and these two variables are highly correlated with each other (>0.73) in the current sample. In order to address this potential multicollinearity, we create a ratio of the number of licensing staff per million in total research funding. The estimate for this ratio is significant for invention disclosure receipt (-1.00%, $p < 0.05$) and startup formation (-0.99%, $p < 0.10$), but not for licensing activities. This negative relationship is expected, as adding more licensing staff to support technology transfer activities does not make sense without a corresponding expansion in research funding. The universities in this current study have on average about one licensing staff member for every \$40 million in research funds. The estimate on the licensing staff/ research funding ratio suggests that universities with higher ratios of licensing staff to research dollars are less effective at obtaining invention disclosures and forming startups. The effect change indicates a 1% positive change in the ratio of licensing staff to research funding may reduce invention disclosure receipt by 1%. An interesting follow up question would be to determine the best ratio for a university to be most efficient and effective in technology commercialization efforts; to find the saturation point at which adding additional licensing staff creates diminishing returns. The estimates on the percentage of industry sponsored research are significant and positive for invention disclosure activity ($p < 0.05$) and startup formation ($p < 0.10$) and suggest a one unit change in the percentage of industry funding at the university may positively influence invention disclosure submission by 9%, and startup activity by 3.32%, all else equal. This finding confirms findings from previous studies on the influence of industry-sponsored research on invention disclosure receipt (Friedman & Silberman, 2003), on licensing activities (Chukumba & Jensen, 2005), and on startup formation (Powers & McDougall, 2005a; O'Shea *et al.*, 2005; Jensen & Jones, 2011). The finding for industry funding from this current study and others suggests that university–industry interactions may have a positive influence upon a university's entrepreneurial efforts and culture of support for faculty collaborations with industry partners.

TLO experience is controlled by including the age of the office, and is found to be positive and strongly significant for invention disclosure receipt ($p < 0.001$), each additional year potentially increasing disclosure activity by 3.12%, suggesting older TLOs may be more experienced and effective at obtaining invention disclosures than TLOs with less experience. Older TLOs who have more experience working with faculty members for commercializing their inventions may have a positive influence due to previous successes (Chukumba & Jensen, 2005; Thursby & Thursby, 2007). The age of the TLO may also reflect universities with more experience and time cultivating cultural acceptance towards faculty entrepreneurship rather than direct engagement of the TLO. The age of the TLO is not shown to have a significant relationship with either licensing activity or startup formation. This supports findings by some (Markman, 2005a; Markman *et al.*, 2009), that the age of the TLO is not significantly related to licensing revenues.

Previous technology transfer activities and historical pipeline inputs show positive and significant relationships with commercialization outcomes. The elasticity estimates on the logged average historical metrics from 2003 to 2006 indicate that prior commercialization activity can have a significant influence upon subsequent activity. Each estimate for the pipeline inputs is positive and strongly significant ($p < 0.001$). The elasticity estimate for prior invention disclosure (0.858) for licensing activity suggests a high positive relationship between invention disclosure in 2003–2006 and subsequent licensing efforts; not one-to-one, but a positive influence nonetheless. The elasticity estimate for prior invention disclosure (0.658) for startup formation indicates a positive relationship between invention disclosure receipt in 2003–2006 and subsequent startup formation, supporting findings by Jensen and Jones (2011) that invention disclosures are a critical input for university startup formation. The elasticity coefficient for previous licensing efforts in the startup regression indicates a negative relationship between previous licensing efforts and subsequent startup formation (-0.234%, $p < 0.05$), the estimate indicating a 1% increase in prior licensing activities may reduce subsequent startup formation by 0.23%. This suggests university TLOs who have had success in the past with licensing efforts may be strategically focused upon licensing rather than startup formation. This finding provides support for Chukumba and Jensen's (2005) suggestion that university TLOs who have success in past licensing activity may be locked into that activity, and not be focused upon startup formation; potentially using that commercialization path as a last resort. This also provides some additional support for the finding by Bercovitz *et al.* (2001), that equity use as a licensing mechanism to startups is diminished with higher prior licensing activity.

The two most prevalent combinations of organizational structure and educational background of TLO director in this study are TLOs reporting to an office of research, with either a TLO director with a PhD, or a TLO director with an MBA educational background. When these two most prevalent structures are compared with the remaining structures, only one, the TLO reporting to an office of research with an MBA directing the office, is shown to be more effective than the remaining 15 structures at obtaining invention disclosures. No significance is indicated for either licensing activity or startup formation between these two common structures and the others. Results from the comparison of the TLO reporting to an office of research with an MBA director are included below (Table 14). The combination of the two characteristics together does not significantly alter the estimates on the other variables in the regression, however the significance of industry sponsored research levels on startup formation is dropped.

Table 14.   TLOs reporting to an office of research with MBA director.

	(1)		(2)		(3)	
	Invention disclosures		Licenses		Startups	
Report to Research & Director MBA	0.450*	56.83%	−0.242	−21.49%	0.0760	7.90%
	(0.215)		(0.230)		(0.170)	
Director tenure	−0.0179	−1.77%	0.0117	1.18%	−0.0132	−1.31%
	(0.0169)		(0.0157)		(0.0134)	
Private	0.452*	57.15%	−0.274+	−23.97%	−0.158	−14.62%
	(0.176)		(0.146)		(0.122)	
Medical School	0.564*	75.77%	−0.259	−22.82%	0.122	12.98%
	(0.213)		(0.230)		(0.111)	
Law School	0.364*	43.91%	0.0268	2.72%	0.229*	25.73%
	(0.160)		(0.172)		(0.105)	
Licensing Staff/ M$ Research Funding	−11.17*	−1.00%	−7.829	−1.00%	−3.161	−0.96%
	(4.885)		(5.311)		(2.230)	
Industry Research %	2.309**	9.06%	−0.822	−0.56%	1.184	2.27%
	(0.851)		(0.942)		(0.822)	
TLO Age	0.0294***	2.98%	−0.00418	−0.42%	0.00728+	0.73%
	(0.00652)		(0.00577)		(0.00420)	
Log Avg Inv. Disc.T1			0.914***	1.49%	0.657***	0.93%
			(0.0943)		(0.115)	
Log Avg Licenses T1					−0.224+	−0.20%
					(0.113)	
_cons	3.218***		−0.542		−1.154***	
	(0.397)		(0.486)		(0.295)	
N	76		75		75	
R^2	0.501		0.658		0.637	
adj. R^2	0.441		0.611		0.580	
F	12.12		31.96		12.84	

Standard errors in parentheses
+ $p < 0.10$, * $p < 0.05$, ** $p < 0.01$, *** $p < 0.001$

Discussion

The findings on the educational background of the TLO director suggest commercialization skills taught through an MBA program may be beneficial for obtaining invention disclosures, licensing efforts, and forming university startups. The current study provides some evidence of a positive relationship between business and commercialization skills taught through an MBA educational degree and increased disclosure and startup activity in comparison to TLO directors with a PhD, and in licensing efforts when compared to a TLO director with a JD. Our findings suggest TLO directors with PhDs are more successful in licensing endeavors than TLO directors with JDs, possibly due scientific background knowledge and research logic in understanding academic innovations. Our findings from this analysis provide some support for prior studies which suggest universities invest in hiring TLO licensing professionals with advanced business skills (Markman *et al.*, 2009) or in educational opportunities or programs designed to increase the broad-based commercialization skillsets of the TLO (Siegel *et al.*, 2007b; Litan & Cook-Deegan, 2011). The finding of a negative between TLO directors with JDs and licensing activity is considerable in this analysis, indicating a TLO director with a JD may be less effective than TLO directors with all other educational backgrounds in licensing university inventions. This finding would indicate that while legal knowledge is an important element for the technology transfer process in intellectual property protection and contractual language, legal wrangling in negotiation practices may limit successful licensing opportunities.

Results from a number but not all previous studies on university institutional and historical characteristics are supported by this study. The presence of a law school has a positive relationship with both invention disclosure and startup activity. The findings for private schools suggest private institutions may be effective in obtaining invention disclosures from research faculty, but less effective at licensing and startup formation than public institutions. This may be reflective of an increased emphasis for public institutions to have an economic development impact and would be an interesting question for a follow up study. The presence of medical school is shown to be a positive influence upon invention disclosure receipt, but not for licensing or startup efforts, suggesting medical schools may have high rates of invention disclosures, but those inventions may not necessarily turn into commercial opportunities at any higher rate than disclosures from other departments. The finding for medical schools confirms those of Kim (2013); medical schools had no significant influence on the licensing activities of 90 universities between 1999 and 2007. The influence of the medical school on commercialization outcomes may have lessened as other institutions increase their commitment to technology transfer. Bulut and Moschini (2009) find the combination of a medical school and a private university has a positive relationship with licensing revenues, suggesting this combination of characteristics may have a larger pipeline of disclosures with which to work, and may be able to negotiate a higher rate of return with successful licensing efforts.

Corroborating previous studies, this analysis finds the effects of experience and history have a strong influence upon an institutions' ability to successfully commercialize academic innovations (O'Shea *et al.*, 2005). Prior TLO invention disclosure history is shown to have a strong influence upon subsequent licensing and successful startup formation, as noted in previous studies (Friedman & Silberman, 2003; Chukumba & Jensen, 2005; O'Shea *et al.*, 2005; DiGregorio & Shane, 2003); confirming the criticality of invention disclosure for the technology transfer process. The findings suggest that the technology transfer activities of US research universities continue to evolve and expand, and correspondingly the influence of university characteristics on commercialization outcomes will continue to change.

Limitations in this current study include the small number of TLOs reporting to multiple offices; 6 out of the 76 universities included in this study are organized under this reporting relationship. Further analysis with additional TLOs under multiple reporting structures may help to properly evaluate this structure's influence upon commercialization outcomes. Some care should be taken with interpretations of this analysis, as relationships between organizational structures may be contingent upon the type of institution, its size, research funding levels, and the existence of various schools within the institution. The sample evaluated in this analysis is from 76 research universities, not an extremely large set to be able to effectively compare the 16 different possible organizational structures to each other. There may also be endogeneity in the model in that the reporting structure may have evolved at the university in response to the culture, history, strategy and needs of the institution, and hiring of the TLO director may have been influenced by the same characteristics. There may be a causal loop between organizational characteristics of the TLO and technology commercialization metrics. For example, universities more highly engaged in entrepreneurial activities in the past may have purposely aligned their office with an economic or business development function to facilitate those activities. Therefore, while a relationship is indicated between some of the different organizational structures of the TLO and commercialization outcomes, more work is needed to infer any causal directions.

References

Bercovitz, J. & Feldman, M. 2008. Academic entrepreneurs: Organizational change at the individual level. *Organization Science*, 19(1), 69–89.

Bercovitz, J., Feldman, M., Feller, I. & Burton, R. 2001. Organizational structure as a determinant of academic patent and licensing behavior: An exploratory study of Duke, Johns Hopkins, and Pennsylvania State Universities. *Journal of Technology Transfer*, 26, 21–35.

Bradley, S. R., Hayter, C. S. & Link, A. N. 2013. Models and methods of university technology transfer. *Foundations and Trends® in Entrepreneurship*, 9(6), 571–650.

Bulut, H. & Moschini, G. 2009. US universities' net returns from patenting and licensing: A quantile regression analysis. *Economics of Innovation and New Technology*, 18(2), 123–137.

Cameron, A. & Trivedi, P.K. 2010. *Microeconometrics Using Stata*. Stata Press.

Chukumba, C. & Jensen, R. 2005. University invention, entrepreneurship, and start-ups. NBER Working Paper Series, #11476.

Cyert, R. & March, J. G. 1963. *A Behavioral Theory of the Firm*. Prentice Hall, Englewood Cliffs, NJ.

DiGregorio, D. D. & Shane, S. 2003. Why do some universities generate more start-ups than others? *Research Policy*, 32(2), 209–227.

Feldman, M., Feller, I., Bercovitz, J. & Burton, R. 2002. Equity and the technology transfer strategies of American Research Universities. *Management Science*, 48(1), 105–121.

Feldman, M. & Bercovitz, J. 2010. Organizational structure as a determinant of academic patent and licensing behavior: A survey of American research universities. Report to the National Research Council, The National Academies.

Friedman, J. & Silberman, J. 2003. University technology transfer: Do incentives, management, and location matter? *Journal of Technology Transfer*, 28, 17–30.

Galunic, D. C. & Rodan, S. 1998. Resource recombinations in the firm: Knowledge structures and the potential for Schupeterian innovation. *Strategic Management Journal*, 19(12), 1193–1201.

Greene, W. H. 2003. *Econometric Analysis*, 5th edition. Pearson Education, NJ.

ipHandbook. 2012. *ipHandbook of Best Practices*. [online] Available at: http://www.iphandbook.org/handbook/topicguides/techtransfermanagers/ch03/#key and http://www.iphandbook.org/handbook/topicguides/techtransfermanagers/ch06/#key. Accessed on 2 August 2013.

Jensen, R. A. & Jones, M. 2011. University startups and entrepreneurship: New data, new results. In *March 9. Conference Paper to be presented at the Searle Center on Law, Regulation, and Economic Growth Fourth Annual Conference on Entrepreneurship and Innovation, Northwestern University School of Law*, Chicago, Illinois.

Kim, Y. 2013. The ivory tower approach to entrepreneurial linkage; productivity changes in university technology transfer. *Journal of Technology Transfer*, 38, 180–197.

Lam, A. 2000. Tacit knowledge, organizational learning, and societal institutions: An integrated framework. *Organizational Studies*, 21(3), 487–513.

Litan, R. & Cook-Deegan, R. 2011. Universities and economic growth. In *Kauffman Foundation's Rules for Growth, Promoting Innovation and Growth through Legal Reform 2011 The Kauffman Task force on Law Innovation and Growth*. Ewing Marion Kauffman Foundation.

Livne, O. 2007. Cost-conscious strategies for patent application filings. In *Intellectual Property Management in Health and Agricultural Innovation: A Handbook of Best Practices*, A Krattiger, RT Mahoney, L Nelsen, *et al.* (eds.). MIHR, Oxford, U.K. Available at: www.ipHandbook.org. Last Accessed August 2013.

March, J. & Simon, H. 1958. *Organizations*. John Wiley & Sons, New York, NY.

Markman, G. D., Gianiodis, P. T. & Phan, P. H. 2009. Supply-side innovation and technology commercialization. *Journal of Management Studies*, 46, 4.

Markman, G. D., Gianiodis, P. T., Phan, P. H. & Balkin, D. B. 2004. Entrepreneurship from the ivory tower: Do incentive systems matter? *Journal of Technology Transfer*, 29, 353–364.

Markman, G. D., Gianiodis, P. T., Phan, P. H. & Balkin, D. B. 2005a. Innovation speed: Transferring university technology to market. *Research Policy*, 34, 1058–1075.

Markman, G. D., Phan, P. H., Balkin, D. B. & Gianiodis, P. T. 2005b. Entrepreneurship and university-based technology transfer. *Journal of Business Venturing*, 20(2), 241–263.

McGee, D. R. 2007. Invention disclosures and the role of inventors. In *Intellectual Property Management in Health and Agricultural Innovation: A Handbook of Best Practices*, A. Krattiger, R. T. Mahoney, L. Nelsen, *et al.* (eds.). MIHR, Oxford, U.K. Available online at www.ipHandbook.org. Last Accessed August 2013.

Metz, B., Davidson, O. R., Martens, J., Rooijen, S. N. M. V. & McGrory, L. V. W. 2000. Methodological and technological issues in technology transfer. *A Special Report of IPCC Working group III, Cambridge University Press*, Published for Intergovernmental panel on Climate Change 2000.

Merrill, S. A. & Mazza, A. M. (eds.). 2010. *Managing University Intellectual Property in the Public Interest*. National Academies Press.

O'Shea, R. P., Allen, T. J., Chevalier, A. & Roche, F. 2005. Entrepreneurial orientation, technology transfer and spinoff performance of U.S. universities. *Research Policy*, 34, 994–1009.

Owen-Smith, J. & Powell, W. W. 2001. To patent or not: Faculty decisions and institutional success at technology transfer. *The Journal of Technology Transfer*, 26(1–2), 99–114.

Powers, J. B. & McDougall, P. 2005a. University startup formation and tech licensing with firms that go public: a resource-based view of academic entrepreneurship. *Journal of Business Venturing*, 20 (2005), 291–311.

Powers, J. B. & McDougall, P. 2005b. Policy orientation effects on performance with licensing to start-ups and small companies. *Research Policy*, 34 (2005), 1028–1042.

Rodan, S. & Galunic, C. 2002. Knowledge heterogeneity in managerial networks and its effect on individual performance. In *Academy of Management Proceedings*, 2002, Z1–Z7. Academy of Management.

Rothaermel, F. T., Agung, S. D. & Jiang, L. 2007. University entrepreneurship: A taxonomy of the literature. *Industrial and Corporate Change*, 16(4), 691–791.

Siegel, D. S. 2012. Academic entrepreneurship: Lessons learned for university administrators and policymakers. *Creating Competitiveness: Entrepreneurship and Innovation Policies for Growth*, 116.

Siegel, D. S., Waldman, D. & Link, A. 2003. Assessing the impact of organizational practices on the relative productivity of university technology transfer offices: An exploratory study. *Research Policy*, 32(1), 27–48.

Siegel, D. S., Waldman, D. A., Atwater, L. E. & Link, A. N. 2004. Toward a model of the effective transfer of scientific knowledge from academicians to practitioners: Qualitative evidence from the commercialization of university technologies. *Journal of Engineering and Technology Management*, 21, 115–142.

Siegel, D., Wright, M., Chapple, W. & Lockett, A. 2008. Assessing the relative performance of university technology transfer in the US and UK: A stochastic distance function approach. *Economics of Innovation and New Technology*, 17(7–8), 717–729.

Siegel, D. S., Wright, M. & Lockett, A. 2007a. The rise of entrepreneurial activity at universities: Organizational and societal implications. *Industrial and Corporate Change*, 16(4), 489–504.

Siegel, D. S., Veugelers, R. & Wright, M. 2007b. Technology transfer offices and commercialization of university intellectual property: Performance and policy implications. *Oxford Review of Economic Policy*, 23(4), 640–660.

Siegal, D. S. & Phan, P. H. 2005. Analyzing the effectiveness of university technology transfer: Implications for entrepreneurship education. University Entrepreneurship and Technology Transfer: Process, Design, and Intellectual Property, (Advances in the Study of Entrepreneurship, Innovation & Economic Growth, Volume 16), Emerald Group Publishing Limited, pp. 1–38.

Swamidass, P. 2013. University startups as a commercialization alternative: Lessons from three contrasting university case studies. *Journal of Technology Transfer*. Available at: http://link.springer.com/article/10.1007/s10961-012-9267-6#.

Thursby, J. G. & Kemp, S. 2002. Growth and productive efficiency of university intellectual property licensing. *Research Policy*, 31(1), 109–124.

Thursby, J. G. & Thursby, M. C. 2007. University licensing. *Oxford Review of Economic Policy*, 23(4), 620–639.

Wooldridge, J. M. 2006. *Introductory Econometrics, A Modern Approach,* 3rd edn. Thompson South-Western.

Zheng, W., Yang, B. & McLean, G. N. 2010. Linking organizational culture, structure, strategy, and organizational effectiveness: Mediating role of knowledge management. *Journal of Business Research*, 63(7), 763–771.

Chapter 6

Academic Entrepreneurship in Eastern Europe: Motivations and Success of University Spin-Offs in Hungary

Adam Novotny

Business School, Nord University

N-8049 Bodø, Norway

Institute of Economic Science, Eszterházy Károly University of Applied Sciences

H-3300 Eger, Hungary

adam.novotny@nord.no

The entrepreneurial process is stimulated and sustained by individual motivations, which incrementally (or in larger steps) lead entrepreneurs towards achieving a desired combination of explicit and implicit goals, satisfaction and the feeling of success. Based on a questionnaire survey of 80 academic entrepreneurs, this chapter examines the interrelations between entrepreneurial motivations and (objective and subjective) success in a post-socialist context. Findings show that supplementing university salaries is the strongest motivation for faculty members to become a part-time entrepreneur, followed by (in decreasing order) research-related benefits, the need for independence, and the need for achievement. In addition to monetary rewards, the application of knowledge to practical purposes (including professional development, problem solving, and recognition) is a prevalent component of subjective success. In view of their financial and human resources, and motivations for growth and innovation, the majority of the spin-off firms in Hungary is not Schumpeterian in nature. A neuralgic aspect of academic entrepreneurship in the country is the contribution of the university, which shows no relation to success indicators and is generally regarded as negative or neutral by faculty members.

Introduction

This chapter discusses the motivations, characteristics and success of small firms created by university faculty members in Hungary. It draws attention to the role of motivations in evaluating the success of academic entrepreneurship. Besides the relevant international and Hungarian literature, the author presents the findings of a recent survey he conducted in Hungary among founders of university spin-offs. To understand the characteristics of academic entrepreneurship in Hungary, first, it is important to look briefly at the evolution of the higher education system of transition economies. Empirical studies on university–industry technology transfer mostly focus on universities in North America and Western Europe, while much less attention has been paid to other parts of the world, including the post-socialist transition economies in Eastern Europe (Rothaermel *et al.*, 2007).

Universities in Eastern Europe nurture German (Humboldtian) traditions, while after the Second World War they were strongly influenced by the Soviet model of higher education. All these influences provide a unique mix of values and motivations for faculty members in these countries to engage in academic entrepreneurship. University systems with German traditions are reluctant to embark on organizational change, since academics here enjoy a relatively high level of freedom and tend to believe that besides impartial research and teaching they have no other social or economic obligations (Nybom, 2006; Lepenies, 1992; van Vught, 2004). High specialization, decentralized and fragmented organizational structure — including faculties, institutes, departments and working groups — and the high level of autonomy of leading professors and their research collectives result in an unfavorable environment for the entrepreneurial transformation of the institution as a whole; however, they can encourage entrepreneurship at the individual or group level.

During the socialist period, higher education institutions in Eastern Europe were nationalized, the research function was placed outside the university sector and university–industry relations weakened (Barakonyi, 2004). The operation of universities became bureaucratic and subsumed to political priorities, while the majority of research was concentrated within academies of sciences (Gaponenko, 1995). The term 'academic entrepreneurship' therefore may be confusing in an Eastern European context, where 'academic' is generally related to the Academy of Science and not to university researchers (Balázs, 1996). Balázs (1993, 1996) gives a thorough analysis of the characteristics of academic entrepreneurship in Hungary during the socialist period and shortly after the change of the political system in 1989. Already in the middle of the socialist period, the New Economic Mechanism (1968) made it possible for the research sector to solve the technical problems of manufacturing companies through contract research. Although these contributions were small-scale and *ad hoc* in nature (companies did not have innovation strategies at that time), they laid the foundations of entrepreneurship at Hungarian universities.

Immediately after the change of the political system, faculty members with prior industrial experience felt encouraged to create their own firms. Despite its uncertainties and the complete lack of resources for innovation at national, corporate and university level, the immature market economy offered new opportunities for those with an entrepreneurial spirit (there was no minimum capital for start-ups, taxation was favorable for firms, there were no university intellectual property regulations, etc.). In addition, freedom and self-regulation in teaching and research was reinforced after the regime change, albeit without consideration for the new challenges faced by modern mass higher education (Barakonyi, 2004). The main driving force behind the proliferation of small faculty-run enterprises at this time was an attempt to complement low university salaries and allow for flexible transactions with industry partners (Balázs, 1996). These 'quasi spin-off firms', created as a part of faculty members' survival strategy during the 1990s, can, in a stabilizing economy, hinder the evolution of technology transfer towards large-scale, multidisciplinary projects (Inzelt, 1999). Hrubos *et al.* (2004) also point to the general practice of entrepreneurship at Hungarian universities in which industry-related research projects are highly fragmented and usually serve the goals of relatively small interest groups such as departments and individuals.

In order to facilitate the involvement of universities in the commercialization of research, as well as to follow international trends, the Hungarian government introduced a new law on research and technological innovation in 2005. Based on the American Bayh-Dole model, the 'Innovation Act' allows universities to retain title to inventions resulting from research activities pursued within the framework of the university. It defines the key concepts of innovation such as applied research and development (R&D), technology commercialization and 'utilizing enterprise' (spin-off firm). The Act also requires universities to create their own intellectual property (IP) management regulations which include instructions on IP reporting and valuation, the rights and obligations of faculty members and the rules regarding profit sharing. The experts who devised the methodological guidelines of these policies invoked the practice of the U.S., where universities traditionally make use of such policies (HIPO, 2005). They followed the American model despite findings that the European continental system of higher education, and especially that typically found in Eastern Europe, is fundamentally different from that of the U.S. (Bonaccorsi & Daraio, 2007; Franzoni & Lissoni, 2009; Erdős & Varga, 2010). In Europe, faculty members are public employees and enjoy high job security; university salaries and tuition fees are regulated (limited) by law, and there is low competition for the best teachers and researchers.

A questionnaire survey of 1,562 faculty members conducted by the author at Hungarian universities (see Novotny, 2011, 2013) found that the majority (73%) of academics in the fields of medical sciences, engineering, natural sciences and agrarian science have at least some experience in university–industry technology transfer, such as consultancy, contract research, government funded applied research and development, spin-off firms and patenting. One in five scientists (21.4%) reported working in an academic spin-off, which is a relatively large proportion in comparison to international findings. These small firms are probably not homogeneous regarding their motivations, levels of innovation and other characteristics, and their high number does not necessarily mean that intensive knowledge flows from the university sphere to the industry.

In what follows, first I focus on the theories of entrepreneurial motivations and success, and prepare the ground for answering the question why university faculty members start spin-off firms. In the empirical part of the paper I examine the dimensions of success and motivations in the case of university spin-offs, and analyze the relationship between them. Here I present some important characteristics of Hungarian academic firms and test their relations with motivation and success. The analysis of the Hungarian example is based on a 2014 survey of 80 spin-off founders; in addition, as part of the literature review, I present some findings of a wide-scale survey conducted on university–industry technology transfer in the country in 2009. The last section of the chapter contains the summary and conclusions of the empirical findings.

Literature Review

Spin-off motivations

Entrepreneurial behavior can be approached in three fundamental ways (Chell, 2008): Economists study entrepreneurs' functions in the economy, i.e., the allocation of resources for production to achieve maximum profit. Sociology emphasizes context — the social, economic and institutional environment of entrepreneurs — in which motivations are shaped by opportunities, family background, social capital, social norms, etc. Psychological approaches analyze the 'inner world' of entrepreneurs including personality, motivations, attitude and perceptions. In what follows, I discuss entrepreneurial motivations in academic context, and also present the specialities of spin-off motivations in the Hungarian university sector.

The first step in the spin-off process is the establishment of the firm, which largely depends on the needs and motivations of the individual faculty member. Based on questionnaires and interviews with 100 Hungarian university researchers, Buzás (2004) points to the lack of entrepreneurial spirit as one of the main barriers to spin-off formation: faculty members have a negative attitude towards entrepreneurship in general, they have a low tolerance for risks and a high fear of failure, business ties and insecurity, and especially when compared to the freedom and relative security which their academic positions provide.

The main motivations of faculty members as researchers are recognition within the scientific community, personal financial gain and obtaining funds for research (Link *et al.*, 2006). Based on McClelland's (1961) theory, the achievement motivation, i.e., the desire to solve difficult tasks, overtake others and gain recognition, influences both occupational choice and performance as an entrepreneur. A career in research inevitably involves facing challenging tasks; however, in the weak organizational culture that persists at Hungarian universities, ambitious faculty members feel encouraged to pursue their own goals: they tend to concentrate their innovativeness on the pursuit of their own careers, which often involve ventures outside the university (Szabó, 2010).

In an early study, Doutriaux and Peterman (1982) found that the desire for freedom and independence are important drivers of starting spin-off ventures. While academic entrepreneurs can enjoy the support of the university (e.g., reputation, infrastructure), they still have the benefit of smaller size, including independent, flexible and fast decision making. The need for independence can also be strengthened by negative experiences about the entrepreneurial competences of the university, such as cumbersome decision making practices, risk avoidance, and insufficient capital for research (Novotny, 2013). The need for achievement and the need for independence are widely acknowledged entrepreneurial motives, and they are positively related to spin-off formation and success as well (Roberts, 1991; Morales-Gualdrón *et al.*, 2009; Chiesa & Piccaluga, 2000).

Mainstream microeconomics posits that the primary motive of all businesses is profit. Accordingly, there is evidence that increasing or maintaining the founder's wellbeing is an important motivation among spin-off entrepreneurs (Etzkowitz, 1998; Franklin *et al.*, 2001; Egeln *et al.*, 2003; Shane, 2004; Owen-Smith & Powell, 2001). However, Lam (2011) argues that financial

motivations are of secondary importance to reputational and career benefits, and also to intrinsic motivations such as solving the problems of applied
research. In Hungary, in order to make up for their relatively low remunera-
tion when compared to their years of schooling, accumulated knowledge
and social status, faculty members are strongly motivated by financial gain:
9 out of 10 academic entrepreneurs agree at least partly that the primary
motivation of technology transfer is money (Novotny, 2013).

Based on their literature review, D'Este and Perkmann (2011) find that
faculty members establish spin-offs for two basic reasons: for profit and to
support their research. Motivations specific to the academic sector may be
of higher importance than money: professional development/learning, the
application of knowledge for practical use, obtaining new ideas/goals for
research, and gaining access to funds and laboratory equipment are all
regarded as important drivers of spin-off creation (Morales-Gualdrón *et al.*,
2009; Baldini *et al.*, 2007). A key question is whether faculty members can
effectively integrate the commercialization of research with publishing and
teaching, and whether university policies facilitate the integration of these
three missions. The pressure for commercialization in Hungary causes role
conflicts in many faculty members (Novotny, 2013), who find it challenging
to allocate sufficient time and efforts to preparing for lectures, writing
papers and solving industry problems at the same time. Although spin-off
founders are also motivated by higher academic prestige and status (Baldini
et al., 2007; Fini *et al.*, 2009), university promotion systems in general do not
reflect the growing importance of the market orientation of research, therefore academic entrepreneurs are expected to be as productive scientifically
as their non-entrepreneurial colleagues. Hungarian universities are hesitant
about how the 'academic heartland' can be stimulated to develop entrepreneurial attitude (Hrubos *et al.*, 2004); apart from growing financial necessity
and loopholes in university regulations, universities typically do not apply
specific tools to encourage academic entrepreneurship (Szabó, 2013).

Entrepreneurial motivations are often classified on the basis of psychological theories. One of the widely used dichotomies is the 'push–pull' model
(Pirnay *et al.*, 2003), which claims that motives or internal forces push a person into action, while incentives or external forces pull him/her towards a
desired goal. Concerning spin-off firms, pull factors include the application
of knowledge for practical uses, the desire for achievement, independence
and wealth, career development (reputation and promotion), a promising
market opportunity, etc., while job-related dissatisfaction (e.g., low salary,
lack of opportunities for promotion) and various types of pressures to

engage in entrepreneurship feature on the push side (Weatherston, 1995; Chiesa & Piccaluga, 2000; de Silva, 2013). As stated by a similar approach popularized by the Global Entrepreneurship Monitor (Ernesto & Bosma, 2014), push motives create 'necessity driven' entrepreneurs, while opportunities make 'opportunity driven' entrepreneurs. Necessity driven entrepreneurship is more prevalent in countries with lower GDP per capita and necessity entrepreneurs' subjective wellbeing is generally lower than that of their counterparts (Reynolds *et al.*, 2002). The necessity-opportunity dichotomy is sometimes referred to as 'subsistence' versus 'transformational' entrepreneurship. The former refers to individuals who become entrepreneurs in order to provide income to maintain themselves and close family members, while transformational entrepreneurs are Schumpeterian in nature: through innovative ideas they transform markets and can shape the whole economy (Schoar, 2009). In addition to complementing university salaries, necessity-related motives can include more advantageous cost accounting and taxation in small businesses and the possibility of employing family members. Transaction costs, such as avoiding the psychological and time costs of tackling university bureaucracy may also be significant motivations.

Many see the future university 'as a generator of spin-off enterprises' that create income and employment (Etzkowitz, 2002). But not all entrepreneurs are equally growth-oriented. For example, the academic entrepreneurs interviewed by Buzás (2004) expressed reluctance to give up their secure academic positions and concentrate all their resources on building a business. Some of them would only leave the university and be with their firms full time if they were supported by a competent and likeable business manager. So-called 'lifestyle' entrepreneurs do not want their firms to exceed an easily manageable size that could pose dangers to their well-established ways of life or to the balance between work and family (Henricks, 2002). Financial motives and growth are secondary for lifestyle entrepreneurs (Kuratko & Hodgetts, 1998).

Besides psychological or motivational explanations, Shane (2004) highlights the importance of career-related factors such as career cycles, academic status, intellectual capital, and entrepreneurial experience in the formation of spin-off firms. According to career-related models, academics are more likely to found spin-offs if they are in the later stages of their careers, have higher academic ranks, possess ample intellectual capital and have more industrial work experience. Hungarian findings also support career-related motivations: researchers' previous industry experience and age relate positively to spin-off formation (Novotny, 2011).

There are several supporting environmental conditions for spin-off formation, but their detailed description would go beyond the scope of this paper. These include opportunity recognition (Shane & Venkataraman, 2000; Fini *et al.*, 2009), intellectual properties, university culture and policies (Shane, 2004; Landry *et al.*, 2006), access to venture capital, investors and other business partners (Carayannis *et al.*, 1998), and the presence of role models and supporting social norms (Brockhaus & Horwitz, 1986).

Entrepreneurial success

Entrepreneurial success can be interpreted from both 'macro' and 'micro' perspectives. The former focuses on the impact of companies on the wellbeing of society, i.e., economic growth, employment growth, poverty reduction, etc. In this paper success is examined from the individual's perspective, as the relationship between entrepreneurial motivations and success can only be understood at the level of the firm and entrepreneur. The success of business organizations is normally measured by indicators such as turnover, profit, market capitalization, market share, number of employees, etc. (Helm & Mauroner, 2007). The advantage of financial indicators is that they can be relatively easily measured and used for comparisons.

While subjective career success is acknowledged in career related literature, authors studying entrepreneurial success tend to focus on business performance (König *et al.*, 2012). However, as shown by the literature review of motivations, not all individuals attach the same importance to growth, and not all entrepreneurs are willing to take the same risks (Baum *et al.*, 2001). For example, in the case of Hungarian spin-offs, 'success is stability and continuity but not, as yet, growth' (Balázs, 1996). Lifestyle entrepreneurs are primarily motivated by independence, and the non-financial rewards of their work (Morrison *et al.*, 1999). Evidence suggests that entrepreneurial success should be approached in a subjective way as well, taking into consideration the basic needs and motivations of the founder.

When measuring entrepreneurial success in an academic context, the degree to which an invention has been transferred to the market has to be assessed as well. It is also important from a macro-economic point of view, whether the technology has been successfully transferred to the customer, whether it has achieved the desired outcome on the market (Choi-Lee, 2000). The problem with this approach is that it can take several years (even 7–12 years) until a promising idea turns into a new product or competitive advantage, success is hard to predict in the earlier phases of a business (Swadimass & Vulasa, 2009). According to the rule of thumb,

100 inventions lead to 10 patents and only one successful product (Blake, 1993), so it is not surprising that one-fourth of start-up companies fail in the first year of business and only three out of 10 will celebrate their tenth birthday (University of Tennessee, 2015).

Method

The findings presented in this chapter are based on a questionnaire survey carried out by the author in Spring 2014. The survey intended to collect information from Hungarian academic entrepreneurs in the fields of engineering, medical science, natural sciences and agrarian science; these fields are generally considered to be more entrepreneurial than others, i.e., better suited for the commercialization of research results. There were approximately 8,700 faculty members (8,000 in teaching positions and 700 in research positions) from 61 university faculties at 15 universities identified as working in the above mentioned fields at the time of the survey (Educational Authority, 2012), however, it was unfeasible to determine the exact number of the population, i.e., academic entrepreneurs and university spin-off firms. The survey defined university spin-offs as firms created to commercialize the research results, technology and expertise developed by university faculty members. I focused on researchers who have retained their university position and hence are part-time entrepreneurs. It was not a requirement for the science-based firm to have any formal or informal agreement with the university, which makes the population difficult to estimate. I only included firms that span out of state-owned universities (non-state universities in Hungary are mostly run by various churches and religious groups).[1]

The survey collected information about academic entrepreneurs' motivations and success with the help of an online database of university faculty members developed in 2009 (see: Novotny, 2011, 2013). E-mails were sent to 1,500 faculty members until a sufficient number of spin-off founders were reached. The final sample comprises 80 academic entrepreneurs from 10

---

[1] State-owned higher educational institutions underwent a process of integration at the turn of the new millennium, thus becoming fewer in number but larger in size. The total number of institutions (public, church and privately funded) was around 90 throughout the 1990s, but subsequently dropped to around 70. In the academic year 2013/2014 there were 66 institutions and 181 faculties, 30% of which (i.e., 20 universities and 10 colleges) were state-run (HCSO, 2014). Higher education institutions called 'universities' are generally larger in terms of the number of faculties and students and more research oriented than 'colleges', hence their technology transfer potential is also greater.

Hungarian universities.[2] Those faculty members were included in the sample who, in addition to working in a firm that commercialized research results, were willing to disclose information about their entrepreneurial behavior. The youngest respondent is 30, the oldest is 68 years of age. The mean age is 50, as is the median. The sample has a relatively high share of men (83.8%), as they also have a higher proportion within the population (70%) and among academic entrepreneurs in general (83.2%) (Novotny, 2011). Respondents are distributed normally in terms of academic ranks: associate professors represent the highest share (37.5%) in the sample. Two thirds of the respondents have a PhD, and one in 10 academic entrepreneurs works officially in a research position.

First, I analyzed the data by descriptive statistics. Then I applied multivariate methods including the factor analysis and cluster analysis of motivational scales to identify the pattern of motivations and the distinct groups of respondents based on motivations respectively. I tested the relations between success indicators and success factors with correlation coefficients, contingency tables, and independent samples *t*-tests (or its non-parametric alternative, the Mann–Whitney test). I assessed subjective success definitions through content analysis.

Findings and Discussion

The motivations of university spin-offs

When analyzing academic entrepreneurs' motivations, the underlying question is whether motives specific to the academic sphere are more important for university spin-off creation than those found in general entrepreneurship literature. The Likert scale used to measure motivations contained 20 items, elaborated on the basis of literature, which were narrowed down to 16 by factor analysis (Table 1). The mean scores of the items show that financial necessity (dissatisfaction with income) is the most important for the creation of spin-offs, followed by motivations related to research. Achievement and independence seem to be of lesser importance.

The motivational items in Table 1 were filtered and classified with the help of Principal Axis Factoring (PAF). Based on the literature review, the latent dimensions behind the items were: the need for achievement, the

---

[2]Budapesti University of Technology and Economics, University of Debrecen, Szent István University, University of Pécs, University of West Hungary, University of Szeged, Eötvös Loránd University, University of Miskolc, Universirty of Kaposvár and Semmelweis University.

Table 1. The importance of motivations to start a science-based firm as reported by faculty members (1 = strongly disagree, 7 = strongly agree).

1.	I could not make ends meet from my university salary.	5.44
2.	I needed extra income to provide for an acceptable quality of life.	5.33
3.	I wanted my research efforts to yield tangible results.	5.29
4.	To complement my research activities.	5.09
5.	To exploit my knowledge for financial gain.	5.04
6.	To further develop research results towards application.	4.84
7.	To put my ideas into practice.	4.84
8.	To work and make decisions on my own.	4.51
9.	I could best make use of my skills by working independently.	4.19
10.	To be my own employer.	4.13
11.	To identify and exploit new market opportunities.	4.06
12.	I was energized to have my own company.	4.05
13.	To solve scientific problems myself.	3.94
14.	To have more challenge at work.	3.90
15.	I wanted to try myself in competition.	3.78
16.	To build my own business.	3.76
17.	To have more funds and better equipment for my research.	3.60
18.	To have higher prestige and reputation.	3.29
19.	To advance my career as a researcher.	3.10
20.	To get rich.	2.54

need for independence, the prospect of higher income and the support for research. The dimensions gained after PAF (Table 2) are somewhat different from the initial model: items related to the prospect of higher income have split, as push motives loaded on *necessity* and pull ones on *achievement.* High achievers are probably pulled by the potential reward of getting rich, rather than being pushed into entrepreneurship by financial necessity. The *achievement* factor embraces various motivations that are often treated separately in the literature: the pursuit of opportunities, the desire for wealth, prestige, reputation, challenge, and building an enterprise are closely related to one another.

Necessity (mean of items: 5.38) is the strongest motivational dimension in starting a spin-off firm, followed by *research* related benefits (4.59), the desire for *independence* (4.19) and the need for *achievement* (3.77). Differences between the four dimensions are significant ($p < 0.05$).

Table 2. The Pattern Matrix of entrepreneurial motivations in the academic sector. (Principal Axis Factoring, Promax with Kaiser Normalization.)

Factors	Items	Factor loadings	Means
Achievement ($\alpha = 0.83$)	To identify and exploit new market opportunities.	0.795	4.06
	To exploit my knowledge for financial gain.	0.661	5.04
	To get rich.	0.616	2.54
	To have higher prestige and reputation.	0.616	3.29
	To build my own business.	0.574	3.76
	To have more challenge at work.	0.498	3.90
Independence ($\alpha = 0.84$)	I could best make use of my skills by working independently.	0.821	4.19
	To work and make decisions on my own.	0.757	4.51
	To be my own employer.	0.628	4.13
	To solve scientific problems myself.	0.623	3.94
Research ($\alpha = 0.80$)	To further develop research results towards application.	0.818	4.84
	To complement my research activities.	0.709	5.09
	To put my ideas into practice.	0.587	4.84
	To have more funds and better equipment for my research.	0.549	3.60
Financial necessity ($\alpha = 0.79$)	I needed extra income to provide for an acceptable quality of life.	0.853	5.33
	I could not make ends meet from my university salary.	0.760	5.44

Table 3. The descriptive statistics of motivational dichotomies.

	1...	Mean	Mode	Median	SD	...7
1.	Tax optimization	4.79	6	5	1.9	Implement innovative idea
2.	Necessity	3.88	4	4	1.63	Market opportunity
3.	Increasing wealth	3.58	4	4	1.44	Support of research
4.	Convenient lifestyle	3.56	3	3	1.68	Continuous growth

I also tested the motivational dichotomies, examined in the literature review, statistically. The descriptive statistics of semantic differentials (Table 3) reveal that respondents in general are more motivated by implementing an innovative idea (60.1%) than by tax optimization (22.6%). The means of the other differentials are relatively close to the midpoint of the scale, so it is

Table 4. Clusters of academic entrepreneurs based on motivational dichotomies.

Semantic differentials (7-point scale)	'Subsistence' academic entrepreneurs 62.5%	'Transformational' academic entrepreneurs 37.5%
	Scale means	
convenient quality of life ↔ continuous growth	2.58	5.20
necessity ↔ appealing market opportunity	3.08	5.20
tax optimization ↔ innovation	3.94	6.20
increasing personal wealth ↔ support for research	2.98	4.57

difficult to make clear assumptions in these cases. The most balanced dichotomies are 'necessity *versus* opportunity' (26.3% chose the midpoint) and 'increasing wealth *versus* supporting research' (37.5% could not decide between them). On the other hand, twice as many academic entrepreneurs are motivated by a convenient life than by continuous growth (56.3% and 27.5% respectively).

I performed a two-step cluster analysis on the sample to categorize academic entrepreneurs into sufficiently different groups based on the dichotomies related to motivations. Not surprisingly, the semantic differentials are related to one another ($p < 0.01$); the opposite poles of the scale items in Table 4 describe the two basic types of academic entrepreneurs: *subsistence* and *transformational*. The two faculty segments differ significantly from each other regarding every dichotomy, which implies that two thirds of the respondents are not that growth and research oriented, opportunity driven, innovative academic entrepreneurs (Table 4). *Transformational* entrepreneurs are more strongly motivated by the support for research, the need for independence and the need for achievement ($p < 0.01$), and less strongly by financial necessity ($p < 0.05$) than *subsistence* academic entrepreneurs.

The success of science-based firms

Entrepreneurial success was measured in three ways by the survey: by objective criteria, and based on faculty members' subjective definitions of entrepreneurial success and their satisfaction with the outcome of technology transfer (Table 5).

Table 5.   The objective and subjective indicators of entrepreneurial success.

Type of success	Indicators
Objective success	firm's average annual revenue
	change in revenue since firm establishment
	employee headcount at the time of the survey
	change in employee headcount since firm establishment
	firm's age at the time of the survey
Subjective entrepreneurial success	Based on your own definition of success, do you consider yourself a successful academic entrepreneur? (1 = not at all; 7 = absolutely successful)
Subjective technology transfer success	How satisfied are you with the degree to which your expertise/invention/research result has been transferred to the market by your firm? (1 = not at all; 7 = absolutely satisfied)

Table 6.   The relationship between the objective and subjective success of spin-off firms (Spearman's rho).

	Subjective entrepreneurial success	Subjective success of technology transfer
Revenue	0.355**	0.243*
Growth of revenue	0.288**	0.327**
Employee headcount	0.408**	0.288**
Growth of employee headcount	0.333**	0.164
Firm's age	0.062	0.059

*Correlation is significant at the 0.05 level (two-tailed).
**Correlation is significant at the 0.01 level (two-tailed).

There is a strong correlation between the two subjective success indicators ($r = 0.66$), which implicates that transferring technologies to the market is an important determinant of subjective entrepreneurial success in the university sector. Findings also reveal that subjective and objective measures relate to one another (Table 6). The strongest association is between subjective entrepreneurial success and employee headcount, so leading and being responsible for people can reward academic entrepreneurs with the feeling of success. Subjective technology transfer success is relatively closely linked to the growth of revenue. As for the relationship among objective success indicators, sales revenue and employee headcount are positively related. There is a negative relationship between the firm's age and its growth rate: growth tends to slow down by time.

The objective success indicators show that the typical spin-off firm has a relatively low revenue (1–5 million forints), no employees (36.3% of the firms are one-person businesses) and was founded around the turn of the millennium. Since its formation, there has been a small increase in its turnover.

When academic entrepreneurs were asked to describe what they mean by success, a relatively large proportion (40%) mentioned pecuniary benefits, such as gaining revenue and profit, complementing university salaries, and making ends meet. On the other hand, many associate success with extending their research towards useful applications and obtaining recognition for it, either from customers or in the academic sphere. Around 20% regard customer satisfaction or the creation of "marketable" results as an important benchmark, and also about one-fifth think that the application of their knowledge/research results to practice is success. To summarize, in addition to monetary rewards, subjective success definitions typically involve the need for achievement, the desire to do something important and valuable, and the solving of problems. According to their own interpretation of success, less than half (46.4%) of the respondents regard themselves as successful academic entrepreneurs, while 20% opt for the unsuccessful side of the scale, with about one third unable to decide. Similarly, somewhat less than half (47.6%) of the respondents are satisfied with the outcomes of the technology transfer they initiated in their firms, while the proportion of dissatisfied academic entrepreneurs is 29% (one fourth indicated the midpoint of the scale).

The role of motivations in entrepreneurial success

According to the correlation coefficients shown in Table 7, motivations related to *research, achievement* and *independence* (see Table 2) are all associated with subjective success. *Achievement* and *independence* have the closest relation with subjective entrepreneurial success, while *research* has a relatively strong link with technology transfer success. These three motivational dimensions also significantly correlate with the objective success measures, such as revenue and employee headcount. To summarize, support for research appears to be the most important entrepreneurial motivation in an academic context. While *necessity* is important at the creation of the venture, it has no link with its success later on.

I found significant ($p < 0.05$) differences between the faculty segments in terms of the success indicators (Table 8): *transformational* entrepreneurs have higher levels of perceived success, both entrepreneurial and technology transfer, and their firms are also likely to be larger in objective terms.

Table 7.   Associations of entrepreneurial motivations and success (Spearman's rho).

	Subjective success		Objective success			
	Entrepreneurial success	**Technology transfer success**	**Revenue**	**Change in revenue**	**Employee headcount**	**Firm's age**
Necessity	0.029	0.078	−0.093	−0.073	0.025	0.170
Research	0.398**	0.421**	0.363**	0.312**	0.367**	−0.015
Independence	0.422**	0.222*	0.249*	0.175	0.305**	0.071
Achievement	0.462**	0.353**	0.222*	0.216	0.259*	0.029

*Correlation is significant at the 0.05 level (two-tailed).
**Correlation is significant at the 0.01 level (two-tailed).

Table 8.   The relationships of faculty segments based on motivations and spin-off success.

	'Subsistence' academic entrepreneurs	'Transformational' academic entrepreneurs
Average annual revenue (most frequent response)	HUF 1–5 million	HUF 6–50 million
Change in revenue (most frequent response)	slight increase	slight increase, large increase
Employee headcount (most frequent response)	0	2
Age of firm (mean years)	13.7	11.1
Subjective entrepreneurial success (mean)	3.96	4.90
Subjective technology transfer success (mean)	3.96	4.73

Motivations and innovativeness

A university spin-off is often regarded as 'a new company founded to exploit a piece of intellectual property created in an academic institution' (Shane, 2004, p. 4). The role of IP rights in economic growth can be especially important in technology-intensive sectors (Máté, 2014). Still, as seen in Table 9, only about half of academic entrepreneurs own some sort of IP rights, most of which are in the forms of know-how (38%) and patent (15.2%). Know-how is more typical in engineering firms, while patents are relatively prevalent in firms involved in pharmaceutical research and biotechnology. Firms owning IP rights, including know-how ($p < 0.05$),

Table 9. The intellectual property rights of science-based firms operated by university faculty members ($N = 80$).

	Responses		Percent of spin-offs
	N	*%*	
Know-how	30	32.3	38.0
Patent	12	12.9	15.2
License	4	4.3	5.1
Utility model	3	3.2	3.8
Trademark	2	2.2	2.5
None	42	45.2	53.2
Total	93	100.0	117.7

Table 10. The innovativeness of spin-off firms and its relationship with entrepreneurial motivations.

Product/service	%	'Subsistence' academic entrepreneurs	'Transformational' academic entrepreneurs
Not innovative	36.3	48.0	16.7
Innovative on regional (NUTS 2) level	8.8	10.0	6.7
Innovative in Hungary	27.5	24.0	33.3
Innovative in Europe	7.5	4.0	13.3
Innovative on a global scale	20.0	14.0	30.0
Total	100.0	100.0	100.0

patent ($p < 0.01$), or utility model ($p < 0.05$), self-reported to be more innovative than ones without them. Spin-offs with IP rights have also grown faster, and their founders feel more successful, i.e., have higher subjective entrepreneurial and higher subjective technology transfer success rates ($p < 0.05$).

Nearly two thirds of the respondents (63.7%) rated their market offer as novel at least on a regional level, and one fifth consider their products or services innovative on a global scale (Table 10). The cross-tabulation of segment membership and spin-off innovativeness shows that offering novel products and services on the market is more inherently linked to *transformational* spin-offs than to *subsistence* ones ($p < 0.05$). Similar to IP rights, innovativeness is positively related ($p < 0.01$) to objective success (revenue, employee headcount, growth) and to subjective entrepreneurial success.

Table 11.   The distribution of spin-off firms by knowledge-based industries.

	Responses		Percent of
	N	%	respondents
Agriculture	18	14.9	22.5
Electronics, ICT	18	14.9	22.5
Energy and environment	16	13.2	20.0
Architectural services	13	10.7	16.3
Medical and health services	13	10.7	16.3
Chemicals, pharmaceutics	12	9.9	15.0
Mechanics, automation, materials	12	9.9	15.0
Biotechnology, biomedical engineering	9	7.4	11.3
Food industry	5	4.1	6.3
Other	5	4.1	6.3
	121	100.0	151.3

Industry type and spin-off success

The industrial distribution of the sample is shown in Table 11. Respondents are relatively evenly distributed among the studied fields of science.

Firms engaged in medical and health services, biotechnology and biomedical engineering are relatively less successful as regards to most success criteria (Table 12). Spin-offs in the sectors of architecture, ICT and electronics, chemicals and pharmaceutics are the most successful overall, considering both subjective and objective indicators. As compared to others, food engineering firms have low revenue but a high growth rate. Respondents from the field of architecture feel the most successful as entrepreneurs, whereas engineers in the ICT, electronics, mechanics, automation and materials sectors are the most satisfied with the degree of technology transfer achieved. Based on objective measures, the most successful companies are engaged in architecture, chemicals and pharmaceutics, and ICT and electronics.

University support and spin-off success

In order to grow, small businesses generally require external resources and support from various institutions, experts, competitors, customers, etc., in the form of information, knowledge, skills or money. An important aspect of academic entrepreneurship is the relationship between the spin-off firm and the university. According to the findings, the university has contributed

Table 12.   The success of academic ventures by knowledge-based industries.

	Percentage of respondents	Feels successful as an academic entrepreneur (Percentage of respondents)	Regards tech-transfer as successful Percentage of respondents)	Objective success		
				Firms with average revenues over HUF 10 million/year	Firms with positive growth rate (%)	Firms with employment growth (%)
Agriculture	22.5	38.9	44.4	5.6	61.1	38.9
Architecture	16.3	69.2	53.8	46.2	46.2	61.5
Biotech, biomedical engineering	11.3	11.1	33.3	33.3	33.3	22.2
Chemicals, pharmaceutics	15.0	50.0	58.3	50.0	58.3	50.0
Energy, environment	20.0	43.8	37.5	31.3	37.5	37.5
Food engineering	6.3	60.0	60.0	20.0	100.0	40.0
ICT, electronics	22.5	50.0	66.7	44.4	61.1	55.6
Mechanics, automation, materials	15.0	50.0	66.7	58.3	33.3	25.0
Medical and health services	16.3	23.1	30.8	30.8	38.5	7.7
Other	6.3	40.0	20.0	0.0	60.0	0.0
Total/average	151.3	43.6	47.2	32.0	52.9	33.8

Table 13.   **The relationship between the university and the spin-off firm.**

	Frequency	%
The university contributed to the firm (e.g., with infrastructure, IP).	24	30.0
The university has an ownership stake in the firm.	4	5.0
1 = The university is a huge hindrance to academic entrepreneurship.	10	12.5
2	15	18.8
3	21	26.3
4	25	31.3
5	5	6.3
6	3	3.8
7 = The university helps a lot in entrepreneurial activities.	1	1.3

to 30% of spin-off firms with some tangible or intangible assets, still, only 5% of academic entrepreneurs share the ownership of their firm with the mother institution (Table 13). The majority of the firm owners are dissatisfied with the support received from the university: almost 9 out of 10 respondents regard the role of the university negative or neutral in academic entrepreneurship.

According to chi-square tests and correlation coefficients, the university environment does not influence the success of spin-offs: whether the university has contributed to the firm with tangible or intangible assets, or if it has a share in it does not relate to the objective or subjective performance of the firm. Even the perceived amount of help academic entrepreneurs receive from the university is unrelated to their success.

An interview survey of nearly 40 Hungarian university spin-offs (Becsky-Nagy & Erdős, 2012) found that about two-thirds of the academic entrepreneurs whose firm had relatively strong university ties were encouraged by a colleague, the university technology transfer office, or an investor/businessperson to spin-out. However, apart from informal discussions with university colleagues, these academic entrepreneurs were not inclined to cooperate with the university either.[3]

---

[3] Cooperation in most cases included the use of university infrastructure (laboratory and office equipment) and the employment of PhD students; while about half of the respondents were engaged in government financed R&D and joint publications with university co-workers (Becsky-Nagy & Erdős, 2012).

Table 14. Human and financial resources of academic spin-off firms.

Share of firms with at least one employee	63.7%
Share of firms with employees having industrial work experience	43.8%
Share of firms with employees having a PhD degree	40.0%
Share of firms drawing on the help of external experts	26.3%
Share of firms taking loans from financial institutions	12.5%
Share of firms receiving venture capital	8.8%

The human and financial capital of academic firms .

As seen in Table 14, less than half of the academic ventures reported to hire one or more employees with industrial work experience; 4 out of 10 respondents employ researchers with a PhD degree. The number of employees with industrial work experience have a significant ($p < 0.05$) and positive relationship with every objective and subjective success indicator (except for the firm's age); its link is relatively strong with subjective entrepreneurial success ($r = 0.45$). The number of employees with a PhD degree is significantly associated to the firm's revenue ($r = 0.33$, $p < 0.01$).

An important barrier to the growth of university spin-offs in Hungary is academic entrepreneurs' insufficient business management skills and experiences (Imreh & Kosztopulosz, 2012). In spite of their insufficient business skills, spin-offs resort to external experts on an *ad hoc* basis: about one-quarter of the academic entrepreneurs have asked the advice of consultants and other experts in the areas of business development, business law, etc. Younger and larger firms are more likely to draw on external expertise ($p < 0.01$). Nearly half of the spin-offs (46.3%) have prepared a business plan, and about one fourth (23.8%) carried out a market research with or without the help of external business professionals. Spin-off companies that make business plans are larger in terms of revenue and employee headcount, and also grow faster ($p < 0.01$).

Lastly, 12.5% of the respondents have drawn on bank loans and 8.8% on venture capital. Academic entrepreneurs who have received a loan have larger firms, higher revenue and more employees (19.1 versus 5.9, on average). Similarly, those who resort to the support of venture capitalists have more employees than their counterparts (29.3 versus 5.4). Despite the fact that technology-oriented firms with high growth potential are more likely to receive venture capital than other companies (Becsky-Nagy, 2014), private equity is not a typical way of financing spin-off firms in Hungary. Instead, firms rely primarily on their own resources, non-refundable state funds, and

3F (family, friends, and fools) in the seed and start-up phases (Becsky-Nagy & Erdős, 2012).[4]

Summary and Conclusions

Eastern European countries offer a special context for examining academic entrepreneurship, although the individual dimensions of entrepreneurial motivation and success are very similar all around the world. In this chapter I presented the findings of a questionnaire survey of 80 academic entrepreneurs from 10 Hungarian research universities carried out in 2014.

I reviewed the possible motivations of university faculty members to start a firm, and found that the literature is somewhat inconsistent regarding the basic entrepreneurial motivations, not to mention the motivations of academic ventures. The Humboldtian and socialist traditions of Hungarian universities provide faculty members with motives that do not match the 'idyllic' prospects of knowledge-intensive start-ups. In Hungary, a relatively high proportion (two-thirds) of the faculty members who found firms can be regarded as *subsistence* entrepreneurs, who are relatively strongly motivated by necessity and by the need to maintain their own and their families' living standards. A smaller proportion of academic entrepreneurs resembles the classic type of spin-off owners (called *transformational* in this chapter) popularized in the literature of the Western World (Western Europe and North America). While supplementing university salaries is an important motivation for a relatively large share of Hungarian academic firm founders, entrepreneurial success is mostly related to the research-intensity of their firms: both objective and subjective success increase if the founder is more motivated by the desire to support his/her research activity through the firm.

Besides motivations and objective success indicators, I examined the subjective aspects of entrepreneurial success in an academic environment. In addition to financial rewards, university entrepreneurs consider success as something related to the academic profession, including such elements as learning, gaining recognition or solving problems. Accordingly, the need

---

[4] Spin-off companies that have stronger university ties appear to have a dependent relationship with the central state; they see their most important financing possibilities in grant applications and non-refundable government sources: many expect the government to support them directly with 'soft' money, and only a few of them try to obtain external funding from the market (Becsky-Nagy, 2013).

for achievement and the need for independence are relatively strongly related to their perceived (subjective) entrepreneurial success.

Motivations and success are associated with the innovativeness and IP rights of spin-off firms. *Transformational* spin-offs, compared to *subsistence* ones, are more strongly motivated by growth, R&D, market opportunities and implementing innovative ideas, are better equipped with intellectual properties, offer more innovative products and services, and are more successful in both objective and subjective terms. If we look at firms in terms of their industrial profile, it is not easy to draw clear conclusions. Firms of one industry are more successful according to one or two criteria, while firms in other industries show better performance regarding other criteria. In general we can state that engineering firms appear to be more successful than firms in the medical and biomedical sciences, and biotechnology. This is somewhat unexpected, as the rise of university–industry technology transfer in the U.S. is partly attributed to the emergence of biotechnology (Rosenberg, 2003; Renault, 2006).

The finding that approximately 9 out of 10 faculty run firms operate outside the institution, i.e., without shared ownership or profit with the university, draws attention to the unsettled relationship between academic entrepreneurs and the university. As faculty members and especially entrepreneurial ones regard university policies and decision making practices to be slow and bureaucratic for making efficient market transactions, they are liable to divert their innovative efforts away from the university into their own firms. More surprising is that support received from the university does not seem to affect the success of spin-off firms. This finding is especially interesting in the light of the recent changes in the national innovation policy that encourage universities to increase their involvement in commercializing inventions resulting from university research.

The results of this study suggest that about one-third of the university spin-offs in Hungary are small (one-person) businesses. Less than half of them have achieved some growth in terms of revenues and only 35% have hired new employees since their creation. Drawing on external funds such as venture capital, and complementary human resources are only typical of larger firms. The low growth potential of many university spin-offs can be largely attributed to the fact that their founder–managers are only part time and non-professional entrepreneurs, who understandably do not want to give up their relatively secure university positions and jeopardize their social status and university income to focus on their firms full time. Consequently, they have several academic obligations in addition to running a firm. As academic career is primarily based on publications, many faculty members are inclined to complement their salaries by applying for government grants to carry on with their favorite research topics, while taking risks, satisfying real industry needs, and meeting uncomfortable industry deadlines are less popular among them. The majority of the university entrepreneurs in Hungary seem to have relatively weak intrinsic motivations and limited resources in terms of time, skills, and money to develop their firms and become transformational academic entrepreneurs.

References

Balázs, K. 1993. Lessons from an economy with limited market functions: R&D in Hungary in the 1980s. *Research Policy*, 22, 02/1993, 537–552.

Balázs, K. 1996. Academic entrepreneurs and their role in 'knowledge' transfer. *STEEP Discussion Paper*, No. 37. University of Sussex, Brighton.

Baldini, N., Grimaldi, R. & Sobrero, M. 2007. To patent or not to patent? A survey of Italian inventors on motivations, incentives, and obstacles to university patenting, *Scientometrics*, 70(2), 333–354.

Barakonyi, K. 2004. Egyetemi kormányzás. Merre tart Európa? (The running of universities. Where is Europe heading?). *Közgazdasági Szemle (Economic Review — monthly of the Hungarian Academy of Sciences)*, LI(6), 584–599.

Baum, J. R., Locke, E. A. & Smith, K. G. 2001. A multidimensional model of venture growth, *Academy of Management Journal*, 44(2), 292–303.

Becsky-Nagy, P. 2013. Venture capital in Hungarian academic spin-offs. *Annals of the University of Oradea Economic Science*, 1(2), 351–360.

Becsky-Nagy, P. 2014. Growth and venture capital investment in technology-based small firms. *Annals of the University of Oradea Economic Science*, 2(2), 828–836.

Becsky-Nagy, P. & Erdős, K. 2012. Az egyetemi spin-off cégek magyar valósága (The reality of university spin-offs in Hungary). In *Spin-off cégek, vállalkozók és technológiatranszfer a legjelentősebb hazai egyetemeken (Spin-off firms, entrepreneurs and technology transfer at major Hungarian universities)*, Z. Makra (ed.), 207–234. Universitas Szeged.

Blake, D. A. 1993. The university's role in marketing research discoveries. *Chronicle of Higher Education*, May 12, A52.

Bonaccorsi, A. & Daraio, C. 2007. *Universities and Strategic Knowledge Creation — Specialization and Performance in Europe*. Cheltenham: Edward Elgar.

Brockhaus, R. H. & Horwitz, P. S. (1986). The psychology of the entrepreneur. In *The Art and Science of Entrepreneurship*, A. Sexton and R. Smilor (eds.), pp. 25–48. Ballinger, Cambridge, MA.

Buzás, N. 2004. A vállalkozói szellem szerepe a spin-off cégek alapításában. In *A szociális identitás, az információ és a piac*, L. Czagány and L. Garai (eds.), pp. 257–266. Szeged, SZTE Gazdaságtudományi Kar Közleményei, JATEPress.

Carayannis, E., Rogers, E. M., Kurihara, K. & Allbritton, M. 1998. High-technology spin-offs from government R&D laboratories and research universities. *Technovation*, 18(1), 1–11.

Chell, E. 2008. *The Entrepreneurial Personality. A Social Construction.* Second edition. London: Routledge.

Chiesa, V. & Piccaluga, A. 2000. Exploitation and diffusion of public research: The case of academic spin-off companies in Italy. *R&D Management*, 30(4), 329–340.

Choi, Y. & Lee, J.-J. 2000. Success factors for transferring technology to spin-off applications: The case of the technology property rights concession program in Korea. *The Journal of Technology Transfer*, 25(2), 237–246.

D'Este, P. & Perkmann, M. 2011. Why do academics engage with industry? The entrepreneurial university and individual motivations. *Journal of Technology Transfer*, 36, 316–339.

De Silva, L. R. 2013. The dynamisms of entrepreneurial motivation: A case of spin-off formation by academics operating in a resource constrained environment. *Triple Helix International Conference 2013*.

Doutriaux, J. & Peterman, D. 1982. Technology transfer and academic entrepreneurship. In *Proceedings of Frontiers of Entrepreneurship Research*, Babson College Conference, 430–448.

Educational Authority. 2012. Statistics of Hungarian higher education. Available at: http://www.oktatas.hu/felsooktatas/felsooktatasi_statisztikak. Accessed on 15 May 2015.

Egeln, J., Gottschalk, S., Rammer, C. & Spielkamp, A. 2003. *Spinoff-Grundungen aus der offentlichen Forschung in Deutschland. (Spin-off foundations from public research in Germany)*. Working Paper. Available at: http://ub-madoc.bib.uni-mannheim.de/966/. Accessed on 11 May 2015.

Erdős, K. & Varga, A. 2010. Az egyetemi vállalkozó — legenda vagy valóság az európai regionális fejlődés elősegítésére? (University entrepreneurs — legend or fact in aiding European regional development?) *Közgazdasági Szemle (Economic Review — monthly of the Hungarian Academy of Sciences)*, LVII(5), 457–472.

Ernesto, A. J. & Bosma, N. 2014. *Global Entrepreneurship Monitor, Global Report 2013*. Available at: http://www.gemconsortium.org/docs/download/3106.

Etzkowitz, H. 1998. The norms of entrepreneurial science: Cognitive effects of the new university–industry linkages. *Research Policy*, 27(8), 823–833.

Etzkowitz, H. 2002. *MIT and the Rise of Entrepreneurial Science*. Routledge, London & New York.

Fini, R., Grimaldi, R. & Sobrero, M. 2009. Factors fostering academics to start up new ventures: an assessment of italian founders' incentives. *Journal of Technology Transfer*, 34(4), 308–402.

Franklin, S. J., Wright, M. & Lockett, A. 2001. Academic and surrogate entrepreneurs in university spin-out companies. *Journal of Technology Transfer*, 26(1–2), 127–141.

Franzoni, C. & Lissoni, F. 2009. Academic entrepreneurs: critical issues and lessons for Europe. In *Universities, Knowledge Transfer and Regional Development: Geography,*

Entrepreneurship and Policy, A. Varga (ed.), pp. 163–190. Cheltenham: Edward Elgar.

Gaponenko, N. 1995. Transformation of the research system in a transitional society: The case of Russia. *Social Studies of Science,* 25(4), 685–703.

HCSO. 2014. Tables (STADAT) — Times series of annual data — Research and development, Hungarian Central Statistical Office. Available at: https://www.ksh.hu/stadat_annual_3_4. Accessed on 20 October 2014.

Helm, R. & Mauroner, O. 2007. Success of research-based spin-offs. State-of-the-art and guidelines for further research. *Review of Managerial Science,* 1(3), 237–270.

Henricks, M. (2002). *Not Just a Living: The Complete Guide to Creating a Business That Gives You a Life.* Perseus, Cambridge, MA.

HIPO. 2005. Módszertani Útmutató a közfinanszírozású kutatóhelyek szellemitulajdon-kezelési szabályzatainak kidolgozásához (Methodological guidelines for the formulation of IP management policies at public research organizations). National Research, Development and Innovation (NRDI) Office. http://nkfih.gov.hu/hivatal/kiadvanyok-kfi/modszertani-utmutato. Accessed on 10 February 2015.

Hrubos, I., Polónyi, I., Szentannai, Á. & Veroszta, Z. 2004. *A gazdálkodó egyetem (The Entrepreneurial University).* Új Mandátum Pub., Budapest.

Imreh, S. & Kosztopulosz, A. 2012. Az egyetemi spin-off folyamatokat akadályozó tényezők szakértői interjúk tükrében (Barriers to university spin-off processes in the light of expert interviews). In Makra Zs. (ed.), *Spin-off cégek, vállalkozók és technológia-transzfer a legjelentősebb hazai egyetemeken (Spin-off firms, entrepreneurs and technology transfer at major Hungarian universities).* Szeged: Universitas. pp. 151–174.

Inzelt, A. 1999. Kutatóegyetem a finanszírozás tükrében (Researching university as reflected by financing). *Közgazdasági Szemle (Economic Review — monthly of the Hungarian Academy of Sciences),* XLVI(4), 346–361.

Kõnig, S., Langhauser, M. & Cesinger, B. 2012. Subjective success in an entrepreneurial career — the case of work-life-balance: Results from a large scale survey in Germany (summary). *Frontiers of Entrepreneurship Research,* 32(5), Article 12.

Kuratko, D. F. & Hodgetts, R. M. 1998. *Entrepreneurship: A Contemporary Approach.* Fort Worth: Dryden Press.

Lam, A. 2011. What motivates academic scientists to engage in research commercialization: 'Gold', 'ribbon' or 'puzzle'? *Research Policy,* 40(10), 1354–1368.

Landry, R., Amara, N. & Ouimet, M. 2007. Determinants of knowledge transfer: Evidence from Canadian university researchers in natural sciences and engineering. *Journal of Technology Transfer,* 32(6), 561–592.

Lepenies, W. 1992. *Aufstieg und Fall der Intellektuellen in Europa. (The Rise and Fall of Intellectuals in Europe),* Edition Pandora — European Lectures I, Frankfurt am Main, New York and Paris.

Link, A. N., Siegel, D. S. & Bozeman, B. 2006. An empirical analysis of the propensity of academics to engage in informal university technology transfer. *Rensselaer*

Working Papers in Economics 0610, Rensselaer Polytechnic Institute, Department of Economics.

Máté, D. 2014. Can intellectual property rights impact directly on productivity: A case study in manufacturing industries. *Vezetéstudomány (Budapest Management Review)*, 45(11), 25–32.

McClelland, D. C. 1961. *The Achieving Society*. Van Nostrand, Princeton, NJ. Reprint: Martino Fine Books, December 10, 2010.

Morales-Gualdrón, S. T., Gutiérrez-Gracia, A. & Roig Dobón, S. 2009. The entrepreneurial motivation in academia: a multidimensional construct. *International Entrepreneurship and Management Journal*, 5(3), 301–317.

Morrison, A., Rimmington, M. & Williams, C. 1999. *Entrepreneurship in the Hospitality, Tourism and Leisure Industries*. Butterworth-Heinemann, Oxford.

Novotny, A. 2013. Az egyetemi-ipari technológiatranszfer sajátosságai Magyarországon (The features of university-industry technology transfer in Hungary). *Közgazdasági Szemle (Economic Review — monthly of the Hungarian Academy of Sciences)*, LV(10), 1119–1139.

Novotny, A. 2011. Vállalkozó egyetemek Magyarországon: technológiatranszfer-aktivitás és — attitűd a magyar egyetemi kutatók körében (Entrepreneurial Universities in Hungary: Technology Transfer Activity and Attitude among Hungarian University Researchers). Ph.D. dissertation. Budapest University of Technology and Economics.

Nybom, T. 2006. Creative intellectual destruction or destructive political creativity? Critical reflections on the future of European 'knowledge production'. In *The European Research University*, S. Strömholm, G. Neave, K. Blückert and T. Nybom (eds.). New York: Palgrave Macmillan.

Owen-Smith, J. & Powell, W. 2001. To patent or not: Faculty decisions and institutional success at technology transfer. *The Journal of Technology Transfer*, 26(1–2), 99–114.

Pirnay, F., Surlemont, B. & Nlemvo, F. 2003. Toward a typology of university spin-offs. *Small Business Economics*, 21(4), 355–369.

Renault, C. S. 2006. Academic capitalism and university incentives for faculty entrepreneurship. *Journal of Technology Transfer*, 31(2), 227–239.

Reynolds, P., Bygrave, W. D., Autio, E. & Hay, M. 2002. *Global Entrepreneurship Monitor: 2002 Executive Monitor*. London Business School, London.

Roberts, E. 1991. *Entrepreneurs in High Technology*. New York: Oxford University Press.

Rosenberg, N. 2003. America's entrepreneurial universities. In *The Emergence of Entrepreneurship Policy. Governance, Start-ups, and Growth in the U.S. Knowledge Economy*, D. M. Hart (ed.), pp. 113–140. Cambridge University Press, New York.

Rothaermel, F. T., Agung, S. D. & Jiang, L. 2007. University entrepreneurship: A taxonomy of the literature. *Industrial and Corporate Change*, 16(4), 691–791.

Schoar, A. 2009. The divide between subsistence and transformational entrepreneurship. In: J. Lerner and S. Stern (eds.), *Innovation Policy and the Economy*, NBER book vol. 10, 57–81.

Shane, S. A. 2004. *Academic Entrepreneurship: University Spinoffs And Wealth Creation,* New Horizons in Entrepreneurship Series. Cheltenham: Edward Elgar.

Shane, S. A. & Venkataraman, S. 2000. The promise of entrepreneurship as a field of research. *Academy of Management Review,* 26(1), 13–17.

Swamidass, P. & Vulasa, V. 2009. Why university inventions rarely produce income? Bottlenecks in university technology transfer. *The Journal of Technology Transfer,* 34(4), 343–363.

Szabó, T. 2010. *A felsőoktatási intézmények és oktatóik innovációs teljesítményét befolyásoló szervezetszociológiai, szociológia, közgazdasági és munkagazdasági tényezők és sajátosságok (Sociological and economic factors and characteristics influencing the innovation performance of higher education institutions and academic faculty).* In *Felsőoktatási intézmények és az innováció (Higher Education Institutions and Innovation),* Á. Kotsis and I. Polónyi (eds.). University of Debrecen, Faculty of Economics and Business Administration, COMPETITIO Books 11.

University of Tennessee. 2015. Startup business failure rate by industry. Statistic Brain Research Institute. Available at: http://www.statisticbrain.com/startup-failure-by-industry/ (Original source: Entrepreneur Weekly, Small Business Development Center, Bradley University, University of Tennessee Research).

Vught, F. V. 2004. Closing the European knowledge gap? Challenges for the European universities of the 21th century. In *Reinventing the Research University,* L. E. Weber and J. J. Duderstadt (eds.). Economica, London, Paris, Geneve.

Weatherston, J. 1995. Academic entrepreneurs: Is a spin-off company too risky? International Council of Small Business, *Proceedings of the 40th International Council on Small Business,* Sydney, 18–21 June 1995.

Chapter 7

University Spin-Outs in the UK

Mike Wright

Enterprise Research Centre, Imperial College Business School, London
University of Ghent, Belgium
mike.wright@imperial.ac.uk

Kun Fu

Loughborough University, United Kingdom
k.fu@imperial.ac.uk

This chapter provides an overview of the creation and performance of university spin-out firms in the full population of UK Higher Education Institutions (HEIs). We provide an overview of the literature relating to academic spin-outs in the UK and identify areas regarding the spin-out landscape that have not been addressed. We consider trends in the demographics of UK university spin-outs. Areas for policy development and for further research are discussed. Given the changing landscape regarding government views about the role of universities and the entrepreneurial objectives of many faculty and, especially, students, we suggest there is a need for an evolution of what is regarded as university start-up activity, with consequences for support activities and for the kind of data collected by researchers.

Introduction

The creation of new ventures to commercialize university research is potentially an important mechanism for technology diffusion that is seen to have significant economic impact at national and regional levels (Garnsey & Heffernan, 2005; Smith & Ho, 2006; Vincett, 2010; Wright *et al.*, 2008).

In the UK, universities have increasingly enforced their ownership rights to the IP generated by academic scientists, abolishing the professor's privilege in 1977 (Lockett *et al.*, 2013). While there has been attention to the nature and policies adopted by UK universities regarding spin-out promotion, there has been little analysis of the demographics of the spin-outs created and their outcomes in terms of success and failure.

This chapter seeks to fill this gap by providing an overview of the creation and performance of university spin-out firms in the full population of UK Higher Education Institutions (HEIs).

This chapter unfolds as follows. In the next section we provide a brief overview of the literature relating to academic spin-outs in the UK and identify areas regarding the spin-out landscape that have not been addressed. We then turn to consider trends in the demographics of UK university spin-outs first outlining the method we adopted to collect data followed by our analysis. In the final section we discuss areas for policy development and for further research.

Previous Evidence on University Spin-outs in the UK

Prior studies of university spin-outs in the UK have been carried out at both the macro university level and at the enterprise level. Siegel and Wright (2015) recently review studies on academic entrepreneurship worldwide, including the UK. We build on and extend their review relating to UK studies.

UK universities experienced a rapid increase in focus on the creation of spin-outs from the late 1990s, accompanied by a growth in the establishment of technology transfer offices at this time (Lockett *et al.*, 2014). Much of the early evidence on spin-out activity in the UK relates to the university level. The focus of these studies was on the drivers of the extent of spin-out activity by different types of universities and the resources and capabilities of their technology transfer offices (TTOs).

Evidence shows that universities most successful in generating the largest numbers of startups have clear, well-defined strategies regarding the formation and management of spin-outs (Lockett *et al.*, 2003). "Old" universities especially have well established research reputations, world-class scientists, and are typically receptive to entrepreneurial startups. New universities, that is those established prior to the elimination of the binary divide between universities and polytechnics in 1992, tend to be weaker in academic research and less flexible with regard to entrepreneurial ventures. Franklin *et al.* (2001) find that the most significant barriers to the adoption of entrepreneurial-friendly policies are cultural and informational and that the universities generating the most start-ups (i.e., old universities) are those that have the most favorable policies regarding surrogate (external) entrepreneurs. This dichotomy between pre and post 1992 universities has probably now become quite a blunt categorization since in the intervening more than two decades the distinction in terms of research activity has become blurred. As the results of the (approximately) five yearly assessment of the quality of research across UK universities, the Research Excellence Framework (REF), shows, many newer universities have developed research strengths in particular areas. Accordingly, there is a need to the extent of spin-out activity from a different perspective, such as in terms of quartiles of universities' standings.

Incentives provided for academic entrepreneurs matter. Lockett *et al.* (2003) find that equity ownership was more widely distributed among the members of the spin-off company in the case of the more successful universities. UK evidence also suggests that the academics developing high-tech ventures are typically key researchers in their fields (Vohora *et al.*, 2004).

There is an important relationship between the resources and capabilities of U.K. TTOs and the rate of startup formation at their respective universities (Lockett & Wright, 2005). There is a positive correlation between startup formation and university spending on protection of intellectual property rights, TTO business development capabilities, and the amount allocated to faculty in royalty distribution formulae. But they also found that universities with the highest number of spin-outs obtaining venture capital finance were the ones with the most developed routines and capabilities. However, this study did not provide insights into the extent of venture capital versus business angel funding for spin-outs, nor did it analyze other aspects of spin-out performance.

On a note of caution, there is also UK evidence however that the nature and extent of spin-outs may be influenced by the various actors involved in academic entrepreneurship seeking to shape this activity, in order to meet their own goals, which may be at variance with those of policymakers and senior university management (Lockett *et al.*, 2014).

Further, there are some question marks over the efficiency of TTOs in promoting academic entrepreneurship. Focusing on licensing activity, Chapple *et al.* (2007) show that UK TTOs on average display low levels of absolute efficiency in this area with decreasing returns to scale evident. Taking into account the university's propensity to generate start-up companies based on technologies developed at these institutions as well as licensing activities, Siegel *et al.* (2008) find that US universities are more efficient than UK universities.

At the spin-out venture level, UK evidence shows both that spin-outs vary in the nature of their business models and that these business models change as the ventures evolve (Druilhe & Garnsey, 2004; Vohora *et al.*, 2004). Longitudinal qualitative interview data from the UK and Norway by Rasmussen *et al.* (2011) indicates that spin-out evolution following creation requires the development of competencies or capabilities that facilitate the *creation* of new development paths that depart from existing practices in the academic context. First, career academic entrepreneurs need to acquire the ability to attract new team members with industrial experience who in turn can identify and interact with industrial partners in order to develop an opportunity refinement competency. Second, career academic entrepreneurs need to evolve the credibility and entrepreneurial experience that facilitates interaction between the entrepreneurial team and external resource providers. Third, career academic entrepreneurs need to evolve a championing competency from the internal university context to include external champions; this is especially critical because of the general lack of industrial and entrepreneurial experience among academic entrepreneurs.

The networks of academic scientists becoming entrepreneurs become critical to the development of spin-outs. Based on data from UK academic scientists, Nicolaou and Birley (2003) found that variations in the extent to which academics were embedded in tie networks external or internal to the university impact spin-out growth trajectories.

Mosey and Wright (2007) adopt a more fine-grained perspective recognizing that academic entrepreneurs have different levels of experience as entrepreneurs. They find important differences between the structure, content and governance of social networks utilized to develop early stage ventures by types of academic entrepreneurs in the UK with differing levels of entrepreneurship experience. They suggest that habitual entrepreneurs (i.e., those with prior business ownership experience) have broader social networks and are more effective in developing network ties to gain equity finance and management knowledge. Less experienced entrepreneurs, either nascent or novice entrepreneurs, likely encounter structural holes between their scientific research networks and industry networks. These structural holes constrain their ability to recognize opportunities and gain credibility for their ventures. They suggest that while support initiatives, such as TTOs, help attract industry partners to selected novice entrepreneurs, business ownership experience is critical to learning how to build relationships with experienced managers and potential equity investors. The development of social capital for nascent and novice entrepreneurs is influenced by the human capital related to the entrepreneurs' discipline-base. Individual academic entrepreneurs with an engineering and material sciences base were more likely to build network ties outside their scientific research networks than those in biological sciences and pharmacy. However, we lack detailed breakdowns of the extent of spin-out activities in different scientific areas and the extent to which these areas are able to attract external funding from venture capital and business angels.

It has also become evident from further in-depth analysis in both the UK and Norway that weak and strong social ties change over the evolution of the spin-out rather than remaining constant (Rasmussen *et al.*, 2015). Weak ties play a central role in the opportunity refinement competency of academic entrepreneurs since they facilitate opportunity recognition and development. They provide a broader base that enables opportunities to be transitioned from a research orientation to a business orientation. In contrast, strong ties contribute towards resource acquisition and championing competencies at the initial development phase because the lack of track record of the new spin-out venture means they need to draw on existing contacts to acquire the resources they need.

Finally, the location of the UK university from which the spin-out emanates may also influence the development of spin-outs through their impact on the ability to access resources. It has been suggested that spin-offs created in universities outside the so-called 'golden triangle' of London and the South East of England may be at a disadvantage in raising venture finance for growth (Smith & Ho, 2006). However, Mueller *et al.* (2012) show that spin-offs in regions outside London and the South East are as likely to be able to raise venture finance if they are able to signal the quality of their ventures and the expertise of their entrepreneurs. Previous UK research lacks an analysis of the regional distribution of spin-out activity.

Method

To address the gaps in the evidence on the spin-out landscape in the UK identified above, we focus on spin-out firms in which the university had an equity stake. We analyzed firms spun out from the full population of UK higher education institutions during a 13-year period from the beginning of 2000 to the end of 2012. Similar population-wide studies of university spin-outs have been also carried out in other European countries. Bolzani *et al.* (2014) analyzed the population of 935 Italian university spin-offs established since 2000 drawing upon data from the TASTE project (Taking Stock: External engagement by academics). Borlaug and colleagues

(2009) conducted an overview of the characteristics and performance of university spin-outs established since 1996 in Norway, based on the database maintained by the Research Council of Norway's FORNY-program, which is designed to support universities in commercializing research results.

In the current study, we collected firm-level data mainly from the Spinouts UK Survey (http://www.spinoutsuk.co.uk/). This is the first survey to investigate spin-out activities taking a cumulative 'bottom up' approach, compiling data company by company and updating it regularly. It includes all spin-out companies from universities and HEIs across the UK since 2000, with information about firms' origins, activity, and their current status, providing a regularly updated continuous time series of data. This data was further complemented and corroborated by data from FAME (https://fame.bvdinfo.com) and Zephyr (https://zephyr.bvdinfo.com), which provides us with information about merger and acquisition deals that firms had been through and whether or not and the when a firm had received an angel investment or a VC funding round since foundation.

We collected university-level data, first, through the European University Data Collection project (EUMIDA) database. From this source one can access to harmonized, EU-level, time-invariant information on: universities' localization, legal status, year of establishment, educational fields, and whether the university emphasizes Science Technology Engineering and Mathematics (STEM). The EUMIDA database stores information on 2,500 higher education institutions from 29 EU countries. Data refers to year 2008 (for details see, European Commission 2010). We then relied on national sources, collecting time-variant information on universities. Data on size and operations of universities in the UK can be retrieved through the Higher Education Information Database for Institutions (HEIDI) (https://heidi.hesa.ac.uk/Home.aspx). Data on universities' intellectual eminence (i.e., national university quality rankings) has been assessed using the UK University League Tables and Rankings from the Complete University Guide (http://www.thecompleteuniversityguide.co.uk/leaguetables/rankings).

The final dataset comprises 113 universities and their 1359 spin-outs during the period from 2000 to 2012.

Creation of University Spin-outs in the UK

In light of our review of previous literature, we examine the following dimensions of the UK spin-out landscape: overall trends in university spin-outs, sector distributions, location of spin-outs, quality of universities and their spin-outs, and performance. Given that the UK regime for financial reporting exempts smaller private firms from providing full income statements and that many spin-outs fall within this category access to financial data is highly restricted. Indeed, many spin-outs may not be generating income from the revenue from products but rather building the value of their technology (Clarysse *et al.*, 2011). Accordingly, our analysis of performance focuses on the extent to which they are able to attract external sources of finance, notably venture capital and business angel finance, the extent to which they have experienced a successful exit through Initial Public Offering (IPO) or acquisition, and whether or not they have survived as an independent entity.

Trend of University Spin-outs in the UK

The annual number of university spin-outs created in the UK has declined over time. In the 2000–2005 period 120 or more spin-out firms were generally created annually but since 2010 especially numbers have fallen sharply to half this level (see Figure 1).

Sector Distribution of UK Spin-Outs

Spin-out firms were created in a range of industrial sectors. The top three sectors for spin-outs are: Scientific R&D and consulting, Information and Communication Technology (ICT), and manufacturing (see Figure 2). Firms spun out into Scientific R&D and consulting sector accounted for nearly half of total population of UK spin-out firms over the observed 13 years period. It is also interesting to note that there have been a number of ventures in

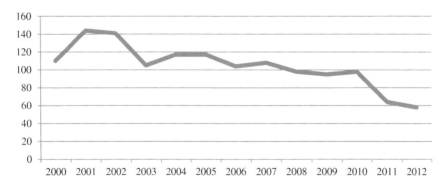

Figure 1.   Total university spin-outs in the UK from 2000 to 2012.

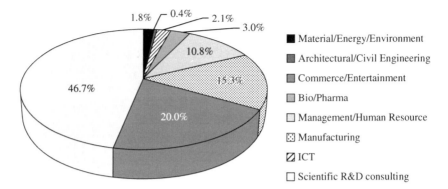

Figure 2.   Sector distribution of UK spin-outs.

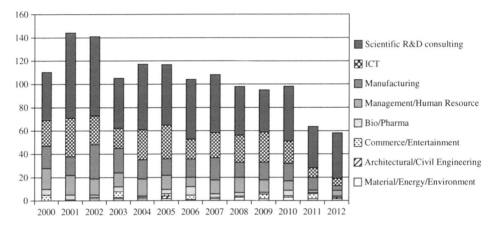

Figure 3.   Sector distribution of UK spin-outs from 2000 to 2012.

sectors not traditionally associated with spin-out activity, notably management and human resources as well as commerce/entertainment. The scientific R&D and consulting sector has been always the dominating sector in terms of attracting spin-out firms over time. Spin-outs entering into ICT sector has seen a quicker decline in more recent years compared to those entering into other sectors (see Figure 3).

Location of University Spin-outs

According to the postcode from the registered company address, England is the home to two thirds (66.7%) of the total spin-out firms over the 13 years of observation period. The Greater London region accommodates about 13.2% of total spin-out firms, followed by South East England in which 11.5% of total spin-out firms are based. Over a quarter (26.9%) of spin-out firms are located in Scotland in the same period of time. Northern Ireland and Wales accounted for only 6% of overall spin-out firms established between 2000 and 2012 (see Figure 4). The decline in the annual number of spin-outs appears to be longer established in respect of English universities, with the decline in the number of spin-outs in Scotland being more recent (see Figure 5).

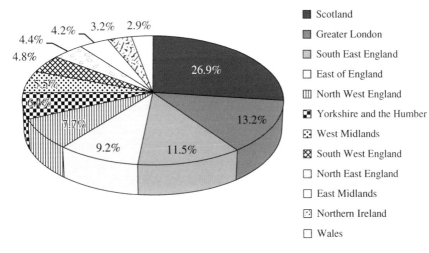

Figure 4.   Regional distribution of university spin-outs in the UK.

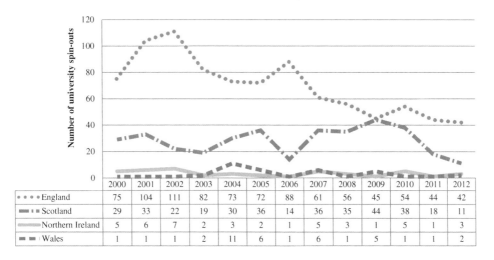

	2000	2001	2002	2003	2004	2005	2006	2007	2008	2009	2010	2011	2012
England	75	104	111	82	73	72	88	61	56	45	54	44	42
Scotland	29	33	22	19	30	36	14	36	35	44	38	18	11
Northern Ireland	5	6	7	2	3	2	1	5	3	1	5	1	3
Wales	1	1	1	2	11	6	1	6	1	5	1	1	2

Figure 5.   Regional distribution of university spin-outs in the UK overtime.

Quality of Universities and their Spin-outs

In this section, we look at the overall quality of universities and how it is related to the volume of spin-out firms.

We classify the universities into four groups based on the their ranking each year in the UK University League Tables (i.e., the top 25%, the top 25–50%, the bottom 50–25%, and the bottom 25% of universities in the UK). This ranking is calculated by taking into consideration a wide range of factors including university entry standards, student satisfaction, research assessment (quality and intensity), graduate prospects, student–staff ratio, academic services spend, facilities spend, good honours degrees, and degree completion. All data sources come from public domain, such as the Higher Education Statistics Agency (HESA), the National Student Survey and the Research Excellence Framework.[1]

From Figure 6 we see that there is a strong association between university's overall quality and the quantity of spin-out firms from the university. The majority (70.8%) of the spin-out firms established during the period from 2000 to 2012 were spun out from the top 25% universities in the UK. The universities ranked in the top 25–50% of all universities launched a bit less than a quarter (22.9%) of total spin-outs in this period. Only about 6.3% of firms were spun out from the universities ranked in the bottom 50% of all universities.

We see that spin-out firms originated from the top universities had experienced quite big and nearly continuous decreases since 2001. The total number of spin-outs in 2012 was less than half the figure in 2001,

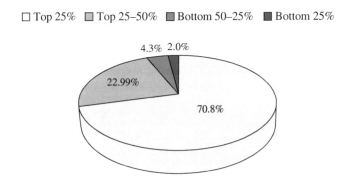

Figure 6.   Quality of universities and their spin-outs.

[1] Methodology of the UK University League Tables is available at http://www.thecompleteuniversityguide.co.uk/league-tables/methodology/.

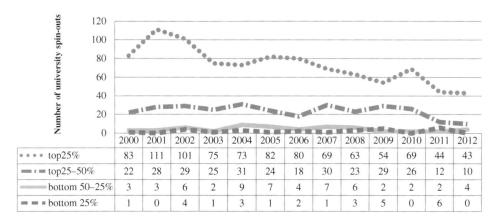

	2000	2001	2002	2003	2004	2005	2006	2007	2008	2009	2010	2011	2012
• • • • top25%	83	111	101	75	73	82	80	69	63	54	69	44	43
━ ı ━ top25–50%	22	28	29	25	31	24	18	30	23	29	26	12	10
▬▬▬ bottom 50–25%	3	3	6	2	9	7	4	7	6	2	2	2	4
━ ━ ▪ bottom 25%	1	0	4	1	3	1	2	1	3	5	0	6	0

Figure 7.   Quality of universities and their spin-outs over time.

reflecting the overall decline in the number of spin-outs noted above (Figure 7).

Performance of University Spin-outs in the UK

To evaluate the performance of university spin-out firms, we expanded the observation time window from the end of 2012 to the time of this study (July, 2015). This enables us to observe the post-entry performance of spin-outs founded in more recent years.

VC-backed university spin-outs

Less than a quarter (24%) of total spin-out firms established between 2000 and 2012 in the UK received at least one round of venture capital funding by the time we carried out this study (July, 2015) (Figure 8). Proportionally speaking, over 30% of spin-out firms in the manufacturing sector between 2000 and 2012 received at least one round of VC funding. During the same period, 28%, 24% and 21% of spin-out firms in Scientific R&D consulting, Bio/Pharmaceuticals and Material/Energy/Environment industry received at least one round of VC funding up until today.

Data shown in Figure 9 indicates that a higher proportion (26%) of spin-out firms from the universities falling in the top 25% of the national university ranking received at least one round of VC funding up until the time of the current study (July, 2015). Interestingly, although there were much fewer spin-out firms originated from the bottom 25% universities

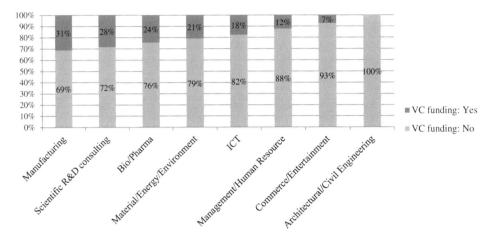

Figure 8.   VC-backed university spin-outs across industrial sectors.

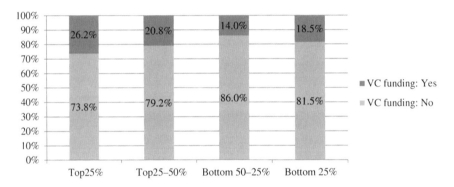

Figure 9.   VC-backed university spin-outs across universities.

compared to other universities, the proportion of firms received VC funding from these universities is not necessarily the lowest (18.5%).

Angel-backed university spin-outs

Angel investments include investments of individual business angel, business angel syndicate, business angel fund, co-investment fund and seed fund (Wright *et al.*, 2015). Compared to VC funding, only a very small share (6.6%) of spin-out firms ever received an angel investment since their foundation (Figure 10), with universities in the top two quartiles being more likely to received it (Figure 11). Comparing Figures 9 and 11 shows that spin-outs in universities in the second quartile are slightly more like to receive business angel funding than those in top quartile universities whereas the position is reversed in respect of venture capital.

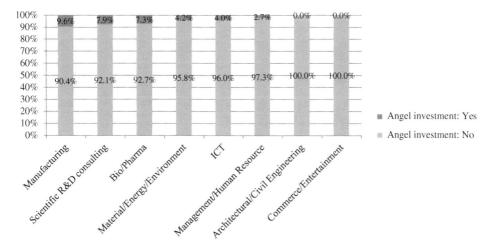

Figure 10.   Angel-backed university spin-outs across industrial sectors.

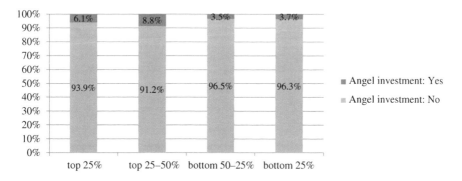

Figure 11.   Angel-backed university spin-outs across universities.

IPOs of university spin-outs

In total, less than 1% of the university spin-outs established between 2000 and 2012, have gone through an IPO by the time of the current study (July, 2015). All of the IPO firms are located in England (i.e., North West England, Yorkshire and the Humber, Greater London, South East England, and South West England).

The sector distribution is quite skewed, with the majority (82%) of the university spin-outs having gone through an IPO coming from the Scientific R&D consulting sector. A small portion is from ICT and manufacture industry. No other sectors have created any university spin-outs that have gone through an IPO (see Figure 12).

Figure 13 shows that spin-outs that went through an IPO during the observation period are concentrated only in universities from the top and

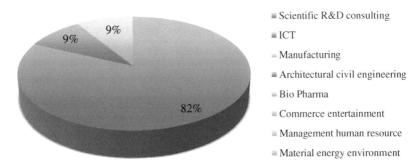

Figure 12.   IPOs of university spin-outs by sector.

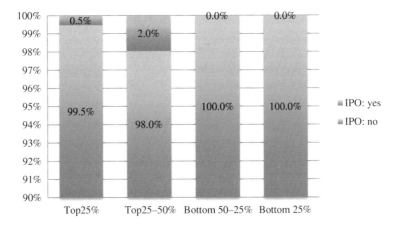

Figure 13.   IPOs of university spin-outs across universities.

second quartile. None of the spin-outs from third and bottom quartile has gone through an IPO.

Mergers and Acquisitions (M&A) deals of university spin-outs

Although much attention is oftentimes devoted to analyzing IPOs as a principal exit route from early stage ventures, in practice most ventures experiencing a successful exit do so through being acquired (Puri & Zarutskie, 2012), especially in Europe (VICO dataset). Following Zephyr terminology, we code any deal where the acquirer ends up with 50% or more of the equity of the target spin-out firm as an "acquisition" as the acquirer now has control of the target spin-out firm. By the time of this study, only about 6.6% of spin-out firms established between 2000 and 2012 had been acquired by other firms. This percentage appears to be substantially lower than that for venture capital backed ventures in the US in particular (Puri & Zarutskie, 2012) and also somewhat less than that for venture capital backed firms in Europe (VICO

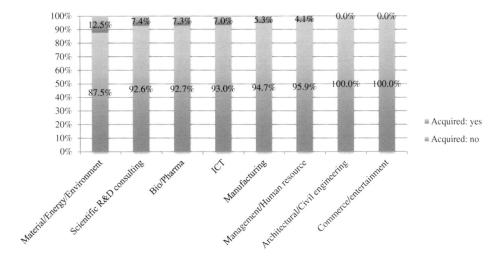

Figure 14. M&A deals of university spin-outs by sector.

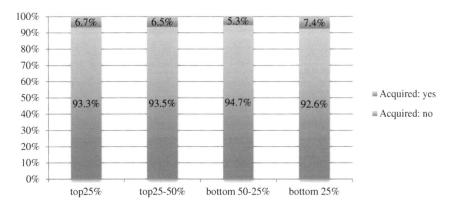

Figure 15. M&A deals of university spin-outs across universities.

database). Firms entering into the Material/Energy/Environment industry have slightly higher chances of being acquired by other firms compared to firms entering into other industries (see Figure 14). Perhaps a little surprisingly, spin-outs in the lowest ranked universities had the highest likelihood of being acquired (Figure 15).

Survival rate of university spin-outs

Among the university spin-out firms established between 2000 and 2012, about two thirds (67%) have survived and one third (33%) have failed (i.e., dissolved or in liquidation) by the time of the current study (July, 2015). This failure rate appears to be substantially greater than that for venture capital backed ventures in the US (Puri & Zarutskie, 2012) and considerably above that for venture capital backed firms in Europe (VICO database). Because of the elapse of time, it is perhaps not surprising that the early spin-outs are more likely to have failed (Figure 16).

About 79% of firms, which spun out into Material/Energy/Environment industry have survived up until today. No less than half of firms spun out into Commerce/Entertainment and Management/Human Resource sector failed by the time we carried out this study. The failure rate was also relatively high for firms entering into Architectural/Civil Engineering industry, at about 40% (see Figure 17).

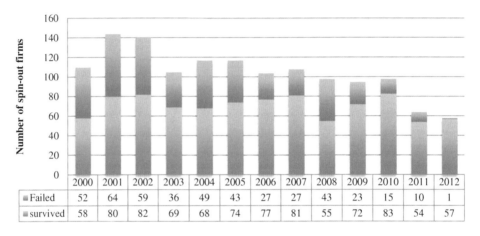

Figure 16.   Spin-outs survival over time.

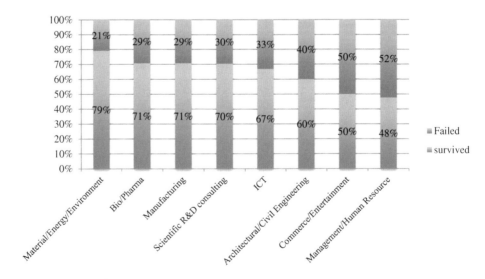

Figure 17.   Survival rate of university spin-outs across industrial sectors.

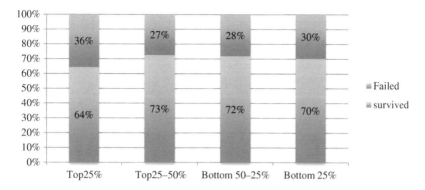

Figure 18.   Survival rate of university spin-outs across universities.

Figure 18 shows that the survival rate of firms spun out from the top 25% universities is a little less than two thirds of the total entries (64%). The survival rates of firms spun out from the rest of the universities are rather similar, which is around 70%.

Discussion and Conclusions

In this chapter, we have examined the literature and trends relating to university spin-outs in the UK. Our aim in reviewing the literature has been to identify areas of the spin-out landscape where systematic data are lacking. We have then presented descriptive analyses of various dimensions of this landscape using a novel longitudinal dataset cover the period 2000–2012.

The decline in the annual number of spin-outs created in the UK over the past decade is quite striking. This may be partly down to the recession during the latter part of the period but also to an increased focus on spin-outs that can create value. In addition, there may be continued shortcomings in the capabilities of TTOs towards seeking out and adding value to potential spin-outs. While demands of the REF have emphasized research output in the form of journal publications, incorporation from the 2014 REF exercise of explicit recognition of the impact of research may to some extent contribute to increased incentives for spinning-out ventures. Recent data from the spin-outs UK survey suggests that there is a slowing down of this decreasing trend. This may be due to the ease with which digital companies can now be started compared to more traditional spin-outs with formal IP. It may also due to the increases in the spread and successes of accelerators and incubators, such as SetSquared. Further, despite the decrease in the total number of university spin-outs, it is worth noting that the UK is more productive in spin-out generation than the US when adjusting for per dollar of GDP and per dollar of tertiary education spending (Autio & Webb, 2015).

Evidence from the experience of academics who were part of the Biotech Yes scheme in the UK (Wright *et al.*, 2012) also indicates a need for further support to enhance the entrepreneurial skills training for academics wanting to commercialize their research as many of the participants in this scheme expressing a serious interest in starting a venture subsequently fail to do so.

More generally, there is a growing need for policy towards academic entrepreneurship in the UK to take a wider focus than on university spin-outs by faculty involving formal IP. Encouragement and support for start-ups which involve less formal IP and which may be smaller and less complex but which nevertheless may have significant local employment benefits (Wright *et al.*, 2008). One further aspect is to encourage mobility of academics to and from corporations as a means of gaining commercial expertise as a precursor to creating a venture (Wright *et al.*, 2012).

The evidence on the decline in spin-outs by faculty also draws attention to the increasing interest in venture creation by students. Universities are responding to and stimulating this trend through the creation of creativity labs and entrepreneurial garages, such as CreateLab at Imperial College, which provides pre-accelerator support for early stage ventures. Given the pattern of spin-out activity outside the most research intensive universities, configuration of TTOs and other support activities to promote student entrepreneurship may be a more feasible route to academic entrepreneurship for those universities without critical mass of world class research.

Given the limited extent of venture capital and business angel funding that we have identified, universities seeking to promote academic entrepreneurship may also seek to develop networks with alternative fund providers. For example, in the UK a number of accelerators are linked to universities, providing short programmes for early stage ventures by faculty, students and alumni that can provide bridge to funding by angels and venture capital firms (Clarysse *et al.*, 2015). As a further possibility, the emergence of crowdfunding platforms also offers further scope for funding very early stage academic entrepreneurship ventures, for example through attracting investment by alumni.

Our depiction of the UK landscape regarding spin-outs also indicates a number of areas for further research. In general, we have identified variations in the extent of spin-outs in relation to sector, location, university quality, funding access, and successful and unsuccessful exit. It was beyond the scope of this chapter to analyze the drivers of these differences but this opens up scope for future research along these dimensions. For example, with respect to sector distribution an interesting avenue for further research would appear to be to compare the challenges in spinning-out ventures in management/human resource and commerce/entertainment sectors compared to more traditional sectors in science and engineering.

We have provided evidence on the survival rate of spin-outs but at present, we lack evidence on the drivers of survival or of the whether spin-outs are more or less likely to survive than other types of firms such as more conventional venture capital backed firms. Recent prior research on firms survival has shown, inter alia, the importance of the composition of the board of directors in terms of their human capital and social capital (e.g., Wilson *et al.*, 2013, 2014). Given the importance attached to the social capital of academic entrepreneurs that we identified above in previous UK research, examination of this issue would appear to be particular salient. As the studies by Wilson and colleagues have shown, it is feasible to link data relating to whether a firm is a spin-out or not to Companies House data on financial performance and fine-grained board composition. One caveat concerning examination of survival of spin-outs concerns the extent to which it is distorted by universities being reluctant to liquidate non-viable ventures by star academics who threaten to go elsewhere.

Finally, we have focused on an analysis of spin-outs officially registered as spin-outs by TTOs. However, as Perkmann *et al.* (2015) find officially identified spin-outs understate the extent of venture creation activity by academics by a substantial margin. Further research is required to examine the extent to which the wider cohort of start-ups by academics experience different issues relating to access to finance, whether they access different forms of finance and whether their exit and survival performance is different.

In concluding, our analysis has provided new insights into the variety of the UK landscape that opens up questions for both policy development and further research. While much has been achieved in developing policy and researching university spin-outs in the UK, much remains to be done. The changing landscape regarding government views about the role of universities and the entrepreneurial objectives of many faculty and, especially, students, strongly suggests the need for an evolution of what is regarded as university start-up activity, with consequences for support activities. For researchers this also poses new challenges for data collection regarding what to encompass in databases of academic entrepreneurship.

References

Autio, E. & Webb, R. 2015. Engineering growth: Enabling world-class UK entrepreneurship in the low-carbon economy. Report by Imperial College Business School for Shell Springboard.

Bolzani, D., Fini, R., Grimaldi, R. & Sobrero, M. 2014. University spin-offs and their impact: Longitudinal evidence from Italy. *Journal of Industrial and Business Economics,* 41, 181–205.

Borlaug, S. B., Grünfeld, L., Gulbrandsen, M., Rasmussen, E., Rønning, L., Spilling, O. R. & Vinogradov, E. 2009. Between entrepreneurship and technology transfer: Evaluation of the FORNY programme, Report 19. NIFU STEP, Oslo.

Chapple, W., Lockett, A., Siegel, D. S. & Wright, M. 2005. Assessing the relative performance of university technology transfer offices in the U.K.: Parametric and non-parametric evidence. *Research Policy,* 34(3), 369–384.

Clarysse, B., Bruneel, J. & Wright, M. (2011). Explaining growth paths of young technology-based firms: structuring resource portfolios in different competitive environments. *Strategic Entrepreneurship Journal,* 5(2), 137–157.

Clarysse, B., Wright, M. & Van Hove, J. 2015. *A Look Inside Accelerators.* Nesta, London.

Complete University Guide. Available at: http://www.thecompleteuniversityguide.co.uk/league-tables/rankings. Accessed on 14 July 2015.

Druilhe, C. & Garnsey, E. 2004. Do academic spin-outs differ and does it matter? *The Journal of Technology Transfer,* 29(3/4), 269–285.

Fame. Available at: https://fame.bvdinfo.com. Accessed on 14 July 2015.

Franklin, S., Wright, M. & Lockett, A. 2001. Academic and surrogate entrepreneurs in university spin-out companies. *Journal of Technology Transfer,* 26(1–2), 127–141.

Garnsey, E. & Heffernan, P. 2005. High-technology clustering through spin-out and attraction: The Cambridge case. *Regional Studies,* 39(8), 1127–1144.

Higher Education Information Database for Institutions (HEIDI). Available at: https://heidi.hesa.ac.uk/Home.aspx. Accessed on 14 July 2015.

Lockett, A., Wright, M. & Franklin, S. 2003. Technology transfer and universities' spin-out strategies. *Small Business Economics,* 20, 185–201.

Lockett, A. & Wright, M. 2005. Resources, capabilities, risk capital and the creation of university spin-out companies. *Research Policy,* 34(7), 1043–1057.

Lockett, A., Wright, M. & Wild, A. 2013. Diffusion and maintenance of knowledge transfer activities in UK higher education. *Business History,* 55, 236–258.

Lockett, A., Wright, M. & Wild, A. 2014. The institutionalization of third stream activities in U.K. higher education: The role of discourse and metrics. *British Journal of Management,* DOI: 10.1111/1467-8551.12069.

Mosey, S. & Wright, M. 2007. From human capital to social capital: A longitudinal study of technology-based academic entrepreneurs. *Entrepreneurship Theory and Practice,* 31, 909–936.

Mueller, C., Westhead, P. & Wright, M. 2012. Formal venture capital acquisition: Can entrepreneurs compensate for the spatial proximity benefits of South East

England and star' golden-triangle universities? *Environment and Planning A* 44, 281–296.

Nicolaou, N. & Birley, S. 2003. Social networks in organizational emergence: The university spinout phenomenon. *Management Science*, 49(12), 1702–1725.

Perkmann, M., Fini, R., Ross, J. M., Salter, A., Silvestri, C. & Tartari, V. 2015. Accounting for universities' impact: using augmented data to measure academic engagement and commercialization by academic scientists. *Research Evaluation*, 24(4), 380–391.

Puri, M. & Zarutskie, R. 2012. On the life cycle dynamics of venture-capital- and non-venture-capital-financed firms. *The Journal of Finance*, 67(6), 2247–2293.

Rasmussen, E., Mosey, S. & Wright, M. 2011. The evolution of entrepreneurial competencies: A longitudinal study of university spin-off venture emergence. *Journal of Management Studies*, 48, 1314–1345.

Rasmussen, E., Mosey, S. & Wright, M. 2015. The transformation of network ties to develop entrepreneurial competencies for university spin-offs. *Entrepreneurship & Regional Development*, 27(7–8), 430–457.

Siegel, D. S. & Wright, M. 2015. University technology transfer offices, licensing, and start-ups. In the *Chicago Handbook of University Technology Transfer and Academic Entrepreneurship*, A. Link, D. S. Siegel and M. Wright (eds.). University of Chicago Press, Chicago, IL.

Siegel, D. S., Wright, M., Chapple, W. & Lockett, A. 2008. Assessing the relative performance of university technology transfer in the U.S. and U.K.: A stochastic distance function approach. *Economics of Innovation and New Technology*, 17 (7/8), 717–729.

Smith, H. L. & Ho, K. 2006. Measuring the performance of Oxford University, Oxford Brookes University and the government laboratories' spin-off companies. *Research Policy*, 35, 1554–1568.

Spinouts UK Survey. Available at: http://www.spinoutsuk.co.uk/. Accessed on 14 July 2015.

Vincett, P. S. 2010. The economic impacts of academic spin-off companies, and their implications for public policy. *Research Policy*, 39(6), 736–747.

Vohora, A., Wright, M. & Lockett, A. 2004. Critical junctures in the development of university high-tech spinout companies. *Research Policy*, 33(1), 147–175.

Wilson, N., Wright, M. & Altanlar, A. 2013. The survival of newly-incorporated companies and founding director characteristics. *International Small Business Journal*, Epub ahead of print 25 February. DOI: 10.1177/0266242613476317.

Wilson, N., Wright, M. & Scholes, L. 2013. Board composition and family firm survival. *Entrepreneurship Theory and Practice*, 37, 1369–1389.

Wright, M., Lockett, A., Clarysse, B. & Binks, M. 2006. University spin-out companies and venture capital. *Research Policy*, 35(4), 481–501.

Wright, M., Clarysse, B., Mustar, P. & Lockett, A. 2007. *Academic Entrepreneurship in Europe*. Cheltenham, Edward Elgar.

Wright, M., Clarysse, B., Lockett, A. & Knockaert, M. 2008. Mid-range universities' in Europe linkages with industry: Knowledge types and the role of intermediaries. *Research Policy*, 37, 1205–1223.

Wright, M., Hart, M. & Fu, K. 2015. A Nation of Angels. London:UK Business Angels Association and Enterprise Research Center.

Wright, M., Mosey, S. & Noke, H. 2012. Academic entrepreneurship and economic competitiveness: Rethinking the role of the entrepreneur. *Economics of Innovation and New Technology*, 21(5/6), 429–444.

Zephyr. Available at: https://zephyr.bvdinfo.com. Accessed on 14 July 2015.

Chapter 8

Canadian Biotechnology University Spin-Offs: Actual Situation and Trends

Ayoub Moustakbal* and Jorge Niosi[†]

*Department of Management and Technology, UQAM,
P.O. Box 8888 Station Centre-Ville, Montréal, QC, H3C 3P8, Canada*
*moustakbalayoub@yahoo.fr
[†]niosi.jorge@uqam.ca

According to the report "OECD Biotechnology Statistics 2009" published by Van Beuzekom & Arundel (2009). Canada is one of the world's biotechnology leaders especially in terms of the number of dedicated biotechnology companies, R&D expenditures, government support, and return per dollar invested. To shed more light on this issue, this chapter aims at drawing up an updated portrait where we present the main characteristics and key trends characterizing Canada biotech. The focus is on the category of university spin-offs (USOs) specialized in human health which represents a key link in the value creation chain of Canadian biotechnology (Niosi, 2006; Statistics Canada, 2007).

In sum, the chapter is divided into three parts. In the beginning we present a theory review addressing the importance of USOs and the factors necessary for their development. Thereafter, we present research methodology and the main characteristics of our research sample. As a conclusion, we discuss the results and determine the implications for different stakeholders, including policy makers, entrepreneurs' founders of spin-offs, and future scientific researchers.

Literature Review

In recent decades, academic entrepreneurship has found greater visibility, and universities are being increasingly considered as a key source of technology transfer process and creation of high-technology firms (Etzkowitz, 2002; Shane, 2004; Mustar *et al.*, 2006; Niosi, 2006; Van Geenhuizen & Soetanto, 2009; Vincett, 2010). As a matter of fact, universities are placing, more and more, greater attention on the linkage between science, technology, and promoting academic entrepreneurship. They are moving from their classic roles of research, teaching, and knowledge dissemination to a more advanced role of creating spin-offs (Lerner, 2004; Shane, 2004; Mustar *et al.*, 2006).

Spin-offs can emerge from organizations other than universities (e.g., hospitals, government labs and firms). Statistics Canada (2008) definition of spin-offs is as follows: "new firms created to transfer and commercialize inventions and technology developed in universities, firms or laboratories." Thus, spin-offs are enterprises established by people who have a strong connection to another organization. The entrepreneurs–founders discover inventions (products or processes) with economic potential that the originating organization chooses not to pursue. The development of these new projects could not be pursued in the originating organization because commercialization is outside their mandate or their core competence (Statistics Canada, 2008).

In the present research, we focus on USOs which are defined as new firms created to exploit commercially some knowledge, technology or research results developed within a university (Pirnay *et al.*, 2003). Universities spin-off is also known under the term of "academic spin-offs", "Research-based spin-offs" or "spin-out" (Nicolaou & Birley, 2003; Shane, 2004; Mustar *et al.*, 2006).

According to Etzkowitz (2002), USOs contribute to local economic development, leading edge research, high value jobs and innovation. In the same vein Vincett (2010) specify that the spin-off have an added value to GDP, much higher (even on a time-discounted basis) than the government funding and directly attributable to it. The governments will also receive more in terms of tax than they spent. So, beyond their socio-economic benefits which come with long term (less quantifiable), the USOs impacts provide a quantitative justification for the public investment (Vincett, 2010). In fact, USOs are seen as an economic actor performing various important functions such as vehicle for technology transfer and technology commercialization, a source of direct income for universities, a generator of employment, a strategic hub to strengthen the relationships with the local stakeholders and, particularly in depressed areas a way to contribute to restructuring regional economies (Van Geenhuizen & Soetanto, 2009). With their strategies of spin-off creations, universities have become key economic actors in shaping the nature of the interaction between the academic world and industrial environment. The rise of the university Technology Transfer Offices (TTOs) and the increasing attempts of universities to capture formal intellectual proprieties on discoveries made within their buildings have had a profound impact on the vocation of universities and the nature of scientific efforts (Shane, 2004; Mustar *et al.*, 2006).

Canadian USOs

In Canada, universities have proved to be quite successful in commercializing their research (Niosi, 2006). Clayman and Holbrook (2004) found that Canadian universities created considerably more spin-off companies than their US counterparts, counting the companies created per dollar of research. To facilitate the process of spin-off venture formation, Canadian universities developed a set of capabilities (Rasmussen & Borch, 2010). They (1) create new paths of action, (2) they balance both academic and commercial interests, and (3) they integrate new resources. Each capability is particularly important for specific phases in the venturing process. Rasmussen and Borch (2010) underline that these capabilities are dependent on prior spin-off experience and reside within several actors both inside and outside of the university. Such a situation could be explained by the fact that Canadian policy makers have devoted a significant amount of resources to promote the commercialization of new technologies and knowledge generated within universities and other public research institutions (Rasmussen, 2008). The examination of the success factors in Canadian academic spin-offs had indicated that Spin-off companies in growing had often obtained patents and received support from the Industrial Research Assistance Program (IRAP), a support program for R&D in smaller firms, managed by the National Research Council of Canada (Niosi, 2006). At federal level, the government support aims to stimulate the commercialization of publicly funded research through two types of programs (Rasmussen, 2008). On one hand, we have programs made to induce structural reforms within the university sector in order to improve the institutional capabilities to facilitate commercialization projects. On the other, there are programs providing support to specific commercialization projects (Rasmussen, 2008).

As can be seen from Table 1, the Spin-offs represented 34% of dedicated biotechnology companies that have been identified by Statistics

Table 1.   Canadian biotechnology spin-offs, by originating organization and sector.

	All firms	Spin-offs	Public research organizations	Businesses and other organizations	Spin-offs
			Number		%
Human health	310	132	114	18	43
Agriculture and food processing	146	36	32	4	25
Environmental/ natural resources	60	8	4	4	13
Other	16	3	3	0	19
All	532	179	154	26	34

Source: Statistics Canada, 2008. Innovation Analysis Bulletin, 10(1), Catalogue No. 88-003-XWE.

Canada in 2005. In other words, one in three came from the spin-offs. The same table shows that in 2005, almost three quarters of recorded spin-offs (74%) specialized in human health.

It seems that the Canadian government initiatives encouraged a bottom-up approach in order to support the commercialization of university research (Rasmussen, 2008). In fact, the government instruments are structured to provide resources for direct use in commercialization projects or to develop professional expertise in technology transfer in the university sector, to facilitate cooperation between commercializing organizations, and finally to experiment new innovative initiatives (Rasmussen, 2008).

In the analysis of the USOs, the role played by TTOs is key. It is an important stakeholder, created at Canadian universities to help regulate and monetize the transfer of knowledge created by the university researchers to the marketplace (Bubela & Caulfield, 2010; Sadek *et al.*, 2015). On a similar note, Niosi and Banic (2005) had already indicated that the routines of Canadian universities are modified with the addition of intellectual property and TTOs intervening as sellers in the newly created knowledge markets. TTOs can play a role in developing a new entrepreneurial ecosystem around mid-sized research universities, based on the perceptions and expectations of the key stakeholders, involved in the technology transfer process, about the role of TTOs. In others words, TTOs can play a critical role in coordinating different bottom-up initiatives to promote entrepreneurship, and in attracting and integrating new external resources to the university. According to Bubela and Caulfield (2010), the interviews with professionals at Canadian TTOs have revealed that, at their best, TTOs support the social and academic missions of their institutions by facilitating knowledge mobilization and research relationships with other sectors, including industry. Yet, Rasmussen (2008) found that several initiatives in Canada have been set up to educate the TTO staff and increase the commercialization competence at universities. According to Rasmussen (2008), the technology transfer within universities is increasingly seen as a function which requires a particular type of boundary-spanning skills.

The survival and sustainability conditions

USOs are an important vehicle for knowledge dissemination and have the potential to generate employment and economic growth. But such results require that USOs cross a number of distinct phases their development (Vohora *et al.*, 2004). Between the different phases, USOs confront "critical junctures" in terms of the resources and capabilities they need to acquire to progress to the next phase. Vohora *et al.* (2004) had inventoried four critical stages confronted by USOs: (1) opportunity recognition; (2) entrepreneurial commitment; (3) venture credibility; and (4) venture sustainability.

Several factors have been identified as essential conditions for USOs development. According to Hayter (2013), these factors are venture capital (VC) support, multiple and external licenses, outside management, joint ventures with other companies, and previous faculty consulting experience. Similarly, Nuria *et al.* (2012) found that the lack of management abilities to bring financial resources and attract strategic alliances make the survival of USOs more difficult than for other companies. It must be stressed that these explanatory factors have been identified as indispensable variables for the growth and survival of biotechnology firms in several past studies (Powell *et al.*, 2002; Niosi, 2003, 2011; Baum & Silverman, 2004; Moustakbal, 2014).

Entrepreneurial team: The presence of a star scientist

Like several previous studies, Zahra *et al.* (2009) and Fontana & Malerba (2010) have shown the decisive impact of the entrepreneurial team on the sustainability and viability of new enterprises specialized in the different high-tech sectors. The concept of entrepreneurial team can refer to the group of people involved in the creation and management of a new venture (Wright *et al.*, 2007). Spin-offs generally have scarce initial resources, and the entrepreneurial team is one of their main business assets (Criaco *et al.*, 2013; Migliorini *et al.*, 2013). The survival of such firms is supposed to be heavily dependent on the skills and the past experiences of their entrepreneurs–founders

(Migliorini *et al.*, 2013). In the same vein, Shane (2004) had argued that the information and learning that USOs entrepreneurial team acquire through interaction with business contacts help them to design a better defined products which meet market needs and ensure a fair balance between technological and commercial dimensions.

In the case of biotechnology companies, the presence of a star scientist in entrepreneurial team seems to be an important driver in the creation and development of the firm (Zucker *et al.*, 1998, 2002; Niosi & Queenton, 2010). On one hand, such managers constitute a kind of generators engines to produce new projects and new innovations. According to Zucker *et al.* (1998, 2002) academic breakthrough discoveries are often transferred to industry through star scientists and the university spin-off. On the other hand, the presence of star scientist is regarded as a kind of guarantee and a credibility indicator by different stakeholders. For instance, VC managers select start-ups with strong technology, but risk failure in the short run. So they require the presence of qualified management including, amongst others, the star scientists in business (Baum & Silverman, 2004). Other studies have shown that the star scientist bring also a decisive intangible asset which is manifested in network of business partners. Aldridge and Audretsch (2011) have studied a data base of high profile scientists receiving large-scale funding from the National Cancer Institute. They suggest that the decision to become an entrepreneur depends on the levels of social capital, as measured by linkages to private industry that increase the propensity of a scientist to become an entrepreneur. However, it is important to make the distinction whether social capital is made of academic or business networks with several stakeholders (Vohora *et al.*, 2004). Social capital is important in the processes of gaining funds, acquiring and hiring surrogate entrepreneurs, accessing information and knowledge. In the same way, Walter *et al.* (2006) had investigated the impact of network capability of team management through a database of 149 USOs. They concluded that network capability influence positively the ability to develop and utilize inter-organizational relationships, and entrepreneurial orientation on organizational performance.

Geographic location

Regional studies have highlighted several benefits and positive externalities arising of agglomeration such as local knowledge spillovers, input–output linkages, and labor market pooling (Marshall, 1920). In case of biotechnology firms, Niosi and Banik (2005) demonstrated that the companies located in regional agglomerations grow faster than isolated ones, and that spin-offs from universities have a better performance than start-ups. The same authors even underline the development of biotechnology regions with complex systems where spin-offs emerge with star scientists that generate knowledge spillovers and they move progressively towards regional technology markets. On his side Stenberg (2014) indicate that the regional environment has more impact on USOs success than receiving public programs.

Thereafter, further studies focused on the establishment of new firms into the cluster of related industries in a location which foster entrepreneurship by lowering the cost of starting a business, enhancing opportunities for innovations, and enabling better access to a more diverse range of inputs and complementary products (Saxenian, 1994; Glaeser *et al.*, 2009; Delgado *et al.*, 2010). The co-location of companies, customers, suppliers, and other institutions also increases the perception of innovation opportunities while amplifying the pressure to innovate (Porter, 2000). Aharonson *et al.* (2008) conducted a comparative analysis of Canadian biotechnology industry across three major metropolitan areas (Vancouver, Toronto, and Montreal). They noted the difference between uninventive locations and inventive ones that offer positive externalities such a greater resource scale and technological focus, as well as greater emphasis on R&D investment and public and private collaboration. Spin-off firms tend to stay close to their alma mater university and that technology transfer through spin-offs is largely a local phenomenon (Zhang, 2009). In a more recent study, Kolympiris *et al.* (2015) used several candidate explanatory variables to examine those factors that may influence the firm location choice for 187 biopharmaceutical firms started by 275 academic entrepreneurs in the US. According to Kolympiris *et al.* (2015), some location-specific factors such as proximity to certain knowledge assets and to the funding VC firms, affect the firm location choice of academic entrepreneurs (Kolympiris *et al.*, 2015).

Venture capital (VC) support

New projects of biotechnology companies are often characterized by intense R&D activities, long product development cycles, high technological and marketing uncertainty and especially very substantial funding needs (DiMasi *et al.*, 2003). So the support of biotechnology companies are not limited to the funding government agencies but also of VC providers because of their great need for financial resources to complete the development of products (Shane, 2004). In addition, the traditional loans involve debt instead of equity, but many banks do not fund firms without a reasonably predictable revenue stream (Statistic Canada, 2007). In such circumstances, the financial intermediaries such as VC firms are almost unavoidable since they offers the support and the most suitable financing for young high-tech companies (Gompers & Lerner, 2001; Baum & Silverman, 2004; Industry Canada, 2006). In other words, VC has become an integral component in the national innovation system (Kenney & Patton, 2011).

We have to highlight that the input of VC companies is not restricted to the role of simple financiers. They offer to provide start-up coaching and advice as well as contacts with other business partners (Gompers & Lerner, 2001; Hsu, 2007). VC managers play an important role in the development and professionalization of managerial skills of their customers (Hellmann & Puri, 2000; Niosi, 2003). About that, Baum and Silverman (2004) point out that Canadian VC companies choose and build successful companies. They adopt an approach of "Scout" and "coach" that explains the success of biotechnology companies. On their side, Rosiello and Parris (2009) conclude that VC companies use their networks of business partners to help young companies dedicated to human health to fill their limitations in terms of financial management and marketing capacities. VC firms can play a key role in the commercialization of innovations (Hsu, 2007). So to achieve this objective, the managers of these financial institutions can even make use of their networks of contacts to help their clients to hire expert leaders (Colombo *et al.*, 2010). However, it is important to specify that the mission of the VC firms is that of a financial intermediate designed to support the launch and development of innovative companies for a specified period (Hellmann & Puri, 2000; Gompers & Lerner, 2001). Thus, VC companies leave these projects financed through two types of exits. On one hand, they can opt for an introduction on the stock market, where they can liquidate their shares in the public market (Hochberg *et al.*, 2007). On the other hand, VC managers can choose merger and acquisition strategies to sell their shares to other investors (Sowlay & Lloyd, 2010). The exit through mergers and acquisitions (M&A) is preferred by the leader–founders start-up and they are guided primarily by economic and industrial as well as financial criteria (Black & Gilson, 1998; Cumming, 2008). It must be considered also that during the economic slowdowns (e.g., 2001 and 2008), the financial markets are reluctant to buy these shares and therefore the exit through initial public offering (IPO) is uncommon. This, VC companies are turning more often towards M&A, which seem to be safer exits and sometimes the only accessible and profitable way to get a return on investment (ROI) (Sowlay & Lloyd, 2010).

Alliance and partnership strategies

According to Powell *et al.* (2005), the complexity of knowledge and low productivity of R&D activities have often stimulated the emergence of a biotechnology industry operating increasingly networked. In fact, strategic alliances can be the major funding sources that complement the funds invested by other financiers (Lemer *et al.*, 2003).

In connection with the previous section, VC societies play an important role in contacting these customers with other business partners through alliances or joint business strategies ("joint venture"). This kind of partnership strategy allows young companies to reduce barriers related to information asymmetry and the risks of opportunism and expropriation (Lindsey, 2008). However, Levitte and Bagchi-Sen (2010) had concluded that managers of biotechnology companies are obliged to provide a kind of "trade off" between strategic alliances for exploration and R&D, versus exploitation ones. Companies that are limited to strategies for collaboration with local universities are less likely to succeed in the stages of development and marketing of new projects (Levitte & Bagchi-Sen, 2010). Furthermore, those managers must develop business models fostering strategic alliances, and not only with local organizations, but also with other geographically distant business partners (Owen-Smith & Powell, 2004). Also, Niosi (2003) had warned that strategic alliances are not enough for the rapid growth of Canadian biotechnology companies. But, he stressed that success (as measured by growth) of biotech firms is linked to human capital, to patenting strategies, to the financial support of VC and large corporate partners as well as exporting.

Sample and Methodology

Our paper is part of large longitudinal study on the disappearance of the Canadian DBFs which we conducted under the framework of a doctoral thesis. The database used in this study has been built over a four-year time frame (2008–2012). It includes more than 1,000 Canadian dedicated biotechnology firms. Our reference period for data and information collection was from 1990 to 2010.

In the present paper we limit the scope of the problem by focusing on USOs dedicated to human health. In other words, we constructed a sample of 213 USOs in order to test our research hypotheses. We chose the spin-offs dedicated to the human health sector which holds the lion's share compared to other sub-sectors of Canadian biotechnology (Niosi, 2003; Statistic

Canada, 2007). In addition, the data is more accessible in the case of spin-offs dedicated to human health.

Data and information about Canadian spin-offs were obtained from several electronic databases (consulted online) specializing in biotechnology (e.g., Biotech Canada, Statistics Canada, Industry Canada, and Biotech Gate). We used also the SEDAR website, the websites of the companies and other public information such as the Canadian Biotechnology Reports (paper format published) by Contact Canada.

In the case of VC financing, we examined the Canadian database 'Thomson VC Reporter'. This database contains different and updated information such as the amount and date of the investment, the financing stage, the investor profile, the objective of the financing, etc.

However, we want to specify that for companies that disappeared, the 'life expectancy' (dependant variable) is the difference between the year of creation and the year of closure or the year of the M&A transaction.

For the surviving firms, the life expectancy is the difference between the year of creation and the year 2010. Regarding the independent variable: "Entrepreneurial team," we refer to the presence of a star researcher, i.e., a researcher having over 30 scientific publications and patents.

Concerning the statistical analysis of data, we used SPSS to conduct the several statistic tests. Moreover, Table 2 summarizes our independent and dependent variables which we codified according to the binary model.

We decided to distinguish between two distinct forms of disappearances of USOs, two dependent variables, namely M&A versus bankruptcies. The assimilation of all cases of disappearances and exit of firms with bankruptcies

Table 2. Summary of the analyses variables.

Dependent variables	Independent variables
Survival (Yes = 1/No = 2)	Star scientist[1] (Yes = 1/No = 2)
M&A (Yes = 1/No = 2)	Advanced stage (Yes = 1/No = 2)
Bankruptcy (Yes = 1/No = 2)	Implementation in major cities (Yes = 1/No = 2)
Life expectancy	VC support (Yes = 1/No = 2)
	Strategic Alliances (Yes = 1/No = 2)

---

[1] The previous work has identified two categories of scientific stars namely (a) "superstars" who are researchers with at least five patents and published more than a year, and (b) the "stars": researchers who have between two and four patents and at least one publication by year (Niosi & Queenton, 2010).

and economic failures can lead us to biased or erroneous conclusions. The factors explaining the failure of start-ups may differ completely from those which are at the origin of M&A (Wennberg *et al.*, 2010; DeTienne, 2010). An acquired company may have succeed its business plan, that was to develop the project until a certain stadium (i.e., clinical essays phase II) and then sell the firm with its semi-developed product or process.

Descriptive Results

First of all, our sample confirms that in Canada the spin-offs dedicated to human health are most often small-sized companies (less than 50 employees). As can be seen in Table 3, this category of spin-offs represents 81% of our total sample. We believe that the leaders of these enterprises face difficulties to realize revenues and to develop their business. We can also note that 61% of surveyed USOs are still in early stage (see Table 3). In this regard, we believe that these initial observations are in continuity of the previous research published by Clayman and Holbrook (2004) which is one of the few longitudinal studies examining the survival of USOs dedicated to biotechnology. These authors had indicated that 70% of surveyed companies were able to survive until 2003. However most of the surviving firms are small and are having serious problems to reach the advanced stages of product development.

In addition, we have to clarify again that the 31% of USOs with at least one product on the market was mainly due to companies specialized in sub-sectors of medical equipment and bioinformatics. The development of new

Table 3.   Size, sub-sectors and the development stages of USOs.

N = 213	n	%
Size by employment		
Small (1–49)	173	81
Medium (50–149)	40	19
Large (+150)	0	0
Sub-sector		
Therapeutics, genomics, proteomics and R&D activities	124	58
Bioinformatics et medical equipments	89	42
Development stage		
Early stage	129	61
Advanced stage	17	8
Commercialization stage	67	31

products in these sub-sectors of human health is less risky and requires less time and funds. So these USOs are more likely to reach the stages of marketing and generate revenues.

To explain the predominance of very small enterprises in early stage, we can make the link with the report of Industry Canada (2006) which had already revealed that many USOs are started prematurely. Too often, Canadian universities adopt a quantitative strategy that focuses on the creation of spin-offs. To achieve national objectives, universities focus on the creation of new businesses which are created early, before they can demonstrate a viability and real market value. The consequences are that USOs have a lower or insignificant patent protection, thus discouraging investors to provide VC as well as they limit their commercial development of new project.

Biotechnology firms frequently engage in intensive R&D efforts to create new products and to meet regulatory requirements for these new products. If they have no sales or their sales are not sufficient to cover costs, firms need alternative sources of funds to maintain these activities (Statistics Canada, 2007). In the same line of thought, Rasmussen and Borch (2010) underlined that the USO research-founders may find that the university is a source of valuable resources, but they are not always aware that the USO project needs to be adapted to a commercial context.

Geographical location and disappearance paths

Table 4 shows that the majority of identified spin-offs (89%) are concentrated in the fourth largest Canadian provinces, particularly in the biggest cities (e.g., Montreal, Toronto, and Vancouver) where are located the most prestigious universities active in R&D. As in previous studies, we can conclude that the spin-offs leaders prefer to locate near the university of origin and in major Canadian cities with the aim to take advantage of positive externalities arising from the ecosystem in place. We believe that these universities may have the capabilities of an anchor tenant (as defined by Agrawal & Cockburn, 2003) that generate favorable conditions for the creation and development of spin-offs. In this direction Landry *et al.* (2006) have studied "why are some university researchers more likely to create spin-off companies than others" through a database of 1554 university researchers funded by the Natural Sciences and Engineering Research Council of Canada (NSERC). Their results suggest that university and industry partnership grants, in combination with traditional funding of university research, provide a more fertile ground for spin-off creation, but that financial support from the private sector might be a good mechanism for fostering knowledge transfer directly to

Table 4.   Location and the forms of disappearance.

Provinces	Location universities/cities	n	%	Survivors (active USOs)		Disappeared (inactive)			
				n	%	M&A		Bankruptcy	
						n	%	n	%
Ontario N = 62	University of Toronto = 43	22	41	19		9	4	12	6
Quebec N = 58	McGill (Montreal) = 39	18	30	14		13	6	15	7
British Colombia N = 44	University of British Columbia (Vancouver) = 35	16	26	12		10	5	8	4
Alberta N = 31	University of Alberta (Edmonton) = 26	12	18	9		6	3	7	3
Others N = 18	n/a			7	3	4	2	7	3
Total N = 213	143			68	122	57	42	20	49	23

private firms. The incubation capacity of university research on spin-off creation is also likely influenced by history dependence for successful technology transfer and by differences in the business models of start-ups (O'Shea *et al.*, 2005; Landry *et al.*, 2006). The affiliation with a university could even have an impact on the propensity of the USOs to be targeted in cross-border M&As. Using a sample of 220 biotech firms that went public in Europe over the period 1995–2006, Cattaneo *et al.* (2015) find the affiliation with a university and, in particular, that with a prestigious and internationalized university improves the attractiveness in the eyes of international acquirers.

Our longitudinal research also indicates that the biotech sector varies widely across Canada. Each metropolitan area has its strengths, and there is, in general, relatively little competition in terms of overlapping research projects or industrial activity (Clayman & Holbrook, 2004; Statistic Canada, 2007). We noticed effectively a kind of specialization trends of major cities or provinces in specific areas of biotechnology dedicated human health. For example in Ontario, we have inventoried more spin-offs dedicated to bioinformatics and medical equipment while in the Quebec province we have noted more spin-offs in human therapy, immunology, cell biology and genetics. We believe that such findings could be explained by the international reputation of each university incubator as active in the production of a specific category of spin-offs. Moreover, we can talk about the routines and a kind of path dependence to business models specific to each university and adapted to the realities of the external environment in each province, especially the institutional framework. In the same vein, Etzkowitz (2002) had noted that each university, as a function of its history and past success, has different resource stocks available and these resource combinations are shown to be a relevant factor in explaining inter-university variation in spin-off activity. These findings support a path dependency argument that current USOs choices of technologies, products and operation are heavily influenced, probably even constrained, by the cumulative effect of previous universities projects (Etzkowitz, 2002).

Beyond the remarkable geographical concentration of USOs dedicated to human health, Table 4 shows that in Canada, 43% of all recorded firms have disappeared between 1990 and 2010. However our longitudinal survey confirmed that the economic bankruptcy is not the only path of disappearance for Canadian biotechnology spin-offs. In fact, 20% of surveyed companies' names no longer appear in the list of survivors due to M&A transactions. This brings us back to previous studies that have drawn similar conclusions. On the one hand, we have Carroll and Hannan (1995) whose results indicate that in the US, bankruptcies of biotechnology companies are uncommon. The disappearance of this kind of companies is manifested mainly by merger and acquisition transactions as well as name changes. Also, Mangematin *et al.* (2003) found that the life cycle of young biotechnology companies can borrow different paths such as bankruptcy, focus on a niche activity, setting place a "blockbuster" or transferring assets through M&A. Regarding the last path of exit, Mangematin *et al.* (2003) had underlined that it is a step in the development process of young companies dedicated to biotechnology, and not necessarily a consequence of failure.

As it can be seen in Table 4, the intra-provincial matching of USOs reveals that the province of Quebec has a higher disappearance rate both through bankruptcy and M&A transactions. First, such a situation could be explained by a high level of USOs density which causes a more severe selection process (as argued within the theory of population ecology). Thus, only the USOs with the necessary conditions (e.g., material, human and/or financial assets) may survive in a more restrictive environment. We also believe that the high exit rate in Quebec could be explained by the specificities of the regional innovation system adopted by the local policy makers. It would be appropriate also to note that in the Quebec province, USOs tend to be more specialized in the areas of human health (e.g., therapeutic) which are more risky and require more money and a longer development process. So the sustainability and viability of these entities is less secure since they have less opportunity to bring products to the market and/or generate revenue through licensing.

We would like to underline the fact that the majority of disappearances recorded (closure and M&A) had occurred after the two crises in the financial market that marked the 2000s. We refer to the periods 2001–2003 and 2008–2010. So it seems that apart the structural problems that are manifested in scientific impasses of projects and/ or the lack of survival factors, the disappearance of a new biotech company is related to economic cycles (Mangematin *et al.*, 2003).

Disappearance causes

Following our consultation of "Thomson VC Report" database, we conclude that 48% of surveyed USOs had the chance to get funding from VC companies (see Table 5). In others words, almost one in two USOs had the chance to access the services of these financial institutions. We have noted that VC investors have multiple profiles such as national or international private institutions as well as the Labour Sponsored VC Corporations (LSVCCs)[2] (e.g., the Fonds de solidarité FTQ) and government agencies, such as the BDC.

As for the 52% of USOs who have not been able to get VC funding, it could be explained by several interrelated factors. First, we emphasized that Canadian USOs are characterized by the dominance of small (under 50 employees), the lack of products in advanced stages and/or on the market and the tendency to start prematurely new projects in some sub-sectors of human health more risky and more demanding in terms of financial and

Table 5. Summary of disappearance causes.

	With VC support		With star scientist		With strategic alliances "exploitation stage"	
	n	%	*n*	%	*n*	%
USOs *N* = 213	96	48%	72	34	68	32

[2] In Canada, LSVCCs or Labour Sponsored Investment Funds (LSIFs) are special corporations designed to provide VC and promote investment in SMEs whose shares are not publicly traded (Ayayi, 2004). LSVCCs receive the funds capitalized by the individual shareholders who are encouraged by the incentives of Canadian federal and provincial tax credits (Sandler, 2004; Cumming & MacIntosh, 2006). Before being generalize across Canada, the model of LSVCCs was adopted for the first time in the Canadian province of Quebec in 1982. This province was in a recession and the lack of capital in SMEs had caused numerous bankruptcies.

human resources. There is also the fact that the Canadian VC industry is not as developed to meet the massive financial requirements of so many USOs. The volume of money invested in each DBF is smaller compared to the situation in the United States. So, in such circumstances, managers of VC funds adopt a selection process in order to choose the best projects to fund and coach. Otherwise, to maximize new business success probabilities and their ROI, VC managers play a role of "Scout" and "coach" (Niosi, 2003; Baum & Silverman, 2004).

Regarding the presence of a star scientist (see Table 5), we noted that barely one-third (34%) of surveyed USOs had the chance to count on the presence of at least one star researcher in the management team. Like VC support, the presence of a skilled management team, especially "star scientists" is one of the major factors in the creation and development of young biotech companies (Zucker *et al.*, 1998, 2002; Niosi & Queenton, 2010). So, we believe that Canadian companies are in a tough competition to attract this kind of strategic human asset. However, it seems that all Canadian biotechnology companies have difficulty in the recruitment and retention of skilled human resources (Conference Board of Canada, 2005). In the case of "star scientists", such a situation could be explained by a strong demand resulting from the large volume of premature new firm foundations while the supply of the Canadian local market is insufficient to meet the needs. In addition, we cannot overlook the international competition imposed by major US and global pharmaceutical companies that offer various attractive financial compensation and working conditions. Consequently, the Canadian biotechnology, which is composed mainly of small firms, could not make the difference in this game.

Strategic Alliances Dedicated to "Exploitation Stage"

At first, it would be appropriate to note that the partnership with universities (alliances dedicated to the exploration stage) do not make difference since all studied spin-offs come from the academic world and continue to cooperate with these organizations. Most of the Canadian USOs remain linked to academic environments (Clayman & Holbrook, 2004; Levitte & Bagchi-Sen, 2010). But in opposite direction, our longitudinal study reveals that only 32% of USOs have developed strategic alliances relationships dedicated to advanced stages (development and marketing). In light of previous results, we believe that such situation seems logical. In other words, we presume that the major biotechnology and pharmaceutical companies do not find any interest in partnership strategies with small USOs dedicated to risky human health sectors, still are in early stage and having less chance to attract star scientists and/or support VC.

Statistical Analyzes and Discussions

In order to determine the nature of the relationship between each form of disappearance (M&A versus bankruptcies) and explanatory factors retained, the descriptive results mentioned above were complemented by a statistical analysis conducted through SPSS (Tables 6 and 7). We try to determine the different factors that can explain every form of disappearance; we compared a sample of 42 USOs recorded as disappearance through M&A (20% of our

Table 6.   Statistical analyses of closed USOs.

$N = 98$

Dependant variable: closed USOs.

	Closed USOs	Major cities	Star scientists	Advanced stages	VC support	Strategic alliances
Closed USOs						
Pearson correlation	1					
Sig. (bilateral)						
N	98					
Major cities						
Pearson correlation	−0.065	1				
Sig. (bilateral)	0.526					
N	98	98				
Star scientist						
Pearson correlation	−0.211*	0.171	1			
Sig. (bilateral)	0.037	0.093				
N	98	98	98			
Advanced stages						
Pearson correlation	−0.409**	−0.013	0.359**	1		
Sig. (bilateral)	0.000	0.899	0.000			
N	98	98	98	98		
VC support						
Pearson correlation	−0.452**	0.212*	0.342**	0.396**	1	
Sig. (bilateral)	0.000	0.036	0.001	0.000		
N	98	98	98	98	98	
Strategic alliances						
Pearson correlation	−0.265**	0.089	0.297**	0.375**	0.343**	1
Sig. (bilateral)	0.008	0.384	0.003	0.000	0.001	
N	98	98	98	98	98	98

*Correlation is significant at the 0.05 level (bilateral).
**The correlation is significant at the 0.01 level (bilateral).

Table 7.   Statistical analyses of disappearance through M&A.

$N = 84$

Dependent variable: M&A USOs.

	VD M&A	Major cities	Star scientists	Advanced stages	VC support	Strategic alliances
VD M&A						
Pearson correlation	1					
Sig. (bilateral)						
N	84					
Major cities						
Pearson correlation	0.325**	1,000				
Sig. (bilateral)	0.003	—				
N	84	84				
Star scientist						
Pearson correlation	0.072	0.446**	1,000			
Sig. (bilateral)	0.517	0.000	—			
N	84	84	84			
Advanced stages						
Pearson correlation	0.331**	0.394**	0.535**	1,000		
Sig. (bilateral)	0.002	0.007	0.000	—		
N	84	84	84	84		
VC support						
Pearson correlation	0.383**	0.383**	0.319**	0.472**	1,000	
Sig. (bilateral)	0.000	0.000	0.003	0.000	—	
N	84	84	84	84	84	
Strategic alliances						
Pearson correlation	0.441**	0.356**	0.351**	0.562**	0.417**	1,000
Sig. (bilateral)	0.000	0.001	0.001	0.000	0.000	—
N	84	84	84	84	84	84

**The correlation is significant at the 0.01 level (bilateral).

total sample) with a random sample of 42 USOs that are still in operation (survivors). Thereafter we did the same exercise for comparing 49 cases of economic bankruptcy (23% of our total sample) with a random sample of the same size (49 USOs) among surviving firms. So we got two dependent variables: disappearances via M&A versus closed USOs.

As can be seen in Table 6, our correlation tests show that compared to survivors, USOs closed following bankruptcy situations, had no products on the market and/or in an advanced stage ($r = -0.409$, $p = 0.000$) did not have the support of VC ($r = -0.452$, $p = 0.000$) and could not form strategic alliances dedicated to exploitation ($r = -0.265$, $p = 0.008$). So all things being equal, disappearances due to bankruptcies seems to concern mainly the small size enterprises that had not fulfilled the conditions essential to the survival of biotechnology companies, especially those dedicated to human health.

It should also be noted that our statistical tests indicate no significant correlation ($r = -0.065$, $p = 0.526$) with the geographical location of USOs in major cities.

In case of disappearances through M&A (dependent variables), the results of statistical tests show (see Table 7) a positive correlation with VC support ($r = 0.383$, $p = 0.002$); strategic alliances ($r = 0.441$, $p = 0.000$); stage advanced and/or product on market ($r = 0.331$, $p = 0.002$) and the location in major Canadian cities ($r = 0.325$, $p = 0.003$). Moreover, our statistical tests indicate no significant relationship with the presence of star scientists.

In the light of the statistical results listed below, we assume that M&A transactions could be regarded as a strategic choice thoughtful and adapted to the realities of Canadian companies whose financial resources are limited. In fact, such a choice also seems justified since the biotechnology product development process is very costly and uncertain. We believe that a business model or entrepreneurial culture based on the creation and development of USOs with the aim of selling them later or merge. So, it could be considered that the trend for M&A in Canadian life sciences could be attributed to the phenomenal success stories of certain biotechnology companies, especially Biochem Pharma. In fact, this biotech company was acquired in 2001 by the British company Shire Pharmaceuticals for $6 billion. So, the characteristics of the external environment (opportunities and threats) can lead to similarities in business models as well as in the strategic guidelines adopted by the researchers–founders of biotechnology spin-offs. These leaders mimic each other in cases of isomorphism a theory initiated by DiMaggio and Powell (1983).

According to Carayannopoulos and Auster (2010), biotechnology is different from other high technology sectors because it has more complex and covers valuable knowledge. The same authors concluded that these factors incite the different stakeholders (e.g., VC investors, big pharma and mangers of biotechnology start-ups) to adopt M&A strategies. For instance, Francesco Bellini, chief executive of Biochem Pharma, had described the sale to Shire Pharmaceuticals as a strategic move that will benefit both the company and its shareholders.[3] Bellini had said in a release: "The pharmaceutical industry

---

[3] http://affaires.lapresse.ca/economie/200901/06/01-673033-biochem-pharma-larbre-mature.php.

is rapidly consolidating and new leaders are emerging. In this environment, scale and leadership are increasingly important." It would be appropriate to think that in Canada the leaders of USOs, managers of VC institutions, and the other stakeholders endorse these business models which seem adequate in specific circumstances (e.g., financial market crisis) and/or with limited resources (e.g., insufficient public support and limited VC industry).

Certainly the USOs having alliances with major pharmaceutical companies and other biotech companies are limited, but they were more likely to disappear in the context of M&A. Such trend could be related to the expansion strategies adopted by major pharmaceutical companies. The leaders of these big pharmaceutical firms are looking to consolidate their patent portfolios and product pipeline in order to face new disruptive technologies that can upset the rules. In other words, the big players seek to appropriate technologies from young biotechnology companies through strategic alliances and/or merger and acquisition transactions (Danzon *et al.*, 2007; Mittra, 2007; Sowlay & Lloyd, 2010).

So this DBF choice could be justified by the Canadian context dominated by the limits of the consumer market (critical mass) and public subsidies. It should be noted that the VC industry is not sufficiently developed to meet the needs of all USOs created and therefore unable to restrain the closure or migration of an enterprise to the American or European market for example. It seems also that the disappearances of Canadian USOs are part of a consolidation phenomenon registered across the global biotechnology and pharmaceutical industries (Ernst & Young, 2012). The market and commercial trade globalization, the increased level of competition to grab market share as well as the economic downturn cyclic generate a situation of consolidation in the global biopharmaceutical industry (McKelvey, 2008).

Conclusions and Policy Implications

In sum, the results of this longitudinal research conducted on a sample of 213 USOs dedicated to human health indicates that Canada is distinguished mainly by a majority of small-sized companies, the domination of early-stage projects, the exceptional geographic concentration in big cities and the difficulties to reach the support of VC and attract strategic alliances dedicated to the exploitation of new projects.

We believe that strategic alliances and interference of various stakeholders in the development life cycle of biotechnology spin-offs could play an important role in governance model adopted by the team management and, therefore, in its forms of disappearance. Some biotechnology companies might not have liquidity problems and decide all the same to be engaged in M&A strategies (Haeussler, 2007). As biotech spin-offs conduct costly, complex and multidisciplinary R&D projects, they are forced to cooperate with multiple stakeholders (e.g., government agencies, VC institutions, and pharmaceutical companies). Nevertheless to preserve their own interests, these different actors could influence the strategic directions and even destiny of spin-offs: continue alone versus sell or merge. According to the same line of reasoning, Lehoux *et al.* (2014) stressed the importance of differentiating business models in the health technology industry and they suggest that it is not only who makes decision that matters, but also how stakeholders' value expectations get embedded in spin-offs' value proposition.

For the policies makers, our study presents relevant and up-to-date portrait of Canadian spin-offs dedicated to human health as well as the factors justifying the survival or disappearance of these companies. We therefore suggest some solutions that can limit the constraints arising from the institutional environment and public policies. In general, Canadian public policies favor the emergence of a system where Canadian researchers and university–industry liaison offices are more oriented towards a quantitative approach mainly favoring the foundation of new dedicated biotechnology firms (Industry Canada, 2006). To remedy this situation, we believe that the Canadian governments at both levels, federal and provincial, should rethink their intervention strategies in the various biotechnology sectors (Lerner, 2010). We believe that it will be more judicious to implement various new programs and policies that address both the development as well as the creation of spin-offs (Vohora *et al.*, 2004). According to Mustar *et al.* (2006), we must distinguish between (1) spin-off creation and (2) spin-off development. The dimensions that differentiate between firms are the type of resources, the business model, and the institutional link.

This distinction is important as it suggests that practitioners may need to differentiate their approaches between the two areas rather than assuming that the development of a spin-off simply requires the continuation of activities, resources, business models, utilized during the creation phase. In other terms, policy makers should think about innovative policies and programs capable of ensuring long-term sustainability and viability of the Canadian biotechnology (Industry Canada, 2006; Niosi, 2009; Ernst & Young, 2012). So they have to adopt reengineering and benchmarking strategies inspired by models adopted by more advanced nations in the field of biotech companies' management. In this regard, Niosi (2009) had reported that Canada's tax credit for R&D and IRAP are useful programs. But they need to be complemented by other direct incentives that may help small technology firms to cross the "valley of death", complete proof of concept and become eligible to VC. The US Small Business Innovation Research (SBIR) program, imitated by Japan, is the best model for such an incentive and Canada should consider its adoption (Niosi, 2009). For their part, Lockett and Wright (2005) had recommended to develop appropriate capabilities of technology transfer officers in spinning-out companies. Universities and policy makers need to devote attention to the training and recruitment of technology officers with the broad base of commercial skills. According to Bubela and Caulfield (2010), the intervention of TTOs does not always produce obvious or traditional commercial outputs. Thus, the existing metrics used to measure the success of TTOs do not capture this reality and, as such, realignment is needed. In the same way, Sadek *et al.* (2015) specify that the ability of TTOs to effectively support the commercialization of university research results is related to the existence of an entrepreneurial culture in the university. Without culture and an entrepreneurial ecosystem, the role of TTOs is more limited to its well-established facilitation role.

Concerning the theoretical foundations, we believe that the examination of the disappearance of USOs seems to be a complex phenomenon that can be addressed in several theoretical schools (Rasmussen, 2011). The life cycle theory, the strategic management and dynamic capabilities, the business network theory as well as the institutional theories explain different aspects of the spin-off venturing process. The combination of various theories may provide a more holistic understanding of the academic entrepreneurship.

Limitations and Reflections Trails

First of all, we believe that our study provides a missing link in the chain of scientific publications dealing with disappearances of USOs. The majority of publications reviewed focus on issues related to the launch and development of such economic entity. So to our knowledge, this study is among the few research projects that has examined in depth the various issues (e.g., forms, reasons, and factors) characterizing the phenomenon of disappearance of young biotech companies. Concerning the research methodology, our results reveal that the factors behind the spin-offs bankruptcies have nothing to do with exits via M&A. So, our approach seems relevant in so far as our conclusions are not biased by the confusion of the two forms of exit.

We are also conscious that our work is an exploratory study that sketches the main features as well as the major trends characterizing the Canadian

USOs. So we want to propose to future research various trails of reflections in order to throw more light on life cycle of this kind of specific business. First, it would be appropriate to focus on each form of disappearance (M&A or bankruptcies) in the goal of achieving further study of the causes and consequences. To address the limitations of a quantitative approach, it would be interesting to conduct qualitative research through interviews with USOs leaders that have declared bankruptcy or who disappeared after M&A transactions. Then considering the regional differences found in our study, we propose to conduct interprovincial comparative studies (e.g., Quebec versus Ontario or British Columbia). We can also examine the phenomenon of USOs disappearance worldwide by comparing Canada with other countries such as France and Germany. Finally, it would be relevant to conduct further study on the links between VC support and the survival of USOs. Such an approach will clarify the VC life-expectancy effect by taking into consideration other more specific criteria such as the investor profiles (national and international private versus institutional), the amounts awarded, the stage funded (early versus advanced) and number of rounds.

References

Agrawal, A. & Cockburn, I. 2003. The anchor tenant hypothesis: exploring the role of large, local, R&D-intensive firms in regional innovation systems. *International Journal of Industrial Organization*, 21, 1227–1253.

Aharonson, B. S., Baum, J. A. & Plunket, A. 2008. Inventive and uninventive clusters: the case of Canadian biotechnology. *Research Policy*, 6(7), 1108–1131.

Aldridge, T. T. & Audretsch, D. B. 2011. The Bayh–Dole act and scientist entrepreneurship. *Research Policy*, 40(5), 1058–1067.

Ayayi, A. 2004. Public policy and venture capital: the Canadian labor-sponsored venture capital funds. *Journal of Small Business Management*, 42(3), 335–345.

Baum, J. A. C. & Silverman, B. S. 2004. Picking winners or building them? Alliance, intellectual, and human capital as selection criteria in venture financing and performance of biotechnology start-ups'. *Journal of Business Venturing*, 19(3), 411–436.

Black, B. & Gilson, R. 1998. Venture capital and the structure of capital markets: bank versus capital markets. *Journal of Financial Economies*, 47, 243–277.

Bubela, T. M. & Caulfield, T. 2010. Role and reality: technology transfer at Canadian universities. *Trends in Biotechnology*, 28(9), 447–451.

Carayannopoulos, S. & Auster, E. R. 2010. External knowledge sourcing in biotechnology through acquisition versus alliance: a KBV approach. *Research Policy*, 39(2), 254–267.

Carroll, G. R. & Hannan, M. T. 1995. *Organizations in Industry: Strategy, Structure and Selection*. Oxford University Press, New York.

Cattaneo, M., Meoli, M. & Vismara, S. 2015. Cross-border M&As of biotech firms affiliated with internationalized universities. *The Journal of Technology Transfer*, 40(3), 409–433.

Clayman, B.-P. & Holbrook, J. A. 2004. The Survival of University Spin-offs and Their Relevance to Regional Development. Centre for Policy Research in on Science and Technology (CPROST).

Colombo, M., Mustar, P. & Wright, M. 2010. Dynamics of science-based entrepreneurship. *The Journal of Technology Transfer*, 35(1), 1–15.

Conference Board of Canada. 2005. *Biotechnology in Canada: A Technology Platform for Growth*. The Conference Board of Canada, Ottawa. Available at http://www.agwest.sk.ca/upload mee image/115-06-Bioteclmology%20in%20 Canada(l).pdf

Criaco, G., Minola, T., Migliorini, P. & Serarols-Tarrés, C. 2013. To have and have not: founders' human capital and university start-up survival. *The Journal of Technology*, 39(4), 567–593.

Cumming, D. 2008. Contracts and exits in venture capital finance. *The Review of Financial Studies*, 21(5), 1947–1982.

Cumming, D. J. & MacIntosh, J. G. 2006. Crowding out private equity: Canadian evidence, *Journal of Business Venturing*, 21, 569–609.

Delgado, M., Porter, M. E. & Stern, S. 2010. Clusters and entrepreneurship. *Journal of Economic Geography*. 10(4), 495–518.

DeTienne, D. R. 2010. Entrepreneurial exit as a critical component of the entrepreneurial process: theoretical development. *Journal of Business Venturing*, 25(2), 203–215.

DiMaggio, P. & W.-W. Powell. 1983. The iron cage revisited: institutional isomorphism and collective rationality. *American Sociological Review*, 48(2), 147–160.

Danzon, P., Epstein, A. & Nicholson, S. 2007. Mergers and acquisitions in the pharmaceutical and biotech industries. *Managerial and Decision Economics*, 28 (4–5), 307–328.

DiMasi, J.-A., Hansen, R. W. & Grabowski, H. G. 2003. The Price of innovation: new estimates of drug development costs. *Journal of Health Economies*, 22, 151–185.

Ernst & Young (2012). Beyond Borders Global Biotechnology Report 2012. Available at [online] http://www.ey.com/Publication/vwLUAssets/Beyond_ borders_2012/$FILE/Beyond_borders_2012.

Etzkowitz, H. 2002. *MIT and the Rise of Entrepreneurial Science*. Routledge, London.

Fontana, R. & Malerba, F. 2010. Entry, demand and survival in the semiconductor industry. *Industrial and corporate change*, 19(5), 1629–1654.

Glaeser, E. L, Kerr, W. R. & Ponzetto, G. A. M. 2009. Clusters of entrepreneurship. *Journal of Urban Economics*, 67(1), 150–168.

Gompers, P. & Lerner, J. 2001. The venture capital revolution. *The Journal of Economic Perspectives*, 15(2), 145–168.

Haeussler, C. 2007. Proactive versus reactive M&A activities in the biotechnology industry. *Journal of High Technology Management Research*, 17(2), 109–123.

Hayter, C. S. 2013. Harnessing university entrepreneurship for economic growth: factors of success among university spin-offs. *Economic Development Quarterly*, 27, 18–28.

Hellmann, T. & Puri, M. 2000. The interaction between product market and financing strategy: the role of venture capital. *Review of Financial Studies*, 13(4), 959–984.

Hochberg, Y., Ljungqvist, A. & Lu, Y. 2007. Whom you know matters: venture capital networks and investment predominance. *Journal of Finance*, 62, 251–301.

Hsu, D. H. 2007. Experienced entrepreneurial founders, organizational capital, and venture capital funding. *Research Policy*, 36, 722–741.

Industry Canada. 2006. The Canadian Biopharmaceutical Industry Technology Roadmap: Technologies to Improve R&D Productivity. Ottawa, Industry Canada, catalogue No. Iu44-31 /2006-MRC.

Kenney, M. & Patton, D. 2011. Does inventor ownership encourage university research-derived entrepreneurship? A six university comparison. Research Policy 40, 1100–1112.

Kolympiris, C., Kalaitzandonakes, N. & Miller, D. 2015. Location choice of academic entrepreneurs: evidence from the US biotechnology industry, *Journal of Business Venturing*, 30(2), 227–254.

Landry, R., Amara, N. & Rherrad, I. 2006. Why are some university researchers more likely to create spin-offs than others? Evidence from Canadian universities. *Research Policy*, 35, 1599–1615.

Lehoux, G., Daudelin, B., Williams-Jones, J. L., Denis, L. & Longo, C. 2014. How do business model and health technology design influence each other? Insights from a longitudinal case study of three academic spin-offs. *Research Policy*, 43, 1025–1038.

Lerner, J. 2010. *Boulevard of Broken Dreams: Why Public Efforts to Boost Entrepreneurship and Venture Capital Have Failed — and What to Do About it*. Princeton University Press, New Jersey.

Lerner, J. 2004. The university and the start-up: lessons from the past two decades. *The Journal of Technology Transfer*, 30(1–2), 49–56.

Lerner, J., Shane, H. & Tsai, A. 2003. Do equity financing cycles matter? Evidence from biotechnology alliances. *Journal of Financial Economies*, 67(3), 411–446.

Levitte, Y. M. & Bagchi-Sen, S. 2010. Demographics, innovative outputs and alliance strategies of Canadian biotech firms. *European Planning Studies*, 18(5), 669–690.

Lindsey, L. 2008. Blurring firm boundaries: the role of venture capital in strategic alliances. *The Journal of Finance*, 63(3), 1137–1168.

Lockett, A. & Wright, M. 2005. Resources, capabilities, risk capital and the creation of university spin-out companies. *Research Policy*, 34(7), 1043–1057.

Mangematin, V., Lemarié, S. Boissin, J.-P., Catherine, O., Corolleur, F., Coronini, R. & Trommetter, M. 2003. Development of SMEs and heterogeneity of trajectories: the case of biotechnology in France. *Research Policy*, 32, 621–638.

Marshall, A. 1920, *Principles of Economics*. MacMillan, London.

McKelvey, M. 2008. Emerging Business Models and Institutional Drivers Bioeconomy 2030, OECD, Paris. Available at [online] http://www.oecd.org/futures/bioeconomy/2030.

Mittra, J. 2007. Life science innovation and the restructuring of the pharmaceutical industry: merger, acquisition and strategic alliance behaviour of large firms. *Technology Analysis and Strategic Management*, 19(3), 279–301.

Moustakbal, A. 2014. The disappearance of dedicated biotechnology firms in Canada, *Int. J. Biotechnology*, 13(1/2/3), 66–89.

Mustar, P., Renault, M., Colombo, M.-G., Piva, E., Fontes, M., Lockett, A., Wright, M. Clarysse, B. & Moray, N. 2006. Conceptualising the heterogeneity of research-based spin-offs: a multidimensional taxonomy. *Research Policy*, 35(2), 289–308.

Nicolaou, N. & Birley, S. 2003. Social networks in organizational emergence: the university spinout phenomenon. *Management Science*, 49, 1702–1725.

Niosi, J. 2006. Success factors in Canadian academic spin-offs. *Journal of Technology Transfer*, 31, 451–457.

Niosi, J. 2003. Alliances are not enough explaining rapid growth in biotechnology firrns. *Research Policy*, 32(5), 737–750.

Niosi, J. 2011. Complexity and path dependence in biotechnology innovation systems, *Industrial and Corporate Change*, 20(6), 1795–1826.

Niosi, J. & Queenton, J. 2010. Knowledge capital in biotechnology industry: impacts on Canadian firm performance. *Int. J. Knowledge-Based Development*, 1(1), 136–151.

Niosi, J. & Banik, M. 2005. The evolution and performance of biotechnology regional systems of innovation. *Cambridge Journal of Economics*, 29, 343–357.

Nuria, C., Valera-Candamio, L., Soares, I. & Rodeiro, D. 2012. Critical analysis of the role of universities in the creation and survival of university spin-offs. Proposal of an academic model of support. *Advances in Management & Applied Economics*, 2(2), 53–82.

O'Shea, R. P., Allen, T. J., Chevalier, A. & Roche, F. 2005. Entrepreneurial orientation, technology transfer and spinoff performance of US universities. *Research Policy*, 34, 994–1009.

Owen-Smith, J. & Powell, W. W. 2004. Knowledge networks as channels and conduits: the effects of spillovers in the boston biotechnology community. *Organization Science*, 15(1), 5–21.

Pirnay, F., Surlemont, B. & Nlemvo, F. 2003. Toward a typology of university spin-offs. *Small Business Economics*, 21(4), 355–369.

Porter, M. E. 2000. Location, competition, and economic development: local clusters in a global economy. *Economic Development Quarterly*, 14(1), 15–34.

Powell, W. W., Koput, K. W. Bowie, J. I. & Smith-Doerr, L. 2002. The spatial clustering of science and capital: accounting for biotech firm-venture capital relationships. *Regional Studies*, 36, 291–305.

Powell, W. W., Koput, K. W., White, D. R. & Owen-Smith, J. 2005. Network dynamics in a field evolution: the growth of interorganizational collaboration in life sciences. *American Journal of Sociology*, 41(1), 1132–1205.

Rasmussen, E. 2011. Understanding academic entrepreneurship: exploring the emergence of university spinoff ventures using process theories. *International Small Business Journal*, 29(5), 448–471.

Rasmussen, E. 2008. Government instruments to support the commercialization of university research: lessons from Canada. *Technovation*, 28(8), 506–517.

Rasmussen, E. & Borch, O. J. 2010. University capabilities in facilitating entrepreneurship: a longitudinal study of spin-off ventures at mid-range universities. *Research Policy*, 39, 602–612.

Rosiello, A. & Parris, S. 2009. The patterns of venture capital investment in the UK bio-healthcare sector: the role of proximity, cumulative learning and specialisation. *International Journal of Entrepreneurial Finance*, 11(3), 185–211.

Sadek, T., Kleiman, R. & Loutfy, R. 2015. The role of technology transfer offices in growing new entrepreneurial ecosystems around mid-sized universities. *International Journal of Innovation and Regional Development*, 6(1), 61–79.

Sandler, D. 2004. Venture Capital and Tax Incentives: A Comparative Study of Canada and the United States. Canadian Tax Foundation, Canadian Tax Papers, No. 108, Toronto, Ontario.

Saxenian, A. 1994. *Regional Advantage: Culture and Competition in Silicon Valley and Route 128.* Harvard University, Cambridge, MA.

Shane, S. 2004. *Academic Entrepreneurship: University Spinoffs and Wealth Creation*, Elgar, Cheltenham.

Statistics Canada. 2008. *Biotechnology spinoffs: Transferring Knowledge from Universities and Government Labs to the Marketplace.* Available at http://www.statcan.gc.ca/pub/88-003-x/2008001/article/10581-eng.htm.

Statistics Canada. 2007. Selected Results of the Biotechnology Use and Development Survey 2005, Ottawa, Statistics Canada, catalogue No. 88F0006XIE.

Stenberg, R. 2014. Success factors of university-spin-offs: regional government support programs versus regional environment. *Technovation*, 34, 137–148.

Sowlay, M. & Lloyd, S. 2010. The current M&A environment and its strategic implications for emerging biotherapeutic companies. *Journal of Commercial Biotechnology*, 16, 109–119.

Van Beuzekom, B. & Arundel, A. 2009. *OECD Biotechnology Statistics 2009.* Paris: Organization for Economic Cooperation and Development.

Van Geenhuizen, M. & Soetanto, D. P. 2009. Academic spin-offs at different ages: a case study in search of obstacles to growth. *Technovation*, 29, 671–681.

Vincett, P. S. 2010. The economic impacts of academic spin-off companies, and their implications for public policy. *Research Policy*, 39(6), 36–747.

Vohora, A., Wright, M. & Lockett, A. 2004. Critical junctures in the development of university high-tech spinout companies. *Research Policy*, 33(1), 147–175.

Walter, A., Auer, M. & Ritter, T. 2006. The impact of network capabilities and entrepreneurial orientation on university spin-off performance. *Journal of Business Venturing*, 21(4), 541–567.

Wennberg, K., Wiklund, J., DeTienne, D. R. & Cardon, M. S. 2010. Reconceptualizing entrepreneurial exit: divergent exit routes and their drivers. *Journal of Business Venturing*, 25(4), 361–375.

Wright, M., Clarysse, B., Mustar, P. & Lockett, A. 2007. Academic Entrepreneurship in Europe. UK Edward Elgar, Cheltenham.

Zahra, S. A., Filatotchev, I. & Wright, M. 2009. How do threshold firms sustain corporate entrepreneurship? The role of boards of directors and knowledge. *Journal of Business Venturing*, 24(3), 248–260.

Zhang, J. 2009. The performance of university spin-offs: an exploratory analysis using venture capital data. *Journal of Technology Transfer*, 34, 255–285.

Zucker, L. G., Darby, M. R. & Armstrong, J. S. 2002. Commercializing knowledge: university science, knowledge capture, and firm performance in biotechnology. *Management Science* 48(1), 138–153.

Zucker, L. G., Darby, M. R. & Brewer, M.-B. 1998. Intellectual human capital and the birth of US biotechnology enterprises. *American Economic Review*, 88(1), 290–306.

Chapter 9

Science-Based Entrepreneurial Firms as Real Options: Assessing the Outcomes of the Norwegian Firm Population from 1995 to 2012

Einar Rasmussen

Nord University Business School 8049 Bodø, Norway

einar.rasmussen@nord.no

Marius Tuft Mathisen

Department of Industrial Economics and Technology Management

Norwegian University of Science and Technology, Norway

marius.mathisen@iot.ntnu.no

Science-based entrepreneurial firms (SBEFs) that are set up to commercialize knowledge created in universities and other public research institutions typically face long development paths. They develop new products and services associated with high levels of technological, market, and organizational uncertainties. Despite strong interest from policy makers and universities to promote the creation of SBEFs, there is little systematic evidence on the value creation patterns and potential impacts of these firms. By using a real options approach, this study provides a detailed assessment of the portfolio of all 471 SBEFs supported by technology transfer offices, incubators and science parks in Norway from 1995 to 2012. By following an entire portfolio

of firms over an extensive period of time, we overcome some of the shortcomings of prior spin-off research. The findings reveal that 97 firms in the
portfolio had reached what could be considered a successful outcome, 126
had failed, while the remaining 251 may still be considered as real options
with an uncertain outcome. Acquisitions appear to be an important mode of
successful outcomes for these ventures; an outcome currently underexplored in the literature. The chapter concludes with implications for policy
makers seeking to maximize the value creation potential of spin-offs from
academic institutions.

Introduction

The possible benefits of academic entrepreneurship have attracted significant attention (Grimaldi *et al.*, 2011; Shane, 2004). Policymakers and universities have spent considerable resources to promote the creation of science-based
entrepreneurial firms (SBEFs) as a tool to create value from investments
made in scientific research (Kochenkova *et al.*, 2015). The impact of SBEFs is,
however, highly debated among both practitioners and researchers (Harrison
& Leitch, 2010). Some argue that SBEFs enhance economic development
through creation of new knowledge-based employment, acting as agents of
technology transfer improving the absorptive capacity of the region (Clausen
& Rasmussen, 2013; Criaco *et al.*, 2013). Thus, these authors see SBEFs play-
ing an important role in the innovation system by transforming scientific
knowledge into commercial application (Hindle & Yencken, 2004). Others
question the impact of SBEFs and argue that exceptional success stories cannot be generalized and that most SBEFs are technology lifestyle firms that
remain small, despite strong public support (Brown & Mason, 2014; Harrison
& Leitch, 2010).

In general, studies of early-stage SBEFs following the growth of such
firms some years after establishment provide rather disappointing results
(Borlaug *et al.*, 2009; Harrison & Leitch, 2010). SBEFs have also been found
to underperform in comparison with other start-ups (Wennberg, Wiklund,
& Wright, 2011), although such comparisons have not produced conclusive
results due to use of a wide range of firm definitions, contexts and time
periods. On the other hand, studies with time frames over several decades
conclude that SBEFs play a key role for economic growth at both regional
and national level (Garnsey & Heffernan, 2005; Lawton Smith & Ho, 2006;
Vincett, 2010).

There is limited evidence on the impacts of SBEFs and the development
paths that lead to such impacts. Conceptual frameworks to assess

the development of such firms are also lacking. In this chapter, we use a portfolio perspective to assess the value creation of the national portfolio of SBEFs established between 1995 and 2012 in Norway. We provide a comprehensive analysis of the national population of SBEFs over a substantial time period, and assess the value creation generated by such firms. We also untangle how different categories of outcomes contribute to the overall value creation of the portfolio.

To account for the particular characteristics of SBEFs, we use a real options framework. This approach provides three important benefits when evaluating the impact of a portfolio of SBEFs. First, the uncertain nature of SBEFs makes it challenging to estimate ex-ante the value and impact of a portfolio of SBEFs. A real options perspective can take into account the decreasing uncertainty along venture development. Second, a real options framework allows for separation between different outcomes in the portfolio. Distinct outcomes contribute in different ways to value creation, where some outcomes have "concealed" impacts that are often overlooked when applying traditional approaches. Third, the non-normal distribution of performance among high-tech firms in general, and SBEFs in particular, can be more appropriately understood with a real-option perspective.

This chapter is further organized as follows. First, we briefly review our theoretical framework with particular emphasis on real options theory. Second, we outline our research method and the empirical context of SBEFs in Norway. Third, we present the results of our analysis of value creation of the portfolio. Lastly, we conclude and provide some implications of our results.

Theoretical Framework

Science-based entrepreneurship and uncertainty

SBEFs can be seen as an extreme type of entrepreneurial ventures because of their high levels of uncertainty across several dimensions. First, SBEFs often commercialize early-stage and novel scientific technology that initially take the form of "proofs and prototypes" (Jensen & Thursby, 2001; Shane, 2004), rather than proven products for commercial application. This gives rise to significant technological uncertainty whether the technology would be functional and profitable at an industrial scale (Lubik & Garnsey, 2015). New technologies developed in industry are likely to be more incremental and applied in nature, and thus closer to practical application. Second, as SBEFs are established to commercialize new scientific knowledge, their innovations can typically be characterized as technology push, rather than market pull. Further, these technologies tend to be radical and general-purpose in nature (Shane, 2004). This creates significant market uncertainty because it is not clear which markets should be targeted for products or services developed based on the technology. Also, the attractiveness of those markets are uncertain, as they might be young and fragmented. Third, compared to new ventures developed in a traditional business context, SBEFs emerging from universities are typically associated with high levels of organizational uncertainty. Academia and business operate with different logics, and access to many of the business related competencies are often in short supply in academic organizations (Rasmussen *et al.*, 2011). Hence, SBEFs are often initiated in an academic environment and face uncertainty with respect to the development of a new venture that will operate in a commercial environment.

Table 1 summarizes three different types of uncertainty associated with SBEFs and contrasts these to other technology ventures emerging from industry. These differences, leading to significantly higher levels of

Table 1.   Types of uncertainty related to SBEFs in comparison with other technology ventures.

	New ventures based on research in academia	New ventures based on research in industry	Implications for SBEFs
Technological uncertainty	Often early-stage and novel technology based on scientific discoveries	Often more incremental, applied and validated technology	Need to verify the viability of the technology at industrial scale
Market uncertainty	Often radical and general-purpose technology looking for market applications. Technology push	Technology developed on the basis of recognized market needs and opportunities. Market pull	Need to identify or develop new market applications and customer needs
Organizational uncertainty	Originates in an academic context with a lack of business infrastructure and competencies	Originates in an industry context with associated business infrastructure and complementary assets	Need to transform the venture from operating in an academic to a commercial context

uncertainty, have important implications for how SBEFs should be assessed by policymakers and investors. While the potential value of high risk investments can be estimated, decision making under uncertainty is extremely difficult (Knight, 1921). Hence, in a short-term perspective, the safest route to maximize return from a portfolio of SBEFs is to invest in cases with lower levels of uncertainty and relatively shorter time to market.

The tradeoff between projects with lower and higher levels of uncertainty is often a tradeoff between more incremental or more radical innovation projects. The innovation literature often points at the long term benefits of investing in radical innovation, also for smaller firms (Rosenbusch *et al.*, 2010). It has also been argued that new and small firms are often better suited to develop more radical innovations than firms that are already well established in the market (Sears & Hoetker, 2014).

For SBEFs the high level of uncertainty is challenging, because the possible returns from investing in such ventures are unknown and will typically be in a distant future. Hence, equity investors and other resource providers can be reluctant to support these ventures (Wright *et al.*, 2006). As SBEFs typically have large funding needs to take their technologies to market, they are especially vulnerable to the "funding gap" (Rasmussen & Sørheim, 2012; Winborg & Landstrom, 2001). Seen from a macro perspective, this potentially leads to underinvestment in such ventures and provides a rationale for governments to support the creation and early development of SBEFs. Indeed, these ventures have become heavily subsidized in most Western countries (Kochenkova *et al.*, 2015). Given the specific role of SBEFs and the heavy public spending to promote such firms, it is very important to assess the results in terms of long-term value creation. In the following, we will assess the portfolio of SBEFs in Norway in the period 1995–2012 and examine the value creation of this portfolio.

Science-based entrepreneurship as real options

The high levels of uncertainty associated with SBEFs make the real options theory a well-suited framework to assess a portfolio of such firms. The uncertainty in early stages makes it difficult to assess the potential long-run value creation of the portfolio. The real options logic implies that an investment in any of these new ventures can be seen as a real option that opens up for future opportunities to make more informed decisions (McGrath, 1999). In contrast to options used as financial instruments, where the owner of the option has the right to exercise a financial transaction, real options provide the opportunity to make operational business decisions. Due to the high levels of uncertainty, the actors investing time and resources in SBEFs can not realistically calculate the value of their investment using either absolute (e.g., discounted cash flow) or relative (e.g., accounting multiples) valuation techniques (Damodaran, 2009; Ge *et al.*, 2005). Rather, they invest in a real option that provides the opportunity of becoming involved in a new venture that potentially can become highly successful. In this perspective, the involvement in the SBEF provides an opportunity, but no obligation, to follow up with new investments when the uncertainty has been reduced.

In a portfolio of SBEFs, the firms can be characterized as either being a real option or as having reached an unsuccessful or successful outcome. The theory on real options in entrepreneurship holds that there is a tendency to spend much energy in trying to pick winners and avoid investing in unsuccessful cases. This leads to underinvestment in developing uncertain cases that might be potentially valuable options (McGrath, 1999). If applied to a portfolio of SBEFs, the real options logic implies that high uncertainty, and thereby high variance, will increase the value of this portfolio. This corresponds to higher volatility of the underlying asset that leads to higher value in the context of financial options. If only the cases with highest likelihood of being successful, i.e., the least uncertain ones, are selected for further development, it may reduce the number of failures in the portfolio. However, it may also lead to the unintended effect that many of the projects with highest potential will not be continued due to high levels of uncertainty. Real options logic argues that the highly uncertain projects should be managed in a way that keep the costs at a lowest possible level, without sacrificing potential opportunities (McGrath & MacMillan, 2000).

Further, a real options perspective is helpful due to the non-normal distribution of returns in a portfolio of new technology-based ventures. Previous research on technology-based entrepreneurship has found that a small portion of successful firms represent the majority of total returns (Astebro, 2003; Mason & Harrison, 2002). This effect is arguably even more pronounced for SBEFs due to the higher levels of uncertainty in their technology, market and organization. As such, the outcome of a few firms can shift the return distribution dramatically. The impact of a portfolio is therefore sensitive to time of measurement, because at any given point in time the portfolio has a set of real options that might prove very valuable at a later stage.

In a portfolio of SBEFs, the majority of firms will not be successful, and most firms spend considerable amount of time before it becomes clear whether it is a success or not. The SBEF portfolio will therefore contain many cases with unknown outcome, which can be characterized as real rather options. From a societal perspective, it is desired that these firms, or rather options, are further developed to clarify their ultimate outcome.

Method

Context: The FORNY-program in Norway

The empirical context for the analysis presented in this chapter is the portfolio of SBEFs connected to the FORNY program in Norway. The FORNY program was a policy and funding initiative to promote science-based entrepreneurship, administrated by The Research Council of Norway (Gulbrandsen & Rasmussen, 2012). The program was established in 1995 and operated until 2012, when the new FORNY2020 program continued with slightly different objectives, more aligned with the increasingly mature infrastructure for science-based entrepreneurship in Norway.

FORNY's objective was to increase wealth creation in Norway by commercializing research results with considerable market potential. To achieve this, the program's activities aimed to:

- Raise awareness and enhance the attitudes and behavior of research communities, making the commercialization of research results an integrated and prioritized task at research institutions;
- Assist in establishing professional organizations and systems for commercialization of research results, including developing competent support mechanisms for scientists having made scientific discoveries with commercial potential;
- Encourage and contribute to increased cooperation between research communities, entrepreneurs, investors, industry and commerce, and public authorities.

The FORNY program worked primarily through the technology transfer offices or equivalent organizations (hereby referred to collectively as TTOs) connected to universities, research institutions and university hospitals (Rasmussen & Gulbrandsen, 2012). As many other European countries, Norway passed changes in legislation related to intellectual property developed at universities in 2004, which essentially led to the establishment of formal TTOs at the major universities. The program was a source of funding for TTOs, both to fund their internal operations and to provide financial support to specific commercialization projects. The FORNY-program

Table 2.   Year of entry and accumulated number of firms in the FORNY-portfolio.

Year	95	96	97	98	99	00	01	02	03	04	05	06	07	08	09	10	11	12
New firms entries	7	18	23	26	25	26	37	34	23	20	37	27	32	33	36	19	26	22
Accumulated	7	25	48	74	99	125	162	196	219	239	276	303	335	368	404	423	449	471
Firm exits	0	0	2	1	3	4	1	8	7	10	8	8	8	5	10	19	7	19

operated with an incentive-pay model for the TTOs where bonuses were awarded for successful establishment of new commercialization projects (Gulbrandsen & Rasmussen, 2012). In total, 471 firms were reported into the program continuously over its history, as shown in Table 2.

The nature of the FORNY program, and the incentive model applied, has certain important benefits. First, the vast majority of all new ventures in Norway having origins at universities, research institutions or hospitals is represented in this portfolio due to the reporting incentive granted by the bonus model. As such, the sample is most likely very close to the Norwegian population of SBEFs. Second, as firms are reported in real-time the portfolio avoids survival and other reporting biases. Third, the period of 1995–2012 is quite long compared to most other studies.

Outcome categories for new ventures

Using the real options perspective, SBEFs can at the time of start-up be seen as real options with unknown outcomes. Over time, the firms will experience outcomes of their commercialization activities. In a simple classification of the portfolio, some firms have achieved a positive outcome, some a negative outcome and some are still real options with an uncertain outcome. These different outcomes are summarized in Table 3 and explained in detail below.

Positive outcome; realized commercialization

A positive outcome implies that the market in some way has accepted the firm's product or service on commercial terms. A general challenge in business research is how to define, measure and interpret the concepts of firm performance and success. For our purposes, it is not critical to develop a complex model to determine the degree of positive outcome. Rather, we assign broad outcome categories for portfolio firms over their life cycle. Although there is no clearly defined trigger level of when a firm can be

Table 3.   Classification of outcomes in a portfolio of SBEFs.

Outcome	Category	Definition
Positive outcome: Realized commercialization	Independent firm	Sustainable operating profit (i.e., the firm has a profit of at least 12,000 EUR for two consecutive years).
	Acquired firm	The firm's activity is acquired by a larger industrial incumbent
Negative outcome: Abandoned commercialization	Abandoned firm	The firm's activity has been abandoned, and the original firm has (or will shortly) been dissolved
Uncertain outcome: Real option	Potential firm	The firm has active operations, but has not reached a point of sustainable profits or acquisition
	Dormant firm	The firm is active, but appears to have no or very limited operating activity

considered to have reached this milestone, it would be reasonable to assume that the firm has some level of commercial sales in the market and is making a profit on its operations. Because small and new ventures often have large variations in activity and sales from year to year, we decided on a minimum earnings (EBIT - Earnings Before Interest and Taxes) requirement of 100,000 NOK (about 12,000 EUR) over two consecutive years to be considered as a realized commercialization. In addition, the firms were manually investigated to confirm that the profit was generated from commercial sales and not other sources of revenue (e.g., public grants). This does not guarantee that the firm will be profitable or survive in the long run. However, as a first approximation, this outcome means that the firm has successfully brought a product or service to an initial market application with a profit.

Moreover, many of the most promising SBEFs are acquired by other firms seeking to make use of or further develop the technology (Meoli *et al.*, 2013). From a societal perspective, this may be a preferred solution because larger and more established firms are often better able to exploit the technology when a SBEF has provided initial proof of concept (Puranam *et al.*, 2006). For many SBEFs an acquisition is also a preferred exit option, especially for stakeholders like venture capitalist investors (Clarysse *et al.*, 2007). We define an acquisition as an event where a larger incumbent acquires all equity (or the net assets) with industrial motives. The latter implies that only non-financial companies can be considered as an acquirer. After an acquisition, the acquired firm can either continue to operate independently or be absorbed into the acquirer's organization.

Negative outcome; abandoned commercialization

A negative outcome implies that the commercialization process pursued by the SBEF is abandoned. This typically coincides with a bankruptcy, dissolution or other formal discontinuation of the firm's registration in the National Register of Business Enterprises.[1] In some cases, it may take some time from the commercialization activities are abandoned until the firm is discontinued legally. Therefore we have defined the firm's commercialization project as abandoned if the firm has no activity for two consecutive years (0 employees and expenditures of less than 100 000 NOK — about 12,000 €). We also used other sources to confirm that the firm has ceased their operations.

Uncertain outcome; real options

The outcome for many of the commercialization processes is still not clear, especially among the younger SBEFs. These firms are considered as real options. According to real options reasoning (McGrath, 1999), activity is preferred over passivity to increase the value of the portfolio. Hence, it would be desirable to resolve uncertainties by investing resources into developing these SBEFs and reach a more conclusive outcome. Therefore, we split this category in two groups; potential firms and dormant firms.

The potential firms are characterized by having significant activity, although they are still not profitable or acquired. These SBEFs have typically received public support or external equity allowing them to invest in technology, market or organizational development. We define these firms as having operating expenses of more than 1 million NOK (about 120,000 EUR) in the last reported fiscal year (2012).

The dormant SBEFs are those with no or low activity. Some of the firms that are recently established are placed into this group because the activity is too recent to have been reported or has not yet started. For older firms, we assume that dormant firms are less likely to reach an outcome in the near future. There may be many reasons for a SBEF to be dormant. Some may have abandoned their activity, while others may lack funding or other

---

[1] The Brønnøysund Register Centre. http://www.brreg.no/english/.

resources to further develop the commercialization project. With the exception of the most recently established firms, the majority of the dormant firms have had no activity for a significant period of time.

Coding of outcome categories

Although the above categories are relatively simple, it is not always straightforward to assess the correct category for a firm. To reduce potential errors, our coding efforts combine information from several data sources. An important source is the annual financial statements for each firm, that provides a reasonable good status report of each firm on an annual basis. In addition, the official corporate announcements to the Register of Business Enterprises reveals important events such as legal mergers, divestments and terminal events such as bankruptcy, de-registration or dissolution. In addition, we used an extensive media and news archive[2] to collect all media and news stories mentioning each firm. The coding was done by research assistants and approved by a senior researcher.

The coding exercise reveals the following distribution of outcomes in the Norwegian SBEF portfolio of 474 firms as of July 2013:

- Positive outcome: 97, whereof 74 as operating firms and 23 as acquisitions.
- Negative outcome: 126.
- Uncertain outcome (real options): 251, whereof 117 as potential and 134 as dormant firms (this includes 46 firms established in 2011 or later).

It is a comprehensive task to determine exactly what happened to all firms. However, we believe our coding is providing a much more precise account of the development in the SBEF portfolio compared to analyses based purely on register data. We have only coded positive outcomes in cases where there is no reasonable doubt that this is the case. Hence, our analysis provides a conservative estimate of the number of positive outcomes in the portfolio.

---

[2] Using Retriever, the largest media surveillance provides in the Nordic region. http://www.retriever-info.com/.

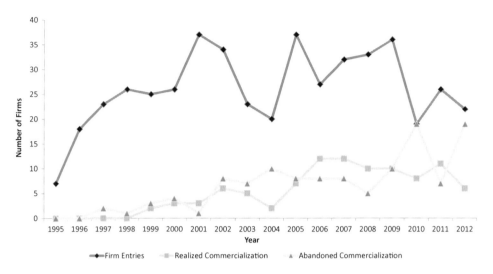

Figure 1.   Number of new entries, realized (positive) and abandoned (negative) commercialization outcomes in the SBEF portfolio per year from 1995 to 2012.

Analysis and Discussion

Status in the SBEF portfolio over time

The Norwegian portfolio of SBEFs is growing over time. Figure 1 shows that the number of new entries since the late 1990s has varied between 19 and 37 each year. Moreover, the number of positive and negative outcomes increases over time, as would be expected because the number of firms in the portfolio increases.

Although the number of firms in the portfolio is growing due to new entries, the number of real options, or firms with an uncertain outcome, depends on the aggregated number of positive and negative outcomes. This is shown in Figure 2, where the number of real options in the portfolio is growing over the first 14 years, reaching 257 firms in 2009. In the subsequent period, the number of positive and negative outcomes was similar to the number of new entries, stabilizing the total number of real options in the portfolio.

The above overview of the entire portfolio provides limited information about the development at the firm level. Figure 3 shows the share of the firms that reaches a positive or negative outcome for any given year after entering the SBEF portfolio as a new firm. Such cohort analysis provides a clearer view of the outcome distribution by firm age.

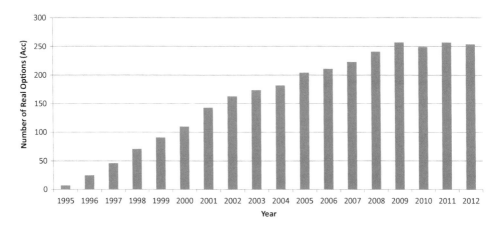

Figure 2.   Accumulated number of firms in the SBEF portfolio with status as uncertain outcome/real option per year.

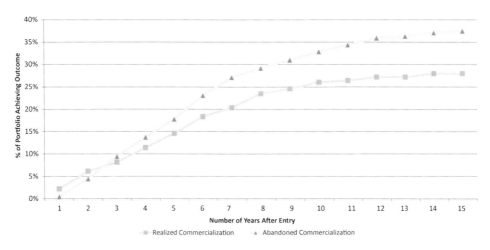

Figure 3.   Percentage of SBEF portfolio with a realized and abandoned outcome by years after establishment.

The patterns are similar for both positive and negative outcomes. The share of firms reaching an outcome increases most rapidly from year 1 to about year 8, when about 29% of the firms have reached a negative outcome and 23% have reached a positive outcome. The number of outcomes are lower in the period from 9 to 12 years after establishment, where the share of negative and positive outcomes seem to stabilize close to 40% and 30%, respectively.

Figure 3 illustrates the relatively long time horizon before SBEFs reach an outcome. Ten years after establishment, about one third of the commercialization projects have been abandoned and one fourth have realized some initial commercial success. The curve also illustrates that if a firm has not reached a positive outcome within the first 8 to 10 years, the likelihood of becoming successful appears limited. However, this visualization does not indicate the magnitude of success. It is possible that later successes have a larger impact on average as they have spent more time developing their technology and business concept. Nevertheless, approx. 40% of the SBEFs in the portfolio still have an uncertain outcome after 10 years, and few of these seems to reach an outcome after 15 years. This indicates that at least a 10-year perspective is needed to assess the initial impact of SBEFs.

Value creation in the SBEF portfolio

Our access to the complete set of firm financial records provides a unique opportunity to follow economic impact of the portfolio over time. As measure of value creation, we use the Norwegian governmental definition of Gross Value Added (GVA), which is used to calculate the gross domestic product. We calculated the GVA across the complete SBEF portfolio to 5.4 billion NOK (about 615 million EUR). This consists of accumulated negative earnings (EBIT - Earnings Before Interests and Taxes) of 3.3 billion NOK summarized with accumulated salaries of 7.8 billion NOK and depreciations of 0.8 billion NOK. Figure 4 illustrates the total GVA for the SBEF portfolio each year

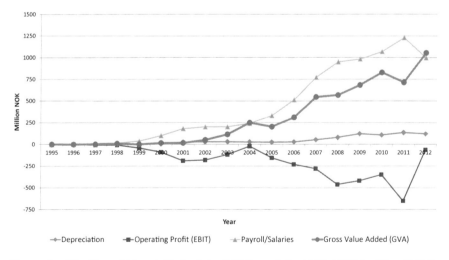

Figure 4.   The Gross Value Added of the SBEF portfolio 1995–2012 (million NOK).

between 1995 and 2012.[3] The values are nominal, and adjusting for inflation only has a minor impact as most of the values occur in relatively recent times (i.e., about 0.2 billion NOK higher GVA). The negative earnings show that most of the firms are in a pre-commercial phase. Most of the GVA is represented by salaries financed by owners and funding sources, rather than from commercial sales.

Using accounting data to assess the value creation in this SBEF portfolio has two major limitations. First, it can be questioned whether accounting data provides relevant information on the status of early stage technology firms, where the potential profit is expected to be realized many years after initial investments. One example in the portfolio is the firm Optinose,[4] which according to the 2011 accounting figures had a negative value-added of close to 100 million NOK, but in July 2013 entered a licensing agreement with an estimated value of 670 million NOK.[5] Second, many firms undergo changes that makes it difficult to follow their development using accounting information, such as mergers, acquisitions and other changes in the formal structure of the business entity. The registered entity often disappears when a firm is acquired, while the business activity may be continued successfully without being traceable using accounting information from the original firm. As discussed below, acquisitions tend to generate value exchanges that represent a significant amount of the total value creation in the portfolio.

Value creation in the different categories of the SBEF-portfolio

To assess a more realistic GVA of the SBEF-portfolio using real options logic, we use the categories of outcomes presented in Table 2. The firms in each of these categories have distinct characteristics that make it challenging to analyze the entire portfolio jointly. For some of these categories, GVA cannot be estimated with comparable methods. As summarized in Table 4, the firms with a positive outcome operating as independent firms can be traced through accounting information, while this is not possible for many of the acquisitions. Firms with a negative outcome can usually be traced until their closure. The uncertain cases can also be traced, but the accounting information is less relevant at these early stages.

---

[3] It should be noted that the 2012 number are not complete due to some firm not having delivered 2012 financial records when the analysis was performed
[4] http://www.optinose.com/
[5] Dagens Næringsliv (Norwegian business newspaper) published June 4, 2013

Table 4.   Calculation of value added in different categories of SBEFs.

Outcome	Category	Possible data sources to assess value added
Positive outcome: Realized commercialization	Independent firm	Can be traced using accounting information
	Acquired firm	Must be traced manually based on acquisition value, which is not comparable to the GVA of firms under going concern
Negative outcome: Abandoned commercialization	Abandoned firm	Can be traced using accounting information until abandonment
Uncertain outcome: Real option	Potential firm	Can be traced using accounting information, but this does not include the option value
	Dormant firm	

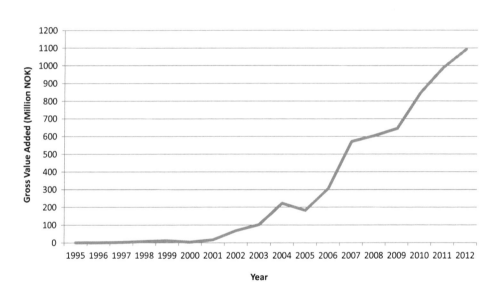

Figure 5.   Sum value creation for all SBEFs with a realized commercialization as operating firms for the period 1995–2012 (Million NOK).

Value creation for positive outcomes: Independent firms

We identified 74 firms in the SBEF portfolio defined as having a positive outcome. These 74 firms represent the main share of GVA among the entire SBEF portfolio with a total of 5.7 billion NOK over the 1995–2012 period.

As shown in Figure 5, the value creation is increasing over time. This is expected because the number of firms in the portfolio with a positive outcome is increasing and there are more firms active in a given year. Moreover, a small number of successes dominate the value creation. One firm, Opera Software[6], represents more than half of the value creation in the portfolio with 3.6 billion NOK. The second highest value creation is about 300 million NOK and only five firms have a value creation of more than 100 million NOK and 15 of more than 50 million NOK.

When looking at the year of establishment of the firms in this category, most of the firms generating positive value creation are of older vintages. This is expected because SBEFs need time to develop their technologies into commercial products generating sales.

Moreover, it becomes more likely that the firms' legal entity merge, demerge, get acquired, establish subsidiaries or go through other restructuring as they get older. Such changes make the annual accounts less precise in estimating the value creation from the underlying commercialization projects. Because of this, these calculations provide a very conservative estimate of the value creation from the SBEF portfolio.

Value creation for positive outcomes: Acquisitions

There is no register or data source identifying acquired firms in a comprehensive manner. To map acquisitions, we searched the Retriever database covering all major newspapers in Norway and performed comprehensive web searches. We searched for articles mentioning current or prior names of all firms in the SBEF portfolio, and identified, downloaded and read about 3500 articles. In addition, we reviewed the ownership structure of all portfolio firms which is available in each annual report. Based on this we were able to identify 23 acquisitions with an industrial motive. Based on their financial accounts, the total value creation in this category is less than 0.4 billion NOK. Such a low number illustrates that many of the acquired firms are integrated in the acquiring firm and the legal firm entity is de-registered or merged. Hence, this sum does not provide any relevant assessment of the value creation in this category of the SBEF portfolio.

An alternative to estimate the value creation in the case of acquired firms is to use the valuation of the firm, i.e., its purchase price. This provides a valuation of the firm that reflects the acquirer's expectation about the present value of future cash flows from the acquired business. Valuations

---

[6] http://www.opera.com/

Table 5.   Acquisition in the SBEF portfolio and purchase price. In all cases, the estimated valuation of the firm at time of purchase have been published in the media.

Acquired firm	Acquiring firm	Location	Estimated valuation (MNOK)
3D-Radar AS	VMetro	Norway	20–70
Adactus AS	Vizrt	Norway	30
Dynamic Rock Support AS	Normet	Finland	90
Genpoint AS	NorDiag	Norway	85
Inside Reality AS	Schlumberger	France/US	150–200
New Index AS	Seiko Epson	Japan	130
Secustream Technologies AS	Conax	Norway	20
Well Diagnostics AS	Dips	Norway	25–30
Zoom Network AS	Kelkoo	Norway	430
GasSecure AS	Dräger	Germany	500
Resman AS	Nordic Capital	Europe	1000

are often difficult to obtain due to confidentiality, but in several of the cases we were able to find an official source, as shown in Table 5.

From Table 5, the known purchase prices for acquisitions in the SBEF portfolio summarizes to about 2.5 billion NOK. It is likely to be a conservative estimate because we are lacking valuations for many of the identified acquisitions, and there might be acquisitions that we have not been able to identify. It is most likely that any unidentified acquisitions are of smaller sizes, as they have not received any media coverage. Further, at least two of the acquisition cases have been through secondary acquisitions releasing even further value.[7]

The examples above illustrate that most acquisitions are completed with larger incumbents within Norway. Many policymakers have been skeptical of technology acquisitions because they fear that knowledge production financed by the government is "sold out of the country", reducing the employment benefits from the investment. Although acquisitions by foreign companies occur, this seems to be relatively rare.

---

[7] The owners of Zoom Network AS received common shares as compensation when acquired by Kelkoo. Kelkoo was later acquired by Yahoo! for a purchase price of 4 billion NOK paid in cash, whereof more than 1 billion NOK to the original Zoom Network shareholders. The buyer of 3D-Radar AS, VMetro, was acquired by US-based Curtiss-Wright.

Value creation for negative outcomes: Abandoned firms

The value creation from abandoned and dissolved firms has a very low impact on the total value creation of the SBEF portfolio. In total, these firms have a positive accumulated GVA of 80 million NOK. It is expected that many ventures will fail in a portfolio with early stage SBEFs associated with high uncertainty. The modest activity in these firms and the positive, rather than negative, value creation among failures indicates however that the losses associated with failures are generally quite low. This may be seen as positive, but it may also be an indication of low willingness to invest in uncertain cases, which may also limit the upside potential.

Value creation for uncertain outcomes (real options): Dormant firms

A relatively large share of the SBEF portfolio consists of firm with very low or no activity. The total value creation of this category in the portfolio is negative with 21 million NOK; an insignificant share of the GVA in the portfolio.

Even though a firm is dormant over a period of several years, there may still be a potential, however uncertain. These firms may be searching for investors, partners or other resources to re-start their activity, or in some cases it might be a matter of timing and luck that leads to re-vitalization of the business. Also, in some cases the majority of activity is taking place at the spawning parent research institution. Hence, there might be future successes in this category, but we believe such cases would be relatively rare.

Value creation for uncertain outcomes (real options): Potential firms

Among the firms in the SBEF portfolio with uncertain outcome, 117 were coded as potential options because there is significant activity in the firm (see Table 2). In total, these firms account for a negative value creation of 750 million NOK. This is primarily driven by a few firms; five companies accounts for a negative value creation of 687 million NOK. These firms all entered the portfolio between 1998 and 2004 and are developing technologies that are far from market ready, typically within the life sciences industry.

This category also consists of firms with positive value creation, but where the activity has not exceeded our financial thresholds for being coded as a realized commercialization. One example is Marine Cybernetics[8],

---

[8] The company was later acquired after this chapter was written: https://www.dnvgl.com/news/dnv-gl-acquires-marine-cybernetics-6171.

with sales revenue of around 80 million NOK, but their first profitable year in 2012. It is only a question of time before this and several other firms will be regarded as a realized commercialization according to our definition.

As discussed earlier, accounting information provides an incomplete picture of the activity in these firms. The companies in the potential options category invest resources developing a unique technology, attempting to reach the market and building an organization able to complete a successful commercialization. Access to financing is crucial for the development of these firms, while raising funding also is a signal of credibility from the venture capital community and shared belief of the firms' value creation potential.

Although it is difficult to obtain exact data about valuation of unlisted private firms, our media archive provides some examples. For instance, Lytix Biopharma[9] was valued at 418 million NOK in a recent share issue. Another example is the previously mentioned Optinose, which received 300 million NOK from a US investor for an undisclosed share of the company. Although exact valuation is unavailable in this example, it nevertheless indicates a substantial valuation of the firm as a whole. The recent increase in accumulated negative value creation among these firms indicates that the SBEF portfolio contains firms that are able to raise significant amount of risk capital based on uncertain but high potential business proposals.

Summary: Value creation in a portfolio of SBEFs

By dividing the SBEF portfolio into different categories based on a real options logic, our analysis reveals that the firm categories have very different implications for the value creation in the portfolio. While most of the firms have low levels of value creation, two types of outcomes have distinct importance. First, positive outcomes in the form of independent firms provide significant value creation of 5.7 billion NOK from 74 firms. Moreover, there are 23 positive outcomes in the form of acquisitions. For these firms the accounting information is incomplete and cannot provide any reasonable estimation on their value creation contributions. We have identified a total purchase price of more than 2.5 billion NOK, which is a conservative number due to unavailable data driven by confidentiality of these transactions. It seems, however, reasonable to assume that the expected value creation among the acquired firms would be significantly higher than the purchase price. In some cases, the acquired firm itself is later the target of a subsequent acquisition

---

[9] http://www.lytixbiopharma.com/.

releasing additional value. Hence, acquired firms are significant source of value creation among positive outcomes, also in comparison with the value creation generated by successful firms operating as independent entities.

The second category of firms that significantly influence the value creation (as calculated on the basis of annual accounts) is the firms with uncertain outcome as potential firms. In this category, 117 firms have an accumulated negative value creation of 750 million NOK. The main activity of many of these firms is, however, to commercialize technology with high uncertainty but potentially high commercial value if successful. Many of these firms have received substantial investments from investors that in some cases provide a valuation of the firms of several hundred million NOK. Still, many of the most promising firms in the SBEF portfolio appears with significant negative value creation contribution based on accounting information when measured at this point in time. Hence, we argue that accounting information is not a particularly relevant source of information to assess these firms, because the real option of becoming a future success is not valued. This raises the question whether traditional GVA numbers is a useful measure to analyze this category of SBEFs. Rather, the amount of external investments received by these ventures may provide a better estimation that takes into account the future value creation potential. However, external investments by private investors are a conservative measure of potential value creation because it only reflects the expected share of value creation that remains with the owners. Additional elements of value creation, such as salaries and taxes, will be added to the GVA if the firm becomes successful.

Conclusions and Implications

This chapter used a real options approach to analyze the value creation of a portfolio of SBEFs in Norway. From our analysis we can provide certain conclusions and implications related to the time span needed to assess value creation in SBEFs, the highly skewed distribution of outcome values, the importance of acquisitions and the high share of firms with low activity. In the following, we discuss these issues in turn and conclude by discussing how our approach can be expanded in future research.

The study confirms that the time span from research to a profitable commercialization is very long (Lawton Smith & Ho, 2006; Vincett, 2010). 10 years after establishment, about 25% of SBEFs are categorized as having a positive outcome and 30% as a negative outcome. The remaining firms are categorized as still having an uncertain outcome and can be considered as real options with a potential for becoming future successes. The incidence of reaching a positive outcome become less likely when it is more than 10 years since the firm was established. This implies that 10 years is a minimum time period to assess the initial outcomes of SBEFs. However, this time period only provides an indication of potential impact, by identifying the cases that have become profitable or acquired. A large share of the value creation is likely to be realized over a significantly longer time period. For the positive outcomes as operating firms, the majority of the value creation in 2011 and 2012 is from firms established in the 1990s and early 2000s, and it seems likely that many of these firms are still early in their life cycle and will create significantly higher value in the years to come. Policymakers should be aware of this when they design and evaluate support programs for science-based entrepreneurship.

Our analysis illustrates another benefit of using the real option perspective. The performance distribution is highly skewed among entrepreneurial firms in general and technology ventures in particular. Our results show that a small number of firms are responsible for extreme shares of the value creation among both independent firms and acquisitions. The implication of this is that the total value creation of the entire portfolio might shift significantly due to single events. For example, within a few months in early 2015, the two firms Resman[10] and GasSecure[11] were acquired for about 1.5 billion NOK in total. This represents a substantial portion of the total acquisition value we have been able to observe in the portfolio. It is uncertain but likely, that firms currently categorized as real options in the SBEF portfolio can realize significant value in similar events over the next years. Hence, the early stage and uncertain nature of the SBEFs in the portfolio implies that projections of the value creation are inherently uncertain.

Compared with other assessments of value creation and performance of SBEF portfolios, our analysis reveals that acquired firms constitute a significant source of value creation. Hence, any evaluation of the outcomes and value creation in SBEFs that do not include or take into account acquisitions is incomplete, and likely to underestimate the performance and impact of SBEFs. Our data is still incomplete, and more research is needed to assess the role of acquisitions in SBEFs and technology commercialization. In particular, little is known about the impact the

---

[10] http://www.resman.no/.
[11] http://gassecure.com/.

acquired firm has on the buyer including the value creation occurring after the acquisition event.

Overall, the value creation from the SBEF portfolio in Norway increases year by year. However, there are few major success cases and relatively few failures in the portfolio compared to other classes of entrepreneurial firms. This might be an indication of a low willingness or ability to invest in firms with high uncertainty. Such reluctance might occur on several levels, from founders and academic entrepreneurs with low growth ambitions, lack of financing and other resources, to difficulties in entering the market with radically new products and services. There are some indications that this trend is changing, as evident with the relatively heavy losses incurred by some of the firms in the portfolio over the last few years.

It may also be questioned why the number of negative outcomes is relatively low. It seems like many firms are able to stay alive with very limited profits and losses. Many of these firms may be technology lifestyle companies (Harrison & Leitch, 2010) or companies staying alive on the relatively generous public support given to this type of ventures. A weakness of our analysis is that we have only looked at outcomes without considering the resources spent on developing these ventures, both from public and private sources. We appreciate that the firms in our portfolio are subsidized by different government grants (Rasmussen & Rice, 2012), and many of the firms have received significant funding from private investors. Future studies therefore need to consider not only the outcomes of the portfolio, but also deduct the investments into the portfolio to get a more complete picture of value creation.

Finally, value creation can be assessed at many levels using a real options approach. We used a societal approach calculating the GVA including salaries and taxes. An analysis from the SBEF shareholders' perspective would result in much lower, or even negative values, because salaries accounts for such a major share of the total GVA. This indicates that these firms are in early stages where the value for the shareholders in most cases is based on future expectations. Shareholder return should also be understood in light of the skewed return distribution already discussed. The few successes will be very profitable for a few shareholders, while mostly negative or insignificant for the vast majority. In essence, venture capital firms are attempting to find these future major successes, while accepting that most of their portfolio will have a negative return.

Although our analysis looked at value creation from a societal perspective, it covers only direct effects measured at firm level. From working with this portfolio of SBEFs, we observe that an important externality from successful commercialization is that new technology becomes available in industry (Autio, 1997). Many SBEFs commercialize scientific inventions and knowledge that have potential societal benefits that may contribute to resolving global challenges related to climate and energy problems; improving health, health care systems and welfare; enhancing research-based professional practice; and promoting knowledge-based trade and industry. Hence, the real value creation of SBEFs may be through their indirect role as a mechanism to translate scientific findings into application in society. Systematic assessments of these effects are virtually absent in the academic entrepreneurship literature (Rasmussen, Bulanova, Jensen, & Clausen, 2012) and require further enquiry.

References

Astebro, T. 2003. The return to independent invention: Evidence of unrealistic optimism, risk seeking or skewness loving? *Economic Journal*, 113(484), 226–239.

Autio, E. 1997. New, technology-based firms in innovation networks symplectic and generative impacts. *Research Policy*, 26(3), 263–281.

Borlaug, S. B., Grünfeld, L., Gulbrandsen, M., Rasmussen, E., Rønning, L., Spilling, O. R. & Vinogradov, E. 2009. Between entrepreneurship and technology transfer: Evaluation of the FORNY programme. *Report 19*, 160. NIFU STEP, Oslo.

Brown, R. & Mason, C. 2014. Inside the high-tech black box: A critique of technology entrepreneurship policy. *Technovation*, 34(12), 773–784.

Clarysse, B., Wright, M., Lockett, A., Mustar, P. & Knockaert, M. 2007. Academic spin-offs, formal technology transfer and capital raising. *Industrial and Corporate Change*, 16(4), 609–640.

Clausen, T. & Rasmussen, E. 2013. Parallel business models and the innovativeness of research-based spin-off ventures. *The Journal of Technology Transfer*, 38(6), 836–849.

Criaco, G., Minola, T., Migliorini, P., & Serarols-Tarrés, C. 2013. "To have and have not": Founders' human capital and university start-up survival. *The Journal of Technology Transfer*, 39(4), 567–593.

Damodaran, A. 2009. Valuing young, start-up and growth companies: estimation issues and valuation challenges. Available at: SSRN 1418687.

Garnsey, E. & Heffernan, P. 2005. High-technology clustering through spin-out and attraction: The Cambridge case. *Regional Studies*, 39(8), 1127–1144.

Ge, D., Mahoney, J. M. & Mahoney, J. T. 2005. New venture valuation by venture capitalists: An integrative approach. *University of Illinois at Urban Champaign Working Paper*, 124, 05-0124.

Grimaldi, R., Kenney, M., Siegel, D. S. & Wright, M. 2011. 30 years after Bayh-Dole: Reassessing academic entrepreneurship. *Research Policy*, 40(8), 1045–1057.

Gulbrandsen, M. & Rasmussen, E. 2012. The use and development of indicators for the commercialisation of university research in a national support programme. *Technology Analysis & Strategic Management*, 24(5), 481–495.

Harrison, R. T. & Leitch, C. 2010. Voodoo institution or entrepreneurial university? Spin-off companies, the entrepreneurial system and regional development in the UK. *Regional Studies*, 44(9), 1241–1262.

Hindle, K. & Yencken, J. 2004. Public research commercialisation, entrepreneurship and new technology based firms: An integrated model. *Technovation*, 24(10), 793–803.

Jensen, R. & Thursby, M. 2001. Proofs and prototypes for sale: The licensing of university inventions. *American Economic Review*, 91(1), 240–259.

Knight, F. H. (1921). *Risk, Uncertainty, and Profit.* Hart, Schaffner & Marx, New York.

Kochenkova, A., Grimaldi, R. & Munari, F. 2015. Public policy measures in support of knowledge transfer activities: A review of academic literature. *The Journal of Technology Transfer*, Advanced online publication.

Lawton Smith, H. & Ho, K. 2006. Measuring the performance of Oxford University, Oxford Brookes University and the government laboratories' spin-off companies. *Research Policy*, 35(10), 1554–1568.

Lubik, S. & Garnsey, E. 2015. Early Business Model Evolution in Science-based Ventures: The Case of Advanced Materials. *Long Range Planning* (In press).

Mason, C. M. & Harrison, R. T. 2002. Is it worth it? The rates of return from informal venture capital investments. *Journal of Business Venturing*, 17(3), 211–236.

McGrath, R. G. 1999. Falling forward: Real options reasoning and entrepreneurial failure. *Academy of Management Review*, 24(1), 13–30.

McGrath, R. G. & MacMillan, I. C. 2000. Assessing technology projects using real options reasoning. *Research-Technology Management*, 43(4), 35–49.

Meoli, M., Paleari, S. & Vismara, S. 2013. Completing the technology transfer process: M&As of science-based IPOs. *Small Business Economics*, 40(2), 227–248.

Puranam, P., Singh, H. & Zollo, M. 2006. Organizing for innovation: Managing the coordination-autonomy dilemma in technology acquisitions. *Academy of Management Journal*, 49(2), 263–280.

Rasmussen, E., Mosey, S. & Wright, M. 2011. The evolution of entrepreneurial competencies: A longitudinal study of university spin-off venture emergence. *Journal of Management Studies*, 48(6), 1314–1345.

Rasmussen, E., Bulanova, O., Jensen, A. & Clausen, T. 2012. The impact of science-based entrepreneurial firms: A literature review and policy synthesis. *Report 3-2012*, 154. Nordland Research Institute, Bodø.

Rasmussen, E. & Gulbrandsen, M. 2012. Government support programmes to promote academic entrepreneurship: A principal–agent perspective. *European Planning Studies*, 20(4), 527–546.

Rasmussen, E. & Rice, M. P. 2012. A framework for government support mechanisms aimed at enhancing university technology transfer: the Norwegian case. *International Journal of Technology Transfer and Commercialisation*, 11(1/2), 1–25.

Rasmussen, E. & Sørheim, R. 2012. How governments seek to bridge the financing gap for university spin-offs: proof-of-concept, pre-seed, and seed funding. *Technology Analysis & Strategic Management*, 24(7), 663–678.

Rosenbusch, N., Brinckmann, J. & Bausch, A. 2010. Is innovation always beneficial? A meta-analysis of the relationship between innovation and performance in SMEs. *Journal of Business Venturing*, 26(4), 441–457.

Sears, J. & Hoetker, G. 2014. Technological overlap, technological capabilities, and resource recombination in technological acquisitions. *Strategic Management Journal*, 35(1), 48–67.

Shane, S. 2004. *Academic Entrepreneurship University Spinoffs and Wealth Creation.* Edward Elgar Publishing, Inc., Cheltenham, UK.

Vincett, P. S. 2010. The economic impacts of academic spin-off companies, and their implications for public policy. *Research Policy*, 39(6), 736–747.

Wennberg, K., Wiklund, J. & Wright, M. 2011. The effectiveness of university knowledge spillovers: Performance differences between university spinoffs and corporate spinoffs. *Research Policy*, 40(8), 1128–1143.

Winborg, J. & Landstrom, H. 2001. Financial bootstrapping in small businesses: Examining small business managers' resource acquisition behaviors. *Journal of Business Venturing*, 16(3), 235–254.

Wright, M., Lockett, A., Clarysse, B. & Binks, M. 2006. University spin-out companies and venture capital. *Research Policy*, 35(4), 481–501.

Chapter 10

The Internationalization of Academic Spin-Offs: Evidence from Italy

Daniela Bolzani

Department of Education Sciences, University of Bologna, Italy
daniela.bolzani@unibo.it

Riccardo Fini* and Rosa Grimaldi†

Department of Management, University of Bologna, Italy
*riccardo.fini@unibo.it
†rosa.grimaldi@unibo.it

Despite growing interest in academic spin-offs (ASOs), research has overlooked the determinants, strategies, and outcomes of their internationalization choices. In this chapter, we review existing literature on the topic of internationalization of ASOs, connecting it to international business and international entrepreneurship literature, identifying relevant theoretical and empirical knowledge gaps. We then carry out a descriptive investigation about the characteristics and internationalization patterns of ASOs in the Italian context, drawing on a survey on 120 companies. Based on the review and our results, we highlight research areas deserving future investigation.

Introduction

The last three decades have been marked by increasing interest in academic spin-offs (ASOs) as a relevant setting to study entrepreneurial endeavors (e.g., Bercovitz & Feldman, 2008; Grandi & Grimaldi, 2005; Mosey & Wright, 2007). ASOs are new firms created to exploit patented or unpatented knowledge, technology, or research results that originated within a university in the commercial market (Pirnay *et al.*, 2003; Shane, 2004a).

ASOs have been devoted attention at different levels of analysis, ranging from institutional, organizational to individual perspectives. Studies have looked at policies supporting ASOs (e.g., Colyvas *et al.*, 2002; Shane, 2004b; Wallmark, 1997), support mechanisms to be implemented within universities such as TTOs and incubators (e.g., Degroof & Roberts, 2004; Fini *et al.*, 2011; Geuna & Rossi, 2011; Markman *et al.*, 2005), individual-level characteristics of (would-be) academic entrepreneurs (e.g., Clarysse & Moray, 2004; Colombo & Piva, 2012; Grandi & Grimaldi, 2003; Nicolaou & Birley, 2003; Roberts, 1991; Zucker *et al.*, 1998).

All this notwithstanding, research on academic spin-offs has overlooked the outcomes of entrepreneurial behaviors in terms of companies' performances (Djokovic & Souitaris, 2008; Grimaldi *et al.*, 2011). Studies of ASOs' performance and growth present mixed findings regarding survival rates, profitability, and growth rates (for reviews, see Bolzani *et al.*, 2014; Djokovic & Souitaris, 2008). This also applies to internationalization strategies, which are possible growth patterns for these companies (Buckley & Ghauri, 1993; Sapienza *et al.*, 2006). Specifically, there is a paucity of studies regarding internationalization antecedents, strategies, and growth outcomes in ASOs (Bjørnåli & Aspelund, 2012; Cumming *et al.*, 2009; Rothaermel *et al.*, 2007).

In an attempt to support international growth trajectories of ASOs, policy makers worldwide have set up science and technology infrastructures to support the foreign entrance and expansion into foreign markets (e.g., Algieri *et al.*, 2013; Markman *et al.*, 2005; Rasmussen *et al.*, 2006). It is therefore important to get an appropriate understanding of internationalization strategies — of its characteristics in terms of extent, scope, speed and determinants — so that effective policies can be implemented (Teixeira & Coimbra, 2014). In addition to its potential benefits for policy-makers, this topic is of interest to the international business and international entrepreneurship literature.

Similar to other high-technology start-ups, ASOs are often faced with internationalization choices due to the idiosyncrasies of their industries, such as an accelerated pace of worldwide technological innovation, high costs of R&D, very specific products/services, and shortened product life cycles, which make a domestic orientation not sufficient for company's growth and survival

(Johnson, 2004). These early-stage companies therefore target new, emerging and frequently international markets, relying on their specialization as niche markets (Bell, 1995; Crick & Jones, 2000; Fratocchi *et al.*, 2015; Oviatt & McDougall, 1994). It has also been put forward that entrepreneurs in these sectors target international markets in a more proactive manner in order to exploit their personal knowledge or relationships, or due to a lack of knowledge of the trade sector (i.e., being unaware of domestic opportunities) (Crick & Crick, 2014). They therefore start to sell abroad their products/services very close to inception, not having the time to learn from the development of their domestic market before expanding internationally (Crick & Jones, 2000).

Unlike other high-technology start-ups, ASOs, because of their idiosyncratic origin (i.e., affiliation with a parent university), have fewer resources and less experience, beyond their technology field, in areas such as management, marketing, commercialization, or access to finance and equity capital (van Geenhuizen & Soetanto, 2009; Vohora *et al.*, 2004). Thus, whereas the human capital of founders is the main business asset for ASOs (e.g., Colombo & Piva, 2012; Grandi & Grimaldi, 2003; Shane & Stuart, 2002; Shane, 2004a, 2004b), it might also endanger survival and growth prospects. However, this might change over time: for example, by changes in the management team (e.g., hiring experts in management or commercial areas) or training and learning-by-doing of founding team members (e.g., Visintin & Pittino, 2014).

Moving from all of these premises, the goal of this contribution is twofold. First, it aims to review existing literature on the topic of internationalization of ASOs. Second, it aims to provide information about the characteristics of internationalized ASOs and their internationalization patterns, drawing on a sample of 120 Italian ASOs. Based on the review and our results, we will highlight research areas deserving future investigation.

The chapter is organized as follows. We first overview the international business and international entrepreneurship literature. We then discuss the literature on the topic of internationalization of ASOs. Based on these two reviews, we identify theoretical and empirical literature gaps to be addressed by future research. Next, we present our empirical descriptive analyses and discuss our results. We conclude our chapter by summarizing main ideas and findings from our work.

Literature Review

Theoretical approaches to firms' internationalization

Internationalization scholars have proposed two different approaches to explain commercial expansion into foreign markets. First, the process

(Uppsala) internationalization model has explained international entry as a gradual process, with managerial decision-making based on reduced uncertainty thanks to market knowledge gradually accumulated through firm-level experiential knowledge of foreign markets (Johanson & Vahlne, 1977). This stream of literature suggests that firms initially target psychologically close markets, then gradually plan and implement entry into psychologically further markets. The expansion into international markets takes place through gradual steps ranging from indirect, low-risk, low-commitment modes (e.g., export through agents/intermediaries) to direct, high-risk, high-commitment modes (e.g., foreign direct investments) (e.g., Bilkey & Tesar, 1977; Johanson & Vahlne, 1977). This view would predict that new technology-based companies, because of their limited resource endowments, would first commercialize their products/services into the home market, then gradually enter foreign markets (e.g., starting with exports), slowly embedding commercial knowledge into their activities and capabilities. However, this stream of literature has not been able to explain the phenomenon of "born globals" (i.e., companies internationalizing rapidly since inception with great market coverage) (Crick & Spence, 2005) or of "international new ventures" (i.e., companies internationalizing rapidly since inception but with limited market coverage) (Bell, Loane, McNaughton, & Servais, 2011; Crick, 2009; Knight & Cavusgil, 2004; Oviatt & McDougall, 1994). Therefore, a second stream of literature, born-global perspective, has emerged to explain how new ventures can overcome their lack of resources and their liability of foreignness by drawing on founders' and managers' international skills and resources, such as personal networks and contacts, international education, international work experience, etc. (Madsen & Servais, 1997; Miesenbock, 1988; Oviatt & McDougall, 2005; Reid, 1981).

This second stream of literature in the last decade has drawn on entrepreneurship studies (Jones *et al.*, 2011) to conceptualize internationalization as an entrepreneurial behavior, entailing activities of "discovery, enactment, evaluation and exploitation of opportunities across national borders" (Oviatt & McDougall, 2005, p. 540). Following this description, the processes of entrepreneurial internationalization have to be seen as a result of both the presence of an opportunity and an entrepreneurial individual who can take advantage of that opportunity (Shane & Venkataraman, 2000; Oviatt & McDougall, 2005). Research has therefore taken an individual-level (rather than a firm-level) approach to internationalization.

Literature on international entrepreneurship has flourished in the last two decades, and we can build on several literature reviews (e.g., Coviello &

Jones, 2004; Jones *et al.*, 2011; Keupp & Gassmann, 2009; Peiris *et al.*, 2012) to summarize existing knowledge and possible future research directions. At the theoretical level, the field appears fragmented. Several theories inform international entrepreneurship research, such as resource-based view, knowledge-based view, dynamic capabilities, network and social capital theory, marketing theory and value creation, internationalization process, and entrepreneurship theory (Peiris *et al.*, 2012; Terjesen *et al.*, 2013), but also institutional theory, culture theory, transaction cost economics, and growth theory in comparative international entrepreneurship (Terjesen *et al.*, 2013). In general, scholars have perceived the need to develop integrative models to explain international entrepreneurship while also accounting for individuals, organizations, and the environment (e.g., industry and country) (see Aspelund *et al.*, 2007; Peiris *et al.*, 2012; Terjesen *et al.*, 2013).

At the empirical level, many studies have addressed how internationalization occurs and its antecedents, as well as the elements of international entrepreneurship and its outcomes (Keupp & Gassmann, 2009). Researchers have been interested in the outcomes of internationalization such as the propensity to internationalize, the pattern of internationalization (e.g., export intensity, entry mode, speed of foreign entry, geographical coverage), international performance (e.g., export performance) and company performance (e.g., firm survival; firm financial performance) (Keupp & Gassmann, 2009). Most existing studies have focused on the relationship between antecedents and outcomes (e.g., the importance of manager's characteristics and the patterns of internationalization at the firm level). Antecedents to international entrepreneurship have been studied at the personal level (e.g., managers' socio-cognitive properties, demographics, human and social capital), firm level (e.g., R&D intensity, international experience, market share/size, ownership, advertising intensity), industry level (e.g., foreign and domestic industry structure, government policy, industry competition), and country level (e.g., cultural distance, host country issues) (Fratocchi *et al.*, 2015; Keupp & Gassmann, 2009). Some other studies have focused on the elements of international entrepreneurship relevant to internationalization outcomes, such as firm strategy (e.g., product-market strategy, planning, competitive strategy, international orientation), entrepreneurial orientation, resources, and capabilities (e.g., resource stock, technology, factor endowments, resource constraints, firm capabilities), competitive advantage (e.g., comparative advantage, intellectual property, innovation), organizational learning (e.g., learning capabilities; technological learning, knowledge growth, and integration), and inter-firm organization (e.g., collaborative agreements, networks, spillovers) (Keupp & Gassmann, 2009).

In sum, most international entrepreneurship research has focused on internationalization antecedents and has been "outcome driven" (Keupp & Gassmann, 2009): that is, striving to explain the scope, extent, patterns, and performance implications of internationalization (e.g., identifying the factors influencing the mode, speed, extent, or scope of internationalization). Methodologically, studies have focused on small new firms, equating this with entrepreneurial companies but overlooking other corporate contexts for the analysis of entrepreneurial behaviors. In addition, the majority of studies have been cross-sectional, thus failing to capture the dynamic nature of the internationalization process (Coviello & Jones, 2004; Keupp & Gassmann, 2009).

Building on existing literature shortcomings, several avenues for future research have been suggested by scholars: among these are (1) process studies to investigate how internationalization is intertwined with entrepreneurial events, how it evolves over time (Coviello, 2006; Jones & Coviello, 2005; Keupp & Gassmann, 2009; Mathews & Zander, 2007), and investigating how internationalizing and non-internationalizing firms differ in their formation and growth processes (Jones *et al.*, 2011). This would require appropriate research designs, both quantitative or qualitative, based on longitudinal data; (2) understanding the role of resource (e.g., social, human, financial) endowments versus later acquisition of experiential learning for international entrepreneurship, at individual, organizational, and environmental levels (Bruneel *et al.*, 2010; Keupp & Gassmann, 2009); (3) understanding international entrepreneurship by not only focusing on small, new firms but also on larger companies. For example, an interesting research context, as suggested by Keupp and Gassmann (2009), is represented by spin-off companies, which can draw on the parent firms' resources, networks, and knowledge base despite their limited size and age.

Internationalization in the context of ASOs

To produce a comprehensive literature review on ASO internationalization, we scanned several electronic databases (EBSCO Econlit, ProQuest ABI/Inform Global, Scopus), searching for specific keywords encompassing both the international entrepreneurship literature (e.g., internationalization, international entrepreneurship, export, abroad, foreign, cross-national) and the academic entrepreneurship literature (e.g., USO, USOs, ASOs, ASOs, academic spin-off/ spinoff/startup/start-up/firm, university, university spin-off/spinoff/startup/

start-up/, academic entrepreneur/entrepreneurship). We also searched Google Scholar to identify other sources such as working papers, conference presentations, or technical reports. Because of the potential difficulties in retrieving books, especially in printed form, we excluded book and book chapters from our review. We focused on articles with research questions that were mainly oriented toward investigating the phenomenon of internationalization in academic spin-offs (e.g., international entry or growth as the dependent variable or as the data of interest in cross-case analysis). Using these criteria, we found 14 articles relevant for our review, 12 of which had been published in international, peer-reviewed journals and 2 of which had been presented at international conferences. As summarized in Table 1, the articles are recent (the earliest 2006) and primarily published in international business/entrepreneurship journals (e.g., *Journal of World Business; Journal of International Entrepreneurship*). We can therefore observe that the intended contribution of researchers studying this topic was directed to the field of international entrepreneurship rather than to that of academic entrepreneurship.

Many of the retrieved studies do not clarify which theoretical framework underlies the study's development, thus dealing with research questions in a seemingly phenomenological manner. The papers with some theoretical development reflect a variety of theories, mirroring the fragmentation of theoretical approaches used to study international entrepreneurship seen above. With regard to methodology, the retrieved studies present qualitative, longitudinal research designs or cross-sectional, quantitative designs (mainly through surveys). Although the qualitative longitudinal studies help explain the entrepreneurial and internationalization processes, they do not allow for generalization. By contrast, whereas quantitative studies allow for generalizability, they do not clarify process-based mechanisms.

The retrieved studies discuss individual-, organizational-, and contextual-level factors that influence ASOs' internationalization. For individual-level factors, scholars have investigated the characteristics, resources, and skills of entrepreneurial or top management teams. Like findings in international entrepreneurship, having top management and entrepreneurial teams with international experience has a positive effect on firm internationalization. In fact, as found by Van Geenhuizen *et al.* (2014), lacking internationalization skills and the understanding of business principles has a negative impact on export outcomes. However, a notable exception is shown by Nordman and Melén (2008), who find that founders of born-global companies have high levels of technological knowledge but not necessarily international-market knowledge. To drive the internationalization process, there might be a substitution effect of high technological competence over

Table 1.   Summary of retrieved articles about internationalization of ASOs (by year of publication).

Author(s) and year	Research question	Theoretical underpinning	Research approach	Sample	Variables and method
Nummela, N., Loane, S., & Bell, J. (2006). Change in SME internationalisation: an Irish perspective. *Journal of Small Business and Enterprise Development, 13*(4), 562–583	What is the individual action and the manager's perception of change during internationalization?	Organizational change	Qualitative: case studies (longitudinal)	3 high-tech companies (among which 2 founded by academics) in Ireland	Variables: n.a. Method: cross-case analysis
Lawton Smith, H., Romeo, S., & Bagchi-Sen, S. (2008). Oxfordshire biomedical university spin-offs: An evolving system. *Cambridge Journal of Regions, Economy, and Society, 1,* 303–319.	What is the performance of academic spin-offs and how is this co-evolving and interacting with their selection environment?	Evolutionary economics	Quantitative: survey and secondary data (cross-sectional)	114 technology-based university spin-offs in UK	Variables: n.a. Method: descriptive statistics
Nordman, E. R., & Melén, S. (2008). The impact of different kinds of knowledge for the internationalization process of Born Globals in the biotech business. *Journal of World Business, 43,* 171–185	How do the levels of international and technological knowledge of founders and managers at Born Global firms are related to the firms' discovery and exploitation of foreign market opportunities?	Opportunity discovery	Qualitative: case studies (longitudinal)	8 biotech companies (among which 4 founded by academics) in Sweden	Variables: n.a. Method: cross-case analysis

Reference	Research focus	Internationalization	Methodology	Sample	Variables / Method
Styles, C., & Genua, T. (2008). The rapid internationalization of high technology firms created through the commercialization of academic research. *Journal of World Business*, 43, 146–157	Developing a precise model of internationalization behavior of high-tech companies developed through the commercialization of academic research.	Internationalization behavior	Qualitative: case studies (longitudinal)	4 academic spin-offs in Australia	Variables: n.a. Method: cross-case analysis
Fafaliou, I., Melanitis, N. E., & Tsakalos, V. (2009). Commercializing research results in immature technology transfer markets: Cases from the Greek experience. *International Journal of Entrepreneurship and Innovation Management*, 11(2), 213–227	How to develop successful technology transfer (TT) polices in immature TT markets such as Greece? How do organisations design and implement their strategic interaction portfolio in order to benefit more from the TT agreements?	Not specified	Qualitative: case studies	8 academic spin-off companies in Greece (most successful case stories)	Variables: n.a. Method: description of cases

(Continued)

Table 1.   (*Continued*)

Author(s) and year	Research question	Theoretical underpinning	Research approach	Sample	Variables and method
Bruneel, J., Yli-Renko, H., & Clarysse, B. (2010). Learning from experience and learning from others: How congenital and interorganizational learning substitute for experiential learning in young firm internationalization. *Strategic Entrepreneurship Journal, 4,* 164–182	Can young firms compensate for their lack of firm-level international experience by utilizing other sources of knowledge in international expansion, i.e., experiential, congenital and interorganizational learning?	Organizational learning theory	Quantitative: survey (cross-section)	114 technology-based companies (among which academic spin-offs) in Flanders (Belgium)	Dependent variable: extent of internationalization (foreign sales weighted by the psychic and geographic distance of the foreign market). Independent variables: (1) experiential learning (number of years with different entry modes); (2) congenital learning (number of years of founders' international experience); (3) interorganizational learning (extent of learning from different partners). Control variables: firm age; founding capital; changes in management team; industry. Method: multiple regression

Taheri, M., & Geenhuizen, M. Van. (2011). How human capital and social networks may influence the patterns of international learning spin-off among academic spin-off firms. *Papers in Regional Science*, 90(2), 287–312	Developing a model that clarifies the adoption of international knowledge relationships and the spatial reach involved	Not specified	Quantitative: survey (cross-section)	100 academic spin-off companies from two incubators in The Netherlands and Norway	Dependent variable: international knowledge networks (yes/no; spatial reach). Independent variables: (1) innovation position (newness of products/processes and R&D expenditure); (2) human capital (size of founding team, work experience at start, disciplinary founders' background, PhD experience); (3) social network profile (density, heterogeneity, frequency and duration of relationships). Control variables: firm size; location. Method: logistic and ordered logistic regression

(*Continued*)

Table 1.   (*Continued*)

Author(s) and year	Research question	Theoretical underpinning	Research approach	Sample	Variables and method
Pettersen, I. B., & Tobiassen, A. E. (2012). Are born globals really born globals? The case of academic spin-offs with long development periods. *Journal of International Entrepreneurship, 10,* 117–141	(1) What type of networks do academic spin-offs acquire during their life cycle, from pre-founding to growth and internationalization? (2) What are the role and importance of these networks during the academic spin-offs' life cycle? (3) How do networks acquired in the pre-founding period affect the academic spin-offs' growth and internationalization?	Not specified (diverse insights on born global and network theories)	Qualitative: case-studies (longitudinal)	3 academic spin-off companies in Norway	Variables: n.a. Method: cross-case analysis

| Bjørnåli, E. S., & Aspelund, A. (2012). The role of the entrepreneurial team and the board of directors in the internationalization of academic spin-offs. *Journal of International Entrepreneurship, 10,* 350–377 | What is the role of the entrepreneurial management team and the board of directors in the internationalization of new technology-based firms in a small and open economy? | Resource-based and resource-dependence view | Quantitative: survey (cross-section) | 135 academic spin-off companies in Norway | Dependent variable: (1) likelihood of international strategic alliances; (2) likelihood of international sales. Independent variables: (1) TMT heterogeneity (functional, industrial, age, education); (2) board of directors' heterogeneity; (3) involvement in service and strategy tasks by board of directors. Control variables: firm age; firm size; firm developmental stage; TMT size; board size; number of both TMT and board; TMT and board international experience. Method: hierarchical logistic regression. |

(Continued)

Table 1.   (*Continued*)

Author(s) and year	Research question	Theoretical underpinning	Research approach	Sample	Variables and method
Van Geenhuizen, M., Ye, Q., & Au-Yong-Oliviera, M. (2014). A skills approach to growth of university spin-off firms: Export as an example. In *14th ICTPI Conference*	(1) Which skills are most important to growth of university spin-offs? (2) To what extent are university spin-off firms engaged in exports and what is the influence of skills that are lacking? Which other factors are involved? (3) In which way can the outcomes regarding lacking skills be translated into action-based learning in new courses?	Skills approach to firm growth	Mixed method: face-to-face interviews based on questionnaire + case studies (cross-section)	85 academic spin-off companies in Finland, The Netherlands, Poland and Portugal	Dependent variable: share in exports in 2011 (% of turnover) Independent variable: internationalization skills; sales skills; understanding economic principles of high-tech business. Control variables: USOs' broad firm profile (country; firm age; firm size; firm industry; pre-start founders' working experience). Method: hierarchical regression. Description of case studies.
Oxtorp, L. A. (2014). Dynamic managerial capability of technology-based international new ventures — a basis for their long-term competitive advantage. *Journal of International Entrepreneurship, 12,* 389–420	What are the dynamic capabilities that support long-term competitive advantage of technology-based international new ventures?	Knowledge-based view	Qualitative: case study (longitudinal)	1 technology-based company (founded by an academic entrepreneur) in Denmark	Variables: n.a. Method: case analysis

| Teixeira, A. A. C., & Coimbra, C. (2014). The determinants of the internationalization speed of Portuguese university spin-offs: An empirical investigation. *Journal of International Entrepreneurship, 12,* 270–308 | What are the determinants of the internationalization speed of academic spin-offs? | Not specified | Quantitative: survey (cross-section) | 111 academic spin-offs in Portugal | Dependent variable: speed (time lag since establishment) and earliness (within 3 years since establishment) of internationalization. Independent variables: (1) previous entrepreneurs' experience in the same industry; (2) type of education (technology-related; business/management-related; both); (3) size of entrepreneurial team; (4) knowledge intensity (R&D) and innovation rate (patenting); (5) previous CEO industry experience; (6) global market orientation and niche positioning; (7) size of ASOs; (8) age of ASOs; (9) past performance; (10) TTO support; (11) perceived importance of science & technology support; |

(*Continued*)

Table 1. *(Continued)*

Author(s) and year	Research question	Theoretical underpinning	Research approach	Sample	Variables and method
Cattaneo, M., Meoli, M., & Vismara, S. (2015). Cross-border M&As of biotech firms affiliated with internationalized universities. *The Journal of Technology Transfer, 40,* 409–433.	Does the prestige and the internationalization of a university affect the propensity of affiliated firms to be targeted in cross-border M&As?	Not specified	Quantitative: secondary data (cross-section)	74 public biotech companies in UK, France, Germany, Italy, Belgium, The Netherlands, and Sweden (among which 53 academic spin-offs)	Dependent variable: cross-border M&A deals within 5 years after IPO. Independent variables: (1) affiliation with a university; (2) university prestige; (3) university internationalization. Control variables: firm size; firm age; firm growth rate; VC
					(12) perceived obstacles (university–industry relationship; labor market rigidity; financial constraints; managerial handicaps; physical infrastructures and distance to markets); (13) characteristics of parent university (patent pool; scientific publications; centers of research excellence); (13) region; (14) industry. Method: multivariate regressions (OLS and logistic regression).

Reference	Research question		Method	Sample	Variables and method
(continued)					backed; top-ranked underwriter; biotech cluster; R&D investments; patenting; education of TMT and board; international experience of TMT and board; industry experience of TMT and board; size of TMT and board. Method: heckman two-stage regression
Suzuki, S., & Okamuro, H. (2015). Determinants of academic startup's orientation toward international business expansion. In *DRUID 2015 conference proceedings*	What are the factors that impact the orientation of academic startups to expand internationally?	Not specified	Quantitative: survey (cross-section)	457 academic start-ups in Japan	Dependent variable: orientation toward international business (1-4 categories). Independent variables: (1) technological capabilities; (2) firm-level received public support; (3) supportive regional environment; (4) parent university's research standards. Control variables: firm size; firm age; firm reported profitability; industry. Method: ordered logit model

international market competence. At the same time, however, the authors do not investigate whether other forms of international experience were gained by the entrepreneurial teams: for example, through studying and visiting academic institutions and conferences abroad, which would nonetheless have enabled them to develop a "global mindset" (e.g., Arora *et al.*, 2004; Gupta & Govindarajan, 2002) rather than practical international experience. We see this as an interesting area worth of further investigation. From other studies emerged the importance of scientific, technical, or industrial experience and the background of ASOs' management teams for driving internationalization. For example, Taheri and Van Geenhuizen (2011) found that the development of international knowledge networks and their spatial reach are brought forward by small teams with PhD-level education. Focusing on industry experience, Bjørnåli and Aspelund (2012) found that teams with either highly similar or highly diverse industry experience, or functionally diverse board members were more likely to internationalize ASOs' sales. A strong technical culture in ASOs' founding teams was also highlighted by Nummela, Loane, and Bell (2006). However, the authors demonstrate that, over time, the internal culture can change from technically oriented to commercially oriented through the establishment of external associations and co-operations leading to internationalization and learning. In fact, linked to the lack of knowledge of and experience with international markets, ASOs' entrepreneurial teams generally suffer from a lack of commercial experience. Along these lines, successful internationalization might be driven, for example, by employing managers with commercial skills (Styles & Genua, 2008) or by establishing an external advisory board (Oxtorp, 2014). By contrast, non-internationalized ASOs were characterized by the presence of technology developers with little commercial experience and little motivation to get involved in it, especially when the technology was outside his/her usual field of interest and work. A final relevant remark regards the development of dynamic managerial capabilities in ASOs. As observed by Oxtorp (2014), managerial capabilities are fuelled by continuous and wide-reaching environmental scanning involving academic and industrial sources, by managers from different levels and functions. In sum, based on the findings of our literature review, we argue that more could be done to understand the timing and causal effects of entrepreneurial and management teams' changes on company's entrepreneurial choices and performance.

For organizational-level factors, similar to what has been found in high-technology start-ups (e.g., Mudambi & Zahra, 2007), possessing unique intangible assets (e.g., R&D and innovation assets) has a positive effect on internationalization. However, because of lengthy technology development

and time-to-market processes, ASOs might be spending many years developing the technology (Pettersen & Tobiassen, 2012) and, thus, their R&D
intensity might not appear as linked to internationalization speed statistically
(Teixeira & Coimbra, 2014). Importantly, to be able to enter foreign markets, ASOs should have mature technologies (Styles & Genua, 2008) and not
try to commercialize them at an early stage. In addition, internationalization
is fostered in companies with management teams that implemented structures, processes, and decision rules for selecting R&D projects and allocating
resources for their development (i.e., exploration versus exploitation);
understood the firm's core competences and legally protected them; and set
processes and structures for effective internal communication, knowledge
sharing, and collegial decision making (Oxtorp, 2014). Other company-level
characteristics that matter for internationalization performance are firm age
(Suzuki & Okamuro, 2015; Teixeira & Coimbra, 2014) and sector of activity
(Teixeira & Coimbra, 2014). An important and distinguishing feature in
ASOs is their affiliation with a parent university (Pettersen & Tobiassen,
2012). Drawing on the corporate spin-off literature, spun-out companies
benefit from the parent institution's resources, networks, and reputation
(Schulz *et al.*, 2009; Zahra, 2005). Being affiliated with a parent university
endows ASOs at inception with resources that can be drawn from the university, either directly (e.g., use of laboratories and other infrastructures; use of
knowledge) or indirectly (e.g., through the entrepreneurial team's networks
and affiliation with the parent university). Human and social capital available to the company might therefore be constituted by several additional
linkages to scientific knowledge than would be available to and enjoyed by
other newly established companies. Thus, ASOs maintain networks with
both academia and industry during all of the company's developmental
stages (Pettersen & Tobiassen, 2012); their purposes, however, are different.
Networks within academia develop technology, bringing it to maturity to be
commercialized and to publish results; doing so is fundamental for legitimi-
zation and credibility not only within technical and scientific communities,
but also from market actors, such as customers and financing institutions
(e.g., venture capitalists) (Pettersen & Tobiassen, 2012; Styles & Genua,
2008). Networks within industry develop customized and applied solutions
to be commercialized and to advertise them to potential customers
(Pettersen & Tobiassen, 2012). From the studies overviewed, an emerging
area that merits investigation is the characteristics of (academic) entrepreneurs' personal networks or parent university's networks, and their potentially different internationalization outcomes (e.g., Styles & Genua, 2008).

Taking a more macro-level perspective, available studies suggest that
environmental support from universities, incubators, and science-parks

positively impacts companies' ability to export and realize investments abroad (e.g., Fafaliou *et al.*, 2010; Lawton Smith *et al.*, 2008; Watkins-Mathys & Foster, 2006). For example, the prestige, research standards and internationalization of the parent university have a positive impact on internationalization outcomes (Cattaneo *et al.*, 2015; Suzuki & Okamuro, 2015). Teixeira and Coimbra (2014) found that technology transfer office (TTO) support was critical in speeding up ASOs' international entry. In the future, we see a potential avenue of research in the investigation of how support from the academic environment, in particular through the provision of scientific and technical knowledge, might eventually clash with ASOs' business and market knowledge and requirements (e.g., intellectual property rights rules, specific market regulation, business practices) (Lockett *et al.*, 2005; Van Geenhuizen & Soetanto, 2009). Mixed results have been found with regard to government support (e.g., Crick & Jones, 2000; Holtbruegge & Kreppel, 2012; Suzuki & Okamuro, 2015). In terms of environmental-level factors that impact ASOs' internationalization, we believe that there is great potential for future research. For example, as suggested by Suzuki and Okamuro (2015), public or university support might produce differentiated effects depending on a set of other factors, such as the nature of the parent institution (e.g., public or private universities), macro-environmental national or local munificence, types of available support (e.g., tax relief; use of equipment land and/or facilities; etc.).

Internationalization of ASOs: New Evidence from Italy

From our review of existing literature on the topic of ASO internationalization, we have identified four issues that warrant further empirical investigation. First, more quantitative longitudinal studies are necessary to better explicate the processual nature of internationalization and its relationship with other entrepreneurial events. Second, few of the available studies have compared the characteristics and entrepreneurial patterns of internationalized and non-internationalized ASOs. Third, although the retrieved studies present a variety of research questions and investigated internationalization dimensions, few considered differences between international entry mode (e.g., imports, exports, partnerships, Foreign Direct Investment (FDI)), extent (e.g., size of exports or FDI investments), scope (i.e., geographical coverage), and speed. Lastly, we note that no available international study on ASO internationalization was carried out in the Italian context. In the following, we will therefore aim to provide some exploratory evidence about these issues.

Method

We draw on data available from the TASTE project (TAking STock: External engagement by academics)[1], which includes longitudinal, multi-level information on the population of 935 ASOs established since 2000 (i.e., after the introduction of the national regulation for commercialization of research through academic spin-offs) (Law 297/1999; for further details see Baldini *et al.*, 2013; Bolzani *et al.*, 2014). We define an ASO as a company that has an affiliation with a university through an equity share held either by the university or by one individual previously or currently employed (as faculty or technician) by the university (Fini *et al.*, 2009).

For the present empirical investigation, we draw on a set of primary and secondary data available from the TASTE database. The primary data come from a survey carried out in 2013 on 467 active companies established between 2000 and 2008[2]. We sent out two questionnaires: one firm-level (i.e., to collect information about the company's achievements and characteristics) and one individual-level (i.e., to collect information about the entrepreneurs' activity in the surveyed businesses). One hundred twenty companies, either represented by one member of the entrepreneurial team (83%), a manager (8%), a designated employee (6%), or a member of the management team (3%) answered our firm-level questionnaire (response rate = 25.8%). From this questionnaire, we used information about companies' development over time and achievement of significant business milestones (e.g., timing of personnel employment, external financing, establishment of collaborations, commercialization of products/services, etc.). One hundred sixty one entrepreneurs answered our individual-level questionnaire (response rate = 7.8%). From this questionnaire, we used details related to internationalization patterns, intentions, attitudes, and skills. Because 32 companies had multiple respondents who completed our individual-level questionnaires, we aggregated their answers (triangulating and averaging reported answers) to obtain one unique answer per company (i.e., 120 detailed questionnaires). The secondary data come from the Italian Company's house and are related to both individual entrepreneurs and their companies.

---

[1] See website: http://www.project-taste.eu.

[2] ASOs established 2000–2008 were surveyed to develop a longitudinal survey protocol following-up a first wave of surveys sent out in year 2009 (for further details see Bolzani *et al.*, 2014).

Table 2.   **Legal, sectoral and industrial characteristics of respondent ASOs.**

Legal form	No. of ASOs	Total (%)
Share-based	115	95.8
Cooperative/consortium	2	1.7
Unlimited liability	3	2.5
Geographical location (NUTS 1)		
ITC — Northwestern Italy	38	31.7
ITD — Northeastern Italy	40	33.3
ITE — Central Italy	21	17.5
ITF — Southern Italy	15	12.5
ITG — Insular Italy	6	5.0
Industry		
Professional, scientific and technical activities	66	55.0
Information and communication services	29	24.2
Manufacturing	20	16.7
Other service activities	3	2.5
Wholesale and retail trade	2	1.6
Total	**120**	**100.0**

Results

The 120 companies that responded to the survey were founded, on average, in 2005 (s.d. 2.25). They originated from 35 universities (for details see Table A.1 in Appendix). Following the geographical localization of parent institutions, respondent ASOs were located mainly in Northern Italy (65%) (see Table 2). Respondents were mostly represented by limited liability companies active in professional, scientific, and technical activities, but also in information and communication services and manufacturing (Table 2).

Internationalization patterns

Seventy-three companies (60.8%) reported having carried out at least one international business activity during their existence. We identified three main entry modes through which ASOs engaged in foreign markets: implementing international sales, establishing a collaboration with international partners, or opening a productive/commercial subsidiary abroad. In our sample, companies either adopted only one strategy or implemented a blending of strategies (see Table 3). The most common entry strategies

Table 3. International entry modes adopted by ASOs.

Entry mode	No of ASOs	Total (%)
International sales and international collaborations	32	43.8
International sales only	22	30.2
International collaborations only	13	17.8
International sales, international collaborations, and foreign subsidiaries	4	5.5
Foreign subsidiaries only	2	2.7
	73	**100.0**

were international sales and international collaborations, or a combination of the two.

With regard to speed of internationalization, the internationalized companies can be defined as born globals, because 63% started a business activity abroad within 3 years after establishment and 82.2% within 5 years after foundation.

Fifty-two out of seventy-three internationalized companies (71.2%) provided details about geographical coverage at the time of the survey. Companies could choose among the following range of geographical areas: European Union (86.5%); Eastern and Balcanic Europe (32.7%); USA and Canada (51.9%); Central America (3.8%); South America (17.3%); China (26.9%); India (17.3%); South-Eastern Asia (11.5%); Middle East (15.4%); North Africa (9.6%); South Africa (9.6%); Sub-Saharan Africa (3.8%). From further analysis of the types of companies operating in different markets (Table 4), it appears that companies pursuing professional, scientific, and technical service activities were more oriented towards working in European and Northern American markets whereas companies operating in manufacturing were more present in the Chinese, Indian, Southern-Asia, Middle East, and African markets.

We asked entrepreneurs who were personally involved in internationalization decision-making within their company to provide details about three of the most important inward or outward internationalization events that occurred for the company. Forty-six out of seventy-three internationalized companies (63%) provided complete details. Of respondent companies, 13% reported one international entry, 28.3% two, 17.4% three, and 41.3% had more than three. For first entry mode, companies entered through partnerships (39%), direct (22%) or indirect (9%) exporting, licensing (13%), importing (13%), and opening a commercial branch (4%). The

Table 4.   **Geographical scope by sector of activity.**

	Profess., scientific, technical	ICT	Manuf.	Other serv.	Total (a)	% (b)
European Union	21	10	12	2	45	86.5
	46.7%	22.2%	26.7%	4.4%	100.0%	
Eastern and Balcanic Europe	7	2	8	0	17	32.7
	41.2%	11.8%	47.1%	47.1%	100.0%	
USA and Canada	15	6	6	0	27	51.9
	55.6%	22.2%	22.2%	0.0%	100.0%	
Central America	0	2	0	0	2	3.8
	0.0%	100.0%	0.0%	0.0%	100.0%	
Southern America	3	1	4	1	9	17.3
	33.3%	11.1%	44.4%	11.1%	100.0%	
China	5	2	6	1	14	26.9
	35.7%	14.3%	42.9%	7.1%	100.0%	
India	3	1	4	1	9	17.3
	33.3%	11.1%	44.4%	11.1%	100.0%	
South-Eastern Asia	0	1	4	1	6	11.5
	0.0%	16.7%	66.7%	16.7%	100.0%	
Middle East	2	1	5	0	8	15.4
	25.0%	12.5%	62.5%	0.0%	100.0%	
North Africa	1	1	3	0	5	9.6
	20.0%	20.0%	60.0%	0.0%	100.0%	
South Africa	2	0	3	0	5	9.6
	40.0%	0.0%	60.0%	0.0%	100.0%	
Sub-saharian Africa	1	1	0	0	2	3.8
	50.0%	50.0%	0.0%	0.0%	100.0%	

(a) Multiple answers were allowed from respondents ($n = 52$).

(b) Calculated on companies providing detailed answers on the geographical scope of current activities ($n = 52$).

main target markets were the European Union (47.8%) and the USA (17.4%). In line with the larger sample described above, 80.4% of companies carried out the first international entry within 5 years after establishment. The first international entry was a sporadic event for 22% of respondents; for the majority, however, entry entailed a process with a duration of less than 1 year (15%) or more than one year (63%). In fact, in 71% of cases, the international relationship remained active at the time of the survey. For companies' second internationalization event, modes of entry were similar to the ones described for first entry (47% partnership, 28% direct export, 13% indirect export, 6% import, 3% licensing, 3% commercial foreign branch). Target markets were the European Union (48%) and Northern America (18%), as well as the Middle East (12%), China (9%) and Central and South America (9%). The majority of companies implemented their second international entry not too long after the first one (on average within 2 years). As with the first entry, the second entry also typically occurred over a period of time (59% more than one year; 13% less than 1 year) and was still active at the time of the survey (85%). Companies reported that the third entry involved direct (27%) and indirect (18%) exports, partnerships (45%), licensing (5%), and opening of commercial branches (5%). Geographic scope was diversified in European countries (45%), North America (18%), Central and South America (9%), and South Asia (9%). On average, it took just over a year to start the third international entry following the second entry, with companies starting long-term relationships (68% lasting more than one year and 73% still active at the time of the survey). Our analyses showed that companies entering more than one foreign market tended to target different and farther countries rather than following a path-dependent strategy with respect to the first country entered.

Internationalized and non-internationalized companies

We compared companies' main characteristics to spot any differences between internationalized and non-internationalized ASOs. A chi-square test yielded non-significant differences in terms of geographical localization and industry. We investigated whether the entrepreneurial teams of internationalized and non-internationalized companies differed in terms of team size, invested equity, and team composition. In the following, we consider differences between internationalized and non-internationalized companies, treating them as two separate groups (i.e., not accounting for the reality that "internationalized companies" likely changed their status from non-internationalized to internationalized over time)[3].

We first analyzed the average number of shareholders in each company from 2000 to 2012 (Figure 1). We found that internationalized ASOs had a slightly smaller shareholder team than non-internationalized companies, but

---

[3] We also carried out analyses by considering internationalized companies as changing status over time and obtained comparable results to those shown in this paragraph. Details are available upon request.

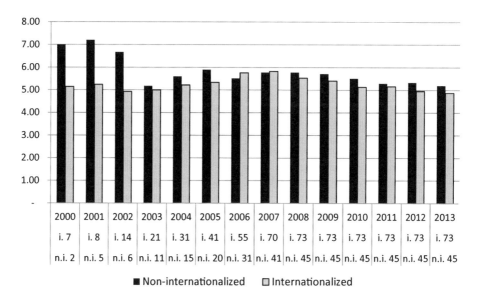

Figure 1.   Average number of shareholders in non-internationalized and internationalized ASOs.

Note: Missing values for two companies. The number of companies is reported under each year (n.i. = non-internationalized ASOs; i. = internationalized ASOs).

the difference was not significant (5.34 versus 5.62 shareholders, $p = 0.18$). By contrast, in terms of the average amount of equity invested in each company in the same period (Figure 2), we found that internationalized ASOs had a significantly higher amount of invested equity than did non-internationalized ones (54,950 € versus 28,240 €, $p < 0.001$). With regard to team composition, we analyzed whether internationalized and non-internationalized ASOs differed with respect to the presence of financial shareholders (e.g., business angels, venture capitalists, banks, and other financial bodies), industrial shareholders, individual shareholders, or public shareholders (e.g., universities, public research centers, incubators, technology parks, or other public bodies). Looking at financial shareholders, none of the respondent companies had equity stakes held by business angels, venture capitalists, or banks. Therefore, in our sample, financial shareholders were represented by public or private financial investors (e.g., private or public investment funds), with an overall small amount of invested equity (on average, for the pooled sample, 363 €, s.d. 4,004). Financial shareholders were present only in ASOs that went international over time, with a statistically significant difference in terms of average invested equity capital with non-internationalized ones (574 € versus 0 €, $p < 0.05$). With regard to public shareholders, respondent ASOs had a variety of public shareholders like universities, public research centers,

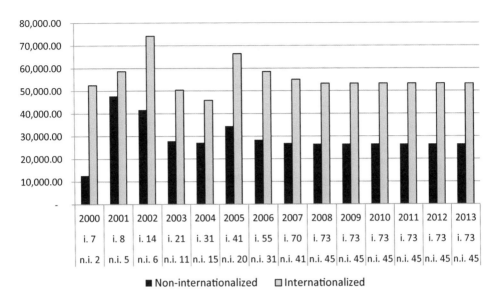

Figure 2.   Average equity in non-internationalized and internationalized ASOs.

Note. Missing values for two companies. The number of companies is reported under each year (n.i. = non-internationalized ASOs; i. = internationalized ASOs).

or other public bodies (e.g., municipalities or local government authorities), but no equity shares were held by incubators or technology parks. While the number of participating public shareholders did not differ between internationalized and non-internationalized companies (for both groups, the average number of shareholders was 0.4), the average invested equity was significantly higher in internationalized ASOs (2,454 € versus 944 €, $p < 0.001$). For the presence of industrial shareholders, although internationalized companies had, on average, a lower number of industrial partners (0.41 versus 0.71, $p < 0.001$), there was no statistically significant difference in terms of average amount of invested equity (internationalized ASOs 7,428 € versus non-internationalized ASOs 8,296 €, $p = 0.63$). Lastly, looking at the relevance of individual shareholders, their average number did not differ in internationalized versus non-internationalized companies (4.52 versus 4.50, $p = 0.94$), but the amount of invested capital was significantly higher for internationalized ASOs (44,494 € versus 18,742 €, $p < 0.001$).

We compared the international experience of internationalized and non-internationalized companies at the time of the survey; using a 7-point Likert scale, we measured the extent of perceived professional experience abroad of the company's (i) shareholders, (ii) managers, and (iii) employees. Similarly, we measured foreign language skills at the company level through a 7-point Likert scale measuring extent of perceived language skills of the company's (i) shareholders, (ii) managers, and (iii) employees.[4] Companies did not report any significant difference in any of these perceived skills.

To investigate attitudes towards internationalization, we used a 4-item, 7-point Likert scale developed by Burpitt and Rondinelli (1998) measuring the perceived attractiveness of international expansion. The scale used the following items: (i) we are very interested in moving the firm into foreign markets; (ii) we feel the possible gains of doing business overseas are well worth the costs; (iii) we feel our most attractive opportunities for growth lie in overseas market; and (iv) firms like ours that are trying to do business overseas are really on to something. The scale was unidimensional and presented a satisfactory Cronbach alpha (0.87). In line with expectations, we found that internationalized companies display a significantly higher global attitude towards internationalization (mean 5.71; s.d. 1.14) than do non-internationalized ASOs (mean 4.34; s.d. 1.53; t-test $p < 0.001$).

We investigated how the internationalization process was linked to other company-level milestones, and compared internationalized versus non-internationalized ASOs to check for any differences in reaching milestones. As shown in Table 5, international entry generally occurred later than other entrepreneurial steps, such as domestic commercialization, employment of personnel, establishment of domestic research and commercial collaborations, prototyping and structuring of an R&D unit, and obtaining external financing. International commercial partnerships were realized slightly earlier than product/service commercialization. It took longer, about one more year, to establish foreign subsidiaries. We investigated whether internationalized and non-internationalized ASOs differed in the timing of achieving these business milestones (Table 5). From the comparison, we see that internationalized ASOs prototyped earlier but were slower in patenting and establishing R&D units. However, these differences were not statistically significant. We also tested for differences by comparing born-globals at 3 and 5 years with non-internationalized companies; the resulting differences were not significant with the exception of year of first employee (mean for 3 years since inception born global ASOs: 2006.21; non-internationalized ASOs 2007.37; $p < 0.1$; mean for 5-years since inception born global ASOs: 2006.20; non-internationalized ASOs 2007.5; $p < 0.1$).

We investigated intentions and attitudes towards future internationalization opportunities for non-internationalized ASOs. We received answers from 28 companies (59.6% of non-internationalized sample). Interestingly, 53.6% of these respondents declared that they had no intention to carry out

---

[4] Companies employing no managers or no employees were not included in the test.

Table 5. Timing to reach business milestones.

Variable	Total sample			Internationalized ASOs			Non-internationalized ASOs		
	No.	Mean	s.d.	No.	Mean	s.d.	No.	Mean	s.d.
Year of foundation	120	2004.70	2.25	73	2004.59	2.25	47	2004.87	2.26
Year first R&D unit/office	48	2005.94	2.85	37	2006.14	2.94	11	2005.27	2.57
Year first domestic sale	100	2005.66	2.89	65	2005.52	2.57	35	2005.91	3.42
Year first prototype	75	2006.00	3.05	52	2005.79	3.01	23	2006.48	3.15
Year first domestic business collaboration	79	2006.42	2.65	54	2006.28	2.91	25	2006.72	1.99
Year first collaboration with public research center	64	2006.50	2.60	47	2006.21	2.60	17	2007.29	2.49
Year first employee	91	2006.70	3.29	61	2006.38	3.26	30	2007.37	3.31
Year first manager	24	2006.92	3.20	20	2006.90	3.51	4	2007.00	0.82
Year first external financing	29	2007.10	2.61	21	2006.67	2.29	8	2008.25	3.20
Year first collaboration with University	18	2007.17	2.98	15	2007.33	3.04	3	2006.33	3.06
Year first international business collaboration	47	2007.70	3.15	47	2007.70	3.15			
Year first patent filed	42	2007.93	2.49	25	2008.04	2.56	17	2007.77	2.46
Year first international sale	58	2007.98	3.02	58	2007.98	3.02			
Year first subsidiary abroad	5	2008.40	4.93	5	2008.40	4.93			

any international activity in the future. These companies do not perceived international expansion opportunities as attractive to them, as measured by the 4-item scale (Burpitt & Rondinelli, 1998) described above (mean 3.35; s.d. 1.36). Non-internationalized ASOs display significantly weaker attitudes towards internationalization than ASOs having intentions to internationalize at some point in the future (mean 5.46; s.d. 0.26; t-test $p < 0.000$). Companies with the intention of internationalizing in the future, however, do not appear to have any internationalization prospects in the short term (see Table 6). Looking at possible future entry modes, companies would internationalize through indirect exports or partnerships, mainly to be realized in Europe. In sum, answers highlight preferences towards low-commitment, low-risk entry modes into psychologically close markets.

As a last set of analyses, we compared internationalized and non-internationalized ASOs in terms of two performance measures from

Table 6.   Forecasted internationalization prospects for non-internationalized ASOs.

Speed	No ASOs	%	Entry mode	Geographical scope
Within 6 months	2	7.1	Direct export (50%)	Worldwide (100%)
			Partnership (50%)	Central Europe (100%)
Within 1 year	2	7.1	Indirect export (50%)	Central Europe (100%)
			Opening a productive subsidiary (50%)	Central Europe (100%)
Within 3 years	9	32.1	Indirect export (22%)	Central Europe (50%), Worldwide (50%)
			Partnership (44%)	Central Europe (50%), USA (25%), Turkey (25%)
			Licencing (22%)	Worldwide (100%)
			Opening a productive subsidiary (12%)	Central Europe (100%)
Never in the future	15	53.6		
	28	**100.0**		

2000 to 2012: number of employees and sales turnover. The number of employees was retrospectively reported by companies surveyed in 2013. We find that internationalized companies were, on average, larger in size than non-internationalized ones (3.29 versus 1.40 employees on average, $p < 0.001$). Sales revenues were retrieved from the AIDA — Bureau Van Dijk database. Our analyses showed that internationalized companies displayed significantly higher average yearly performance than non-internationalized ones (331,306 € versus 183,121 €, $p < 0.001$).

Discussion and Conclusion

In this chapter, we aimed to make two contributions to the literature on academic entrepreneurship: (a) to review the literature on the topic of internationalization of ASOs, and (b) to carry out an in-depth investigation of ASOs' internationalization in the Italian context by drawing on a sample of 120 surveyed companies.

Despite several calls for greater attention to the performances of ASOs (e.g., Djokovic & Souitaris, 2008; O'Shea *et al.*, 2008), to date, few studies have investigated this topic empirically. This is a potentially relevant gap in literature because academic spin-offs have been found to be more innovative and more internationalized than companies that were established via different methods (Lejpras, 2014). Our literature review retrieved fourteen recent studies that discussed environmental-, organizational-, and individual-level factors that influence the internationalization of ASOs. Among the environmental factors that impact ASOs' international entry, support from infrastructures such as science parks, universities, and university TTOs seems to play a pivotal role. However, more research should disentangle the effects of different types of supporting institutions (e.g., national versus local; public versus private) and policy tools (e.g., tax relief; use of labs, facilities, etc.), also accounting for contextual munificence (e.g., through cross-national studies). An additional research direction could lie in understanding different perceptions of international opportunities or of the needed business and market knowledge and skills from companies and for supporting institutions.

At the organizational level, reviewed studies have confirmed the importance of unique, intangible assets; mature technologies; and functioning organizational structures, processes, and decision rules for entering international markets. As an important and unique characteristic of ASOs, affiliation with the parent university has been found to influence the resources available to companies at inception and throughout the lifespan. Along these lines, a promising area for future research would be the characteristics of individuals' and organizations' networks with external stakeholders and their potentially different outcomes related to internationalization.

Similar to previous studies on international entrepreneurship, the reviewed studies confirmed the positive effect of top management's and entrepreneurial teams' international experience on internationalization outcomes. Given the academic origin of ASOs, future studies could do more to disentangle how international experience is accumulated by ASOs' teams and which forms of international experience matter for these companies (e.g., periods of studying and academic visiting abroad, conferences, international teaching assignments, international research projects, etc.). Additionally, the retrieved works highlighted the importance of scientific, technical, or industrial experience in driving internationalization. Thus, future studies could investigate whether there is a complementary or substitution effect between technological competences and international market competences. In addition, future research could examine the timing and causal effects of entrepreneurial and management teams' changes (e.g., cultural changes from an academic-oriented to a commercial-oriented culture, employment of partners or managers with a commercial background, etc.).

Through our empirical analyses of 120 Italian ASOs, we aimed to illuminate the process-based nature of internationalization, its relationship with other entrepreneurial events, and any differences in the characteristics and patterns of internationalized and non-internationalized companies. We have been able to illustrate several relevant points and offer a descriptive base for future studies on the topic. First, Italian ASOs are likely to internationalize (60.8% of the sample), in line with previous studies showing that these companies operate in global market niches. As also found by previous studies (e.g., Bjørnåli & Aspelund, 2012; Fafaliou *et al.*, 2010), the most used entry modes consist of exports but also the development of international partnerships. As understood through our surveys, these two entry modes are not mutually exclusive because establishing a partnership can convey subsequent sales to the partners and vice versa. Internationalized ASOs can be described as "born globals" because they internationalize in several markets within three to five years after inception. They cater to a variety of global markets, mainly focused on Western countries (Europe and North America) but also on emerging countries (China, India, South America). The majority of companies internationalized in several countries with increasingly broad geographic scope. An interesting feature of internationalization patterns disclosed by respondent companies is the long-lasting duration of international operations.

Our investigation did not show any significant difference between internationalized and non-internationalized ASOs in terms of industry and geographic location. Although the number of shareholders did not differ between internationalized and non-internationalized companies, the amount of invested equity was significantly higher in internationalized companies. We also found that the composition of shareholding teams differed between internationalized and non-internationalized ASOs. In particular, internationalized companies benefit from the presence of financial shareholders and from a higher amount of equity invested by public institutions and individual shareholders. As self-reported by surveyed entrepreneurs, both internationalized and non-internationalized ASOs seem to benefit from internationally skilled entrepreneurial teams, managers, and employees.

In terms of milestones and performance, we found that the timing for reaching significant company milestones does not differ for internationalized and non-internationalized ASOs. However, key performance variables such as the number of employees and sales revenues are significantly higher in internationalized companies.

Our findings show that non-internationalized companies display a significantly less positive attitude towards international opportunities and challenges. When considering future internationalization possibilities, these companies look at low-risk, low-commitment entry modes into psychologically close markets in the medium- and long-term. These data point to the possibility that, because ASOs are generally companies well-endowed in terms of internationally skilled individuals (e.g., having international experience as researchers and scientists), internationalization is not simply driven by these observable characteristics of team and personnel members but, rather, by other more unobservable characteristics (e.g., opportunity perception, motivation, etc.).

In light of our literature review and empirical results, we offer several considerations for future research. First, academic spin-offs represent an interesting parallel to similar studies about high-technology companies. ASOs' linkages with parent academic institutions would be an interesting avenue for future research. In fact, whereas many studies have investigated the impact of the parent university on spin-off establishment (for a review, see Rasmussen & Borch, 2010), there is scant information about their subsequent impact on ASOs' growth, especially in international markets. Thus, the role of the parent university in supporting ASOs' knowledge- and network-development could be clarified (e.g., Pettersen & Tobiassen, 2012). For example, because our work has demonstrated that internationalized companies count on a higher invested amount of equity from universities and other public shareholders, future studies could highlight the explanatory mechanisms as to how the parent university can provide legitimacy, credibility, and reputation in international markets (e.g., by impacting perceptions of customers or financing bodies). Additionally, contrasting academic and commercial logic and how these affect ASOs and their institutional environment would be interesting areas to explore. In fact, although the two logics have been compared in previous studies (e.g., Sauermann & Stephan, 2013; Fini & Toschi, 2016), they seem to be both leading to successful internationalization patterns (e.g., through publishing or scientific conferences) (Pettersen & Tobiassen, 2012). Second, studies have found that ASOs have long pre-founding periods whereas technology and business ideas gradually take shape. From this viewpoint, the founding date might not be the ideal indicator of maturity for market entrance (Pettersen & Tobiassen, 2012) because technology development and "readiness for market" could be better captured by prototyping or patenting dates. Therefore, it would be interesting to account for technological readiness when investigating ASOs' internationalization speed, keeping in mind that they might be targeting domestic and international markets equally.

References

Algieri, B., Aquino, A. & Succurro, M. 2013. Technology transfer offices and academic spin-off creation: the case of Italy. *Journal of Technology Transfer*, 38, 382–400. Available at: http://doi.org/10.1007/s10961-011-9241-8.

Arora, A., Jaju, A., Kefalas, A. G. & Perenich, T. 2004. An exploratory analysis of global managerial mindsets: A case of U.S. textile and apparel industry. *Journal of International Management*, 10, 393–411. Available at: http://doi.org/10.1016/j.intman.2004.05.001.

Aspelund, A., Madsen, T. K. & Moen, Ø. 2007. A review of the foundation, international marketing strategies, and performance of international new ventures. *European Journal of Marketing*, 41(11/12), 1423–1448. Available at: http://doi.org/10.1108/03090560710821242.

Baldini, N., Fini, R. & Grimaldi, R. (2013) The transition towards entrepreneurial universities: An assessment of academic entrepreneurship in Italy. In A. N. Link, D. S. Siegel and M. Wright (eds), Chicago Handbook of University Technology Transfer and Academic Entrepreneurship, pp. 218–244. Chicago, IL: University of Chicago Press. DOI: 10.7208/Chicago/9780226178486.001.0001

Bell, J. 1995. The internationalization of small computer software firms. *European Journal of Marketing*, 29(8), 60–75.

Bell, J., Loane, S., McNaughton, R. & Servais, P. 2011. *Toward a Typology of Rapidly Internationalizing SMEs*, N. Nummela (ed.). Routledge, New York.

Bercovitz, J. & Feldman, M. 2008. Academic entrepreneurs: organizational change at the individual level. *Organization Science*, 19(1), 69–89. Available at: http://doi.org/10.1287/orsc.1070.0295.

Bilkey, W. J. & Tesar, G. 1977. The export behavior of smaller-sized Wisconsin manufacturing firms. *Journal of International Business Studies*, 8(1), 93–98.

Bjørnåli, E. S. & Aspelund, A. 2012. The role of the entrepreneurial team and the board of directors in the internationalization of academic spin-offs. *Journal of International Entrepreneurship*, 10, 350–377. http://doi.org/10.1007/s10843-012-0094-5

Bolzani, D., Fini, R., Grimaldi, R., Santoni, S. & Sobrero, M. 2014. *Fifteen Years of Academic Entrepreneurship in Italy: Evidence From the TASTE Project.*

Bolzani, D., Fini, R., Grimaldi, R. & Sobrero, M. 2014. University spin-offs and their impact: Longitudinal evidence from Italy. *Journal of Industrial and Business Economics*, 41(4), 179–205.

Bruneel, J., Yli-Renko, H. & Clarysse, B. 2010. Learning from experience and learning from others: How congenital and interorganizational learning substitute for experiential learning in young firm internationalization. *Strategic Entrepreneurship Journal*, 4, 164–182. Available at: http://doi.org/10.1002/sej.

Buckley, P. J. & Ghauri, P. N. 1993. Introduction and overview. In *The Internationalization of the Firm: A Reader*, P. J. Buckley & P. N. Ghauri (eds.), pp. ix–xxi. Academic Press, London.

Burpitt, J. W. & Rondinelli, D. A. 1998. Export decision-making in small firms: The role of organizational learning. *Journal of World Business*, 33(1), 51–68.

Cattaneo, M., Meoli, M. & Vismara, S. 2015. Cross-border M&As of biotech firms affiliated with internationalized universities. *The Journal of Technology Transfer*, 40, 409–433. Available at: http://doi.org/10.1007/s10961-014-9349-8.

Clarysse, B. & Moray, N. 2004. A process study of entrepreneurial team formation: The case of a research-based spin-off. *Journal of Business Venturing*, 19(1), 55–79.

Colombo, M. G. & Piva, E. 2012. Firms' genetic characteristics and competence-enlarging strategies: A comparison between academic and non-academic high-tech start-ups. *Research Policy*, 41(1), 79–92. Available at: http://doi.org/10.1016/j.respol.2011.08.010.

Colyvas, J., Crow, M., Gelijns, A., Mazzoleni, R., Nelson, R. R., Rosenberg, N. & Sampat, B. N. 2002. How do university inventions get into practice? *Management Science*, 48(1), 61–72.

Coviello, N. E. 2006. The network dynamics of international new ventures. *Journal of International Business Studies*, 713–731. Available at: http://doi.org/10.1057/palgrave.jibs.8400219.

Coviello, N. E. & Jones, M. V. 2004. Methodological issues in international entrepreneurship research. *Journal of Business Venturing*, 19, 485–508. Available at: http://doi.org/10.1016/j.jbusvent.2003.06.001.

Crick, D. 2009. The internationalisation of born global and international new venture SMEs. *International Marketing Review*, 26(4/5), 453–476.

Crick, D. & Crick, J. 2014. The internationalization strategies of rapidly internationalizing high-tech UK SMEs: Planned and unplanned activities. *European Business Review*, 26(5), 421–448. Available at: http://doi.org/10.1108/EBR-12-2012-0073.

Crick, D. & Jones, M. V. 2000. Small high-technology firms and international high-technology markets. *Journal of International Marketing*, 8(2), 63–85.

Crick, D. & Spence, M. 2005. The internationalisation of "high performing" UK high-tech SMEs: a study of planned and unplanned strategies. *International Business Review*, 14(2), 167–185.

Cumming, D., Sapienza, H. J., Siegel, D. S. & Wright, M. 2009. International entrepreneurship: managerial and policy implications. *Strategic Entrepreneurship Journal*, 3, 283–296. Available at: http://doi.org/10.1002/sej.75.

Degroof, J.-J. & Roberts, E. B. 2004. Overcoming weak entrepreneurial infrastructures for academic spin-off ventures. *Journal of Technology Transfer*, 29, 327–352.

Djokovic, D. & Souitaris, V. 2008. Spinouts from academic institutions: A literature review with suggestions for further research. *Journal of Technology Transfer*, 33(3), 225–247. Available at: http://doi.org/10.1007/s10961-006-9000-4.

Fafaliou, I., Melanitis, N. E. & Tsakalos, V. 2010. Commercialising research results in immature technology transfer markets: cases from the Greek experience. *International Journal of Entrepreneurship and Innovation Management*, 11(2), 213–227. Available at: http://doi.org/10.1504/IJEIM.2010.030069.

Fini, R., Grimaldi, R., Marzocchi, G. L. & Sobrero, M. 2012. The determinants of corporate entrepreneurial intention within small and newly established firms. *Entrepreneurship Theory and Practice*, 36, 387–414. Available at: http://doi.org/10.1111/j.1540-6520.2010.00411.x.

Fini, R., Grimaldi, R., Santoni, S. & Sobrero, M. 2011. Complements or substitutes? The role of universities and local context in supporting the creation of academic spin-offs. *Research Policy*, 40(8), 1113–1127. Available at: http://doi.org/10.1016/j.respol.2011.05.013.

Fini, R., Grimaldi, R. & Sobrero, M. 2009. Factors fostering academics to start up new ventures: An assessment of Italian founders' incentives. *Journal of Technology Transfer*, 34(4), 380–402. Available at: http://doi.org/10.1007/s10961-008-9093-z.

Fini, R. & Toschi, L. 2016. Academic logic and corporate entrepreneurial intentions: A study of the interaction between cognitive and institutional factors in new firms, *International Small Business Journal*, 34(5), 637–659.

Fratocchi, L., Ancarani, A., Barbieri, P., Di Mauro, C., Nassimbeni, G., Sartor, M., Vignoli, M. & Zanoni, A. 2015. Manufacturing back-reshoring as a nonlinear internationalization process, *Progress in International Business Research*, 10, 365-403

Geuna, A. & Rossi, F. 2011. Changes to university IPR regulations in Europe and the impact on academic patenting. *Research Policy*, 40(8), 1068–1076.

Grandi, A., & Grimaldi, R. 2003. Exploring the networking characteristics of new venture founding teams: A study of Italian academic spin-off. Small Business Economics, 21(4), 329–341.

Grandi, A. & Grimaldi, R. 2005. Academics' organizational characteristics and the generation of successful business ideas. *Journal of Business Venturing*, 20, 821–845. Available at: http://doi.org/10.1016/j.jbusvent.2004.07.002.

Grimaldi, R., Kenney, M., Siegel, D. S. & Wright, M. (2011). 30 years after Bayh-Dole: Reassessing academic entrepreneurship. *Research Policy*, 40(8), 1045–1057. Available at: http://doi.org/10.1016/j.respol.2011.04.005.

Gupta, A. K. & Govindarajan, V. 2002. Cultivating a global mindset. *Academy of Management Executive*, 16(11), 116–126.

Holtbruegge, D. & Kreppel, H. 2012. Determinants of outward foreign direct investment from BRIC countries: An explorative study. *International Journal of Emerging Markets*, 7(1), 4–30. Available at: http://doi.org/10.1108/17468801211197897.

Johanson, J. & Vahlne, J.-E. 1977. The internationalization process of the firm — a model of knowledge development and increasing foreign market commitments. *Journal of International Business Studies*, 8(1), 23–32.

Johnson, J. E. 2004. Factors influencing the early internationalization of high technology start-ups: US and UK evidence. *Journal of International Entrepreneurship*, 2(1–2), 139–154.

Jones, M. V. & Coviello, N. E. 2005. Internationalization: Conceptualising an entrepreneurial process of behavior in time. *Journal of International Business Studies*, 36(3), 284–303.

Jones, M. V., Coviello, N. & Tang, Y. K. 2011. International entrepreneurship research (1989–2009): A domain ontology and thematic analysis. *Journal of Business Venturing*, 26(6), 632–659. Available at: http://doi.org/10.1016/j.jbusvent.2011.04.001.

Keupp, M. M. & Gassmann, O. 2009. The past and the future of international entrepreneurship: A review and suggestions for developing the field. *Journal of*

Management, 35(3), 600–633. Available at: http://doi.org/10.1177/0149206308330558.

Knight, G. A. & Cavusgil, S. T. 2004. Innovation, organizational capabilities, and the born-global firm. *Journal of International Business Studies*, 35(2), 124–141.

Lawton Smith, H., Romeo, S. & Bagchi-Senb, S. 2008. Oxfordshire biomedical university spin-offs: An evolving system. *Cambridge Journal of Regions, Economy and Society*, 1(2), 303–319. Available at: http://doi.org/10.1093/cjres/rsn010.

Lejpras, A. 2014. How innovative are spin-offs at later stages of development? Comparing innovativeness of established research spin-offs and otherwise created firms. *Small Business Economics*, 43(2), 327–351. Available at: http://doi.org/10.1007/s11187-013-9534-4.

Madsen, T. K. & Servais, P. 1997. The internationalization of born globals: An evolutionary process? *International Business Review*, 6(6), 561–583.

Markman, G. D., Gianiodis, P., Phan, P. & Balkin, D. 2005. Innovation speed: Transferring university technology to market. *Research Policy*, 34(7), 1058–1075.

Mathews, J. A. & Zander, I. 2007. The international entrepreneurial dynamics of accelerated internationalisation. *Journal of International Business Studies*, 38, 1–17. Available at: http://doi.org/10.1057/palgrave.jibs.8400271.

Miesenbock, K. J. 1988. Small businesses and exporting: A literature review. *International Small Business Journal*, 6, 42–61. Available at: http://doi.org/10.1177/026624268800600204.

Mosey, S. & Wright, M. 2007. From human capital to social capital: A longitudinal study of technology-based academic entrepreneurs. *Entrepreneurship Theory and Practice*, 31(6), 909–935. Available at: http://doi.org/10.1111/j.1540-6520.2007.00203.x.

Mudambi, R. & Zahra, S. A. 2007. The survival of international new ventures. *Journal of International Business Studies*, 38, 333–352. Available at: http://doi.org/10.1057/palgrave.jibs.8400264.

Nicolaou, N. & Birley, S. 2003. Academic networks in a trichotomous categorisation of university spinouts. *Journal of Business Venturing*, 18(3), 333–359.

Nordman, E. R. & Melén, S. 2008. The impact of different kinds of knowledge for the internationalization process of Born Globals in the biotech business. *Journal of World Business*, 43, 171–185. Available at: http://doi.org/10.1016/j.jwb.2007.11.014.

Nummela, N., Loane, S. & Bell, J. 2006. Change in SME internationalisation: an Irish perspective. *Journal of Small Business and Enterprise Development*, 13(4), 562–583. Available at: http://doi.org/10.1108/14626000610705750.

O'Shea, R. P. O., Chugh, H. & Allen, T. J. 2008. Determinants and consequences of university spinoff activity: a conceptual framework. *Journal of Technology Transfer*, 33, 653–666. Available at: http://doi.org/10.1007/s10961-007-9060-0.

Oviatt, B. M. & McDougall, P. P. 1994. Toward a theory of international new ventures. *Journal of International Business Studies*, 25(1), 45–64.

Oviatt, B. M. & McDougall, P. P. 2005. Defining international entrepreneurship and modeling the speed of internationalization. *Entrepreneurship Theory and Practice*, 29(5), 537–553.

Oxtorp, L. A. 2014. Dynamic managerial capability of technology-based international new ventures — a basis for their long-term competitive advantage. *Journal of International Entrepreneurship*, 12, 389–420. Available at: http://doi.org/10.1007/s10843-014-0133-5.

Peiris, I. K., Akoorie, M. E. M. & Sinha, P. 2012. International entrepreneurship: A critical analysis of studies in the past two decades and future directions for research. *Journal of International Entrepreneurship*, 10(4), 279–324. Available at: http://doi.org/10.1007/s10843-012-0096-3.

Pettersen, I. B. & Tobiassen, A. E. 2012. Are born globals really born globals? The case of academic spin-offs with long development periods. *Journal of International Entrepreneurship*, 10, 117–141. Available at: http://doi.org/10.1007/s10843-012-0086-5.

Pirnay, F., Surlemont, B. & Nlemvo, F. 2003. Toward a typology of university spin-offs. *Small Business Economics*, 21, 355–369.

Rasmussen, E. & Borch, O. J. 2010. University capabilities in facilitating entrepreneurship: A longitudinal study of spin- off ventures at mid-range universities. *Research Policy*, (2015). Available at: http://doi.org/10.1016/j.respol.2010.02.002.

Rasmussen, E., Moen, Ø. & Gulbrandsen, M. 2006. Initiatives to promote commercialization of university knowledge. *Technovation*, 26(4), 518–533. Available at: http://doi.org/10.1016/j.technovation.2004.11.005.

Reid, S. D. 1981. The decision-maker and export entry and expansion. 1*Journal of International Business Studies*, 12(2), 101–112.

Roberts, E. 1991. *Entrepreneurs in High Technology, Lessons From MIT and Beyond.* Oxford University Press, Oxford.

Rothaermel, F. T., Agung, S. D. & Jiang, L. 2007. University entrepreneurship: A taxonomy of the literature. *Industrial and Corporate Change*, 16(4), 691–791. Available at: http://doi.org/10.1093/icc/dtm023.

Sapienza, H. J., Autio, E., George, G. & Zahra, S. A. 2006. A capabilities perspective on the effects of early internationalization on firm survival and growth. *Academy of Management Review*, 31(4), 914–933.

Sauermann, H. & Stephan, P. 2013. Conflicting logics? A multidimensional view of industrial and academic science. *Organization Science*, 24(3), 889–909.

Schulz, A., Borghoff, T. & Kraus, S. 2009. International entrepreneurship: Towards a theory of SME internationalization. *International Journal of Business and Economics*, 9(1), 1–13. Available at: http://doi.org/Article.

Shane, S. 2004a. *Academic Entrepreneurship: University Spinoffs and Wealth Creation.* Edward Elgar, Cheltenham.

Shane, S. 2004b. Encouraging university entrepreneurship: The effect of the Bayh-Dole act on university patenting in the United States. *Journal of Business Venturing*, 19(1), 127–151.

Shane, S. & Stuart, T. 2002. Organizational endowments and the performance of university start-ups. *Management Science*, 48(1), 154–170.

Shane, S. & Venkataraman, S. 2000. The promise of enterpreneurship as a field of research. *The Academy of Management Review*, 25(1) 217–226.

Styles, C. & Genua, T. 2008. The rapid internationalization of high technology firms created through the commercialization of academic research. *Journal of World Business*, 43, 146–157. Available at: http://doi.org/10.1016/j.jwb.2007.11.011.

Suzuki, S. & Okamuro, H. 2015. Determinants of academic startup's orientation toward international business expansion. In *DRUID 2015 Conference Proceedings*.

Taheri, M. & Van Geenhuizen, M. 2011. How human capital and social networks may influence the patterns of international learning spin-off among academic spin-off firms. *Papers in Regional Science*, 90(2), 287–312. Available at: http://doi.org/10.1111/j.1435-5957.2011.00363.x.

Teixeira, A. A. C. & Coimbra, C. 2014. The determinants of the internationalization speed of Portuguese university spin-offs: An empirical investigation. *Journal of International Entrepreneurship*, 12, 270–308. Available at: http://doi.org/10.1007/s10843-014-0132-6.

Terjesen, S., Hessels, J. & Li, D. 2013. Comparative international entrepreneurship: A review and research agenda. *Journal of Management*, 1–46. Available at: http://doi.org/10.1177/0149206313486259.

Van Geenhuizen, M. & Soetanto, D. P. 2009. Technovation academic spin-offs at different ages: A case study in search of key obstacles to growth. *Technovation*, 29(10), 671–681. Available at: http://doi.org/10.1016/j.technovation.2009.05.009.

Van Geenhuizen, M., Ye, Q. & Au-Yong-Oliviera, M. 2014. A skills approach to growth of university spin-off firms: Export as an example. In *14th ICTPI Conference*.

Visintin, F. & Pittino, D. 2014. Technovation Founding team composition and early performance of university — based spin-off companies. *Technovation*, 34(1), 31–43. Available at: http://doi.org/10.1016/j.technovation.2013.09.004.

Vohora, A., Wright, M., & Lockett, A. (2004). Critical junctures in the development of university high-tech spinout companies. *Research Policy*, 33, 147–175. http://doi.org/10.1016/S0048-7333(03)00107-0

Wallmark, J. T. 1997. Inventions and patents at universities: the case of Chalmers University of Technology. *Technovation*, 17(3), 127–139.

Watkins-Mathys, L. & Foster, M. J. 2006. Entrepreneurship: The missing ingredient in China's STIPs? *Entrepreneurship & Regional Development*, 18, 249–274. Available at: http://doi.org/10.1080/08985620600593161.

Zahra, S. A. 2005. A theory of international new ventures: a decade of research. *Journal of International Business Studies*, 36(1), 20–28. Available at: http://doi.org/10.1057/palgrave.jibs.8400118.

Zucker, L. G., Darby, M. R. & Brewer, M. B. 1998. Intellectual human capital and the birth of U.S. biotechnology enterprises. *American Economic Review*, 88(1), 190–305.

Appendix

Table A.1.   **Parent universities of respondent ASOs.**

University	No. of ASOs	Total (%)
University of Bologna	14	11.7
Polytechnic of Milan	12	10.0
Polytechnic of Turin	9	7.5
University of Padua	8	6.7
University of Ferrara	7	5.8
University of Milan	6	5.0
University of Pisa	5	4.2
University of Siena	5	4.2
University of Salento	4	3.3
University of Cagliari	4	3.3
University of Modena and Reggio Emilia	4	3.3
Sant'Anna School of Pisa	3	2.5
University of Sannio and Benevento	3	2.5
University of Florence	3	2.5
University of Parma	3	2.5
University of Pavia	3	2.5
University of Udine	3	2.5
Polytechnic of Bari	2	1.7
Catholic University of Sacred Hearth	2	1.7
University of Calabria	2	1.7
University of Bergamo	2	1.7
University of Perugia	2	1.7
Polytechnic University of Marche	2	1.7
University of Eastern Piedmont "Amedeo Avogadro"	1	0.8
University of Bari	1	0.8
University of Genoa	1	0.8
University of L'Aquila	1	0.8
University of Milan-Bicocca	1	0.8
University of Naples "Federico II"	1	0.8
University of Palermo	1	0.8
University of Rome "three"	1	0.8
University of Sassari	1	0.8
University of Turin	1	0.8
University of Trento	1	0.8
University of Verona	1	0.8
Total	**120**	**100.0**

Chapter 11

The Economic Performance of Portuguese Academic Spin-Offs: Do Science & Technology Infrastructures and Support Matter?

Aurora A. C. Teixeira

CEF.UP, Faculdade de Economia,
University of Porto & INESC TEC, Portugal
ateixeira@fep.up.pt

Academic and political interest in Academic Spin-offs (ASOs) has increased significantly in the last few years. In 2007 the Portuguese government established, jointly with the University of Texas at Austin, the University Technology Enterprise Network (UTEN), a network of professional Technology Transfer Offices focused on the commercialization and internationalization of Portuguese Science and Technology. The present chapter assesses the role of S&T infrastructures and support on the economic performance of a sample of Portuguese ASOs associated to the UTEN. Econometric estimations revealed that certain types of S&T infrastructures (incubators) and support mechanisms (access to skilled labor; business mentoring and counselling) were critical for the economic performance of ASOs. In contrast, other contextual factors, namely the characteristics and endowments of host universities and the level of development of regions where the companies located failed to influence their economic performance. Such results highlight the need for continuing and sustainable public investment/efforts aimed at strengthen technology transfer and commercialization process in Portugal.

Introduction

University Spin-offs (USOs) (O'Shea *et al.*, 2008) or Academic Spin-offs (ASOs) (Ndonzuau *et al.*, 2002) are firms whose products or services are based on scientific/technical knowledge generated within a university setting (Samson & Gurdon, 1993; Steffensen *et al.*, 1999), where the founding members may (or may not) include the academic inventor.

Existing literature in this field is on rise (Fryges & Wright, 2015) but it nevertheless tends to focus on countries where the phenomenon of academic spin-offs is fully consolidated, most notably the US and Canada (Doutriaux & Peterman, 1982; Louis *et al.*, 1989; Shane & Khurana, 2003; Shane, 2004a; Lehrer & Asakawa, 2004 ; Ding & Stuart, 2006; Zhang, 2009; Landry *et al.*, 2006; Gibson & Naquin, 2011). Studies on Europe are increasing but are comparatively less common (Jones-Evans, 1998; Klofsten & Jones-Evans, 2000; Vohora *et al.*, 2004; Clarysse *et al.*, 2005; Ratinho & Henriques, 2010; Ganotakis, 2012; Bigliardi *et al.*, 2013), despite the strong policy interest in the promotion and development of this type of firms (Lockett *et al.*, 2005; Wright *et al.*, 2007).

In the European context, the promotion of ASOs has revealed to be a daunting, complex task (Morales-Gualdrón *et al.*, 2009), especially because European research institutions have shown limited capacity for transferring scientific and technological knowledge to industry (Jones-Evans *et al.*, 1999). Among the reasons pointed for this shortcoming stand cultural differences between universities and private sectors which, in part, reflect the lack of an entrepreneurial spirit within the university environment (Morales-Gualdrón *et al.*, 2009), and the poor industry–university relations that characterize several EU countries, exacerbating the lack of university entrepreneurial orientation (Teixeira & Costa, 2006; Nosella & Grimaldi, 2009).

Although there are numerous and high quality studies that identify factors underlying the creation of ASOs (see, for instance, Fini *et al.*, 2011), few have examined the consequences of the activities accomplished, most specifically their economic performance (Martínez & Miranda, 2014). Three main groups of determinants of firms economic performance are usually highlighted: entrepreneur or founder factors (Colombo & Grilli, 2010; Dahl & Sorenson, 2011; Gimmon & Levie, 2010; Ganotakis, 2012); firms attributes (Lee *et al.*, 2001; Zheng *et al.*, 2010; Taheri & van Geenhuizen, 2011; Pirolo & Presutti, 2010; Ganotakis, 2012); and contextual factors (Li & Atuahene-Gima, 2001; Zheng *et al.*, 2010). Science and Technology (S&T) support mechanisms and infrastructures, such as Technology

Transfer Offices (TTOs), Incubators or Science Parks, are included in this latter group of determinants but so far have received scanty attention from the literature in the area (Minguillo & Thelwall, 2015).

The analysis presented in this chapter aims to fill in the above gap by assessing the relevance of Science & Technology infrastructures and support technological for the economic performance of ASOs. It therefore contributes to the literature by adding empirical evidence on the process of technology transfer in an unexplored setting, Portugal, a fast follower country in terms of innovation (Bento & Fontes, 2015).

To achieve this goal, a direct email survey was designed and applied to all 309 ASOs associated to the members of the University Technology Enterprise Network (UTEN). The survey aimed to analyze quantitatively what were the main drivers of the ASOs' economic performance in the period between 2008 and 2011. The UTEN was established in 2007, a collaboration between the Portuguese government and the University of Texas at Austin, and includes among its members all Portuguese public universities as well as the most important research institutions located in Portugal.

The next section presents a literature review on the relevance of contextual factors for ASOs' economic performance. The study's methodological considerations are described in Section 3, and in Section 4, the results of the survey are analyzed and discussed. In the Conclusion the main findings and implication for innovation policy are put forward.

The Economic Performance of ASOs and the Relevance of Contextual Factors: a Review

The studies that analyze the distinct dimensions (e.g., international, innovation or economic) of ASOs performance can be grouped into three main categories (see Teixeira and Coimbra, 2014): entrepreneur-specific factors, business-related factors, and contextual factors. Given the focus of this chapter, the literature review presented below synthetizes mainly the relevance of contextual factors (namely science and technology support mechanisms and infrastructures — TTOs, Incubators or Science Parks), for ASOs economic performance.[1]

Resources in ASOs are usually in short supply, and the literature mentions the lack of investment capital and of non-technical knowledge and skills most often (e.g., Lockett *et al.*, 2005). Thus, in their early years, spin-offs

---

[1] See Table A.1 (in Appendix) for an overview of the relevant studies.

need to have access to these resources, critically depending on the presence of key suppliers, such as customers and investors, and to develop capabilities in networking with them (Walter *et al.*, 2006). To overcome these shortcomings, Technology Transfer Offices (TTOs), incubators, Science Parks or similar organizations may act as mediators or direct suppliers of resources at relatively reduced costs (Soetanto & van Geenhuizen, 2009).

Meyer (2003), focusing on support mechanisms and the impact they have on the development of four selected US and European start-ups in a science-based environment, found that the support, in this case from incubators, is fundamental for a firm's performance. Start-up advice at an early stage, ideally before the company is set up, may get the company off to a better start. In the same line, according to Bathula *et al.* (2011), support mechanisms play a key role in assisting the budding entrepreneur, providing a range of services such as shared offices, access to research labs, hardware and software, knowledge and network pools, as well as to other start-up companies. Such support gives the start-up a relatively secure environment and a head start over others. Ganotakis (2012) found a strong positive impact of science and technology infrastructures, most notably science parks, on firms' performance.

The literature emphasizes the importance of business networks and collaboration (e.g., Fornoni *et al.*, 2012; Ganotakis, 2012) for the performance of ASOs. This literature stream suggests that the innovative capabilities of a firm can be enhanced when it engages in inter-firm networks or strategic alliances, i.e., voluntary arrangements between firms involving the exchange, sharing or co-development of products, technologies, or services (Gulati, 1998). ASOs are typically associated to support mechanisms such as incubators, science parks and TTOs, and may have the opportunity to benefit from their social networks. Network relations act as a bridge to access information and resources that supplements the entrepreneurs' or young firms' own resources (Rasmussen *et al.*, 2011). Access to venture capital or targeting potential partners with managerial skills are aspects that can be decisive for potential entrepreneurs (Carayannis *et al.*, 1998), and can be conducted or facilitated not only by universities but also by TTOs, or other support mechanisms. As Cooper *et al.* (2012) reveal in their study, focusing mainly on university business incubators, these support mechanisms strive to develop robust business and social networks to bring value to their resident companies in the form of intellectual and material resources.

University–industry collaborations may be of key importance, resulting not only in additional revenue for the university and technological spillovers which stimulate additional R&D investment and job creation at local level (Caldera & Debande, 2010), but especially by constituting an opportunity for ASOs to engage with the market. University–industry cooperation has been widely studied and identified as a key element in improving the innovation ability of enterprises and regions (Xu *et al.*, 2010). A university network that is built based on this type of cooperation facilitates access to a variety of partners (Van Burg *et al.*, 2008), setting the grounds for solid external relationships with, for instance, institutional investors, firms and consulting organizations (Nosella & Grimaldi, 2009). Tödtling *et al.* (2011) analyzed open innovation, i.e., well-developed regional knowledge infrastructure and excellent universities that provide easy access to knowledge and qualified personnel. In their study, they found that the collaboration of companies and universities or research institutes contribute to an open innovation environment connecting not only long-term investment in fundamental research and education but contributing also to university start-ups connecting ideas from companies in the region with new insights from fundamental research to develop successful commercial applications. This knowledge infrastructure facilitates the continuation of successful development paths and investments in a broader knowledge base to open up new fields and opportunities for young companies.

Therefore, we hypothesize that:

Hypothesis 1: *The existence of S.&T support mechanisms and the importance of the relations established by ASOs influence their economic performance.*

Scientific and technological achievements and outcomes of universities can be critical for their spin-off activities, since they may constitute a relevant source of business opportunities (Gómez-Gras *et al.*, 2008). According to the literature (e.g., O'Shea *et al.*, 2005), the technological production of universities, measured by the number of patents, has a positive impact on spin-off activity. In line with these findings, we hypothesize that:

Hypothesis 2: *ASOs that are associated to universities with a higher pool of advanced applied/commercialized knowledge (Patents) tend to outperform the other ASOs.*

Regional factors might be potential determinants of ASOs' performance, because they may enjoy externalities from proximity to diverse infrastructures such as universities, research institutes and companies, benefiting from knowledge spillovers (Lynskey, 2004). Indeed, Maine *et al.* (2010), analyzing spill-over effects in clusters, found that when cluster effects are measured in terms of distance, proximity to a relevant cluster is associated with enhanced growth. Additionally, Malmberg *et al.* (2000) reported that urbanization economies have a significant impact on firm performance, more specifically, export performance. Thus, we posit that:

Hypothesis 3: *ASOs located in more economically developed regions outperform those from less developed regions.*

In terms of 'control' variables, the studies analyzed include the sector (Gimmon & Levie, 2010) as well as firms' age (Baum *et al.*, 2000; Colombo & Grilli, 2000; Clarysse *et al.*, 2011; Ganotakis, 2012) and size (Lee *et al.*, 2001; Maine *et al.*, 2010; Clarysse *et al.*, 2011).[2]

Methodological Underpinnings

The empirical analysis undertaken in this study aims to assess the relevance of the determinants of the economic performance of Portuguese ASOs. To achieve this goal, a direct email survey was designed and applied to all ASOs associated to the members of the University Technology Enterprise Network (UTEN), analyzing quantitatively what were the main drivers of the economic performance of ASOs in the period between 2008 and 2011.

Given the lack of an official statistical source/body that gathered information on academic spin-offs (ASOs), in 2009, UTEN researchers started to identify the ASOs associated to universities that were part of the network. This extensive and time-consuming task was conducted in collaboration with each university's TTOs, incubators and science parks. Although the identification process was paved with difficulties given the absence of a common definition of ASO among the participants involved, based on an interactive process developed between the researchers and each UTEN stakeholder, it was possible to establish a group of ASOs — i.e., firms whose products or services are based on scientific/technical knowledge generated within a university setting — associated to each member university of UTEN (which means that all public universities were represented).

By 2012, 309 ASOs associated to UTEN's Portuguese members were identified, whose distribution is set out in Table 1. From this total, 286 comprise our effective/target population, as 23 firms were unreachable, having presumably ceased operations. It is important to note that since 2009 this number has been evolving and our database has been constantly updated to reflect the new firms created and the firms that in the meanwhile ceased their activities. From 2009 onwards, each ASO has been contacted every

---

[2]In Table A.2 (in Appendix), a synthesis of studies which deal with the relation between ASOs economic performance and age and size is presented.

Table 1.   Representativeness and distribution of ASOs by TTO and University (reference year: 2012).

Associated University [target population; sample; response rate (%)]	UTEN partner associated to technology transfer	Population by 2012	Target population	Sample	Effective Response rate. (%)	Percentage in the 'target population' [sample]
U. Minho [37; 18; 48.6%]	Avepark/Spinpark	14	12	7	58.3	12.9 [18.2]
	TecMinho	29	25	11	44.0	22.4 [31.7]
U. Porto [64; 32; 50.0%]	UPIN	3	3	2	66.7	
	UPTEC	54	53	23	43.4	
	INESC Porto	9	8	7	87.5	
U. Aveiro [11; 7; 63.6%]	UATEC	11	11	7	63.6	3.8 [6.9]
U. Beira Interior [26; 5; 19.2%]	UBI-GAPPI	5	5	2	40.0	9.1 [5.1]
	Parkurbis	23	21	3	14.3	
U. Coimbra [27; 8; 29.6%]	OTIC-UC	5	5	3	60.0	9.4 [8.1]
	IPN	23	22	5	22.7	
U. Nova Lisboa [48; 11; 22.9%]	Gab. de Empreendedorismo (FCT-UNL)	20	20	6	30.0	16.8 [11.1]
	Madan Parque	29	28	5	17.9	
U. Lisboa [2; 2; 100%]	IMM	2	2	2	100.0	0.7 [2.0]

(Continued)

Table 1. *(Continued)*

Associated University [target population; sample; response rate (%)]	UTEN partner associated to technology transfer	Population by 2012	Target population	Sample	Effective Response rate. (%)	Percentage in the 'target population' [sample]
ISCTE [4; 1; 25.0%]	INDEG	4	4	1	25.0	1.4 [1.0]
U. Técnica de Lisboa [35; 6; 14.3%]	OTIC-UTL	1	1	0	0.0	12.2 [6.1]
	Inovisa	3	3	2	66.7	
	TT@IST	4	4	4	100.0	
	Taguspark	30	27	0	0.0	
U. Algarve & U. Évora [30; 11; 36.7%]	CRIA	32	24	10	41.7	10.5 [11.1]
	UÉvora	3	3	0	0.0	
	Sines Tecnopólo	3	3	1	33.3	
U. Madeira [2; 0; 0.0%]	GAPI Madeira	1	1	0	0.0	0.7 [0.0]
	TECMU Madeira	1	1	0	0.0	
All		309	286	101	35.3	100 [100]

Notes: The difference between the population and the 'target population' is explained by the fact that 23 ASOs were unreachable, presumably having gone out of business.

year (between September and October) in order to answer a questionnaire designed for the purpose. In 2012, after two months (September–October 2012) of contacts, 101 responses were obtained representing a response rate of 35.3%.

The questionnaire sent to the targeted firms was divided into three main parts. The first included firm-specific data. The second part dealt with questions regarding the support mechanisms for ASOs, namely science parks, TTOs and/or incubators. ASOs were asked to classify the importance of these organizations/technological infrastructures regarding the ease of access to infrastructures, specialized competences and national or international networks, contact with a creative environment, and support in terms of recruitment, of access to public subsidies, financial support, and mentoring. The third part included financial, operational and human resources data about the firm, namely the year of establishment, and year of the first sales/exports/international subsidiary. Additional information on turnover, R&D expenditure, number of patents, and value of royalties in each year from 2008 to 2011 was also collected. Human resources-related data included the number of founders and employees in Full Time Equivalent (FTE).

Based on the literature, and in a simplified way, the general econometric specification used is as follows:

$$Performance_i = \hat{\beta}_0 + \frac{\hat{\beta}_1\,S\&T\ infrastructure + \hat{\beta}_2\,\textbf{S \& T support} + \hat{\beta}_3\,\text{University} + \hat{\beta}_4\,Region +}{Context} \\ + \hat{\beta}_5\,\textbf{Sector} + \hat{\beta}_6\,Age + \hat{\beta}_7\,Size + \hat{e}_i$$

where, i is the subscript for each ASO and ei is the sample error term. Bold indicates vector-variables.

Our dependent variable 'economic performance' is measured, following Ganotakis (2012), as the log of sales per individual (in FTE) in 2011. The proxies for the determinants of performance (i.e., the model's independent variables) are described in Table 2, together with the study's main hypotheses.

Empirical Results

Descriptive results

In 2011, the total sample of respondent firms employed 960 individuals (264 founders plus 696 collaborators), sold about 27 million Euros, invested

Table 2. Hypotheses and proxies for the relevant variables of the model.

Determinant group		Hypothesis	Proxy for the variable	Source
Contextual factors	S&T support	H1a: ASOs that resort to technology transfer support from S&T infrastructures (TTOs; S&T Parks; Incubators; More than one S&T; Any S&T support) outperform the other ASOs.	ASO resort to the support of the S&T infrastructures (dummy — 1: yes; 0: no)	Questionnaire
		H1b: ASOs that attribute greater importance to S&T support mechanisms (Resource access; Network and business advice; Financial/capital advice and support; IPR support) regarding a given set of items.	High relevance attributed to the given item (dummy — 1: if ASO considered it highly important; 0: otherwise)	Questionnaire
	University characteristics	H2: ASOs that are associated to Universities with a higher pool of scientific knowledge or higher proportion of research excellence tend to outperform the other ASOs.	International patent pool per 1000 researchers (2010) (in ln)	Universities' web sites
	Regional factors	H3: ASOs located in more economically developed regions outperform those from less developed regions.	Index of purchasing power per NUT III regions (in ln)	INE
	Sector (default: ICT/Software/Digital Media)	Energy — Dummy variable: 1 if the ASO operates in …	… Energy/Environment/Sustainability	Questionnaire
		Bio	… Bio/Pharma or Medical devices/diagnostics	
		Micro	Microelectronics/Robotics	
		Agri Food	… Agri-Food	
		Consultancy	… Consultancy related activities including training and other specialized services	
Control variables	Firms	ASOs business experience	Number of years since creation (in ln)	Questionnaire
		ASOs size	Number of employees plus founders in terms of FTE (in ln)	

6 million Euros in R&D activities (representing a global average R&D intensity of 23%), and owned 15 patents. Most of these firms operate in ICT/ Software/Digital Media (43%), Energy/Environment/Sustainability (17%), and Bio/Pharma (10%) (see Table A.3).

These respondent ASOs are young, having been founded mainly after 2006, with 2008 as the year recording the highest number of new ASOs (25, i.e., 25%). About 78% of the total respondent firms were created in 2007 or later, presenting an average age of 6 years in business.

The respondent ASOs are, as expected, quite small. In FTE, the size of the respondent ASOs is five individuals (including founders). The respondent ASOs presented yearly sales per person (in FTE) of about 31,000 €. This figure, although well below the national value for SMEs (87,000 €), varied significantly depending on the sector considered, reaching 117,000 € in Medical devices/diagnostics and 21,000 € in ICT/Software/Digital Media.

Almost all the firms surveyed acknowledged they had benefited from technology transfer infrastructures, most notably incubators (62%) and Science Parks (40%) (cf. Figure 1). The demand for services from Intellectual Property Offices was relatively rare (16%), which might reflect in part the type of activity they develop, not relying on highly complex, novel technology, requiring the management and activation of property

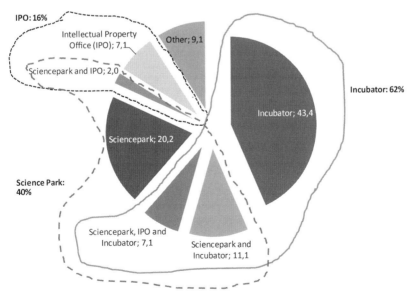

Figure 1.   Distribution (in %) of ASOs by use of S&T infrastructures.

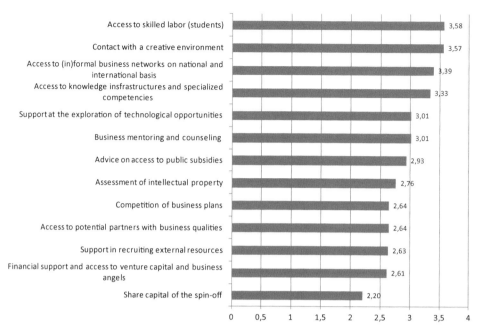

Figure 2. Importance attributed by ASOs to available technology transfer support mechanisms.

Note: 1: very low importance … 5: very high importance.

right mechanisms, and/or the firms' intrinsic weaknesses in terms of resources and competencies for intellectual property rights implementation and management; in order to apply to highly complex and advanced/ specialized support, firms are often required to have a minimum level of competencies and an adequate organizational structure.

The most important support mechanisms associated to technology transfer infrastructures were, according to the respondent firms, 'Access to skilled labor (students)', 'Contact with a creative environment', and 'Access to (in)formal business networks on a national and international basis' (cf. Figure 2).

About 63% of the firms considered 'Access to skilled labor (students)' as an important or very important support mechanism associated to the S&T system. 'Contact with a creative environment' was also highly important for 60% of the firms, whereas about 55% of the respondent firms attributed high importance to 'Access to knowledge infrastructures and specialized competencies' and 'Access to (in)formal business networks on a national and international basis'.

Economic performance of ASOs and S&T infrastructures and support: estimation results

The estimation of the econometric model based on linear regression identifies the critical drivers of the economic performance of Portuguese ASOs over the period in analysis, 2008–2011 (Table 3). Given that the correlations between independent variables were not problematic as to posit multicollinearity problems in the econometric model, the estimated models included all the relevant variables. We nevertheless estimated five different specifications according to the S&T infrastructure the firms used: TTOs exclusively (Model 1), Science Parks exclusively (Model 2), Incubators exclusively (Model 3), two or more S&T infrastructures (Model 4), and any S&T infrastructure (Model 5). The models revealed a reasonable goodness of fit with 43–46% of the variance in economic performance being explained by the variables included in the models.

As mentioned earlier, almost all (about 90%) of the Portuguese ASOs received support from some type of S&T infrastructure, whether they were TTOs, Science Parks, and Incubators exclusively, or in an integrated manner. Our results convey that although S&T infrastructures and support mechanism matter for the ASOs' economic performance, which is in line with some existing literature (e.g., Colombo & Grilli, 2010; Ganotakis, 2012), not all types of infrastructure and mechanisms seem to be relevant for Portuguese ASOs in the period in analysis (Table 3).

We found that ASOs that received support exclusively from incubators (Model 3) or from more than one S&T infrastructure (Model 4) tend to present on average higher sales per worker (in full time equivalent), which might be associated to having receiving business mentoring and counselling that are critical in the earlier stages of business development. The incubators in specific tend to reduce the operating costs of tenant firms by providing facilities and shared services at low cost as well as aiding in market expansion; moreover, the incubator provides tenant firms with research and development support, which results in the enhancement of innovation capability (Kim & Jung, 2010). Albeit non-significant in statistical terms, support from TTOs (exclusively or in combination) emerged negatively related to the ASOs' economic performance. This may be in line with Trott *et al.*'s (2008, p. 2) argument that such support removes start-up firms from the "harsh commercial environment where economic rationality and price-based decision making dominates", and that supported firms might suffer from "product myopia… focus[ing] too early on a product category or a

Table 3.   Determinants of the economic performance of Portuguese ASOs: OLS estimations (dependent variable).

	Variables	$\hat{\beta}$ (p-value)				
		Model 1 (only TTOs)	Model 2 (only Science Park)	Model 3 (only Incubator)	Model 4 (More than one S&T support)	Model 5 (Any S&T support)
S&T support mechanisms (dummies: attribute great importance=1)						
S&T infrastructures support	Received support by the given S&T infrastructure (dummy)	-0.409 (0.497)	0.041 (0.923)	0.536* (0.095)	0.751** (0.043)	-0.487 (0.409)
Resource access	Access to knowledge infrastructures and specialized competencies	0.021 (0.954)	0.044 (0.907)	-0.041 (0.911)	0.203 (0.582)	0.108 (0.776)
	Contact with a creative environment	0.578* (0.091)	0.581* (0.090)	0.540 (0.122)	0.464 (0.182)	0.540 (0.130)
	Access to skilled labor (students)	0.785* (0.055)	0.768* (0.064)	0.752* (0.062)	0.750* (0.060)	0.868** (0.041)
	Support in recruiting external resources	-0.181 (0.613)	-0.178 (0.621)	-0.278 (0.436)	-0.285 (0.418)	-0.118 (0.744)
	Access to potential partners with business qualities	-0.276 (0.503)	-0.267 (0.527)	-0.131 (0.751)	-0.221 (0.582)	-0.272 (0.508)
Network & Business advice	Competition of business plans	0.051 (0.891)	0.054 (0.886)	0.104 (0.777)	0.110 (0.762)	0.031 (0.934)
	Business mentoring and counselling	0.401* (0.084)	0.398* (0.090)	0.511* (0.054)	0.306* (0.095)	0.364* (0.096)
	Access to (in)formal business networks on national and international basis	-0.038 (0.914)	-0.047 (0.895)	0.004 (0.990)	-0.052 (0.881)	-0.034 (0.924)
	Support at the exploration of technological opportunities	-0.205 (0.616)	-0.195 (0.642)	-0.273 (0.500)	-0.127 (0.750)	-0.199 (0.625)

		(1)	(2)	(3)	(4)	(5)
Financial & capital advice/support	Advice on access to public subsidies	0.064	0.074	−0.065	0.061	0.067
		(0.862)	(0.847)	(0.862)	(0.865)	(0.856)
	Financial support and access to venture capital and business angels	0.172	0.142	0.246	0.182	0.092
		(0.700)	(0.750)	(0.579)	(0.675)	(0.838)
	Share capital of the spin-off	−0.384	−0.333	−0.566	−0.463	−0.269
		(0.438)	(0.497)	(0.261)	(0.336)	(0.586)
IPR support	Assessment of intellectual property	−0.036	−0.024	0.040	−0.120	−0.056
		(0.926)	(0.953)	(0.918)	(0.755)	(0.887)
University	University's accumulated patents(2010) (ln) [a]	−0.204	−0.183	−0.161	−0.142	−0.182
		(0.169)	(0.208)	(0.259)	(0.316)	(0.205)
Region	Located in highly developed regions	0.971	1.036	1.298*	1.173	0.948
		(0.210)	(0.183)	(0.093)	(0.118)	(0.220)
Sector (default: ICT/Software/Digital Media)	Energy/Environment/Sustainability	0.903**	0.909**	0.837*	0.893**	0.808*
		(0.042)	(0.050)	(0.056)	(0.039)	(0.076)
	Bio/Pharma or Medical devices/diagnostics	0.172	0.179	0.085	0.084	0.127
		(0.715)	(0.708)	(0.856)	(0.855)	(0.789)
	Microelectronics/Robotics	0.355	0.375	0.017	0.147	0.379
		(0.563)	(0.551)	(0.978)	(0.808)	(0.537)
	Agri-Food	0.557	0.526	0.550	0.565	0.434
		(0.361)	(0.396)	(0.358)	(0.339)	(0.479)
	Consultancy related activities including training and other specialized services	1.232**	1.158**	1.133**	1.042**	1.145**
		(0.020)	(0.026)	(0.026)	(0.039)	(0.026)
Firm	Age (ln)	2.071***	2.069***	1.925***	1.856***	2.102***
		(0.000)	(0.000)	(0.000)	(0.000)	(0.000)
	Size (ln)	0.408*	0.404*	0.376*	0.430**	0.428*
		(0.068)	(0.072)	(0.087)	(0.049)	(0.057)
	Adjusted R²	**0.432**	**0.427**	**0.463**	**0.457**	**0.434**

Note. (***) (**) [*]: Significant at 1% (5%) [10%]; *p*-values in brackets; [a] Using the variables 'scientific publications indexed in ISI' and 'proportion of R&D centers classified with excellent by FCT', estimates and significance levels do not change. All models include a constant. $N = 92$.

market segment which precludes the possibility of development for other market opportunities." Thus, Hypothesis 1a is partially supported.

Besides mentoring and counselling, access to skilled labor and, to a lesser extent, contact with a creative environment are S&T support mechanisms that are strongly and positively associated to higher performing ASOs. This means that Hypothesis 1b is supported.

In relation to spill-over effects from universities, we failed to find any statistical evidence for the impact of university characteristics on the economic performance of their associated ASOs. With exception of Model 3 (where ASOs located in highly developed regions outperform the remaining), regional spill-over effects, measured by the index of purchasing power per NUT III regions, did not emerge as statistically significant. Thus hypotheses H2 and H3 are not corroborated.

The sector seems to be an important factor to explain ASOs' economic performance. On average, and compared to ASOs from ICT/Software/ Digital Media, firms in Energy/Environment/Sustainability or Consultancy-related activities (including training and other specialized services) presented higher sales per worker.

In line with previous findings (e.g., Baum *et al.*, 2000; Lee *et al.*, 2001; Maine *et al.*, 2010; Clarysse *et al.*, 2011), the firms' age and size has a strong positive impact on their economic performance, meaning that the more experienced and larger an ASO, the better it performs.

Conclusion and Policy Implications

"After a remarkable effort in investment in research (effectively turning money into knowledge) the time has come for Portugal to take command of the imperative of turning knowledge into money." (José Mendonça, Scientific Director for UTEN, UTEN 2006–2012: A Progress Report, p. 2)

An appropriate and efficient innovation system requires linkage mechanisms to facilitate the transfer of research results from universities to industry and the support of an institutional framework, especially with regard to the commercialization of innovation results (Calvo *et al.*, 2012).

Academic and political interest in ASOs has increased significantly in Europe (Landry *et al.*, 2006; Martínez & Miranda, 2014) and in Portugal (Fontes, 2005; Teixeira & Coimbra, 2014) in the last few years. These companies, created to exploit the results of scientific research, are considered important because they contribute to the creation of employment and wealth, and to local economic development, as well as being key instruments in the transfer of knowledge developed in academia which is crucial for innovation (Shane, 2004b). ASOs, therefore, can be considered the tangible evidence of the implementation of entrepreneurship in universities (Minguillo & Thelwall, 2015; Rasmussen & Wright, 2015). In the Portuguese case, the development of spin-offs is still incipient, although there is strong interest in their promotion and development (Gibson & Naquin, 2011; Peterson *et al.*, 2013).

In Portugal, the creation of science and technology support infrastructures to foster the commercialization of science and academic entrepreneurship has been highly intensive in the last decade (Heitor & Bravo, 2010). Even though such infrastructures have been traditionally linked to economic growth and job creation (Phan *et al.*, 2005), by the mid-2000s, their impact on Portugal had been modest, and their contribution to job creation and economic growth was barely visible (Ratinho & Henriques, 2010).

In order to foster knowledge-based innovation in Portugal, the Portuguese government has strived to not only to promote science and technology research activities, but also encourage the transfer of results to produce innovation, adding economic value to the scientific quality of research results through the establishment of a number of international programs, most notably the UTEN (Henriques, 2013). Created in 2007 by the Portuguese Science and Technology Foundation Fundação para a Ciência e Tecnologia (FCT) with the support of the Portuguese Institute of Industrial Property (INPI) and in partnership with the IC² Institute, the University of Texas at Austin within the scope of the International Collaboratory for Emerging Technologies (CoLab), the UTEN program is focused on building a professional, globally competitive, sustainable technology transfer and commercialization network in Portugal (Bravo *et al.*, 2010). One of the program's missions is "[p]romoting active support and mentoring for select and globally competitive Portuguese business ventures as well as the national and international promotion of technology portfolios from Portuguese research centers and universities." (Bravo *et al.*, 2009, p. 4).

In 2009, as part of the UTEN's "Observation and assessment" activity, the first major data collection on Portuguese ASOs was initiated. This first and subsequent 'censuses' centered on ASOs associated with members of the network, namely universities and research institutes and connected S&T infrastructures (TTOs, Incubators and Science Parks). By 2011, about 300 ASOs had been identified with the aim of conducting an in-depth analysis of their characteristics and to assess the determinants of their economic performance.

A direct questionnaire was applied to the ASOs, to which about one third responded.

The surveyed ASOs yielded rather negligible figures, both in terms of sales and employment. The largest ASO presented, in 2011, a turnover of 4.5 million Euros and employed 103 FTE individuals. On average, the respondent ASO employed 9 individuals (FTE) and sold about 300,000 € in products and services. The econometric analysis further revealed the relevant role of certain types of S&T infrastructures and support mechanisms for ASOs' economic performance. In particular, access to incubators or the combination of more than one S&T infrastructure support, access to skilled labour, and support in terms of business mentoring and counselling emerged as significantly and positively related with ASOs' sales per worker.

Our descriptive and causality results show that the steady investment in innovation, namely in S&T infrastructures have partially payoff. Indeed, support by incubators or by more than two S&T infrastructures significantly contribute to Portuguese ASOs economic performance. Additionally, the access to skilled labor, the services of business mentoring and counselling provided by S&T infrastructures are fundamental to these companies' sustainability. Nonetheless, the considerable public investment and efforts in science and technology areas aimed at spurt universities patents, scientific publications and research centers (Heitor & Bravo, 2010), apparently have not been sufficient to generate productive spillovers and foster the performance of ASOs. Our results indicate that university spillovers (proxied by the stock of scientific publications and patents and the quality of research centers) have not yet yielded noticeable economic returns to ASOs.

In overall, the amount of sales per capita and employment generated by Portuguese ASOs are quite small. This is likely to reflect the yet feeble and embryonic stage of the process of technology transfer and commercialization in Portugal. Continuing and additional efforts have to be done to accelerate innovation and creation of economic and social value based on knowledge produced in Portuguese scientific and R&D institutions.

Acknowledgments

I sincerely acknowledge the valuable research assistance of Marlene Grande in the data gathering phase. I am also indebted to ASOs founders for their valuable collaboration. Finally, I express my gratitude to the support of the University Technology Enterprise Network (UTEN), a component of the UT Austin|Portugal Program founded by the Portuguese Foundation for Science and Technology (FCT).

References

Bathula, H., Karia, M. & Abbott, M. 2011. The role of university-based incubators in emerging economies. *Working Paper no. 22*, Centre for Research in International Education, AIS St Helens.

Baum, J. A. C., Calabrese, T. & Silverman, B. S. 2000. Don't go it alone: Alliance network composition and startups' performance in Canadian biotechnology. *Strategic Management Journal*, 21(3), 267–294.

Bento, N. & Fontes, M. 2015. The construction of a new technological innovation system in a follower country: Wind energy in Portugal. *Technological Forecasting and Social Change*, 99, 197–210.

Bigliardi, B., Galati, F. & Verbano, C. 2013. Evaluating performance of university spin-off companies: Lessons from Italy. *Journal of Technology Management and Innovation*, 8(2), 178–188.

Bravo, M., Gibson, D. V., Francisco, M. J., Amorim, A. P. & Cotrofeld, M. (eds.). 2010. UTEN 2009–2010 Annual Report, IC^2 Institute, The University of Texas at Austin, USA.

Bravo, M., Gibson, D.V. & Cotrofeld, M. (eds.). 2009. UTEN 2008–2009 Annual Report, IC^2 Institute, The University of Texas at Austin, USA.

Caldera, A. & Debande, O. 2010. Performance of Spanish universities in technology transfer: An empirical analysis. *Research Policy*, 39(9), 1160–1173.

Calvo, N., Varela-Candamio, L., Soares, I. & Rodeiro, D. 2012. Critical analysis of the role of universities in the creation and survival of university spin-offs. Proposal of an academic model of support. *Advances in Management & Applied Economics*, 2(2), 53–82.

Carayannis, E. G., Rogers, E. M., Kurihara, K. & Allbritton, M. M. 1998. High-technology spin-offs from government R&D laboratories and research universities. *Technovation*, 18(1), 1–11.

Clarysse, B., Wright, M., Lockett, A., Van de Velde, E. & Vohora, A. 2005. Spinning out new ventures: A typology of incubation strategies from European Research Institutions. *Journal of Business Venturing*, 20(2), 183–216.

Clarysse, B., Wright, M. & Van de Velde, E. 2011. Entrepreneurial origin, technological knowledge, and the growth of spin-off companies. *Journal of Management Studies*, 48(6), 1420–1442.

Colombo, M. G. & Grilli, L. 2010. On growth drivers of high-tech start-ups: Exploring the role of founders' human capital and venture capital. *Journal of Business Venturing*, 25(6), 610–626.

Cooper, C. E., Hamel, S. A. & Connaughton, S. L. 2012. Motivations and obstacles to networking in a university business incubator. *Journal of Technology Transfer*, 37(4), 433–453.

Dahl, M. S. & Sorenson, O. 2012. Home sweet home: Entrepreneurs' location choices and the performance of their ventures. *Management Science*, 58(6), 1059–1071.

Ding, W. W. & Stuart, T. E. 2006. When do scientists become entrepreneurs? The social structural antecedents of commercial activity in the academic life sciences. *American Journal of Sociology*, 112(1), 97–144.

Doutriaux, J. & Peterman, D. 1982. Technology transfer and academic entrepreneurship. *Frontiers of Entrepreneurship Research*, 430–448.

Fini, R., Grimaldi, R., Santoni, S. & Sobrero, M. 2011. Complements or substitutes? The role of universities and local context in supporting the creation of academic spin-offs. *Research Policy*, 40(8), 1113–1127.

Fontes, M. 2005. Distant networking: The knowledge acquisition strategies of 'out-cluster' biotechnology firms. *European Planning Studies*, 13(6), 899–920.

Fornoni, M., Arribas, I. & Vila, J. E. 2012. An entrepreneur's social capital and performance: The role of access to information in the Argentinean case. *Journal of Organizational Change Management*, 25(5), 682–698.

Fryges, H. & Wright, M. 2014. The origin of spin-offs: A typology of corporate and academic spin-offs. *Small Business Economics*, 43(2), 245–259.

Ganotakis, P. 2012. Founders' human capital and the performance of UK new technology based firms. *Small Business Economics*, 39(2), 495–515.

Gibson, D. V. & Naquin, H. 2011. Investing in innovation to enable global competitiveness: The case of Portugal. *Technological Forecasting & Social Change*, 78(8), 1299–1309.

Gimmon, E. & Levie, J. 2010. Founder's human capital, external investment, and the survival of new high-technology ventures. *Research Policy*, 39(9), 1214–1226.

Gómez-Gras, J. M., Galiana Lapera, D. R., Mira Solves, I., Verdú Jover, A. J., Sancho Azuar, J. 2008. An empirical approach to the organisational determinants of spin-off creation in European universities. *International Entrepreneurship and Management Journal*, 4(2), 187–198.

Gulati, R. 1998. Alliances and networks. *Strategic Management Journal*, 19(4), 293–317.

Heitor, M. V., and Bravo, M. 2010. Portugal on the crosstalk of change, facing the shock of the new: People, knowledge and ideas fostering the social fabric to facilitate the concentration of knowledge integrated communities. *Technological Forecasting and Social Change*, 77, 218–247.

Henriques, L. (org.). 2013. Diagnóstico do Sistema de Investigação e Inovação. Desafios, Forças e Fraquezas Rumo a 2020, Foundation for Science and Technology (FCT), Lisbon.

Jones Evans, D., Klofsten, M., Andersson, E. & Pandya, D. 1999. Creating a bridge between university and industry in small European countries: The role of the industrial liaison office. *R&D Management*, 29(1), 47–56.

Jones-Evans, D. 1998. Universities, technology transfer and spin-off activities: Academia entrepreneurship in different European regions. *Targeted Socioeconomic Research Project No. 1042. Final Report*. University of Glamorgan, Business School, and European Commission. Available at: http://www.lambertreview.org.uk/

pdffiles/uni/utheschoolforbusinandregiondevelreport.pdf. Accessed on 20 October 2012.

Kim, H.-Y. & Jung, C. M. 2010. Does a technology incubator work in the regional economy? Evidence from South Korea. *Journal of Urban Planning and Development*, 136(3), 273–284.

Klofsten, M. & Jones-Evans, D. 2000. Comparing academic entrepreneurship in Europe: The case of Sweden and Ireland. *Small Business Economics*, 14(4), 299–309.

Landry, E., Amara, N. & Rherrand, I. 2006. Why are some university researchers more likely to create spin-offs than others? Evidence from Canadian universities. *Research Policy*, 35(10), 1599–1615.

Lee, C., Lee, K. & Pennings, J. M. 2001. Internal capabilities, external networks, and performance: A study on technology-based ventures. *Strategic Management Journal*, 22(6–7), 615–640.

Lehrer, M. & Asakawa, K. 2004. Rethinking the public sector: Idiosyncrasies of biotechnology commercialization as motors of national R&D reform in Germany and Japan. *Research Policy*, 33(6–7), 921–938.

Li, H. & Atuahene-Gima, K. 2001. Product innovation strategy and performance of new technology ventures in China. *Academy of Management Journal*, 44(6), 1123–1134.

Lockett, A., Siegel, D., Wright, M. & Ensley, M. D. 2005. The creation of spin-off firms at public research institutions: Managerial and policy implications. *Research Policy*, 34(7), 981–993.

Louis, K. S., Blumenthal, D., Gluck, M. E. & Stoto, M. A. 1989. Entrepreneurs in academe: An exploration of behaviors among life scientists. *Administrative Science Quarterly*, 34(1), 110–131.

Lynskey, M. J. 2004. Determinants of innovative activity in Japanese technology-based start-up firms. *International Small Business Journal*, 22(2), 159–196.

Maine, E. M., Shapiro, D. M. & Vining, A. R. 2010. The role of clustering in the growth of new technology-based firms. *Small Business Economics*, 34(2), 127–146.

Malmberg, A., Malmberg, B. & Lundequist, P. 2000. Agglomeration and firm performance: Economies of scale, localisation and urbanisation among Swedish export firms. *Environment and Planning A*, 32(2), 305–321.

Martínez, I. R. & Miranda, M. 2014. The academic spin-off in Andalusia: Economic and financial characteristics. *Revista De Estudios Regionales*, 99, 75–101.

Meyer, M. 2003. Academic entrepreneurs or entrepreneurial academics? Research-based ventures and public support mechanisms. *R&D Management*, 33(2), 107–115.

Minguillo, D. & Thelwall, M. 2015. Which are the best innovation support infrastructures for universities? Evidence from R&D output and commercial activities. *Scientometrics*, 102(1), art. no. A053, 1057–1081.

Morales-Gualdrón, S. T., Gutiérrez-Gracia, A. & Dobón, S. R. 2009. The entrepreneurial motivation in academia: A multidimensional construct. *International Entrepreneurship and Management Journal*, 5(3), 301–317.

Ndonzuau, F. N., Pirnay, F. & Surlemont, B. 2002. A stage model of academic spin-off creation. *Technovation*, 22(5), 281–289.

Nosella, A. & Grimaldi, R. 2009. University-level mechanisms supporting the creation of new companies: An analysis of Italian academic spin-offs. *Technology Analysis and Strategic Management*, 21(6), 679–698.

O'Shea, R. P., Chugh, H. & Allen, T. J. 2008. Determinants and consequences of university spinoff activity: A conceptual framework. *Journal of Technology Transfer*, 33(6), 653–666.

O'Shea, R. P., Allen, T. J., Chevalier, A. & Roche, F. 2005. Entrepreneurial orientation, technology transfer and spinoff performance of U.S. universities. *Research Policy*, 34(7), 994–1009.

Peterson, R., Bravo, M. & Cotrofeld, M. (eds.). 2013. UTEN 2013 Annual Report, IC² Institute, The University of Texas at Austin, USA.

Phan, P. H., Siegel, D. S. & Wright, M. 2005. Science parks and incubators: Observations, synthesis and future research. *Journal of Business Venturing*, 20(2), 165–182.

Pirolo, L. & Presutti, M. 2010. The impact of social capital on the start-ups' performance growth. *Journal of Small Business Management*, 48(2), 197–227.

Rasmussen, E. & Wright, M. 2015. How can universities facilitate academic spin-offs? An entrepreneurial competency perspective. *Journal of Technology Transfer*, 40(5), 782–799.

Rasmussen, E., Mosey, S. & Wright, M. 2011. The evolution of entrepreneurial competencies: A longitudinal study of university spin-off venture emergence. *Journal of Management Studies*, 48(6), 1314– 1345.

Ratinho, T. & Henriques, E. 2010. The role of science parks and business incubators in converging countries: Evidence from Portugal. *Technovation*, 30(4), 278–290.

Samson, K. J. & Gurdon, M. A. 1993. University scientists as entrepreneurs: A special case of technology transfer and high-tech venturing. *Technovation*, 13(2), 63–71.

Shane, S. 2004a. *Academic Entrepreneurship: University Spinoffs and Wealth Creation.* Edward Elgar, Massachusetts.

Shane, S. 2004b. Encouraging university entrepreneurship? The effect of the Bayh–Dole act on university patenting in the United States. *Journal of Business Venturing*, 19(1), 127–151.

Shane, S. & Khurana, R. 2003. Bringing individuals back in: The effects of career experience on new firm founding. *Industrial and Corporate Change*, 12(3), 519–543.

Soetanto, D. P. & van Geenhuizen, M. 2009. Academic spin-offs at different ages: A case study in search of key obstacles to growth. *Technovation*, 29(10), 671–681.

Steffens, M., Rogers, E. M. & Speakman, K. 1999. Spin-offs from research centers at a research university. *Journal of Business Venturing*, 15(1), 93–111.

Taheri, M. & Van Geenhuizen, M. 2011. How human capital and social networks may influence the patterns of international learning among academic spin-off firms. *Papers in Regional Science*, 90(2), 287–311.

Teixeira, A. A. C. & Coimbra, C. 2014. The determinants of the internationalization speed of Portuguese university spin-offs: An empirical investigation. *Journal of International Entrepreneurship*, 12, 270–308.

Teixeira, A. A. C. & Costa, J. 2006. What type of firm forges closer innovation linkages with Portuguese universities? *Notas Económicas*, 24, 22–47.

Tödtling, F., van Reine, P. P. & Dörhöfer, S. 2011. Open innovation and regional culture—findings from different industrial and regional settings. *European Planning Studies*, 19(11), 1885–1907.

Trott, P., Scholten, V. & Hartmann, D. (2008). How university incubators may be overprotective and hindering the success of the young firm: Findings from a preliminary study. (p. 1–5). Engineering Management Conference, 2008. IEMC Europe 2008. IEEE International.

Van Burg, E., Romme, A. G. L., Gilsing, V. A. & Reymen, I. M. M. J. 2008. Creating university spin-offs: A science-based design perspective. *Journal of Product Innovation Management*, 25(2), 114–128.

Vohora, A., Wright, M. & Lockett, A. 2004. Critical junctures in the development of university high-tech spinout companies. *Research Policy*, 33(1), 147–175.

Walter, A., Auer, M. & Ritter, T. 2006. The impact of network capabilities and entrepreneurial orientation on university spin-off performance. *Journal of Business Venturing*, 21(4), 541–567.

Wright, M., Clarysse, B., Mustar, P. & Lockett, A. 2007. *Academic Entrepreneurship in Europe*. Edward Elgar, Cheltenham, UK.

Xu, Z., Parry, M. E. & Song, M. 2010. The impact of technology transfer office characteristics on university invention disclosure. *IEEE Transactions on Engineering Management*, 58(2), 212– 227.

Zhang, J. 2009. The performance of university spin-offs: An exploratory analysis using venture capital data. *Journal of Technology Transfer*, 34(3), 255–285.

Zheng, Y., Liu, J. & George, G. 2010. The dynamic impact of innovative capability and inter-firm network on firm valuation: A longitudinal study of biotechnology start-ups. *Journal of Business Venturing*, 25(6), 593–609.

Appendix

Table A.1.   ASOs' performance: Contextual determinants.

Determinant	Proxy/indicator for the determinant	Unit of analysis (number of observations)	Country in analysis	Data gathering methodology	Method of analysis	Proxy/indicator for performance	Impact	Authors (Year)
S&T Support mechanisms	Science park (dummy)	Entrepreneurs (751) Companies (412)	UK	Direct questionnaire	Quantitative	Number of employees (log)	++	Ganotakis (2012)
	Incubator (dummy)	New technology-based firms (439)	Italy	Secondary database	Quantitative	Growth of the number of employees (log)	0	Colombo and Grilli (2010)
Network/ Cooperation	Density (proportion of partners mutually connected)	ASOs (100)	Netherlands and Norway	Direct questionnaire and interviews	Quantitative	International knowledge network (formal knowledge sources [yes/no]; spatial reach)	–	Taheri and van Geenhuizen (2011)
	Frequency of face-to-face contact						++	
	Duration of relationship (years)						0	
	Network heterogeneity (Herfindahl index of heterogeneity)	Biotechnology firms (170)	US	Secondary database	Quantitative	Total market value of company's equity	++	Zheng *et al.* (2010)
	Network status (number of agreements with partners)						0	
	Relational dimension of access to information (support of personal contacts to get information)	Entrepreneurs (282)	Argentina	Direct questionnaire	Quantitative	Number of employees; turnover; profits (% of sales)	+++	Fornoni *et al.* (2012)
	Strong social ties with business partners	Start-ups (82)	Italy	Direct questionnaire	Quantitative	Growth of total annual sales Number of new products, services or technologies	++ –	Pirolo and Presutti (2010)
	Network efficiency (Hirschman–Herfindahl index)	Startup biotechnology firms (142)	Canada	Secondary database	Quantitative	Firms' revenue, R&D spending and patents' growth	+	Baum *et al.* (2000)

Category	Variable	Sample (firms)	Country	Data source	Method	Dependent variable	Sign	Authors
	Formal cooperative agreements with other companies (dummy)	Entrepreneurs (751) Companies (412)	UK	Direct questionnaire	Quantitative	Number of employees (log)	++	Ganotakis (2012)
Market condition	Biotechnology stock market index	Biotechnology firms (170)	US	Secondary database	Quantitative	Total market value of company's equity	++	Zheng et al. (2010)
Industry density	Number of biotech firms						0	
Environmental turbulence	Predictability of competitors' actions and market demand (5-point Likert scale 1:high, 5: low)	New technology ventures (202)	China	Direct questionnaire	Quantitative	Return on investment, return on sales, profit growth, return on assets, overall efficiency of operations, sales growth, market share growth, cash flow from market operations, and firm's overall reputation	—	Li and Atuahene-Gima (2001)
Regional factors	Distance (miles) from the nearest cluster	New technology-based firms (451)	US	Secondary database	Quantitative	Firm growth (average growth of revenues and employees)	—	Maine et al. (2010)
	Hachmann Index (range of cluster activities)						0	
	Local development (per capita value added, share of manufacturing out of total value added, employment index, per capita bank deposits, automobile–population ratio, and consumption of electric power per head)	New technology-based firms (439)	Italy	Secondary database	Quantitative	Growth of the number of employees (log)	0	Colombo and Grilli (2010)
Sector	Industry sector (1: new industries; 0: traditional industries)	High-technology start-ups (193)	Israel	Secondary database	Quantitative	Survival (1: survived; 0: not survived) Survivors (low growth versus high growth based on sales, employees or funding)	+++	Gimmon and Levie (2010)
	Industry sector (1: human applications; 0:non-human)	Startup biotechnology firms (142)	Canada	Secondary database	Quantitative	R&D spending growth	+	Baum et al. (2000)

Table A.2.   ASOs' performance: Firm-related determinants.

Proxy/indicator for the determinant	Unit of analysis (number of observations)	Country in analysis	Data gathering methodology	Method of analysis	Proxy/indicator for performance	Impact	Authors (Year)
Firms' age (years)	Entrepreneurs (751) Companies (412)	UK	Direct questionnaire	Quantitative	Number of employees (log)	+++	Ganotakis (2012)
	Startup biotechnology firms (142)	Canada	Secondary database	Quantitative	Firms' revenue growth	+	Baum et al. (2000)
	New technology-based firms (439)	Italy	Secondary database	Quantitative	Growth of the number of employees and sales (log)	+/-	Colombo and Grill (2010)
	New technology-based firms (451)	US	Secondary database	Quantitative	Firm growth (average growth of revenues and employees)	—	Maine et al. (2010)
	Corporate (43) and University Spin-offs (73)	Belgium	Direct questionnaire	Quantitative	Sales/employment growth (founding-2005)	+++	Clarysse et al. (2011)
Firms' size (log of FTE)	ASOs (100)	Netherlands and Norway	Direct questionnaire and interviews	Quantitative	International knowledge network (formal knowledge sources [yes/no]; spatial reach)	+	Taheri and van Geenhuizen (2011)
	Technological startups (137)	Korea	Direct questionnaire	Quantitative	Sales growth	+++	Lee et al. (2001)
Firms' size (ln)	New technology-based firms (451)	US	Secondary database	Quantitative	Firm growth (average growth of revenues and employees)	—	Maine et al. (2010)

Table A.3.   Descriptive statistics of the model's variables.

Determinant group		Variables	Mean	Min.	Max.	Kendal's tau_b corr. Coef.	Sig. (2-tailed)
Dependent variable		Sales per capita (ln)	2.605	0.00	5.86	1.000	
Contextual factors — S&T support mechanisms (dummies: attribute great importance=1)	S&T infrastructures support	Received support by TTOs only (dummy)	0.057	0	1	-0.001	0.993
		Received support by Science park only (dummy)	0.193	0	1	0.000	0.996
		Received support by Incubator only (dummy)	0.432	0	1	0.213**	0.016
		Received support by more than one S&T infrastructure (dummy)	0.227	0	1	-0.258***	0.004
		Received support by any of the S&T inf. (dummy)	0.909	0	1	-0.010	0.907
	Resource access	Access to knowledge infrastructures and specialized competencies	0.534	0	1	0.098	0.271
		Contact with a creative environment	0.614	0	1	0.051	0.562
		Access to skilled labor (students)	0.625	0	1	0.093	0.296
		Support in recruiting external resources	0.250	0	1	0.043	0.626
		Access to potential partners with business qualities	0.284	0	1	0.011	0.904
	Network & Business advice	Competition of business plans	0.261	0	1	-0.024	0.783
		Business mentoring and counseling	0.420	0	1	-0.077	0.388
		Access to (in)formal business networks on national and international basis	0.511	0	1	0.003	0.970
		Support at the exploration of technological opportunities	0.420	0	1	-0.063	0.474

(*Continued*)

Table A.3.   (Continued)

Determinant group	Variables	Mean	Min.	Max.	Kendal's tau_b corr. Coef.	Sig. (2-tailed)
Financial & capital advice/support	Advice on access to public subsidies	0.307	0	1	0.037	0.680
	Financial support and access to venture capital and business angels	0.261	0	1	−0.094	0.289
	Share capital of the spin-off	0.159	0	1	−0.159*	0.073
IPR support	Assessment of intellectual property	0.307	0	1	0.041	0.647
University characteristics	University's accumulated international patents per 1000 researchers in 2010 (ln)	1.558	0.00	3.07	0.014	0.855
	University's scientific publication indexed in ISI per researcher(2007–2010) (ln)	1.320	0.093	1.70	0.071	0.354
	Proportion of research centers classified as Very Good or Excellent by FTC	0.582	0.375	0.87	0.086	0.260
Regional factors	Located in highly developed regions	4.692	4.34	4.98	0.240***	0.003
Sector (default: ICT/Software/ Digital Media)	Energy/Environment/Sustainability	0.182	0	1	0.132	0.138
	Bio/Pharma or Medical devices/diagnostics	0.148	0	1	−0.086	0.331
	Microelectronics/Robotics	0.080	0	1	0.157*	0.077
	Agri-Food	0.080	0	1	−0.028	0.752
	Consultancy related activities including training and other specialized services	0.091	0	1	0.028	0.755
Demographics	Age (ln)	1.775	0.693	2.83	0.460***	0.000
	Size (ln)	1.887	0.00	4.63	0.211***	0.005

Control variables

Chapter 12

A Process-Based Approach to Support Entrepreneurship and Innovation Ecosystem Management — A Brazilian Trial

Luiz Marcio Spinosa* and Marcos Mueller Schlemm†

Pontifical Catholic University of Parana, Brazil

* m.spinosa@pucpr.br

† marcos.schlemm@pucpr.br

Rosana Silveira Reis

ISG — International Business School, France

rosana.reis@isg.fr

Innovation ecosystems have emerged worldwide to foster social and economic development. In Brazil these ecosystems originate from the current national innovation policy and are relevant assets to accomplish entrepreneurial efforts. The improvement of management competences within those ecosystems is the main driver of our research. Precisely, we attempt to answer the question "How can Brazilian Innovation ecosystems organize innovation and entrepreneurial processes in order to foster the resulting outcome?" This chapter introduces a process-based approach implemented as an ICT platform in Curitiba, a Brazilian metropolitan area with 3,800 million inhabitants. The platform emerged from several requirements issued from innovation clusters and networked organizations studies. The experience has proven to be a helpful tool to generate better outputs from the complex innovation dynamics that reside in innovation ecosystems.

Introduction

Innovation performance became a crucial determinant of competitiveness and national progress (OECD, 2010). Empirical data show that companies that have a successful innovation record usually enjoy greater competitive advantage, which also guides to a higher company evaluation. Although only 1.7% of Brazilian industries innovate, they are nonetheless responsible for 25.9% of national industrial revenues and for 13.4% of the employment within the sector (IPEA, 2005). Clearly, those companies show a more successful contribution to gains in prosperity when compared to companies that do not carry out innovation.

At same time, Brazil has seen a considerable reduction in its Global Competitiveness Index (Figure 1). When we analyze the composition of the indexes, we notice that innovation affects several indicators. For instance, in 2013 one ton of mineral was priced at $115 and one ton of soybeans at $560. An imported Smartphone (140 g) was valued at about $1,000. Thus, 8.7 tons of mineral, or 1.8 tons of soybeans, was required to balance the trade. This inequality is easily explained by high value-added imports against low value-added commodities exports. We expect that, the improvement of the Brazilian competitiveness through better innovation systems will lead to more value-added products.

Seeking to achieve competitiveness through innovation, several Brazilian polices have been conceived and focused on how to induce the creation of innovation ecosystems in several distinct regions of the country. One indicator of such effort is the number of technology parks. According to the Brazilian Ministry of Science, Technology and Innovation (MCTI) and the Brazilian Association of Science Parks and Business Incubators, there are 94 known technology parks. These initiatives comprise 939 companies and generate 32,237 jobs (17,630 Graduates). About US$ 1.93 billion have already been invested by the public and private sectors (MCTI, 2014).

YEAR	2014	2013	2012	2011	2010	2009
Index	46,778	53,222	56,524	61,043	56,531	56,865
Position	54	51	46	44	38	40

Figure 1. Brazil's position in the global competitiveness index.

Source: Fundação Dom Cabral — FDC, 2015 (English translation: the authors).

Innovation policies have been influenced by the unique Brazilian entrepreneurship context. Since 1999, the Global Entrepreneurship Monitor (GEM) a comparative research project led by London Business School and Babson College, has published a variety of relevant primary data on different aspects of entrepreneurship within and among countries. The project provides harmonized measures that follow rigorous research procedures and methodology (www.gemconsortium.org).

GEM outcomes confirmed that entrepreneurial activity, in different forms (nascent, start-up, intrapreneurship), is positively correlated with economic growth, but this relationship differs according to stages of economic development. In the past two decades, the Brazilian economy has experienced a significant incremental change in its economic profile and growth rates. With stabilizing policies aimed at the national currency and the adoption of the fluctuating exchange rate, the Real has maintained an aggressively high value *vis-à-vis* stronger currencies like the Dollar and the Euro, thus generating a flow of imported products coming from Asia, Europe, and other industrialized economies. With China maintaining impressive GDP growth rates, Brazilian economy has enjoyed the benefits of exporting agricultural and mining products in addition to a few products from the manufacturing sector, like the medium-sized commercial airplanes produced by Embraer. Social-improvement policies, targeting financial aid to low-income populations and incremental business growth ever since the stabilization of the national currency, concurred to expand and consolidate the national market, giving rise to a new and so far unknown entry class, and expanding its traditional middle class. Nonetheless, 40 million Brazilians still live below the poverty line, and social problems like rampant crime are still a challenge for national and local policies. Opportunities for entrepreneurship, on any level, have been in an upward cycle since, and in spite of a recent slowdown clearly visible from 2013 to 2015, there is still an entrepreneurial drive mainly within the young adult population that desires to achieve an independent life style and to have the same opportunities enjoyed by their counterparts in North America and Europe.

The GEM Report published in 2015 based on data collected during the year of 2014, shows that there is still a growth trend within the new entrepreneurial activity (startups with three plus years), even though there has been a slight reduction in newly started companies. Graphic 1 presents the historical evolution of these two categories, where a downward slope from 5.1% in 2002 to 3.7% in 2014 in the number of new startups can be observed. Conversely, the new entrepreneurial activity rate, that is, those which have provided an income to its entrepreneurs for more than three

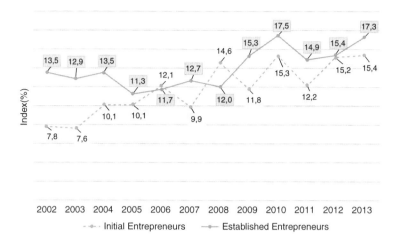

Graph 1.   Evolution of entrepreneurial activity — enterprise second stage.
Source: GEM Brazil Report, 2013.

and less than 42 months, rose from 8.5% in 2002 to 13.8% in 2014. The
GEM Report gives an alert regarding this trend in the near future, since the
economic slowdown is the current and ongoing trend.

According to GEM, the total early-stage entrepreneurial activity corre-
lates with the GNP growth. This leads to the establishment of new firms
given the new business opportunities. In turn, the high growth rates
observed in the period measured are a direct result of an internal market
expansion and of an increased wealth distribution resulting from governmental income and social improvement programs. In the past five years in
spite of a slowdown in the economy, since 2011, the Total Early Stage Activity
(TEA)[1] has maintained its rate at around 17%, suggesting strong entrepreneurial activity in Brazil (see Table 1). The downside is that most of the
Brazilian entrepreneurial effort is still non-sophisticated types of businesses
whose sole aim is to generate income to their owners, more often than not,
being nothing but an alternative or complementary source of income.

Taking the TEA in Brazil, the North Region (18.7%) has contributed the
most, followed by the Southeast (17.9%) and the South regions (17.15%).
The Center-West Region showed the lowest early stage entrepreneurial activity rate, with 15.6%. The highest rates for established entrepreneurs are in
the Northeast (20.3%), followed by the South (18.5%) and the Center-West
regions, with 17.5% (data from 2014 — GEM Brazil Report, in press).

---

[1] The TEA Index is calculated by adding the proportion of adults involved in the creation of
nascent businesses and the proportion involved in surviving companies (GEM Report, 2000).

Table 1.   TEA Development between 2005 and 2014.

BRAZIL	Nascent entrepreneurship rate	New business ownership rate	Early-stage entrepreneurial activity (TEA)	Established business ownership rate	Discontinued Businesses)
2005	3.3	8.2	11.3	10.10	
2006	3.5	8.6	11.7	12.1	
2007	4.3	8.7	12.7	9.9	
2008	2.9	9.3	12.0	14.6	3.5
2009	5.8	9.8	15.3	11.8	4.0
2010	5.8	11.8	17.5	15.3	5.3
2011	4.1	11.0	14.9	12.2	3.8
2012	4	11	15	15	5
2013	5.1	12.6	17.3	15.4	4.7
2014	3.66	13.79	17.23	17.51	4.14

Source: The authors (table based on data from GEM Reports 2005 to 2014).

It becomes clear from these data that the entrepreneurial context in Brazil is less than favorable for new ventures based on new technology, innovation and internationalization. The 2015 GEM Report reveals that most of the entrepreneurial activities are not innovative nor are they expected to develop to a level that would actually increase the job-creation rate. GEM's findings reveal a lack of critical entrepreneurial conditions that need to be improved through public policies in order to strengthen the national innovation culture and business environment.

Several are the challenges revealed by these scenarios. This study aims to answer the question "How can Brazilian Innovation ecosystems organize innovation and entrepreneurial processes in order to foster the expected outcome?" An action-research methodology was used to come up with a possible answer to this question. An illustration of the process-based approach is provided together with a case study of the Curitiba Metropolitan Area. As a result, this chapter presents a feasible management framework based on process organization structured into five sections, and organized as follows): Introduction, or Sec. 1, presenting the research questions and the structure of the work; Sec. 2, introducing the theoretical background. Our goal is to provide the reader with an overview of innovation ecosystems and mainly their conceptual and operational requirements. In Sec. 3, we present the research setting, where we address some answers to the research question. This section ends with the description of a trial, a process-based platform called 'PIA'. Next, in Sec. 4, we analyze clusters and network findings. Finally, Sec. 5 takes the discussion to a conclusion, where we outline and summarize the main findings and managerial implications.

Innovation Ecosystem

Scholars of Entrepreneurship have increased attention to the innovation ecosystems perspective (Nambisan & Baron, 2013). The term 'innovation ecosystem' describes the role of independent factors that work together to empower entrepreneurs and to allow innovation to occur in a sustained way in a given location (Lawlor, 2014). According to Autio and Thomas (2014), an innovation ecosystem can be understood as a network of interconnected entities organized around an organization, which incorporates both production and final users and create value through innovation.

Innovation ecosystems are also defined as a competitive asset in the knowledge economy (Corkill, 2007). For the purpose of this study, and considering that the majority of innovation ecosystems in Brazil are near to or fully inserted in cities, the authors adopt an expanded definition, which considers innovation ecosystems as competitive assets in the knowledge economy integrating both urban and regional territories.

An important assumption in this study is that the conceptual and operational perspectives of an innovation ecosystem's activities are examined by a process-based approach. As for the conceptual point of view the authors argue that the dynamics of the Brazilian innovation ecosystem are derived from the innovation clusters and networked organization areas. In fact, we assume that an innovation ecosystem, even a national innovation ecosystem, can be seen as a set of innovation clusters structured as cooperation networks. As far as the operational point of view is concerned, the study assumes that the innovation management area grows in significance in the Brazilian innovation ecosystem.

One of the World`s most celebrated innovation ecosystems is Silicon Valley, responsible for 9.6% of the GDP of California State, USA (SV, 2015). The GDP of California is comparable to the Brazilian GDP, which occupies the eighth position in the World GDP Ranking 2015. Silicon Valley's genesis and growth is endemic; that is, it is the result of an environment and local culture extremely favorable for world-class entrepreneurship. Its development, strongly influenced by Stanford University, occurred naturally in the 1950s, due to a need of establishing a high-tech industry in the United

States. Later, this whole effort was tapped into with the purpose of enhancing the development of other industrial sectors. The Valley concentrates more than 40% of all the venture capital targeting innovation in the US. It is, therefore, one of the largest venture capital concentrations in the world (Spinosa & Krama, 2014).

Another impressive example is One North, in Singapore, due to the systemic and national development associated to it. It is an initiative that contributed heavily to change the economic and social standards of Singapore. Strong development policies in recent decades, converted a deficit economy frame into a frame that shows the one of the highest GDP per capita in the world. The transformation took place due to a clear option for public policies aimed at the development of knowledge-based society and around innovation (Spinosa & Krama, 2014).

In Brazil, public policy and civil organizations have fostered the innovation ecosystems by encouraging the creation and implementation of technology parks inside or close to several cities. In this scenario, the ecosystem surrounding the Curitiba Metropolitan Area gains in importance for our research.

The Curitiba technopark was created in 2008 by the municipal government in order to stimulate the development of high-tech sectors, in association with Curitiba Development Agency S.A. This ecosystem is important because was integrated into the city environment (Figure 2). It is a 100% urban park and is not set up in a single lot, but instead its facilities are spread around the city, in different neighborhoods. It has a total physical area of 90,000 m² and promotes a favorable environment for innovation, knowledge transfer and development of technology-based activities. The areas are: (i) Logistic Ring: a center for innovation generation, where the two main universities' campuses are located, the Federal University of Paraná (UFPR) and the Pontifical Catholic University of Paraná (PUCPR). This area is also home of the Institute for Technology Development — LACTEC, and the Federation of Industries of the State of Paraná (FIEP-PR); (ii) Central Rebouças Neighborhood Sector: a third university, comprising the Federal University of Technology — Paraná (UTFPR) and a convention center; (iii) Sector CIC North: where a Software Park is located; (iv) Sector CIC South: where the Institute of Technology of Paraná is located together with FIOCRUZ biotech research facilities (Spinosa & Krama, 2014).

The next sections introduce the main conceptual and operational requirements needed to deal with the dynamics of an innovation ecosystem. Such requirements are the backbone of the proposed process-based approach.

Figure 2.   Areas of Curitiba Technopark.
Source: Curitiba Development Agency S.A.

Conceptual requirements

Seven main concepts and assumptions outline the context that has to be taken into account (Spinosa & Quandt, 2003). **The first concept** that innovation clusters and cooperation networks have emerged in the last decade as significant tools to promote regional development through the activation, diffusion and expansion of locally generated knowledge. The basic understanding of what is an innovation ecosystem can be drawn from a review on innovation clusters. According to Engel (2005), clusters of innovation are global economic "hot spots" where new technologies germinate at an outstanding rate and where pools of capital, expertise, and talent foster the development of new industries and new ways of doing business. Normally they are vibrant, effervescent ecosystems composed of startups, businesses that support the startup process, and mature enterprises (Engel, 2015).

In these ecosystems, people, capital, and knowhow are fluidly mobile resources and the pace of transactions is driven by a relentless pursuit of opportunity, networking, staged financing, and short business model cycles. Clusters are generated on linkages and relationships that integrate the isolated technological capabilities of institutions, firms and individuals into a collective, territorial asset (Song & Shin, 2008; Lee *et al.*, 2001). Establishing mechanisms to efficiently coordinate these relationships is essential to create a support environment for different forms of technical exchange, cross-fertilization, risk-sharing and collective learning (Quandt & Spinosa, 2007; Terstriep *et al.*, 2009). This is essentially a territorially-based process, as people who share the same space discover the advantages of "learning by interacting". In the cluster/network-based approach, both concepts are reunited by a focus on interactive learning and the diffusion of different types of knowledge: tacit or codified, scientific or practical, etc. in different spatial and organizational settings. That also implies a focus on the emerging field of knowledge management.

The second concept is that the cooperation and the creation of economies among small- and medium-sized enterprises (SMEs) within clusters contribute to generating competitive advantages through "collective efficiency". SMEs can play a key role in triggering and sustaining economic growth and equitable development in developing regions (Mohannak & Keast, 2008). SMEs, particularly technology-based ones, have a tremendous potential to accelerate economic growth, expand their share of exports and promote a more scattered and equitable pattern of development in developing countries. The creation of technology-intensive firms is essential to building local capabilities to compete in the global economy; they are also essential to strengthening academic–industry–government links and encourage technological innovation. The regions' development potential could be greatly enhanced by adopting a cluster/network-based approach to address its development needs and spatial imbalances, searching for cooperation and partnerships among different government levels, the private sector and non-government organizations. Limitations can be reduced and even surpass the typical areas of access to technological information, and guidance on issues of quality control; access to finance; assistance in the purchase of materials or equipment, in workplace organization, in financial management or in other determinants of effective performance; and market stability (security of demand over a period of time). More importantly, small-scale entrepreneurs in developing countries are often ill prepared to look beyond the boundaries of their firms and capture new market opportunities (Valente & Crane, 2010). The development of networks can improve the competitive position of SMEs and reduce the problems related to their size through mutual help (Mohannak & Keast, 2008).

The third concept refers to the advantages of cooperation among SMEs, typically related to collective economies of scale, to the benefits of dissemination of information and inter-firm division of labor (Mesquita & Lazzarini, 2008). These benefits tend to increase when transaction costs are low, and these in turn tend to decrease with geographic proximity and the establishment of shared infrastructure, common norms and tacit rules for cooperation. Therefore, an innovation cluster is characterized not only by type of industry, geographical concentration of firms and other economic agents that give rise to external economies and favors the creation of specialized technical and financial services (Karaev *et al.*, 2007). It also comprises public and private local institutions to foster knowledge transfers and to support local economic development. A successful cluster is dependent on both, private and public sector (usually universities and research institutions), which join efforts to create innovative environments and to build synergies among agents with complementary capabilities. Their development is gradual and cumulative (Andersson & Karlsson, 2006): over time, the region builds knowledge, skills, institutional support structures, specialized services, financing arrangements, infrastructure and collective norms of cooperation and mutual trust.

As Bianchi (1993) points out, the crucial characteristic of the "Marshallian" type of cluster or *milieu* is the set of competitive and collaborative linkages among agents in a socially- and historically-defined agglomeration, complemented by a set of collective intangible assets that belong to the production system as a whole. The cluster benefits from its complex web of interactions because innovation rarely happens in isolation. It is an experimental, trial and error activity, and each agent may draw innovation inputs from a wider matrix of institutions to take advantage of a division of labor in the generation of knowledge and skills. In that sense, the cluster improves "dynamic" efficiency (or innovative capability) by reducing uncertainty through information sharing and screening, and by establishing a durable relational basis for the construction of competences (Camagni, 1995).

The fourth concept is associated with the literature on high-tech clusters that has described diverse "locational ingredients", which are usually seen as necessary for the development of successful clusters. These ingredients can be categorized as tangible and intangible elements, as proposed by Bortagaray and Tiffin (2000). The tangible elements are: knowledge-based firms; knowledge inputs; specialized consulting services; specialized inputs; markets; cluster support; and financing. The intangible elements are: a supportive social climate; links and interactions among individuals and organizations; quality of life for people working in the community where the cluster operates. Among the tangible elements, the knowledge-based firm is the core element. As Kozul-Wright (1995) points out, "the firm is in a position to fulfill a number of critical conditions for innovation: (i) by acting as an organization for storing knowledge (including tacit knowledge); (ii) as an enduring institution which can reproduce that knowledge and inculcate it in new entrants or share it with other firms, and (iii) as a social agent which can establish trust and cooperation."

In more general terms, two regional components may be considered necessary, but may not be sufficient for a successful cluster. The first is a "critical mass" of human resources, including entrepreneurs, scientists, engineers, technicians and skilled labor. The second is a capable scientific and technological infrastructure, or the "knowledge assets" of a region (Tallman *et al.*, 2004). These may include universities, public and private research labs, libraries, technological incubators, innovation centers and science parks. The main roles of these anchor institutions are to promote technology transfers and to support networking.

The fifth assumption has to do with the fact that regional innovation and growth are not restricted to local sources of knowledge, capital or other factors. In the context of this study, it has become apparent to regional authorities that a focus on the mobilization of local assets to build synergy and achieve competitive advantage by fostering innovation clusters will not suffice. They have to be connected to a broader focus, to the ability of joining increasingly wider spatial networks and thus develop alliances, partnerships and opportunities with outside firms and investors as well as science parks and incubators, universities and research institutes.

The sixth assumption deals with the issue that, as far as sources of knowledge are concerned, the most important factor perceived as affecting a company's performance is access to a skilled labor pool, followed by ties to the local research base and access to qualified suppliers. The least important factor is government incentives, which probably reflects their limited availability. Direct observation and analysis also appear as important ways in which companies gather new knowledge, benefiting from their closeness to other firms in the area (Garvin, 1993). Co-operative alliances are also very important means of acquiring relevant knowledge. Localized flows of knowledge predominate among the region's firms, in connection with the predominance of local transactions and cooperative linkages. Although in some cases a large share of the components is sourced from remote locations, specific knowledge for product development is rarely obtained abroad. Cooperative arrangements are also important for access to relevant knowledge (Manhart & Thalmann, 2015). Alliances with other firms — and to a lesser extent with universities — both locally and outside the region, are highly ranked as sources of knowledge. Again, local partners play a dominant role. Finally, clients are also critical sources of knowledge for product and process development by a significant number of firms (Knudsen, 2007).

For the diverse agents in a cluster, opening up to wider cooperation networks implies differentiated benefits. Although the costs and risks can be high, small firms and startups tend to gain more, because they generally have limited access to technology networks and to international events, and they tend to have a limited ability to interface with the infrastructure due to their small size. They may also lack other key skills and resources — such as marketing or business capabilities, which is often the case for new technology-based firms. It becomes clear, then, that wider cooperation networks may play a major role in improving the "collective efficiency" of existing clusters, by expanding the scope of knowledge search and deepening the capability to generate and manage technical change. It is also clear that the wider level of knowledge flows requires different channels and different types of learning processes. This appears to be a significant shortcoming of many of the firms. In the specific case of technology-intensive industries, the complex environment in which firms and clusters operate highlights the importance of access to a wide range of complementary assets and competencies (Quandt, 2000). Given their limited ability to take advantage of supra-territorial networks, an important function of the institution — the cluster's incubator or managing institution — would be to help screening, codifying and channeling relevant information into the cluster. Some of the technology incubators in the region attempts to perform that function, with limited results.

The seventh concept adopted shows that the establishment of networks enables firms to expand their access to knowledge and resources from a broader range of sources, in addition to an expansion of the available resources to the incubators and clusters themselves (Gibson *et al.*, 1999).

It becomes clear that a broad-based cluster/network-based system may have a strong impact in specific areas such as the following:

- Access to new markets and marketing strategies;
- Access to capital: integrated access to services such as financial planning, support for obtaining grants, opportunities for access to venture, development, and seed capital;
- Expansion of inter-firm linkages: a networked approach is ideal for maximizing the impact of programs and projects, such as partnerships, alliances, and linkages to outside suppliers;
- Technological support: access to services such as technology assessment and forecasting, assistance on technological choices, marketing assessment of innovative projects and access to outside technical information;
- Technology transfer opportunities: networks may be used to stimulate investment in Science & Technology (S&T), Research & Development (R&D), technology transfer and spin-offs;
- Access to talent and know-how: networks may help in the process of identifying and hiring skilled people across regional boundaries. It should also be noted that labor markets are essentially place-based, yet virtual technologies may boost the development of human resources in more remote locations through training centers, distance education, career planning, virtual job markets, and also support business development through the establishment of virtual entrepreneur schools;
- Strengthening local cluster governance structures: the establishment of linkages with other clusters enables a better understanding of stakeholder needs and markets and improves organization methods. As the network demonstrates, such arrangement may also be used to disseminate best practices in business incubation to improve the performance of firms in each cluster; and,
- Optimizing and sharing facilities: the operational support infrastructure may be optimized and many facilities could be shared over the network, including incubators, prototype centers, pilot plants, online library, test laboratories, and online conferencing facilities.

Operational requirements

The previous requirements capture an important part of the complexity of an innovation ecosystem context. This list of concepts is non-exhaustive and can be easily expanded considering more operational requirements issued from different points of view. This work focus on management needs, mainly on innovation management.

Innovation management is a complex phenomenon that has many definitions (Birkinshaw *et al.*, 2008). For organizations, innovation management handles the development of new technologies, new organizations processes and the transformation of several variables on new market opportunities, products and successful services. Innovation is one of the most powerful weapons a company has to face competition (Tidd & Bessant, 2013). Innovation management is considered to be a new field that combines concepts, techniques, methods and models from other disciplines, particularly engineering and administration. Four more operational requirements are assumed to impact the innovation management process, as follows.

Innovation management is a set of processes needed to include all the necessary steps — technical, managerial, commercial and financial — and to coordinate the systemic accomplishment of innovations in organizations (Spinosa & Nogas, 2014). These processes fulfill the function of managing the organization's effort, ranging from the generation of an idea, transforming the idea into a new product, process, service, marketing or organizational form, up to its availability for customers or users in existing markets or new ones. Innovation management seen as a set of processes must occur within the constraints of the organization and its workforce. This occurs through the habits, culture, skills and expectations of managers, employees and customers, their technical skills and their ability to mobilize tangible and intangible assets. All this effort is subject to the conjuncture of economic dynamics, political dimensions and corporate decisions all of which affect firms, countries and the World itself. To understand the management of innovation as a set of processes leads to shape the type of management model to apply.

Various models of innovation management have been developed in recent years. The model used in this study is adapted from the work of Joe Tidd, John Bessant and Keith Pavitt (Tidd & Bessant, 2013). Figure 3 shows eight macro processes that guide innovation in a systemic and continuously way (Spinosa & Nogas, 2014). These are: (1) Innovation culture and training to raise awareness within the organization about the benefits of innovation; (2) Identification of opportunities or promotion of ideas and creativity; (3) Strategic evaluation in order to align new ideas with corporate strategy; (4) Investment and risk analysis; (5) Resource allocation in the innovation management process (financial, intellectual capital, technologies, etc.); (6) Implementation of the new product, process or service; (7) Diffusion of innovation, involving the marketing of new products, processes or services. Sometimes it involves creating a market for them; (8) Learning, which

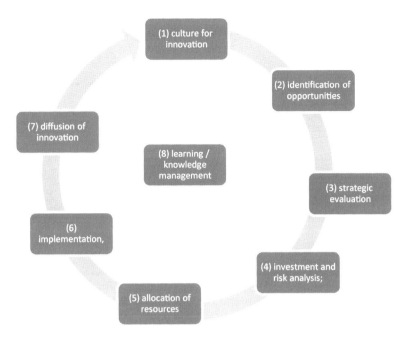

Figure 3.   Innovation management model.
Source: Adapted from Spinosa and Nogas (2014).

consists mainly in gathering knowledge management techniques, and occurs simultaneously with the other phases.

Special attention should be given to knowledge management (Spinosa *et al.*, 2002). Sveiby (1999) identifies two basic approaches to knowledge management. The first one considers knowledge management as specific information process management, where knowledge is equivalent to objects that are identified and treated with the help of information systems. In the second one, knowledge management is equivalent to people management, and knowledge is equivalent to processes, like a dynamic set of qualifications and know-how leading to the learning and creation of abilities. Moreover, from the classification originally proposed by Polanyi (Liebowitz, 1999), it is possible to identify two basic types of knowledge within the organization: explicit (or codified) and tacit (Nonaka & Takeuchi, 1997).

Explicit knowledge corresponds to procedures, data base, patents, reports and relationships with customers, and it is codified, stored, and transmitted in a formal way. It represents a small collection of the organization's full body of knowledge. Tacit knowledge is less formalized. It refers to experience, to the power of innovation and the abilities of people. It is less easily transmitted, mainly through examples (best practices), and it can originate new applications, depending on each context and the experience of each individual. When both tacit and implicit kinds of knowledge are captured and incorporated into the systems, processes, products, norms and the culture of an organization, it becomes possible to take great advantage of the organizational knowledge to support its actions. (Myers, 1996; Stewart, 1998).

The above classification takes on a practical perspective. Knowledge management claims to be the explicit and systematic management of vital knowledge and its associated processes. In this sense, the basic requirement for knowledge management, as far as IT-based solutions are concerned, is to take into account the general knowledge-value chain. In fact, IT-based solutions have to support the creation, organization, broadcasting, use, examination, protection and maintenance of knowledge.

The objective is to connect problems to solutions in an efficient and fast manner. This implies that the knowledge of individuals within corporate knowledge be shared and duly applied by the organization. The reason why enterprises are concerned with such an assertion is to transform ideas into commercialized products, i.e., to recover individual knowledge — intellectual capital — and transform it into products and services that can be further exploited by the organization.

Research Design & Setting

This paper is based on a qualitative paradigm, which according to Bulmer (1977) is used to interpret phenomena and occurs thanks to constant interaction between observation and conceptual formulation, between empirical research and theoretical development, between perception and explanation, and is presented as one among many investigation possibilities.

We adopted the action-research method since it is considered as "learning by doing", in other words, a group of people identifies a problem, does something to solve it, sees how successful their efforts were, and if they are not pleased, they try again (O'Brien, 2001). According to Kurt Lewin (1947) 'action research' is a process by which practitioners attempt to study their problems scientifically in order to guide, correct, and evaluate their decisions and actions. In this sense, action-research is one of many different forms of investigation-action, which could be briefly defined as any continued, systematic and empirically grounded attempt to improve practice (Tripp, 2005).

Action-research occurred from 2010 to 2013, and followed the following steps: (i) Diagnosing: identifying or defining a problem; (ii) action planning: considering alternative courses of action; (iii) taking action: selecting a course of action; (iv) evaluating: studying the consequences of an action; (v) specifying learning: identifying general findings.

The research setting was the Pontifical Catholic University (PUC) in Curitiba (Brazil); the solution, 'named PIA Platform' involved the management of approximately 350 contracts, with 50 active at the same time. All the processes involved approximately 300 people, including researchers and technicians. The main companies participating in the cluster in 2013 were: Nokia, Siemens Sofhar, Lego ZOOM, Cardioprótese, and Biogen.

The main stages of research were: revision and bibliographic analysis of innovation clusters, and management of knowledge; creation of the competence network (Network PUC); organization of juridical and financial instruments; development of knowledge bases; development of public presence on the internet; and development of the intranet.

PIA platform

The PIA platform takes into account the identified requirements and implements a set of processes, in order to support the dynamics of an innovation ecosystem. These processes are embedded in IT-based services articulated with management practices. The overall functioning of the platform can be described as follows:

- Innovation management processes are the core of the platform. They establish how activities take place for formation of an entrepreneurial culture, identification of opportunities, strategic evaluation, resource allocation, implementation and dissemination. Knowledge management processes complement the core and ensures of innovations tasks for creation, codification, diffusion and use of explicit knowledge;
- All the above processes give rise to groups of IT-based Services, and each group is organized in specific layers. The layers can be seen as supporting tools to accomplish the Management Practices;
- The "Public Services" layer was responsible for organizing the interface with the community and members of the innovation cluster. All the institutional information about the organization (mission, values, products and services provided, etc.) was publicly accessible. Navigation by profile is an efficient process to find information about companies, researchers and students. Each interface provides customized information, according to the user's profile;
- The "Resources" layer organizes every piece of information concerning the tangible and intangible assets of the ecosystem. By tangible assets, we mean, facilities, mainly the laboratories at the disposal of the cluster. By intangible assets we mean intellectual capital, mainly the scientific and technical competences handled by the cluster. These assets form three

main databases: projects, patents and competences. Access to this layer is half-public; and,

- The "Private" layer is reserved for managers, and takes into account the need for different control levels. The emphasis is on safe, fast and reliable transfer of technical and commercial information among the innovation ecosystem's members.

One of the critical challenges of this proposal was to integrate the levels with management practices. This integration was sustained by processes, in a logical execution order, and the main element of connection is the knowledge flowing between them. In this sense, the nature of the knowledge is considered and the knowledge management solutions prioritize the knowledge of clients, products, process, relations, and business.

Clients Knowledge: no productive structure is currently conceived without taking into account the client's requirements, which represent one of the major determinants in the innovative process of the enterprises. The clients' feedback is necessary during the design process of products and services, involving expectations about use, maintenance and recycling, as well as in the production planning as a whole. A "suitable information channel" must be opened to achieve those requirements.

Products Knowledge: it is a fact that good knowledge about products can facilitate their commercialization and, mainly, encourage innovative changes leading to new products. So, making knowledge available to the ecosystem's members becomes essential, particularly to sales units. Salesmen, who usually have direct contact with their clients, can think of new products, thus generating innovative knowledge that must be duly captured.

Processes Knowledge: the quality of products and services, as well as the ability of enterprises to understand and capture market needs can be attributed to the amount of flexibility they have in customizing their processes. Flexibility, in turn is only possible as a result of the perfect understanding (knowledge) of the processes.

Relationships Knowledge: usually, the establishment of strategically alliances in innovation ecosystems requires great efforts to identify potential partners in a truthful and fast way. Such requirements are quite important in reworking existing relations, as well as in establishing new agreements on sales and/or purchases among members. The dynamics required is only possible if reliable knowledge about relationships can be provided.

Businesses Knowledge: uniform monitoring of market behavior can cause businesses to redirect their strategies in a faster and efficient form.

That is the case with commodities, where product quotes can bear heavily upon internal and external negotiation processes.

It is important to note that behind all the knowledge categories listed, people knowledge is the actual asset to be managed. In fact, other major challenges are: to promote interactions among workers in order to tap into their tacit knowledge; to convert the tacit knowledge into more explicit knowledge through documents, processes, databases, etc., and to spread the explicit knowledge throughout the ecosystem, taking into account the right place, the right moment, the right people, and the right information content.

Examples of PIA processes:

Diagram 1 shows two of the processes most used in providing support to stakeholders. Using P 1, a company manager (even a citizen) can get information about all the services the ecosystem can provide to his/her enterprise, and more precisely, he/she can access public information about the projects, competences, patents and registers of industrial, technological and biotech products, among others.

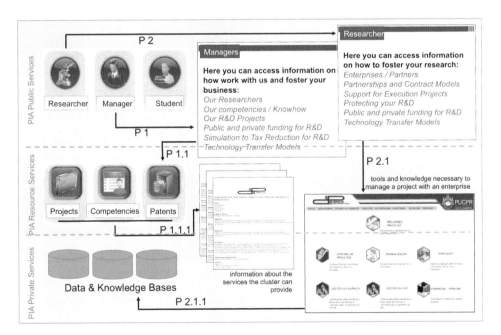

Diagram 1. Examples of processes supporting stakeholders as they disseminate macro-processes.

Source: Adapted from Spinosa *et al.* (2013).

Similarly, using P 2 a researcher can get complete information about the services provided by the ecosystem to support his/her researchers and developments. P 2.1 provides access to several tools and knowledge necessary to manage a project with an enterprise. More, researchers using P 2.1.1 provide information about current research projects and competences. One of the challenges to kicking off the development of a new product and/or service in an innovation ecosystem is establishing a contractual relationship among stakeholders. A complementary process achieves this task by offering stakeholders contracts knowledge base that can be used in several different situations. Implementation also involves controlling the contracts' (projects) financial aspects and schedule. The former specifies the base lines of the contract and the latter controls the inflow and outflow of funds.

Another example of PIA's process concerns the development of new products or new services. It is necessary to make sure that the required know-how, intellectual capital, equipment, technologies, supplies, among others, are available at the right moment in time. A project coordinator (usually a researcher responsible for a contract with an enterprise) can create knowledge communities around the themes of the projects. A coordinator can have access to competences provided by these knowledge communities. In the case of PIA, in 2014, there were 11 knowledge communities.

Most of PIA's processes work in a complementary way with innovation management practices, which are not implemented through IT services. They are mainly people-oriented activities, such as the organization of meetings, conferences, workshops to face the needs of enterprises with offers from researchers. This is the case of processes related to a yearly event carried out in the state of Paraná. In the past 5 years, several actions to foster entrepreneurship among young people and students were held, including competitions, and a quarter showing the results obtained from the stakeholders of the ecosystem. This publication is called PUC Innovation.

Findings Analysis

It could be seen that PIA produced some significant results, as foreseen in a previous study (Spinosa & Quandt, 2003) focusing on clusters and cooperation networks:

- Support of entrepreneurial activity and commercialization: the different networks have facilitated access to new markets and marketing strategies, through the development of specific marketing processes, the development of marketing surveys that benefit the network as a whole and entrepreneurial training.

- Information exchange: This is probably the most important impact of the network-building efforts. The initiatives comprise creation and maintenance of shared intelligence; creation of several different ways for members to share knowledge and lessons learned; facilitation of access to technology transfer opportunities; shared information on funding opportunities, potential partners, possibilities for incubation and spin-offs, etc.
- Capacity building: The proposal facilitated alliances and partnerships, as well as the access to information and the establishment of linkages with incubators and universities.
- Networking: The efforts were focused on obtaining a better understanding of stakeholder needs and markets, while encouraging all parties to participate and share knowledge, so that the network as a whole would be strengthened.
- Incubation: the local incubators have played an important role in the promotion of these actions. They have facilitated the incorporation of professors and senior students into entrepreneurial business, and also provided the physical facilities and specialized services to help startup firms during the first critical years of their creation. As Bortagaray and Tiffin (2000) point out, incubators "may provide a unique source of low-cost, low-risk, high potential value investment prospects for venture capitalists, thus acting as the focal point for a small cluster" in the Latin American context.

Some important challenges remain for PIA:

- It becomes clear that wider cooperation networks and ICT (Information and Communication Technology) may play a major role in the improvement of the "collective efficiency" of existing clusters. The expected next step to improve PIA is expanding the scope of knowledge search and deepening the capability to generate and manage technical change.
- In the specific case of technology-intensive industries, the complex environment in which firms and clusters operate highlights the importance of the access to a wider range of complementary assets and competencies. PIA has to continuously augment the assets and competences involving other stakeholders inside and outside the boundaries of the

clusters; put into effect the links that will really established the innovation ecosystem.

The future competitiveness of networked economies will be determined by their ability to make effective use of new methods and technologies capable of dealing with intangible assets, such as information and knowledge. PIA has to increase the Management Practices level in order to better deal with intangible assets. Finally, PIA has to observe a more abroad and upcoming context:

- For technology-based industries, more than in any other case, knowledge and competence flows matter increasingly more than flows of ordinary goods and services. At the same time, flexibility and rapid responses in the linkages between firms and other institutions, as well as close user-producer relations are crucial to support innovation in new and unstable technologies that involve a great deal of uncertainty. For developing-country firms, the range of knowledge flows still tends to be very limited, not only in terms of their spatial reach, but also with respect to the channels and interfaces through which these flows occur. This in turn constrains the relevance of such flows to the innovation process, since the firms face simultaneously a difficult access to a small number of sources.
- Policy implications connect particularly to the triple role of the scientific and technological infrastructure of any given region in the knowledge-based economy: It comprises the production of knowledge (research and development), its transmission (education and training) and its diffusion (or transfer) so that such knowledge may be applied by the productive sector to generate wealth and development.
- The relative success of the networks strongly suggests that the focus of public support on innovation should include not only strategic science and technology projects, but also specific programs to enhance more knowledge diffusion. This includes efforts to stimulate university-industry-government cooperation and more efficient mechanisms for transfer of technology.
- Technology incubators should expand their outreach role, which is usually limited to the local community including universities, local firms, and clients. Successful incubators need to be integrated into the local infrastructure but also to national and global sources of technologies and markets.

Conclusion

In the last two decades, the Brazilian economy has experienced a significant incremental change in its economic profile and growth rates. The opportunities for entrepreneurship on any scale have been in an upward cycle since, and in spite of a recent slowdown in the economy, there is still an entrepreneurial drive mainly among the young adult population who are aiming life styles and opportunities like their counterparts in North America and Europe.

Contributions from several knowledge domains are under consideration at this moment in Brazil. The trial based on Curitiba's innovation ecosystem is one of them. Based on this experiment we make some recommendations/ alerts adapted from the work of Joe Tidd, John Bessant and Keith Pavitt (Tidd & Bessant, 2013). (1) It is possible and desirable to manage innovation in order to achieve best results and to minimize risks; (2) The major challenge for innovation managers is how to manage it in a systematic and continuous way, according to strategic choices made by the ecosystem's members; (3) Innovation management takes into account a set of processes needed to coordinate the systematic achievement of innovations. This occurs through the habits, culture, skills and expectations of managers, employees and customers, their technical skills and their ability to mobilize tangible and intangible assets; (4) All the effort is subject to economic, political and development features to which the ecosystem, the country, and the world, are subject to; (5) All the changes brought about by innovation generate change in organizations, which need to be flexible; (6) The relentless pursuit of improvement becomes part of the ecosystem's everyday life; (7) Innovation also has multiple approaches, requiring flexibility and speed, due to the rapid advancement of new ideas that emerge at every turn of events, which often have their origin in perception and intuition, due to unforeseen problems occurring in the course of the process. Innovations can at the same time destroy the skills an organization has acquired throughout its existence. The skills are represented by accumulated knowledge about the domain of a particular technology and of existing processes that are being put into practice. The organization's skills should be respected and should be aligned with innovation practices in response to the strategic development directions.

Although still in a small scale, the experience and process-based approach to innovation ecosystems has proven to be a helpful tool. Further studies are, of course, still required to substantiate the present findings.

References

Andersson, M. & Karlsson, C. 2006. Regional innovation systems in small and medium-sized regions. In *The Emerging Digital Economy.* Springer, Berlin-Heidelberg.

Autio, E. & Thomas, L. D. W. 2014. Innovation ecosystems: Implications for innovation management. In *The Oxford Handbook of Innovation Management,* M. Dodgson, D. M. Gann and N. Philips (eds.). Oxford University Press, Oxford, UK.

Bianchi, P. 1993. Industrial districts and industrial policy: The new European perspective. *Journal of Industry Studies,* 1, 16–29. Taylor & Francis Online. Available at: http://www.tandfonline.com/doi/abs/10.1080/13662719300000002. Last access: March 9th, 2016.

Birkinshaw, J., Hamel, G., & Mol, M.J. 2008. Management innovation. *The Academy of Management Review,* 33(4), 825–845.

Bortagaray, I. & Tiffin, S. 2000. Innovation clusters in Latin America. Presented at the *4th International Conference on Technology Policy and Innovation,* Curitiba, Brazil, August 28–31.

Bulmer, M. 1977. *Sociological Research Methods.* Macmillan, London.

Camagni, R. 1995. Global network and local milieu: towards a theory of economic space. In *The Industrial Enterprise and Its Environment: Spatial Perspectives,* S. Conti, E. Malecki and P. Oinas (eds.), pp. 195–214. Avebury, Aldershot.

Corkill, D. 2007. Why can't we do it alone? *IET Engineering Management,* 36–39.

Engel, J. S. 2005. *Global Clusters of Innovation: Entrepreneurial Engines of Economic Grow Around the World.* Edward Elgar Publishing, Cheltenham.

Engel, J. S. 2015. Global clusters of innovation: Lessons from Silicon Valley. *California Management Review,* 57(2), 36–65.

Garvin, D. A. 1993. Building a learning organization. *Harvard Business Review,* July–August.

GEM. 1999–2014. Global Entrepreneurship Monitoring Global Report. Global Entrepreneurship Research Association, London Business School. London (UK). Available at: http://www.gemconsortium.org/. Last access: March 9th, 2016.

Gibson, D. Burtner, J., Conceição, P., Nordskog, J., Tankha, S. & Quandt, C. 1999. Incubating and sustaining learning and innovation poles in Latin America and the Caribbean. In *3rd International Conference on Technology Policy and Innovation,* Austin, Texas.

IPEA. 2005. Indústria: Quem inova fatura mais (Industry: Those who innovate more, bill more). Instituto de Pesquisa Econômica Aplicada Edição 12. Available at: http://www.ipea.gov.br/desafios/index.php?option=com_content&view=article%20&id=2073:cati%20d=28&Itemid=23.

Karaev, A., Koh, S. C. L. & Szamosi, L. T. 2007. The cluster approach and SME competitiveness: A review. *Journal of Manufacturing Technology Management,* 18(7), 818–835.

Kozul-Wright, Z. 1995. *The Role of the Firm in the Innovation Process.* UNCTAD, Geneva.

Knudsen, M. P. 2007. The relative importance of interfirm relationships and knowledge transfer for new product development success. *Journal of Product Innovation Management*, 24(2), 117–138.

Lawlor, A. 2014. Innovation ecosystems: Empowering entrepreneurs and powering economies. *Barclays Report*. M. Woodley (ed.). The Economist Intelligence Unit. Available at: http://www.economistinsights.com/sites/default/files/barclays_1.pdf. Last access: March 9th, 2016.

Lee, C., Lee, K. & Pennings, J. M. 2001. Internal capabilities, external networks, and performance: A study on technology-based ventures. *Strategic Management Journal*, 22(6/7), 615–640. Special issue: Strategic Entrepreneurship: Entrepreneurial Strategies for Wealth Creation.

Lewin, K. 1947. Group decision and social change. In *Readings in Social Psychology*, T. Newcomb and E. Harley (eds.). Henry Holt, New York.

Liebowitz, J. 1999. *Knowledge Management Handbook*. CRC Press, New York.

MCTI. 2013. Indicadores Nacionais de Ciência, Tecnologia e Inovação (National Indicators for Science, Technology and Innovation). Available at: http://www.mct.gov.br/index.php/content/view/740.html. Accessed on April 2014.

Manhart, M. & Thalmann, S. 2015. Protecting organizational knowledge: A structured literature review. *Journal of Knowledge Management*, 19(2), 190–211.

Mesquita, L. F. & Lazzarini, S. G. 2008. Horizontal and vertical relationships in developing economies: Implications for SMEs' access to global markets. *The Academy of Management Journal*, 51(2), 359–380.

Mohannak, K. & Keast, R. 2008. Cooperative networks and clustering of high-technology SMEs: The case of Brisbane Technology Park. In *The Genesis of Innovation: Systemic Linkages Between Knowledge and the Market*, B. Laperche, D. Uzunidis and N. Tunzelmann (eds.). Edward Elgar Publishing Limited, UK.

Myers, P. 1996. *Knowledge Management and Organizational Learning*, Butterworth-Heinemann, London.

Nonaka, I. & Takeuchi, H. 1997. *Criação de Conhecimento na Empresa (Knowledge Creation within the Enterprise)*. Campus, Rio de Janeiro.

O'Brien, R. 2001. An overview of the methodological approach of action research. In *Theory and practice of Action Research*, R. Richardson (ed.). Available at: http://web.net/robrien/papers/arfinal.html. Accessed 6 October 2015.

OECD. 1996. *The Knowledge-based Economy*. OCDE/GD(96)102, excerpted from the 1996 Science, Technology and Industry Outlook, OECD, Paris.

OECD. 2010. *Innovation and the Development Agenda*. Paris.

Quandt, C. 2000. Entreprise-level innovation in emerging clusters: The impact of local and external sources in the diffusion of technological knowledge. Rio 2000 Third Triple Helix International Conference. Rio de Janeiro, BR.

Song, J. & Shin, J. 2008. The paradox of technological capabilities: A study of knowledge sourcing from host countries of overseas R&D operations. *Journal of International Business Studies*, 39(2), 291–303.

Spinosa, L. M. & Quandt, C. O. 2003. Fostering innovation and knowledge sharing in cooperation networks. In *7th International Conference on Technology Policy and*

Innovation, 2003, Monterrey. Proceedings of the 7th International Conference on Technology Policy and Innovation, 2003.

Spinosa, L. M. & Krama, M. 2014. *Ecossistema de Inovação e Meio Urbano: princi-pais desafios para seus gestores (Urban Innovation Ecosystem: Main Challenges for their Stakeholders)*. Relevância Imobiliária Ambiental na 26 implantação de Parques Tecnológicos: com destaque ao Parque Tecnológico 27 do Estado de São Paulo. Universidade de São Paulo.

Spinosa, L. M. & Nogas, P. M. 2014. *Metodologia para Elaboração de Plano de Gestão da Inovação (Methodology for Innovation Management Plan)*. MBA Internacional em Gestão da Inovação. Curitiba.

Stewart, T. 1998. Capital Intelectual: A nova vantagem competitiva das empresas (Intellectual Capital: A new competitive advantage for enterprises), Campus, Rio de Janeiro.

SV, Silicon Valley Index. Joint Venture Silicon Valley, Silicon Valley Institute for Regional Studies, 2015. Available at: http://siliconvalleyindicators.org/pdf/index2015.pdf. Accessed on June 2015.

Sveiby, K. 1999. What is knowledge management? Available at: http://www.sveiby.com.au/Knowledge Management.html.

Tallman, S., Jenkins, M., Henry, N. & Pinch, S. 2004. Knowledge, clusters, and competitive advantage. *The Academy of Management Review*, 29(2), 258–271.

Terstriep, J., Rehfeld, D., Beer, C., Freise, S., Miettinen, J., Thorburn, K. & Wengler, C. 2009. Policy recommendations — Lessons learnt from NICE. *Europe INNOVA, Innovation and Clusters, NICE.*

Tidd, J. & Bessant, J. 2013. *Managing Innovation: Integrating Technological, Market and Organizational Change*, 5th edn. Wiley, New York.

Tripp, D. 2005. *Pesquisa-açao: uma introduçao metodologica (Action Research: a methodology introduction)*. *Educação e Pesquisa*, São Paulo, 31(3), 443–466.

Valente, M. & Crane, A. (2010). Public responsibility and private enterprise in developing countries. *California Management Review*, 52(3), 52–78.

Chapter 13

The Ecosystem Approach: Rethinking Academic Entrepreneurship in Belgium

Jonas Van Hove

University of Ghent, Belgium

ETH Zurich, Switzerland

jvanhove@ethz.ch

Bart Clarysse

Imperial College Business School, London SW7 2AZ, United Kingdom

b.clarysse@imperial.ac.uk

Universities have become more 'strategic' in their pursuit of creating entrepreneurial capital as part of their commitment to make a wider contribution to society. In this part of the book, we will explore the strategic approach of Belgium-based universities and its evolution from closed powerhouses to boundary-spanning organizations. By adopting the case study methodology, we highlight the following strategic options available to Belgium-based universities looking to further develop its university-centered ecosystems: (1) appropriate infrastructure and innovative approaches to ensure diversity; (2) differentiated approach to develop financial support networks; (3) enterprise education; and (4) grassroot entrepreneurial movements. However, in order to fully benefit from the value created within the university ecosystem, each institution will have to find a way to attract all ecosystem practitioners which also captures the value. This study enhances the wider understanding of regional ecosystems and the role of universities.

Introduction: Science-Based Economic Development

The primary goals of knowledge exchange are to create economic benefits from research and to bring impactful innovations to the market. However this is not without its obstacles due to the failure of the European institutions to exploit its research excellence for technological and economic benefits. This contradiction is known as the "European innovation paradox" caused by an apparent lack of entrepreneurial capacity and traditionally unfriendly innovation systems (Caracostas & Mulder, 1998). Virtually all over Europe, governments are focusing on the economic and social role of universities as they are rich sources of knowledge and technology. University research and its commercialization has been viewed to be a key driver of national competitiveness, and been consequently supported by numerous support measures. Although the transfer of scientific and technological know-how is essential, it is still difficult to achieve due to the complex development paths and the many competences needed to transform scientific findings into viable products and services (Vohora *et al.*, 2004). A better comprehension on how to deal with this figures high on the agenda of many European countries. With policies that promote technology transfer, support spin-outs and assess the nature, scale, and beneficiaries of the impact of research, universities have been encouraged to become more active in supporting science-based economic development. Consequently, this led to the "second academic revolution" as described by Etzkowitz *et al.* (2000) which revealed that universities gained the extra role as economic developer alongside their traditional roles as educators and research institutions.

Notable is the trend for Higher Education Institutions (HEIs) to be screened on their non-academic impact as well. To illustrate, the Research Excellence Framework (REF) in the United Kingdom is one of the first examples of this trend as it measures the impact of research outside academia (Grant, 2015). As a result HEIs have widened their scope from an exclusive focus on research and education to a broader commitment to the translation of research into innovation and as such to society as a whole.

Furthermore scholars suggest that the innovation context regulates the outcomes of entrepreneurial action i.e., what the consequences will be when someone decides to pursue a given opportunity (Acs *et al.*, 2014). Thus, to pursue opportunities successfully, a HEI needs to gain access to a number of vital resources such as financial capital, human capital, customers, distribution channels, specialized skills, support services and the like. To access any of these resources, the HEI must approach and link to specialized resources such as people, companies and institutions, thereby creating so-called entrepreneurial ecosystems.

The commitments initiated by universities to promote commercialization on campus and in surrounding regions of the university is described as

academic entrepreneurship (Siegel & Wright, 2015a). While the importance of knowledge and technology exchange is obvious in this setting,
fairly little is known about the strategies that universities can use to establish
a strong innovation and entrepreneurship ecosystem. Against this backdrop, we ask ourselves in this study how to strive for a vibrant entrepreneurial community with a balanced representation of university, corporate,
entrepreneurial and government stakeholders or in other words how to
reposition a university to ensure strategic fit looking at both internal organizational factors and the external market.

To address the above question, this chapter explores the factors determining the propensity of Belgium-based HEIs[1] to create an entrepreneurial
and knowledge-driven ecosystem. More precisely we take a closer look at
Flanders, the largest autonomous region of Belgium, and examine how the
role of Flemish universities has evolved from closed powerhouses to boundary-spanning organizations. This evolution is mainly based on applying
an inter-organizational network perspective. To illustrate, in addition to the
HEIs, Flanders created four independent research institutes: the Flanders
Interuniversity Institute for Biotechnology (VIB), the Interuniversity Institute
for Microelectronics (IMEC), the Flemish Institute for Technology Research
(VITO) in the fields of energy, environment and materials, and the digital
research hub IMINDS. These are set up as network integrators, cumulating
the research efforts across different universities. In this chapter we examine
the case of IMINDS as a representative example of Flanders entrepreneurial
ecosystem and how academic entrepreneurship is supported.

In studies of entrepreneurship, several scholars have adopted the
 case study methodology to examine complex and under-explored topics
(O'Shea *et al.*, 2005, 2007). Taking a comparative approach that considers
both entrepreneurship and education we benchmark IMINDS, a strategic
Flemish research institute connecting all five universities in Flanders, with a
top-level HEI in the United Kingdom (UK), Imperial College London (IC).
Globally recognized as one of the world's most prestigious institutions, IC is
identified by experts as an "emerging giant" demonstrating emerging leadership in entrepreneurship and establishing one of the world's most successful technology innovation ecosystems (Graham, 2013). A more detailed
description of both cases can be found in addendum. Using the information
on the existence and use of various strategies, we will explore the emerging

---

[1] Belgium is a federal country with a highly decentralized research and innovation system. It
is composed of seven autonomous entities: the Federal State, the three regions, and three
communities. Each entity have close to full autonomy in managing their own innovation
policy system. In this book, we will examine Flanders, recognized as the European
Entrepreneurial Region in 2014 by the European Union's Committee of the Regions.

ecosystem in Belgium, make projections on what an entrepreneurial university would look like and examine the barriers to achieving this.

Section 2 assesses the context-dependence of entrepreneurial university centers. We classify the existing approaches towards strengthening entrepreneurial capabilities in universities with the goal of promoting knowledge exchange and achieving economic and societal benefits. We distinguish between (in-) formal institutional and community-led strategies. Section 3 will draw on the experiences of both cases in order to see first whether some systemic similarities emerge and secondly to elude on any regional differences. Finally, Section 4 discusses the practices focusing on how to realize a university-based entrepreneurial ecosystem.

The Importance of Contextualization

In general, the literature indicates that spinning out from academia is a complex phenomenon, because of the number and diversity of human parties involved (academic and surrogate entrepreneurs, (research) students, tech transfer office professionals, university staff, etc.). Understanding the factors that determine the success and long-term performance of spin-outs is an important element to establish a globally competitive institution. It is recognized that entrepreneurship is fundamentally an individual-level phenomenon; if opportunities were not recognized and pursued by individuals, there would be no entrepreneurship. However if the context or the ecosystem does not support entrepreneurship, individual-level efforts will be hampered. Therefore, when thinking of university entrepreneurship, one has to both consider individual-level action and how well the university context supports the transformation of these efforts into real-life businesses. In other words, entrepreneurship is a systemic phenomenon: individual-level action is required for entrepreneurship to happen, but the outcomes of these actions are regulated by context (Aldrich & Martinez, 2001).

Thus, the real question seems to be, not *whether* entrepreneurs innovate, but rather *when* and *where* they do so. Universities used to focus on nurturing spin-offs into successful start-ups via internal approaches such as technology transfer offices (TTOs), science parks, and incubation infrastructures. For years, the logic of closed innovation by the powerhouses of education was tacitly held to be self-evident as "the right way" to bring new ideas and translate research into the mainstream market. Towards the end of the 20th century, a number of factors started to erode the underpinnings of closed innovation. One of the major factors of change may lie within the changing economics of starting up, whereby the costs of experimentation — especially for early stage tech start-ups — have dropped significantly in the last decade

(Fehder & Hochberg, 2014). Other important factors are the changing landscape in start-up support, the evolving needs of participating ventures and the dramatic rise in the number and mobility of knowledge workers. At the same time, venture capitalists have moved towards later stage investment, calling new funds into life to invest in early-stage university start-ups. As such, too much substantial value created at HEIs remained unexploited.

Nowadays when breakthroughs occur at universities, the scientists or students who have made them search for an outside option in case the discovery was not pursued in a timely fashion by the university or other supporting services. If that occurs, they have to explore opportunities outside the institution and have the chance to pursue their discovery on their own for instance in a start-up financed by an incubation model that accelerates its development. In addition, many innovative ideas also come from the market itself, leading only at a later stage to intensive research. Universities noticed a lot of value being created outside its perimeters because of this external commercialization. The closed innovation approach started to lose its effectiveness as the boundaries between spin-outs and its surrounding environment became more porous, enabling innovation to move easily between the two (see The Open Innovation Model by Chesbrough, 2003). Led by these changes, universities started to integrate contextual variables in their strategic thinking. The aim is to become a focal point in entrepreneurial ecosystems, both as an innovation house and an educational provider.

University-centered ecosystem

In management research, the term 'ecosystem' has been used to refer to a network of interconnected organizations that are linked or operated around a local firm or a platform (Moore, 1993; Teece, 2007). Following Markman *et al.* (2008), we define a university-centered ecosystem of research and technology commercialization as a market that includes research joint ventures, strategic alliances, licensing agreements, incubation mechanisms, and the formation of start-up companies. Given that ecosystems comprise multiple participants bound by complex relations that often involve mutual interdependence, it is important to improve our understanding of the various strategies that ecosystem participants can use to promote and facilitate the ecosystem to their advantage (Thomas & Autio, 2013).

It is our objective to provide insight into this important question through the empirical lens provided by ongoing ecosystem creation efforts. As our empirical context, we study the IMINDS initiative through which Flemish universities seek to catalyze knowledge and technology exchange.

Furthermore, by way of comparing IMINDS to a world-renowned HEI like IC, strategic lessons can be drawn on how to enhance entrepreneurial capacity in a university-centered ecosystem.

Both institutions are located in "leading innovation regions" in Europe characterized by their entrepreneurial performance, according to The Regional Entrepreneurship and Development Index (Szerb *et al.*, 2013). In addition, the success of these institutions is viewed to be genuinely a product of effective university-based strategies rather than circumstance. For this study, we believe an institutional perspective provides a useful framework to categorize the different strategies implemented by IMINDS and IC. Based on the integrated model of Guerrero *et al.* (2014) explaining entrepreneurial universities, we will focus on the similarities and differences of the conditional factors whilst confronting both cases. Furthermore, next to the creation of academic spin-outs, universities are also considered to be sources of new venture creation by students and recent graduates. Powerful student-led entrepreneurial drive, supported by an array of activities and resources, is viewed to be an increasingly prominent driver of ecosystem development. In the next section we will describe the different strategies and approaches that may drive the successful creation of an interactive and entrepreneurial ecosystem in a university setting.

In fact, various support mechanisms — customized to the strengths and opportunities of each institution — are installed by universities to stimulate entrepreneurial innovation. These types of practices can be associated with two main strategies: (1) effective institutional strategy that allows multiple, often unconnected, activities to emerge and operate across and beyond the campus; and (2) grassroots movements with the ultimate aim to build an integrated community through an ambitious range of activities.

The primary data source for the study is one-to-one semi structured interviews to tap the expertise of the individuals with direct experience of the respective university-centered entrepreneurial ecosystems. The authors also are affiliated or work closely together with the institutions described, allowing them to gather a large amount of insider insights and a very realistic experience of how things were being done.

Science and impact: robust mechanisms

Formal and informal institutional approach

These approaches refer to the universities' internal management structures, decision-making mechanisms, and educational strategies. According to

Lazzeretti and Tavoletti (2005), the entrepreneurial mission needs to be integral to the organizational structure of the university, hereby influencing a range of support measures. These measures are: (1) facilitation; (2) development of enterprise education; (3) support for technology transfer; (4) appropriate infrastructure; (5) new early stage investment models; (6) promoting (gender) diversity; and (7) customized support for different types of ventures. These measures will be discussed in greater detail in our analysis below.

First, a HEI structure should facilitate the ecosystem by being a visionary leader who engages with the potential ecosystem participants i.e., the intricate web of large corporates, entrepreneurial initiatives, government and start-ups. Importantly, as the focal point of the ecosystem, a HEI should not monopolize or dictate these interactions but employ subtle communication and coordination strategies. This element of *facilitation* brings together a mix of experiential approaches. For instance, the challenges in linking universities and business/industry are well known. In terms of goals and culture, the academic perspective is fundamentally different compared to the commercial mind set of company leaders. Companies need to be sustainable and preferably make a profit whilst universities have different motives such as societal impact and education. This leads to different value systems. However being united around shared goals and objectives seem to be a prerequisite for interactions to emerge. In this respect, IMINDS has been set up as a network integrator with strategic partnerships with all five universities in Flanders. It is a centralized structure that is set up as a coordinated effort to keep the balance between public policy, the universities' societal mission, and private sector interests. The model is a virtual cooperation meaning that the researchers groups stay within the different universities but a holding structure coordinates their efforts. As it is mainly centered on collaborative and demand-driven research, it fosters innovation and entrepreneurship by working closely together with local and international companies, governmental associations, and societal actors. Uniquely to most other institutions, IMINDS has developed a 'flipped knowledge transfer model' wherein it helps solve challenges faced by start-ups (not only large corporates) by giving access to the academic research capacity of Flanders. It is different to conventional contract research as it is specifically tailored to the needs and dynamics of start-ups. This gives them the opportunity to fail fast and adapt their business. Additionally, IMINDS applies a structured approach to stimulate the internationalization of its start-ups. It offers easy access into international locations and gets them the support to operate in an international business context. In the context of IC, the highest decision-making body is advised by a platform responsible for cross-college coordination, co-operation and strategic oversight of support for enterprising students and academics. This advisory board, called Enterprising Student Strategy Group (ESSG), aims to encourage a cultural shift towards entrepreneurship among students, academics, and university management. It consists of four elements: (i) **coordination** takes place by jointly engaging with the students and academics in order to seek new ways to provide a seamless, contemporary, support offer for the enterprising journey; (ii) **co-operation** aims to identify novel, emerging, internal and external partnership opportunities that will enhance the enterprise ecosystem of IC. Having a clear profile around a limited number of areas of excellence and setting up new challenge-led programmes with a focus on entrepreneurship and industry relevance played a pivotal role in building up corporate involvement in the university-centered ecosystem. In addition, as part of the College's societal mission, a number of international university partnerships have been established in order to support and inform other entrepreneurial ecosystems. Furthermore, diverse relations are being managed between IC and the global community of entrepreneurial alumni. One reason for this engagement is the College's approach on fundraising from philanthropic sources, similar to the American university model of philanthropic funding; (iii) **collective intelligence** is there to compare, share and report overall College performance and outcomes from enterprising academics, students and alumni. Metrics have been revised in order to capture the university's institutionalization and commitment to its innovation and entrepreneurship culture and capacity. An example of such a metric is the indicator describing the degree of investment and engagement from senior researchers in spin-outs launched by their students and alumni; and (iv) **awareness building** is an essential action of the ESSG to communicate the broad definition of entrepreneurship within business/industry. Through accurate and timely career information, ESSG emphasizes the key entrepreneurial skills and attributes needed to be successful in any career. This includes, for instance, celebrating and raising the profile of entrepreneurial success stories.

Second, central to university's enterprise approach are the *continuing enterprise education programmes.* Educational applications may lead indirectly to academic entrepreneurship via case-based and traditional teaching, or through action-based programmes (Rasmussen & Sorheim, 2006; Wright, 2014). Within the Flemish university system, incubators are seen as catalysts and enablers for effective entrepreneurship education programmes (Gielen *et al.,* 2013). Asides the more traditional entrepreneurship education, a bigger focus has been laid on the roles of incubators and the exploration of opportunities offered by 'learning-by-doing' in an ecosystem perspective.

Based on the premise that heterogeneity in experiences and teaching methods is critical in entrepreneurship education (Pittaway & Cope, 2007), an action-based education programme has been developed which aims at educating entrepreneurs and at establishing an actual business. Within this line of reasoning, IMINDS has strongly embedded an action-based incubation programme called iStart across the universities. According to the Swedish UBI Index (2014), it ranks 25th on the list of best university business incubators worldwide. The importance of the incubation programme for new academic ventures is great since they cumulate all research efforts across universities and is seen as a follow-on module to any enterprise-related course that the Flemish HEIs are offering. The goal of the incubation process is to assess the feasibility of a business idea and prepare the (commercial) launch of the first product and the establishment of a start-up. The incubator supports entrepreneurs (i.e., academics and students) through the early development of a business idea and participants have the opportunity to attend a number of dedicated workshops given by external experts in a particular subject domain. Additionally, there is the option to take part in a hands-on training programme that is a mix of one-on-one coaching and interactive lectures on business fundamentals. Overall, this business generation strategy typically complements the university mission of technology transfer by commercializing academic inventions. In the case of IC, the focus of enterprise education lays on fostering the entrepreneurial mind set (equally relevant to starting-up, scaling-up or steady-state organizations), from undergraduates to postgraduates and researchers. This targeted approach to each type of students and academics helps to concentrate resources and increase impact. IC is distinct from other institutions through its proactive approach to forming collaborations with Royal College of Art — one of the world's very best design and art schools — in order to combine design thinking and entrepreneurialism. The creation of these triangle projects between engineers, Masters/MBA's and design students drawn from both institutions resulted in a number of early commercialization successes. Another key differentiator here is the central role of the Business School at IC and its world-leading research. It informs and develops these programmes, bringing together innovative thinking and insight with new technologies. Examples are the flagship programmes MSc Innovation, Entrepreneurship & Management at the Business School, the Enterprise and Entrepreneurship Project by the Graduate School and the pioneering Althea — Imperial programme. The latter is specifically designed for women studying at IC to help develop their enterprising idea. More recently, the Business School can also bring the Imperial community to students wherever they are based in the world. A high-tech and connected network of high-calibre students, alumni, academics, and corporate partners has been created through a purpose-built virtual learning platform. To sum up, it is primarily an entrepreneurship education with a strong focus on 'learning-by-doing', which incorporates business generation as a side effect.

Third, as governments and universities became interested in the business of science, they started to look for support to academics in the commercialization of their ideas. This meant the establishment of TTOs in the 1990s with the traditional mission to share knowledge for the benefit of society. However, over time the initial philosophy behind the mission of a TTO increasingly got replaced by a growing emphasis towards protecting IP and financial returns via patents and licenses (Lockett *et al.*, 2015; Siegel & Wright, 2015a). Aligned with the stakeholder theory (Donaldson & Preston, 1995; Freeman *et al.*, 2010), different sets of incentives come into play here, as TTO operations are influenced by a market 'shareholder' (versus university 'stakeholder') oriented focus on creating, managing, and financing spin-outs. It created the rather peculiar situation where the interests of all stakeholders need to be balanced. As there is no optimal formula in place for adjudicating among the stakeholder's disparate interests, some have claimed that the tech transfer model is in fact a continuing experiment (see Siegel and Wright (2015b) for a review). In Flanders, the purpose of independent research institutes, such as IMINDS, is to complement the services of a standard technology transfer entity. It stimulates fundamental research through the virtual model and facilitates technology transfer by for instance filing patents through a co-application with the respective university. In the UK, a game-changing step was executed in 2006 at IC by listing its tech-transfer unit on the Alternative Investment Market of the London Stock Exchange, becoming the first UK university commercialization company to do so. It needed to raise capital in order to exploit the substantial value created at the College. Wright *et al.* (2006) have shown that a lack of capital is often seen by TTO managers as a barrier to start-up activity. Following this line of thinking, the TTO at the College also created a ventures arm with the aim to develop technology within the "Golden Triangle" i.e., University of Cambridge, the University of Oxford, University College London, and IC. However, observers still question whether the listing and the traditional reliance on a TTO, embedded within an investment management company is the right strategic decision for a HEI.

Fourth, during the last decennia, universities have devised more and more proactive policies to stimulate the commercial exploitation of public research through spin-outs. One way to support spin-outs is to develop and invest in appropriate infrastructure. Physical space is considered to be one of the six types of resources key to entrepreneurial success (Clarysse *et al.*, 2005). It is a way to keep start-ups within the vicinity of the incubator of the parent institution, granting access to technological knowledge and academic networking. In the case of Flanders, IMINDS offers incubation space where a mix of co-working spaces, offices, administrative support and a vibrant ecosystem encourages peer interaction and learning (Gielen *et al.*, 2013). Likewise, IC operates an incubator to support its start-ups in terms of funding, intangible services and office space. The incubator model is flexible and offers leases to suit the needs of the start-up, whether it is an established business, a start-up, or simply in need of a virtual office. Virtual membership is an easy, yet cost-effective way of boosting a company's image by having a prestigious business address. The College has also expanded its campus by developing an inner city innovation district, well connected and with good access to London's financial center and venture funding. The centerpiece will be a £200m Research and Translation Hub, where large companies will be able to mingle with spin-outs and its research scientists.

Fifth, universities started to explore novel approaches to early-stage investment due to an increasing variety in the entrepreneurial funding landscape. For instance, institutions feel attracted to the idea of starting an accelerator or partnering up with one. These entities can be considered as the newest generation of incubators to stimulate academic entrepreneurship (Pauwels *et al.*, 2015). Accelerators are innovative investment vehicles and business service providers, which select promising entrepreneurial teams and provide them with pre-seed investment and time-limited support comprising programmed events and intensive mentoring (Clarysse *et al.*, 2015). The focus is even less on space and more on assisting the ventures through their entrepreneurial journey and typically operate early in the life cycle of a new venture. Because of this, it tries to tackle the issue of substantial variation in start-up quality within a given university. Leading universities also start to orient and even fast-track (aspiring) academic entrepreneurs towards particular types of accelerators that may best meet their needs. However, this tends to be more on an ad hoc basis and depending on individuals within the university with an extensive network, thereby lacking a systematic approach. To illustrate the rise of university-linked (pre-) accelerators, reference can be made to the IMINDS 'iStart Light programme', an adapted version of its iStart incubation programme. This is intended for students and part-time entrepreneurs with limited funding, but offers more on-going support and supervision. Additionally, IMINDS has installed Living Labs where innovative products and services get to be tested by end-users in real-life circumstances. This allows individuals to assemble user feedback, fine-tune and co-create their innovations before establishing a business model and rolling it out to their target audience. Similarly, a structured pre-acceleration programme has been formed at IC, called Imperial Create Lab, with the clear objective to 'skill-up' academic entrepreneurs (no funding attached). Initially launched as a student business plan development programme, it now offers students and researchers an entrepreneurial community-platform to test their high-technology ideas. Location services are also part of the accelerator program package, but are limited to co-location in a shared open office space, with the aim to encourage collaboration and peer-to-peer learning.

Sixth, it is fundamental in a HEI environment to ensure (gender) diversity since dissolving the geospatial boundaries give rise to unexpected opportunities as people come in contact with new perspectives ('cross-fertilization'). In addition, an even more pressing matter is the gender inequality in entrepreneurship. Academic entrepreneurs are predominantly male and female tech entrepreneurship still suffers from big social biases that hold back this latent talent base globally (Abreu & Grinevich, 2013; Thebaud, 2015; Stephan & El-Ganainy, 2007). Against this backdrop, there are some exemplars with the aim to promote (gender) diversity. Although IMINDS has made a number of decisive moves in this regard, with its open access to external entrepreneurs to create an ecosystem setting as a major feature, no other pioneering approaches could be identified that were perceived as impactful. In the case of IC, two particular initiatives were developed to tackle the diversity matter, called the Advanced Hackspace and the Imperial — Althea programme. The former is a working model designed for interdisciplinary and inter-departmental collaboration, exploration and experimentation by providing social tools, laboratory equipment, and advanced manufacturing capabilities. The latter is a pioneering programme which promotes and honors innovations developed by promising female students in science, technology, engineering, and mathematics (STEM).

Seventh, research has shown that relatively small differences in the early stages of a venture such as opportunity recognition and resource acquisition can result in significant differences in their subsequent development (Rasmussen *et al.*, 2015). Virtually all early-stage ventures face the challenge of recognizing and effectively addressing opportunities. Entrepreneurs may identify an entrepreneurial opportunity in either an un/under served need or in an un/under exploited technology. This leads to the distinction among entrepreneurial ventures based on the type of opportunity being pursued i.e., tech-push or market-pull ventures (Clarysse *et al.*, working paper). Several factors such as market and technology experience, influence these types of ventures in different ways. This implies, reinforced by the increased diversity of start-ups at universities (Shah & Pahnke, 2014), that the way HEIs support and guide new ventures should be distinct for the type of venture. For instance, market-pull ventures would benefit from support in scanning technological possibilities to build a product that can address the identified market need, while tech-push ventures need resources so they can conduct a broad search into markets. In this respect, IMINDS developed a toolbox consisting of opportunity recognition workshops to help in recognizing societal and business applications based on academic or applied research. Also IC integrated certain practices in this regard however more appreciation and research is required of the different needs of these types of ventures.

Community-led approach

Notwithstanding university level policies and various support measures, the organizational structure of universities (Ambos *et al.*, 2008) may create a schism between these policies and what actually happens on the ground. Setting social cues to encourage a cultural shift towards entrepreneurship among students, academics and even university management has been the primary goal for student-led enterprise clubs and societies. These can be found in universities across the world driving a grassroots entrepreneurial movement within their institution. Such peer-led enterprise communities are usually led by passionate students from across faculties and departments and prone to build valuable connections and share knowledge and skills. In both cases, many enterprise societies could be identified organizing entrepreneurial related and support activities to support, educate and nurture the entrepreneurial mind set of the community within a university.

The model of university enterprise societies can be perceived as a catalyst and an advocate for the increased support of student enterprise.

Concluding Comments and Recommendations

Academic entrepreneurs are often highly dependent on others in their environment to gain the momentum and competences necessary to develop a fledging new business. This analysis shows the proactive role of Flemish HEIs in stimulating academic entrepreneurship by running an incubation model of virtual cooperation. Benchmarking IMINDS with a world-renowned education institute will inform practice by bringing to light the strategic options available to Belgium-based HEIs looking to further develop its university-centered ecosystems.

We have also shown some key foundations which supports the valorization and exploitation of (research) ideas in a university-centered ecosystem:

- Appropriate infrastructure and innovative approaches to ensure diversity — Promoting a diverse scientific community is necessary to realize the objective of developing world-class talent in STEM and business. Reconfigurable shared spaces can ease translation of knowledge and dissolve geospatial boundaries. Complementing this, it is essential to develop more pioneering interventional programmes in order to equalize the gender variance in academic entrepreneurship.
- Exploration of novel approaches to early-stage investment in the surroundings — There is a need for a more differentiated approach (beyond the TTO model) to develop financial support networks. We can see an evolution to a system wherein aside TTOs, there are other enablers for academic entrepreneurship such as incubators, bootcamps, (pre-) accelerators. Thus, the stimulation of business angel and accelerator activity may warrant attention as we believe that the technology transfer model should be more of a dialogue (e.g., by including externals) instead of solely handled by a TTO.
- Enterprise Education — Equip students and academics with an entrepreneurial mind set by embedding entry-level and state-of-the-art enterprise education in experiential programmes. For instance, an action-oriented programme that is tailored to STEM graduates may trigger a revolution in science venturing. We contend that the full potential of scientific venturing has been held back by a lack of time, space and resources for R&D and prototyping. To form multi-disciplinary teams and actually implement solutions to real problems, one of the core issues remains at the top of the funnel: pre-idea and pre-team. The combination of post-graduate education and learnings from the accelerator model (e.g., Entrepreneurs First) can generate science-based start-ups at scale. Furthermore, entrepreneurship teaching around well-defined challenges helps community building across different disciplines and encourages interaction with industry.
- Grassroots entrepreneurial movements — Besides a university governance matching strategies, activities and resources, HEIs need to take the cultural view on entrepreneurship into account. Advocating enterprise

support and building awareness by championing entrepreneurs to build an ecosystem community in a university setting.

The reviewed approaches have their own merits, and they need to be designed based on the configuration of the university and its context. There are no imitable successful methods as universities are heterogeneous (Mustar *et al.*, 2006) and their context is unique. In order to fully benefit from the value created within the university ecosystem, each institution will have to find a way to attract all ecosystem practitioners (i.e., companies, government funding agencies, investors, entrepreneurs, and start-up support programmes) which also captures the value. Incentives and mechanisms need to be developed in order to transform weak ecosystems ties into stronger ones.

Major questions remain on how to be effective in creating and developing a university-centered ecosystem. A deeper understanding of the determinants of success for different types of start-ups and the impact factors influencing such a system is crucial. Factors such as the lack of international commercial expertise, the widely-critiqued IP incentive policies; the search for philanthropic donations; and setting new evaluation metrics, highlight the need for further theory development and empirical analyses. This will help us enhance the wider understanding of regional ecosystems and the role of universities.

Acknowledgments

We are deeply grateful to the faculty, university managers, and research experts who contributed to the study by sharing their experiences, knowledge, and feedback. The authors thank specifically the Entrepreneurship Hub, IC Business School, and the management of IMINDS responsible for its incubation programme.

References

Acs, Z., Autio, E. & Szerb, L. 2014. Innovation in large and small firms — an empirical analysis. *American Economic Review*, 78(4), 678–690.

Aldrich, H. E. & Martinez, M. A. 2001. Many are called, but few are chosen: an evolutionary perspective for the study of entrepreneurship. *Entrepreneurship Theory and Practice*, 25, 41–56.

Ambos, T. C., Makela, K., Birkinshaw, J. & D'Este, P. 2008. When does university research get commercialised? Creating ambidexterity in research institutions. *Journal of Management Studies*, 45, 1424–1447.

Abreu, M. & Grinevich, V. 2013. The nature of academic entrepreneurship in the UK: Widening the focus of entrepreneurial activities. *Research Policy,* 42, 408–422.

Bhatli, D. 2015. *Top University Business Incubators — Global Benchmark 14/15.* UBI Global.

Caracostas, P. & Mulder, U. 1998. Society, the Endless Frontier: A European Vision of Research and Innovation Policies for the 21st Century. *European Commission, Directorate General XII — Science, Research and Development, Lanham MD.* Bruxelles, Bernan Associates (distributors).

Chesbrough, H. W. 2003. The Era of Open Innovation. *MIT Sloan Management Review,* 44.

Clarysse, B., Danneels, E. & De Cock, R. 2015. *A Tale of Two Ventures: Search and Linking in Tech Pull Start-ups.* Innovation and Entrepreneurship Department Working London, UK, Imperial College Business School.

Clarysse, B., Wright, M. & Van Hove, J. 2015. *A Look inside Accelerators.* Nesta, London.

Donaldson, T. & Preston, L. E. 1995. The stakeholder theory of the corporation: concepts, evidence and implications. *Academy of Management Review,* 20(1), 65–91.

Etzkowitz, H., Webster, A., Gebhardt, C. & Terra, B. R. C. 2000. The future of the university and the university of the future: evolution of ivory tower to entrepreneurial paradigm. *Research Policy,* 29, 313–330.

Fehder, D. C. & Hochberg, Y. V. 2014. Accelerators and the Regional Supply of Venture Capital Investment. *Available at SSRN.*

Freeman, R. E., Harrison, J. S., Wicks, A. C., Parmar, B. L. & De Colle, S. 2010. *Stakeholder Theory: The State of the Art.* Cambridge University Press.

Gielen, F., De Cleyn, S. H. & Coppens, J. 2013. Incubators as Enablers for Academic Entrepreneurship. In *8th European Conference on Innovation and Entrepreneurship, Proceedings,* 809–817.

Graham, R. 2013. *Technology Innovation Ecosystem Benchmarking Study: Key findings from Phase 1.* MIT Skoltech report.

Grant, J. 2015. *The Nature, Scale and Beneficiaries of Research Impact: An Initial Analysis of Research Excellence Framework (REF) 2014 Impact Case Studies.* HEFCE report by Kings College London & Digital Science, 29.

Guerrero, M., Urbano, D., Cuningham, J. & Organ, D. 2014. Entrepreneurial universities in two European regions: a case study comparison. *Journal of Technology Transfer,* 39, 415–434.

Lazzeretti, L. & Tavoletti, E. 2005. Higher education excellence and local economic development: the case of entrepreneurial university of twente. *European Planning Studies,* 13(3), 475–493.

Lockett, A., Wright, M. & Wild, A. 2015. The institutionalisation of third stream activities in UK higher education: the role of discourse and metrics. *British Journal of Management,* 26, 78–92.

Markman, G. D., Siegel, D. S. & Wright, M. 2008. Research and technology commercialization. *Journal of Management Studies*, 45(8), 1401–1423.

Moore, J. F. 1993. Predators and prey: a new ecology of competition. *Harvard Business Review*, 71, 75–86.

Mustar, P., Renault, M., Colombo, M., Piva, E., Fontes, A., Lockett, A., Wright, M., Clarysse, B. & Moray, N. 2006. Conceptualising the heterogeneity of research-based spin-offs: a multi-dimensional taxonomy. *Research Policy*, 35, 289–308.

O'Shea, R., Allen, T. J., Chevalier, A. & Roche, F. 2005. Entrepreneurial orientation, technology transfer and spin-off performance of US universities. *Research Policy*, 34, 994–1009.

O'Shea, R., Allen, T. J., Morse, K. P., O'Gorman, C. & Roche, F. 2007. Delineating the anatomy of an entrepreneurial university: the Massachusetts institute of technology experience. *R&D Management*, 37(1), 1–16.

Perkmann, M., Fini, R., Ross, J., Salter, A., Silvestri, C. & Tartari, V. 2015. Accounting for universities' impact: using augmented data to measure academic engagement and commercialization by academic scientists. *Research Evaluation*, ISSN, 1471–5449.

Pittaway, L. & Cope, J. 2007. Entrepreneurship education: a systematic review of the evidence. *International Small Business Journal*, 25(5), 479–510.

Rasmussen, E. & Sorheim, R. 2006. Action-based entrepreneurship education. *Technovation*, 26, 185–194.

Rasmussen, E., Mosey, S. & Wright, M. 2015. The influence of university departments on the evolution of entrepreneurial competencies in spin-off ventures. *Research Policy*, 43(1), 92–106.

Shah, S. & Pahnke, E. 2014. Parting the ivory curtain: understanding how universities support a diverse set of start-ups. *Journal of Technology Transfer*, 39, 780–792.

Siegel, D. S. & Wright, M. 2015a. Academic entrepreneurship: time for a rethink? *British Journal of Management*, 00, 1–14.

Siegel, D. S. & Wright, M. 2015b. University technology transfer offices, licensing, and start-ups. In *Chicago Handbook of University Technology Transfer and Academic Entrepreneurship*, A. N. Link, D. S. Siegel & M. Wright (eds.). 1–40. University of Chicago Press.

Stephan, P. E. & El-Ganainy, A. 2007. The entrepreneurial puzzle: explaining the gender gap. *Journal of Technology Transfer*, 32, 475–487.

Szerb, L., Acs, Z. J., Autio, E., Ortega-Argiles, R. & Komlósi, E. 2013. *REDI, The Regional Entrepreneurship and Development Index — Measuring Regional Entrepreneurship Final Report*. European Commission, Directorate-General for Regional and Urban Policy.

Teece, G. J. 2007. Explicating dynamic capabilities: the nature and microfoundations of (sustainable) enterprise performance. *Strategic Management Journal*, 28, 1319–1350.

Thebaud, S. 2015. Business as plan B: institutional foundations of gender inequality in entrepreneurship across 24 industrialized countries. *Administrative Science Quarterly*, 1–41, 60(4), 671–711.

Thomas, L. D. & Autio, E. 2013. Emergent equifinality: an empirical analysis of ecosystem creation processes.

Vohora, A., Wright, M. & Lockett, A. 2004. Critical junctures in the development of university high-tech spinout companies. *Research policy*, 33(1), 147–175.

Wright, M., Clarysse, B., Lockett, A. & Binks, M. 2006. University spin-out companies and venture capital. *Research policy*, 35(4), 481–501.

Wright, M. 2014. Academic entrepreneurship, technology transfer and society: where next? *Journal of Technology Transfer*, 39, 322–334.

ADDENDUM

IMINDS: a "Network Integrator" for Collaborative Innovation

IMINDS has been established by the Flemish government in 2004 under its original name of Interdisciplinary Institute for Broadband Technology (IBBT). Today, it has developed itself into Flander's digital research center and business incubator. Building on the strengths of its research community located at five Flemish universities, IMINDS has a proven methodology (i.e., 'virtual cooperation') to convert knowhow into real-life products and services.

IMINDS is instrumental in positioning Flanders as one of Europe's leading digital regions. Its main mission is to develop demand-driven research and solution for the digital media and ICT sector and foster the adoption of newly developed technologies. Nowadays, they have been an active member in 380+ local and European research projects and incubated over 75 start-up projects in their incubation programme. With over 1100 research partners (commercial and social-profit organizations), they are supportive (or even active) in knowledge transfer by acting as a network integrator in Flanders.

Imperial College London: a "Well-Connected" Institution

IC was established in 1907 through a merger between a number of colleges including the Royal College of Science and the Royal School of Mines. Later it fused with St. Mary's Hospital Medical School and established the Business School bringing together science, technology, engineering, medicine, and business. It is widely recognized as a UK-leading center that champions outstanding science and technology by commercializing innovative academic research.

This commitment for great discoveries, application to industry and collaborating for the better, is part of the culture and priorities within the university over the past 100 years. In addition, its Business School has been recognized as a research powerhouse in the REF 2014 as 92% of the Business School's research is classed as 'world-leading' and 'internationally excellent'. REF is the UK Government's system for assessing the quality of research in HEIs, occurring every six years. Furthermore, IC unveiled its first entrepreneurship barometer in 2015 illustrating how the school's academic progress to become true value-creators by starting businesses and generating employment. For instance, the barometer reveals that entrepreneurs' scientific record is 40% higher, research and services income is three to four times higher compared to non-entrepreneurs (Perkmann *et al.*, 2015).

Index